Shojo Beat

Kaze Hikaru

10

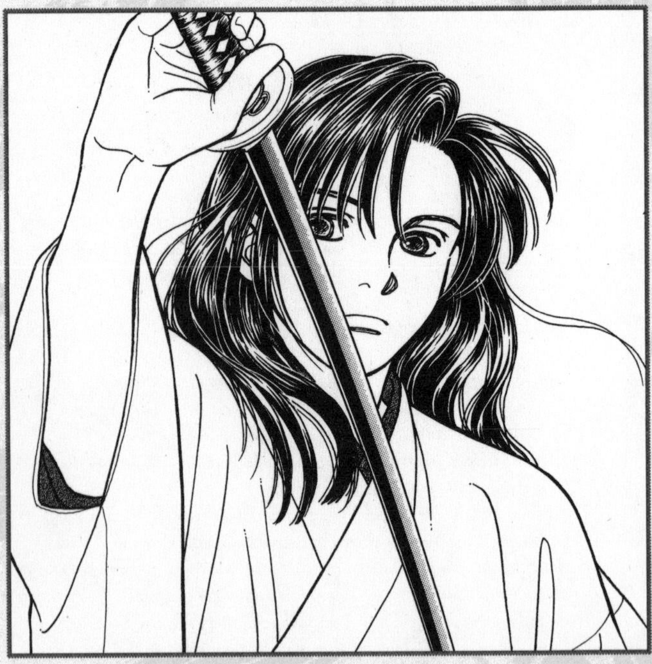

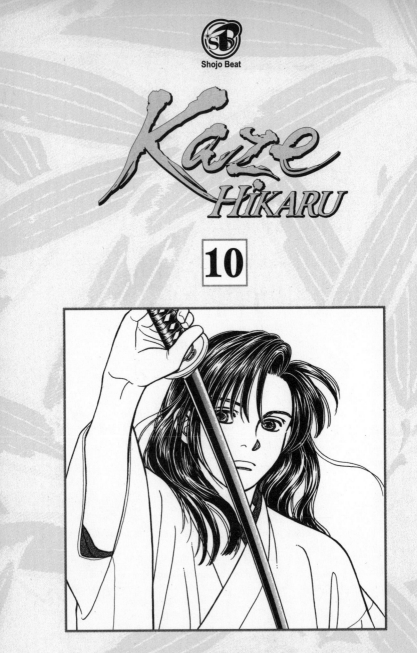

Story & Art by

Taeko Watanabe

Contents

Story Thus Far

It is the end of the Bakufu era, the 3rd year of Bunkyu (1863) in Kyoto. The Shinsengumi is a band of warriors formed to protect the Shogun.

Tominaga Sei, the daughter of a former Bakufu bushi, joined the Shinsengumi disguised as a boy by the name of Kamiya Seizaburo to avenge her father and brother. She has continued her training under the only person in the Shinsengumi who knows her true identity, Okita Soji, and she aspires to become a true bushi.

The Shinsengumi prove their worth through their success in the Ikedaya Affair and the *Kinmon no Hen*. The Bakufu orders the group to expand their troop, resulting in reorganization. Sei finds herself appointed as Vice-Captain Yamanami's *kosho*, and she is depressed that she is no longer working under Okita's command. However, after discovering that the new arrangement was because Yamanami knows her secret and is concerned for her, Sei's resolve is renewed. Sei is deeply moved by Yamanami's wise advice to "be the blade of grass that shows the wind where home is."

Characters

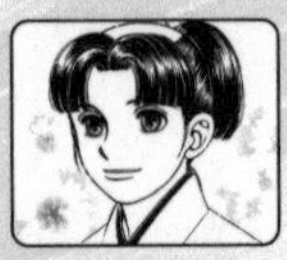

Tominaga Sei
She disguises herself as a boy to enter the Mibu-Roshi. She trains under Soji, aspiring to become a true bushi. But secretly, she is in love with Soji.

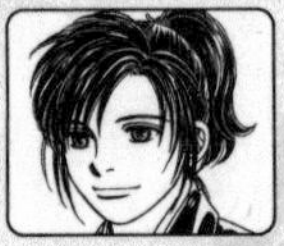

Okita Soji
Assistant vice captain of the Shinsengumi, and licensed master of the Ten'nen Rishin-Ryu. He supports the troop alongside Kondo and Hijikata and guides Seizaburo with a kind yet firm hand.

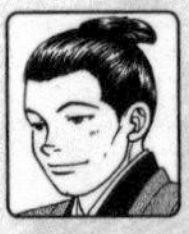

Kondo Isami
Captain of the Shinsengumi and fourth grandmaster of the Ten'nen Rishin-ryu. A passionate, warm and well-respected leader.

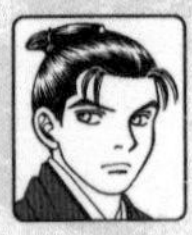

Hijikata Toshizo
Vice captain of the Shinsengumi. He commands both the group and himself with a rigid strictness. He is also known as the "Oni vice captain."

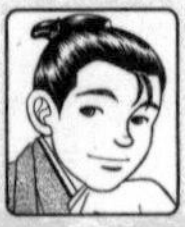

Yamanami Keisuke
Vice captain of the Shinsengumi. A master of the Hokushin Itto-Ryu, he is kind and well learned.

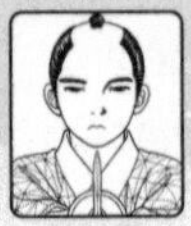

Saito Hajime
Assistant vice captain. He was a friend of Sei's older brother. Sei is attached to him in place of her lost brother.

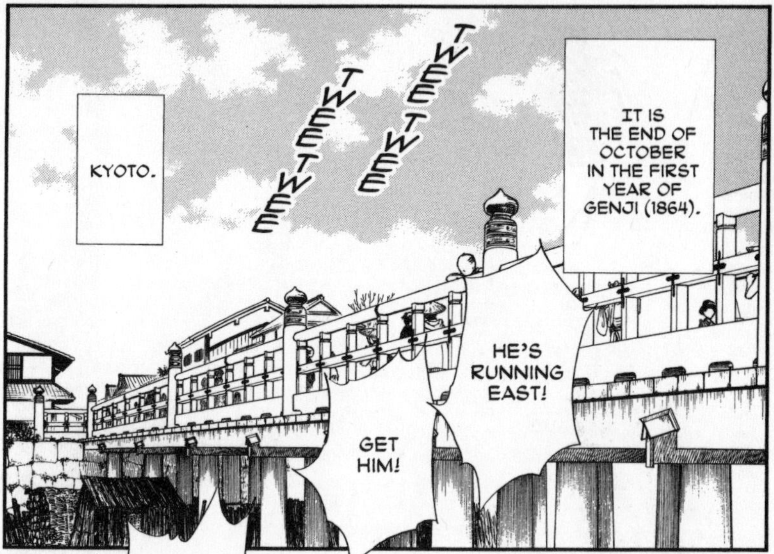
IT IS THE END OF OCTOBER IN THE FIRST YEAR OF GENJI (1864).
TWEETWEE
TWEETWEE
KYOTO.
HE'S RUNNING EAST!
GET HIM!

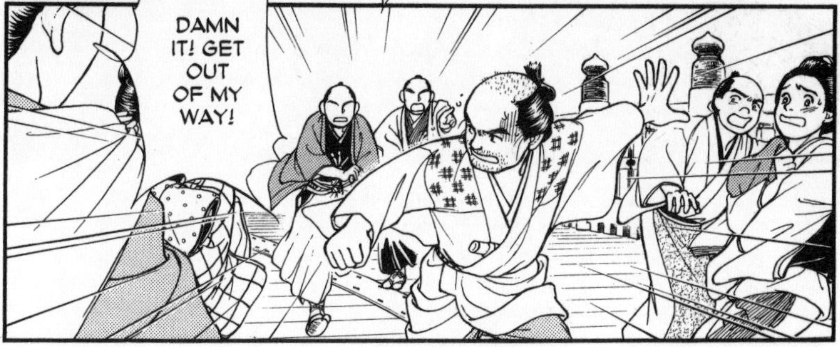
DAMN IT! GET OUT OF MY WAY!

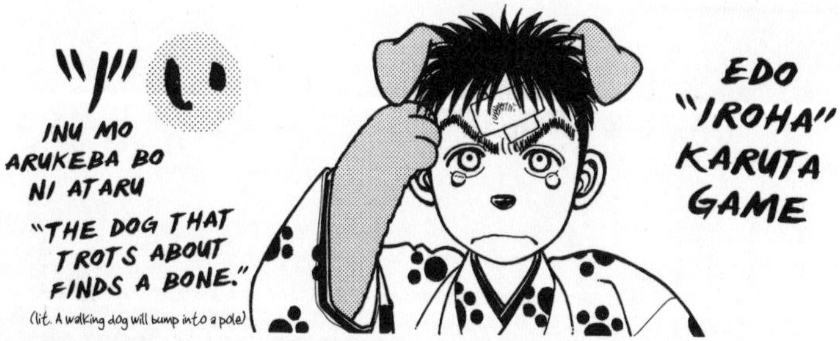
EDO "IROHA" KARUTA GAME
い
INU MO ARUKEBA BO NI ATARU
"THE DOG THAT TROTS ABOUT FINDS A BONE."
(lit. A walking dog will bump into a pole)

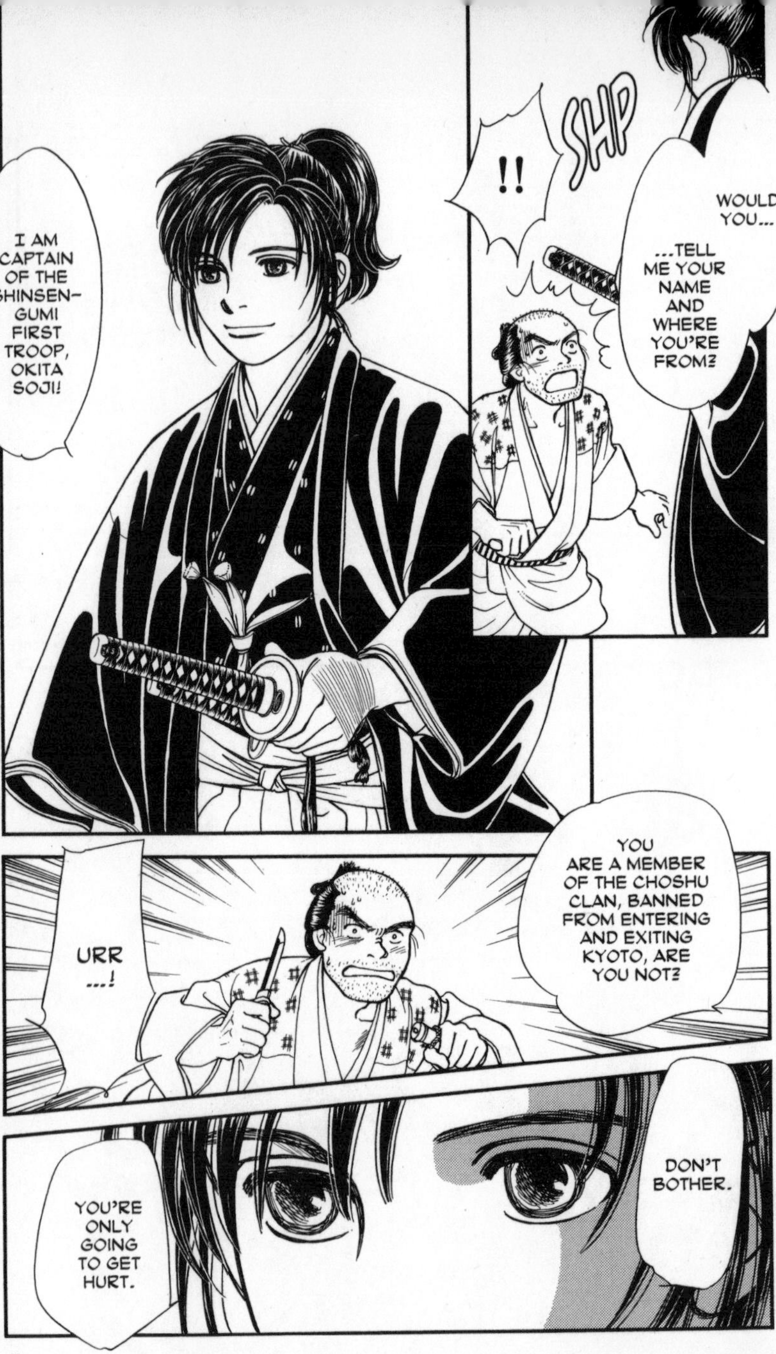
WOULD YOU...
...TELL ME YOUR NAME AND WHERE YOU'RE FROM?
SHP
!!
I AM CAPTAIN OF THE SHINSEN-GUMI FIRST TROOP, OKITA SOJI!
YOU ARE A MEMBER OF THE CHOSHU CLAN, BANNED FROM ENTERING AND EXITING KYOTO, ARE YOU NOT?
URR ...!
DON'T BOTHER.
YOU'RE ONLY GOING TO GET HURT.

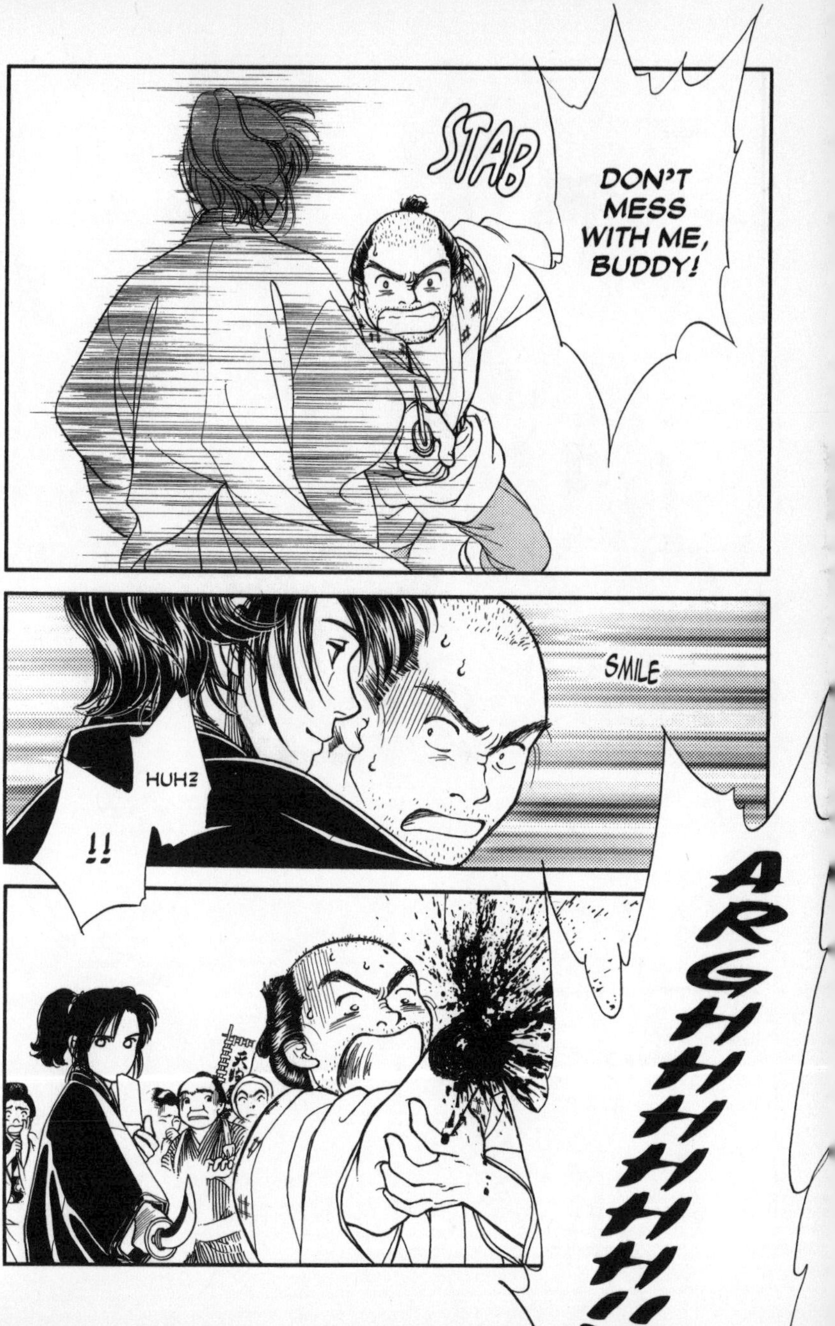
DON'T MESS WITH ME, BUDDY!
STAB
SMILE
HUH?
!!
ARGHHHHHH!!

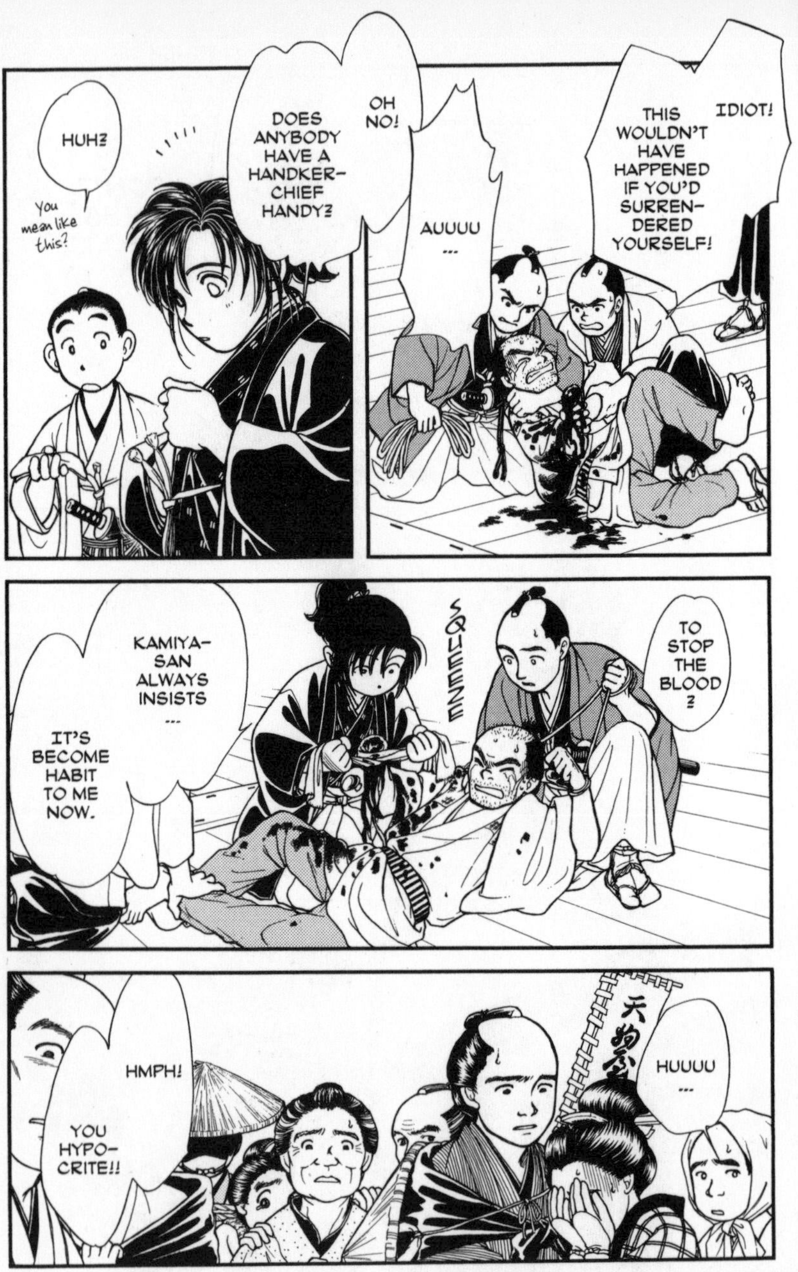
IDIOT!
THIS WOULDN'T HAVE HAPPENED IF YOU'D SURRENDERED YOURSELF!
AUUUU ...
OH NO! DOES ANYBODY HAVE A HANDKERCHIEF HANDY?
HUH?
You mean like this?
TO STOP THE BLOOD?
SQUEEZE
KAMIYA-SAN ALWAYS INSISTS ...
IT'S BECOME HABIT TO ME NOW.
HUUUU ...
HMPH!
YOU HYPOCRITE!!

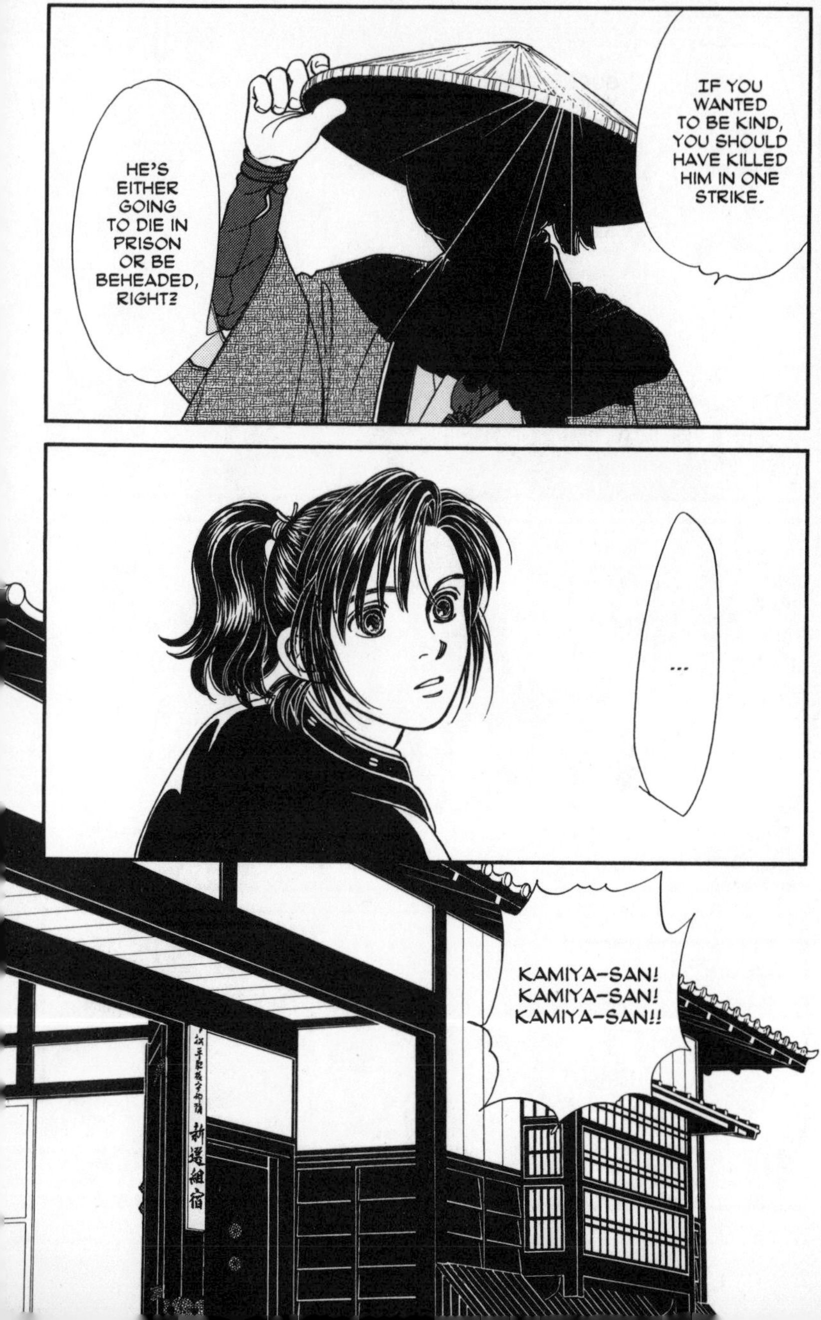
IF YOU WANTED TO BE KIND, YOU SHOULD HAVE KILLED HIM IN ONE STRIKE.
HE'S EITHER GOING TO DIE IN PRISON OR BE BEHEADED, RIGHT?
...
KAMIYA-SAN! KAMIYA-SAN! KAMIYA-SAN!!
新選組宿

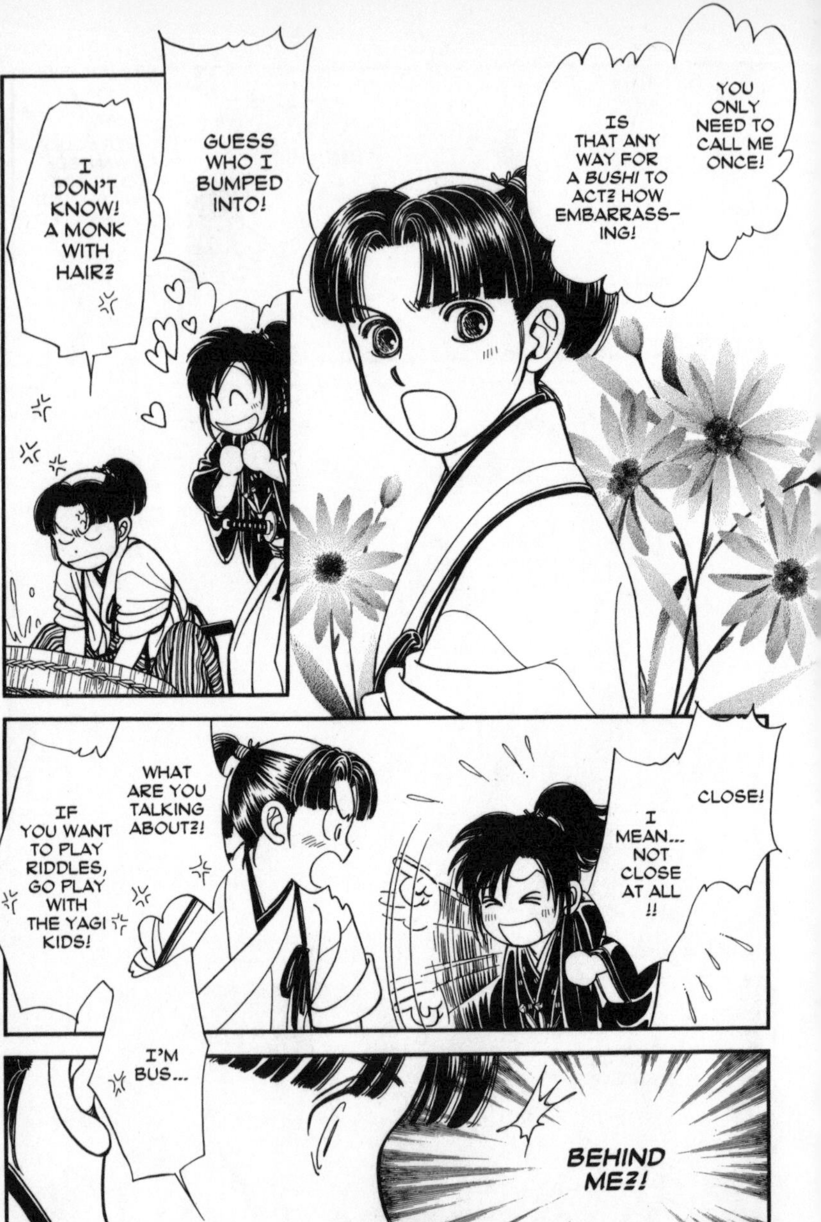
YOU ONLY NEED TO CALL ME ONCE!
IS THAT ANY WAY FOR A *BUSHI* TO ACT?! HOW EMBARRASSING!
GUESS WHO I BUMPED INTO!
I DON'T KNOW! A MONK WITH HAIR?
CLOSE!
I MEAN... NOT CLOSE AT ALL!!
WHAT ARE YOU TALKING ABOUT?!
IF YOU WANT TO PLAY RIDDLES, GO PLAY WITH THE YAGI KIDS!
BEHIND ME?!
I'M BUS...

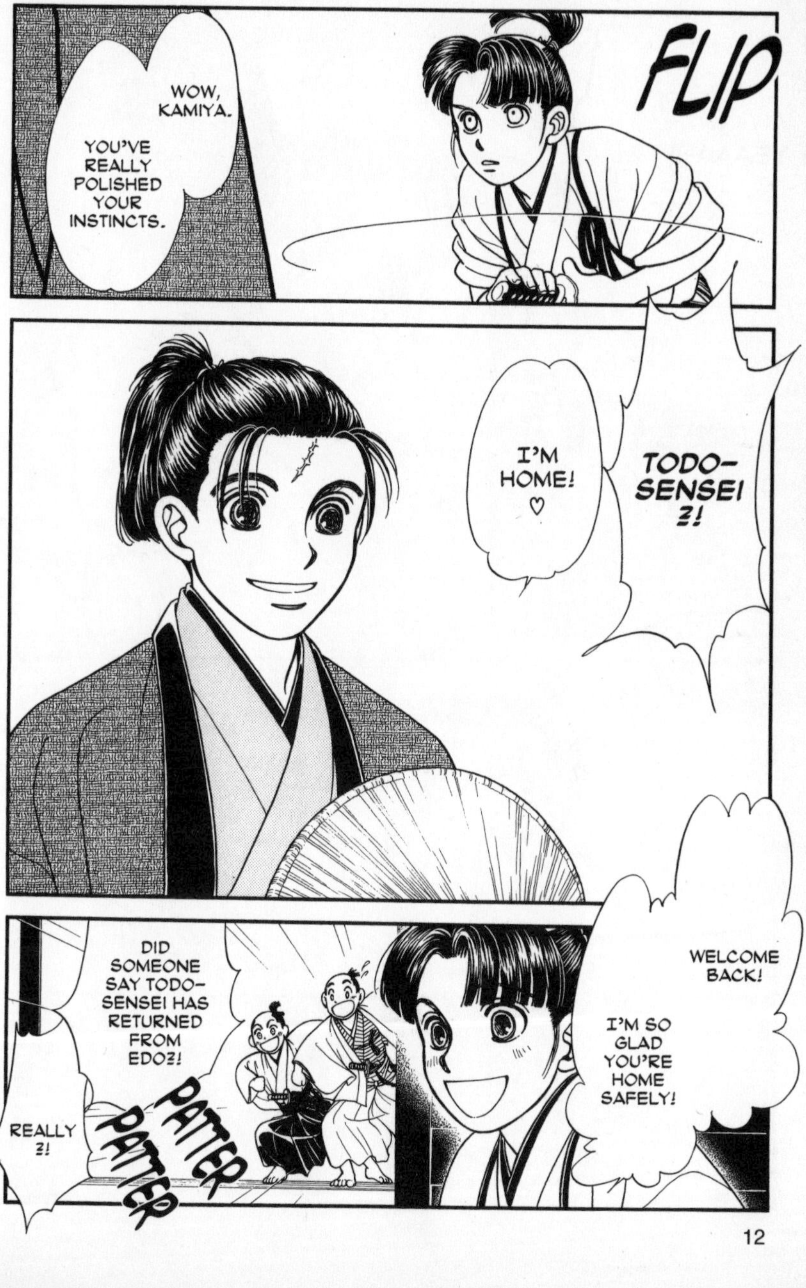
FLIP
WOW, KAMIYA.
YOU'VE REALLY POLISHED YOUR INSTINCTS.
TODO-SENSEI?!
I'M HOME! ♡
WELCOME BACK!
I'M SO GLAD YOU'RE HOME SAFELY!
DID SOMEONE SAY TODO-SENSEI HAS RETURNED FROM EDO?!
PATTER PATTER
REALLY?!

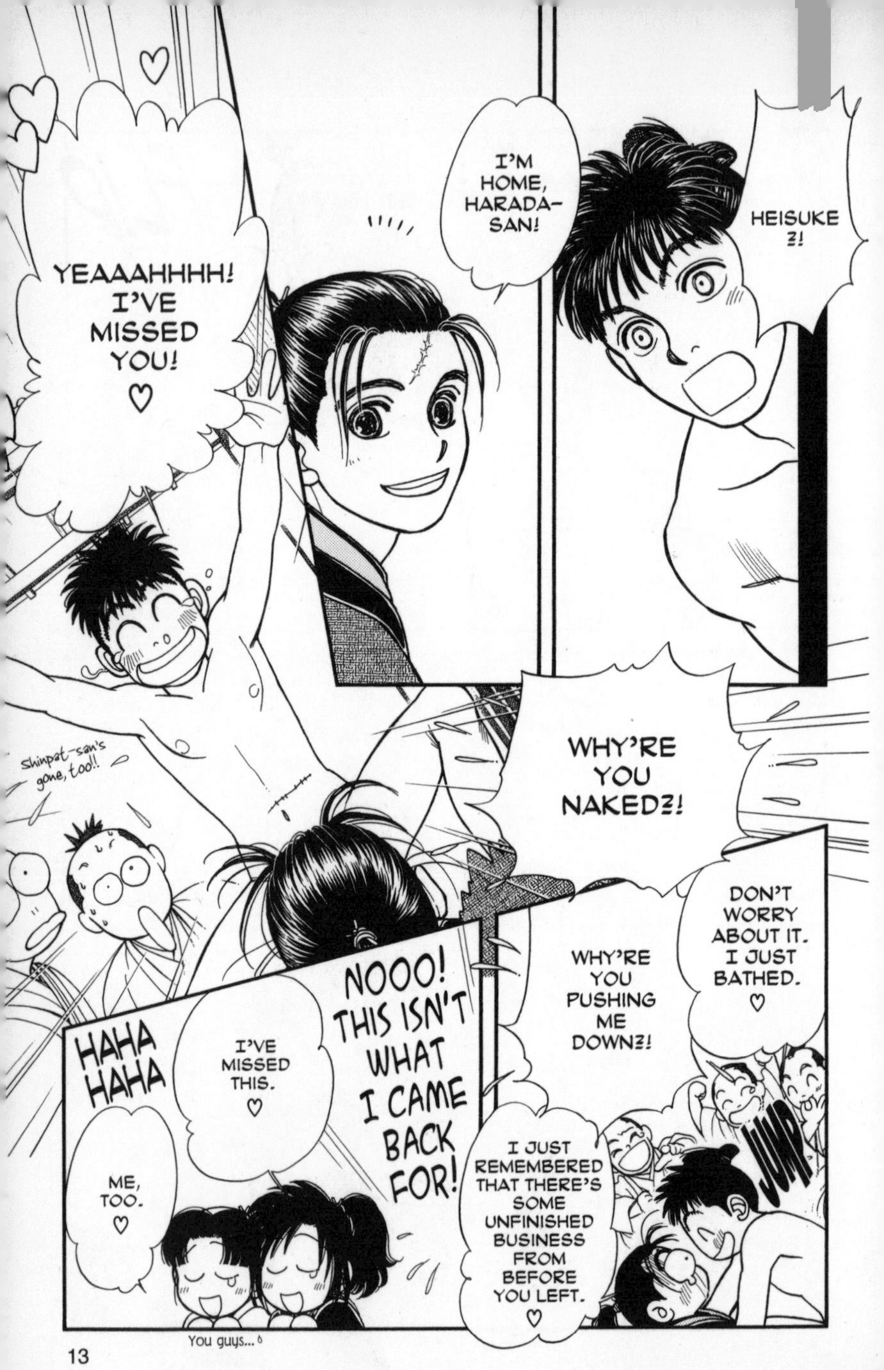
HEISUKE?!
I'M HOME, HARADA-SAN!
YEAAAHHHH! I'VE MISSED YOU! ♡
WHY'RE YOU NAKED?!
Shinpat-san's gone, too!!
DON'T WORRY ABOUT IT. I JUST BATHED. ♡
WHY'RE YOU PUSHING ME DOWN?!
I JUST REMEMBERED THAT THERE'S SOME UNFINISHED BUSINESS FROM BEFORE YOU LEFT. ♡
JUMP
NOOO! THIS ISN'T WHAT I CAME BACK FOR!
I'VE MISSED THIS. ♡
HAHA HAHA
ME, TOO. ♡
You guys...

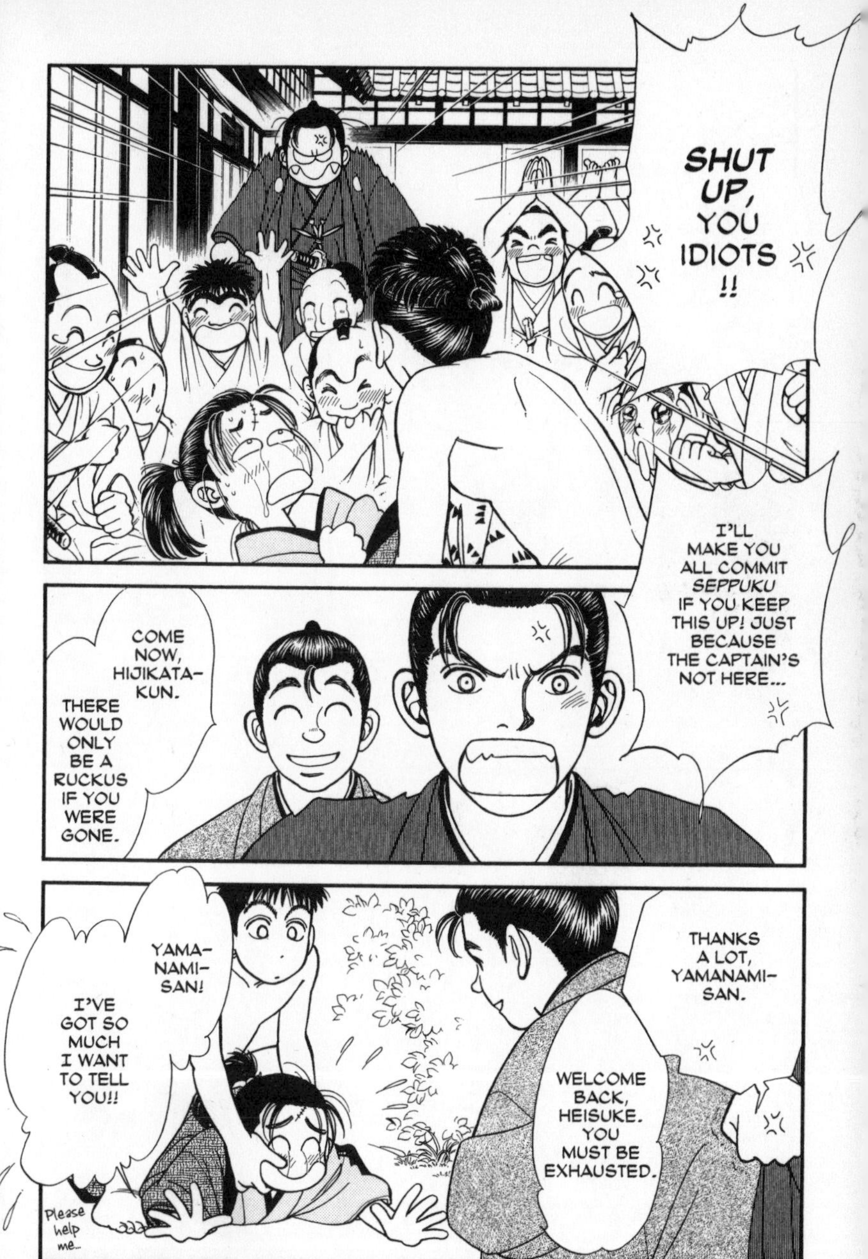
SHUT UP, YOU IDIOTS!!
I'LL MAKE YOU ALL COMMIT SEPPUKU IF YOU KEEP THIS UP! JUST BECAUSE THE CAPTAIN'S NOT HERE...
COME NOW, HIJIKATA-KUN.
THERE WOULD ONLY BE A RUCKUS IF YOU WERE GONE.
THANKS A LOT, YAMANAMI-SAN.
WELCOME BACK, HEISUKE. YOU MUST BE EXHAUSTED.
YAMANAMI-SAN!
I'VE GOT SO MUCH I WANT TO TELL YOU!!
Please help me...

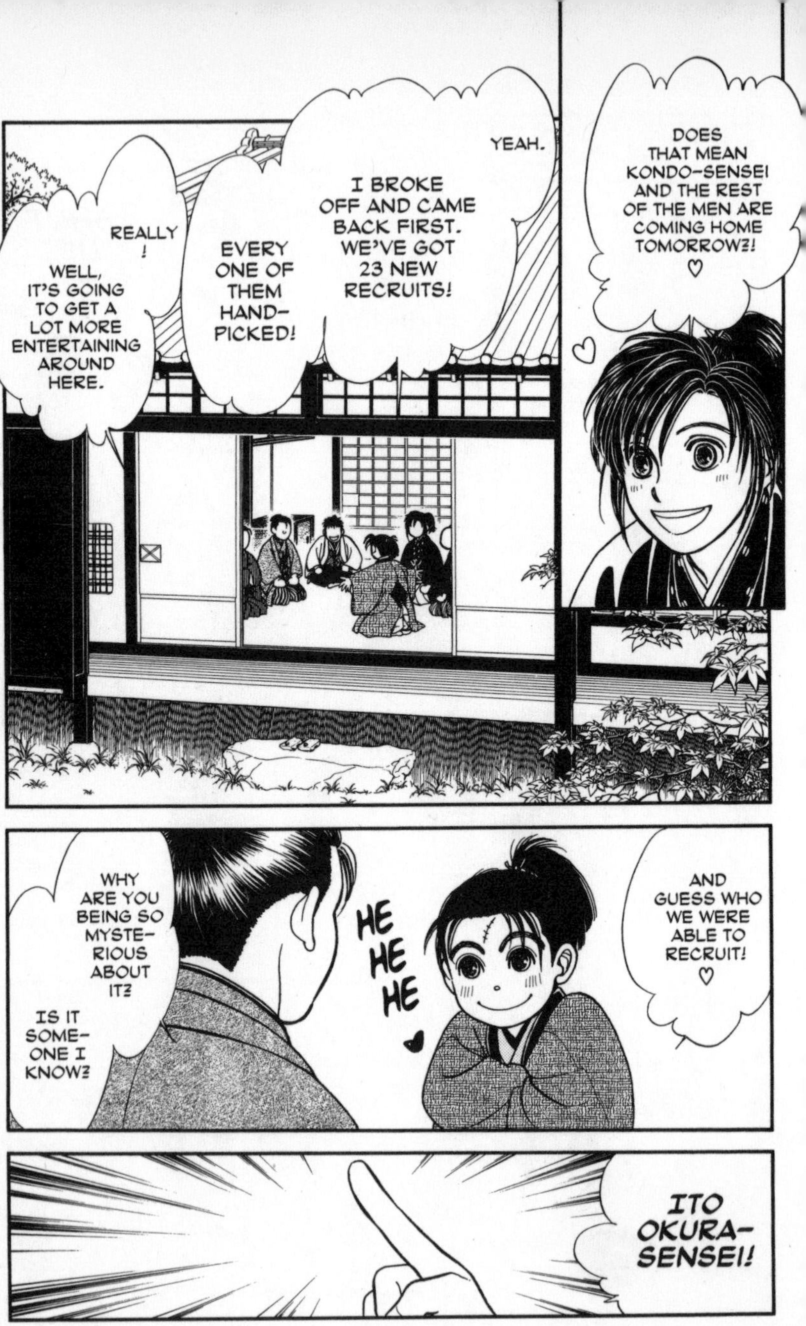
DOES THAT MEAN KONDO-SENSEI AND THE REST OF THE MEN ARE COMING HOME TOMORROW?! ♡
YEAH.
I BROKE OFF AND CAME BACK FIRST. WE'VE GOT 23 NEW RECRUITS!
EVERY ONE OF THEM HAND-PICKED!
REALLY!
WELL, IT'S GOING TO GET A LOT MORE ENTERTAINING AROUND HERE.
AND GUESS WHO WE WERE ABLE TO RECRUIT! ♡
HE HE HE
WHY ARE YOU BEING SO MYSTERIOUS ABOUT IT?
IS IT SOMEONE I KNOW?
ITO OKURA-SENSEI!

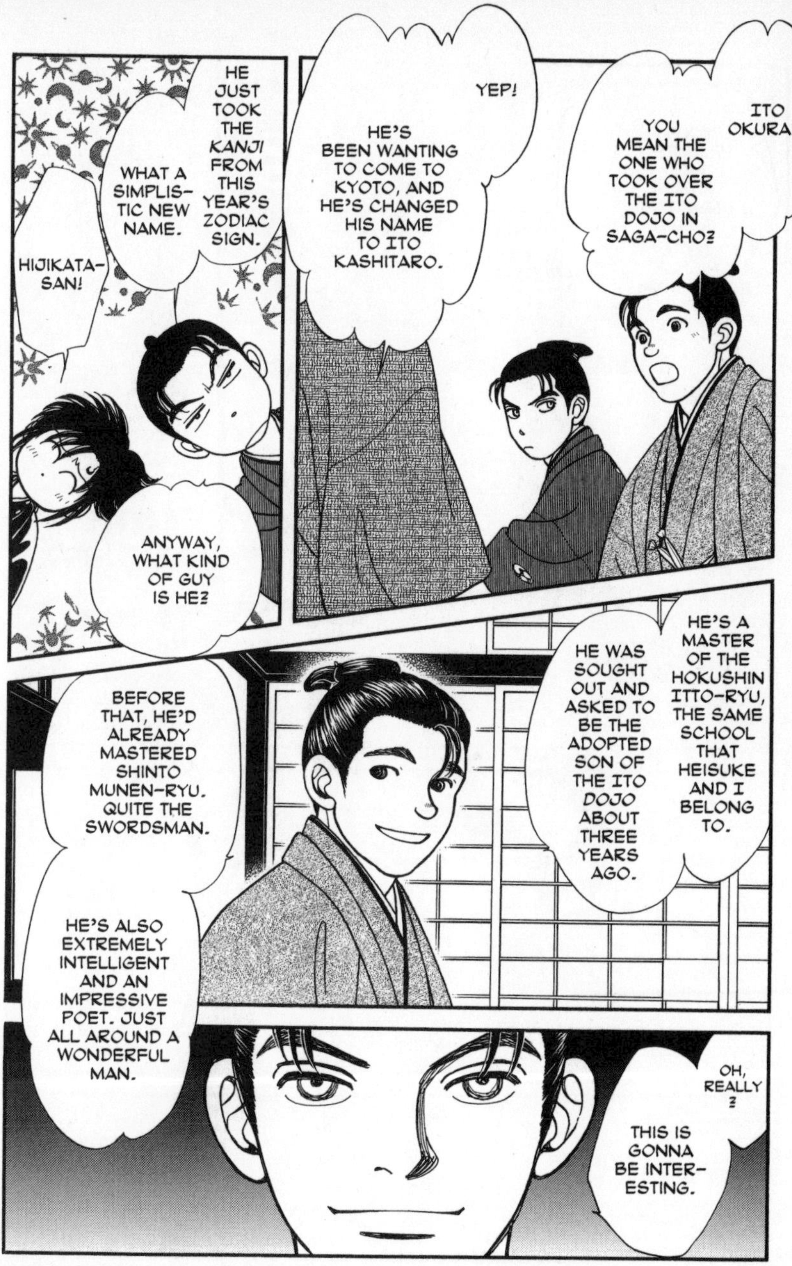
ITO OKURA?!
YOU MEAN THE ONE WHO TOOK OVER THE ITO DOJO IN SAGA-CHO?
YEP!
HE'S BEEN WANTING TO COME TO KYOTO, AND HE'S CHANGED HIS NAME TO ITO KASHITARO.
HE JUST TOOK THE *KANJI* FROM THIS YEAR'S ZODIAC SIGN.
WHAT A SIMPLISTIC NEW NAME.
HIJIKATA-SAN!
ANYWAY, WHAT KIND OF GUY IS HE?
HE'S A MASTER OF THE HOKUSHIN ITTO-RYU, THE SAME SCHOOL THAT HEISUKE AND I BELONG TO.
HE WAS SOUGHT OUT AND ASKED TO BE THE ADOPTED SON OF THE ITO *DOJO* ABOUT THREE YEARS AGO.
BEFORE THAT, HE'D ALREADY MASTERED SHINTO MUNEN-RYU. QUITE THE SWORDSMAN.
HE'S ALSO EXTREMELY INTELLIGENT AND AN IMPRESSIVE POET. JUST ALL AROUND A WONDERFUL MAN.
OH, REALLY?
THIS IS GONNA BE INTERESTING.

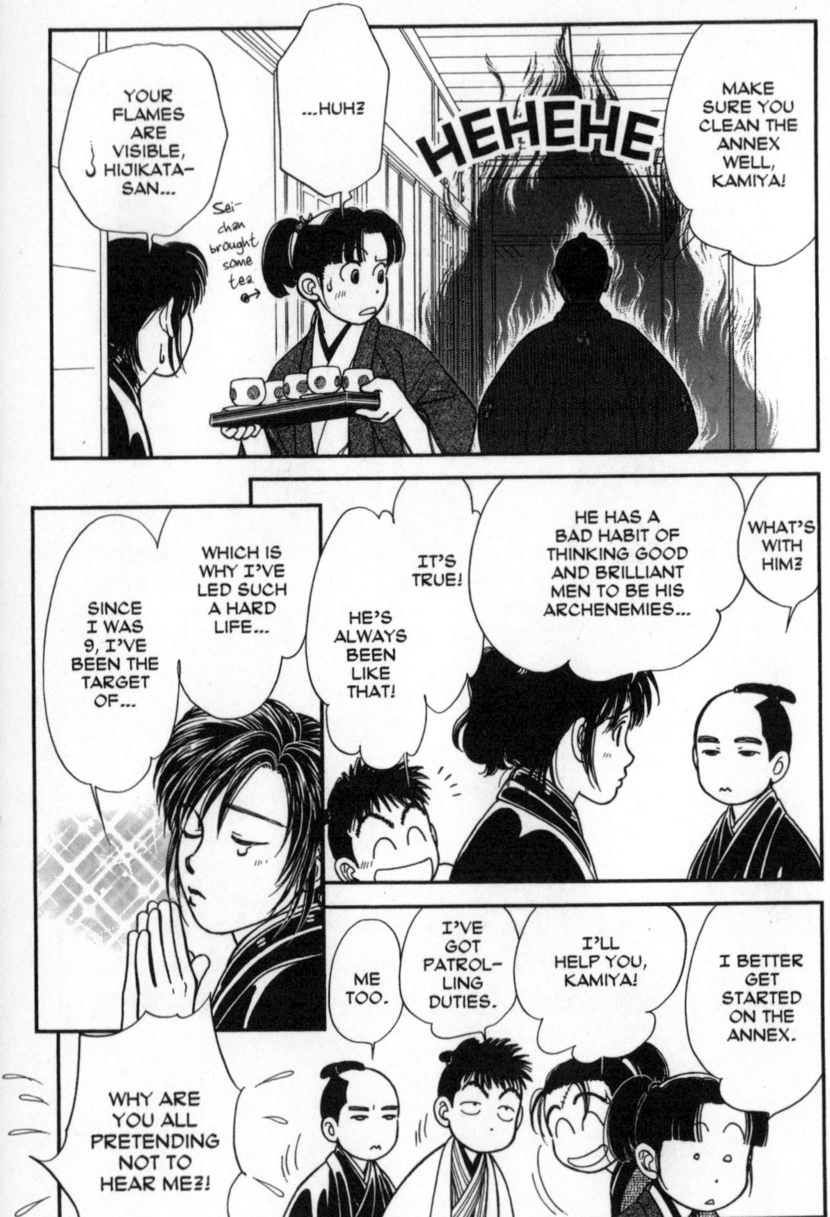
MAKE SURE YOU CLEAN THE ANNEX WELL, KAMIYA!
HEHEHE
...HUH?
Sei-chan brought some tea.
YOUR FLAMES ARE VISIBLE, HIJIKATA-SAN...
WHAT'S WITH HIM?
HE HAS A BAD HABIT OF THINKING GOOD AND BRILLIANT MEN TO BE HIS ARCHENEMIES...
IT'S TRUE!
HE'S ALWAYS BEEN LIKE THAT!
WHICH IS WHY I'VE LED SUCH A HARD LIFE...
SINCE I WAS 9, I'VE BEEN THE TARGET OF...
I BETTER GET STARTED ON THE ANNEX.
I'LL HELP YOU, KAMIYA!
I'VE GOT PATROL-LING DUTIES.
ME TOO.
WHY ARE YOU ALL PRETENDING NOT TO HEAR ME?!

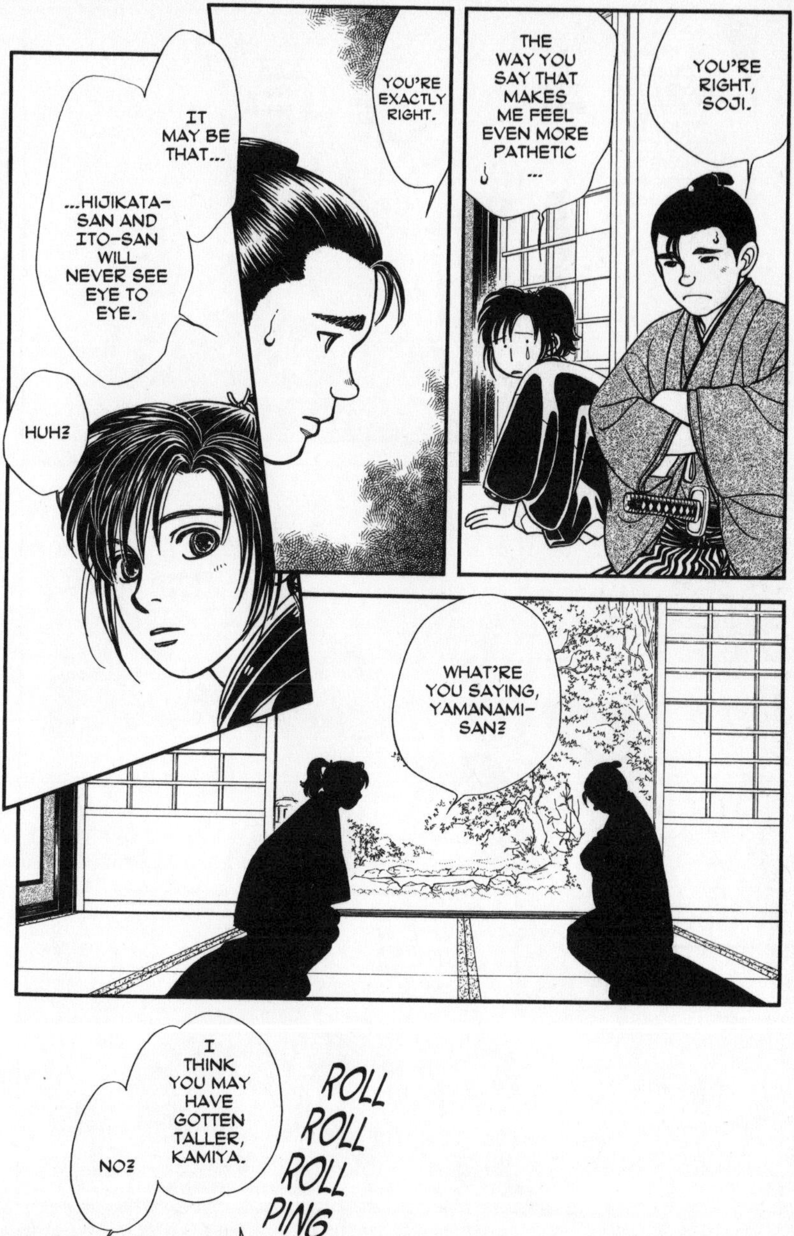
YOU'RE RIGHT, SOJI.
THE WAY YOU SAY THAT MAKES ME FEEL EVEN MORE PATHETIC...
YOU'RE EXACTLY RIGHT.
IT MAY BE THAT...
...HIJIKATA-SAN AND ITO-SAN WILL NEVER SEE EYE TO EYE.
HUH?
WHAT'RE YOU SAYING, YAMANAMI-SAN?
I THINK YOU MAY HAVE GOTTEN TALLER, KAMIYA.
NO?
ROLL ROLL ROLL PING

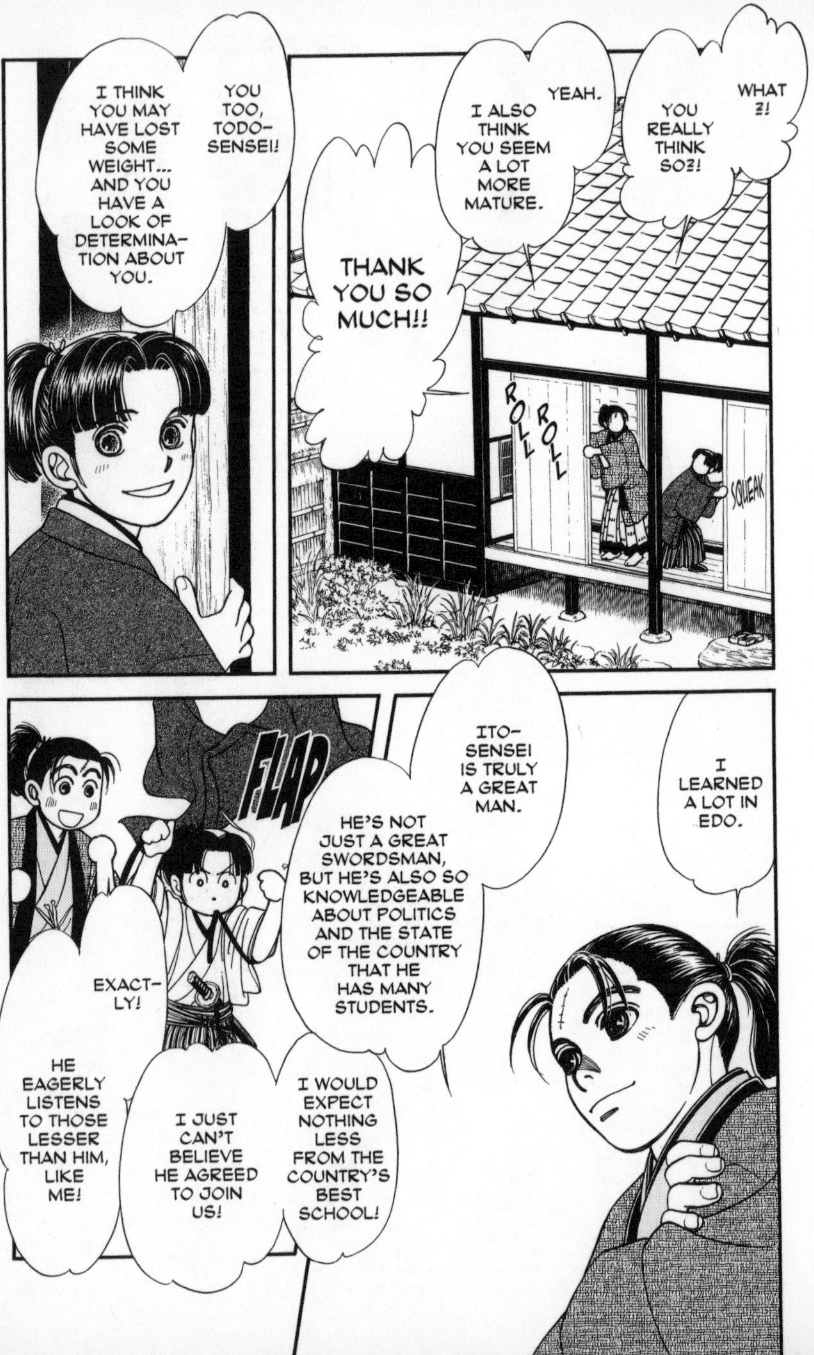
WHAT?! YOU REALLY THINK SO?!
YEAH. I ALSO THINK YOU SEEM A LOT MORE MATURE.
THANK YOU SO MUCH!!
ROLL ROLL
SQUEAK
YOU TOO, TODO-SENSEI!
I THINK YOU MAY HAVE LOST SOME WEIGHT... AND YOU HAVE A LOOK OF DETERMINATION ABOUT YOU.
I LEARNED A LOT IN EDO.
ITO-SENSEI IS TRULY A GREAT MAN.
HE'S NOT JUST A GREAT SWORDSMAN, BUT HE'S ALSO SO KNOWLEDGEABLE ABOUT POLITICS AND THE STATE OF THE COUNTRY THAT HE HAS MANY STUDENTS.
FLAP
I WOULD EXPECT NOTHING LESS FROM THE COUNTRY'S BEST SCHOOL!
I JUST CAN'T BELIEVE HE AGREED TO JOIN US!
EXACTLY!
HE EAGERLY LISTENS TO THOSE LESSER THAN HIM, LIKE ME!

*Short for *sonno joi.*

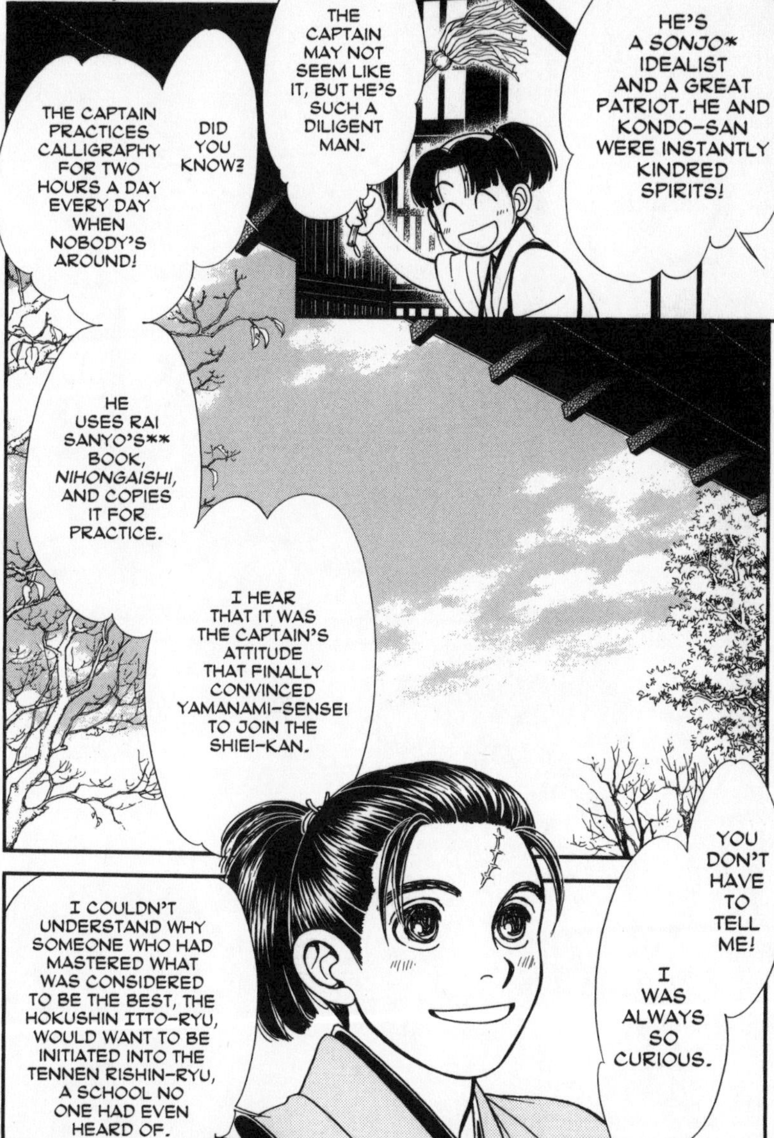
HE'S A *SONJO** IDEALIST AND A GREAT PATRIOT. HE AND KONDO-SAN WERE INSTANTLY KINDRED SPIRITS!
THE CAPTAIN MAY NOT SEEM LIKE IT, BUT HE'S SUCH A DILIGENT MAN.
DID YOU KNOW?
THE CAPTAIN PRACTICES CALLIGRAPHY FOR TWO HOURS A DAY EVERY DAY WHEN NOBODY'S AROUND!
HE USES RAI SANYO'S** BOOK, *NIHONGAISHI,* AND COPIES IT FOR PRACTICE.
I HEAR THAT IT WAS THE CAPTAIN'S ATTITUDE THAT FINALLY CONVINCED YAMANAMI-SENSEI TO JOIN THE SHIEI-KAN.
YOU DON'T HAVE TO TELL ME!
I WAS ALWAYS SO CURIOUS.
I COULDN'T UNDERSTAND WHY SOMEONE WHO HAD MASTERED WHAT WAS CONSIDERED TO BE THE BEST, THE HOKUSHIN ITTO-RYU, WOULD WANT TO BE INITIATED INTO THE TENNEN RISHIN-RYU, A SCHOOL NO ONE HAD EVEN HEARD OF.

**A Confucian philosopher who was a famed poet and author, but who was also interested in historiography. His famous works include, *Nihongaishi, Nihonseiki* and *Sanyo Shishu.*

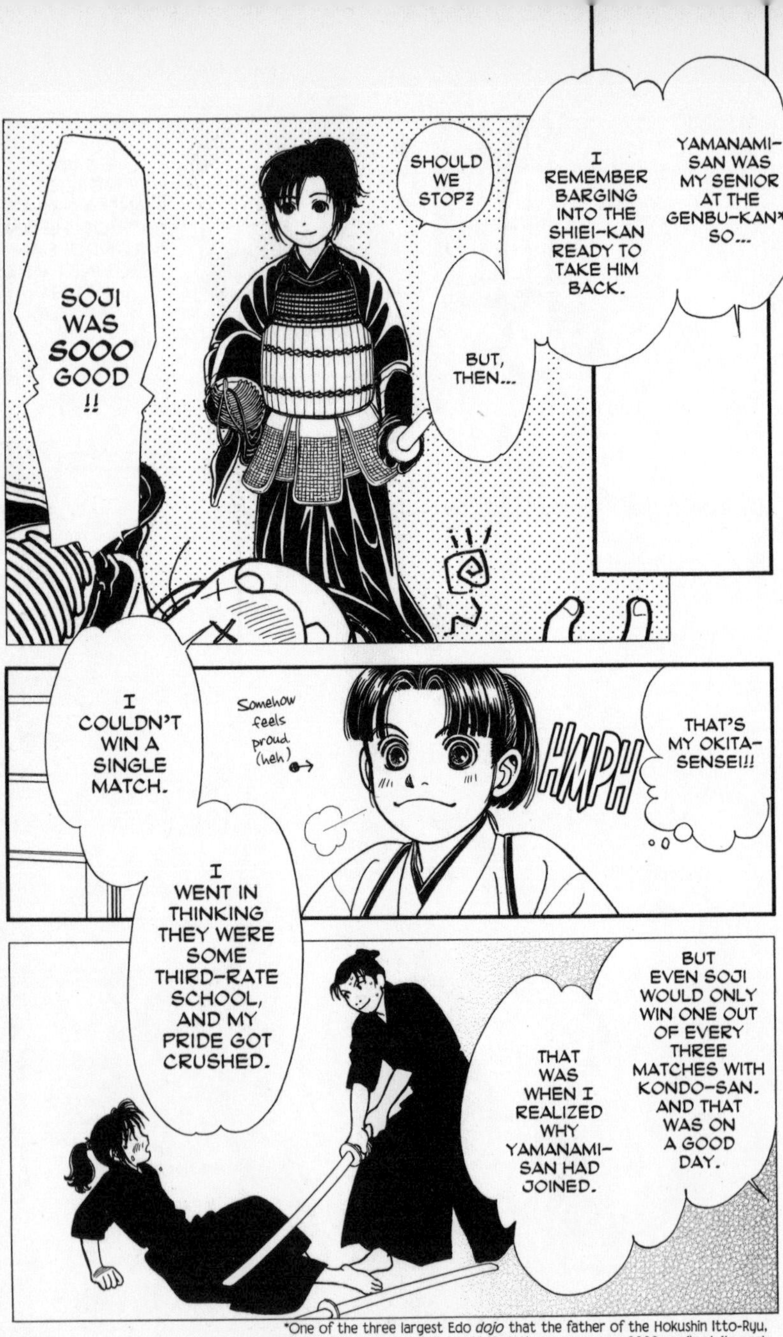
YAMANAMI-SAN WAS MY SENIOR AT THE GENBU-KAN*, SO...
I REMEMBER BARGING INTO THE SHIEI-KAN READY TO TAKE HIM BACK.
BUT, THEN...
SHOULD WE STOP?
SOJI WAS SOOO GOOD!!
THAT'S MY OKITA-SENSEI!!
HMPH
Somehow feels proud (heh)
I COULDN'T WIN A SINGLE MATCH.
BUT EVEN SOJI WOULD ONLY WIN ONE OUT OF EVERY THREE MATCHES WITH KONDO-SAN. AND THAT WAS ON A GOOD DAY.
THAT WAS WHEN I REALIZED WHY YAMANAMI-SAN HAD JOINED.
I WENT IN THINKING THEY WERE SOME THIRD-RATE SCHOOL, AND MY PRIDE GOT CRUSHED.

*One of the three largest Edo *dojo* that the father of the Hokushin Itto-Ryu, Chiba Shusaku, opened. It is said that there were over 3000 pupils at its peak.

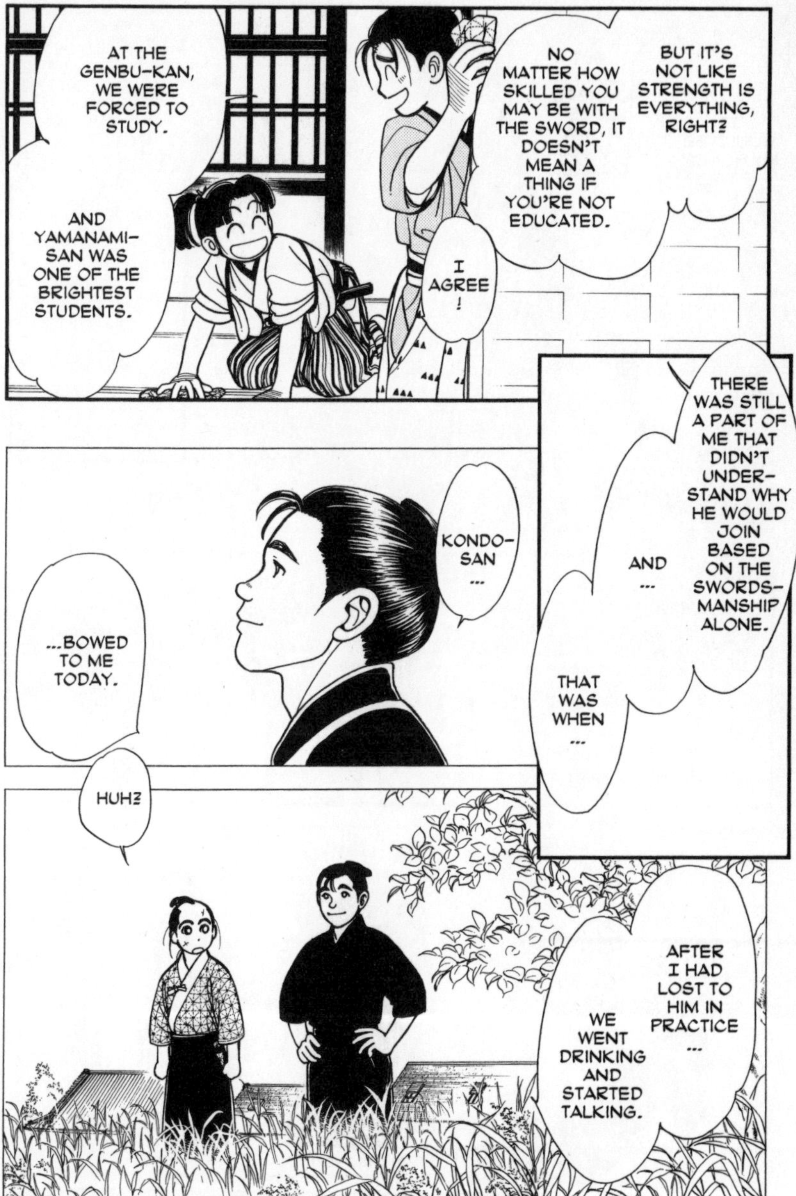
BUT IT'S NOT LIKE STRENGTH IS EVERYTHING, RIGHT?
NO MATTER HOW SKILLED YOU MAY BE WITH THE SWORD, IT DOESN'T MEAN A THING IF YOU'RE NOT EDUCATED.
AT THE GENBU-KAN, WE WERE FORCED TO STUDY.
I AGREE!
AND YAMANAMI-SAN WAS ONE OF THE BRIGHTEST STUDENTS.
THERE WAS STILL A PART OF ME THAT DIDN'T UNDER-STAND WHY HE WOULD JOIN BASED ON THE SWORDS-MANSHIP ALONE.
AND...
THAT WAS WHEN...
KONDO-SAN...
...BOWED TO ME TODAY.
HUH?
AFTER I HAD LOST TO HIM IN PRACTICE...
WE WENT DRINKING AND STARTED TALKING.

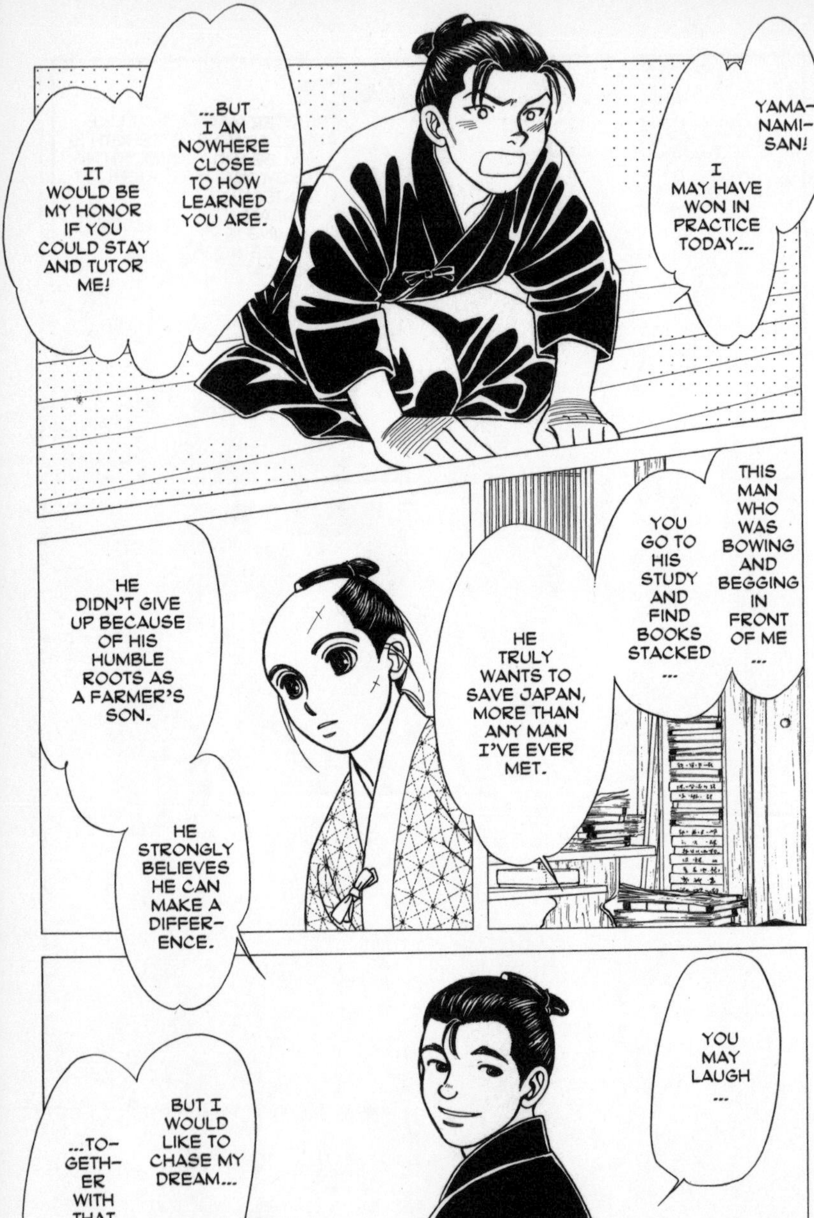
YAMA-NAMI-SAN!
I MAY HAVE WON IN PRACTICE TODAY...
...BUT I AM NOWHERE CLOSE TO HOW LEARNED YOU ARE.
IT WOULD BE MY HONOR IF YOU COULD STAY AND TUTOR ME!
THIS MAN WHO WAS BOWING AND BEGGING IN FRONT OF ME...
YOU GO TO HIS STUDY AND FIND BOOKS STACKED...
HE TRULY WANTS TO SAVE JAPAN, MORE THAN ANY MAN I'VE EVER MET.
HE DIDN'T GIVE UP BECAUSE OF HIS HUMBLE ROOTS AS A FARMER'S SON.
HE STRONGLY BELIEVES HE CAN MAKE A DIFFER-ENCE.
YOU MAY LAUGH...
BUT I WOULD LIKE TO CHASE MY DREAM...
...TO-GETH-ER WITH THAT MAN.

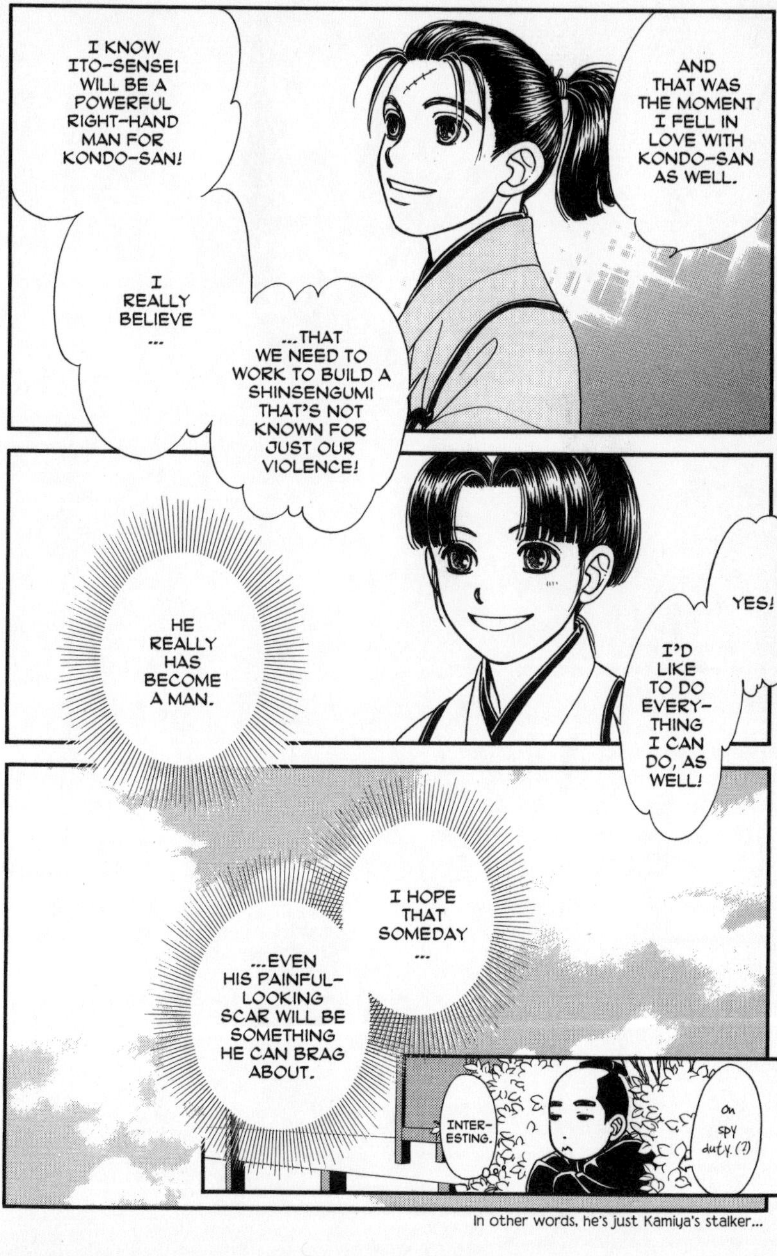
AND THAT WAS THE MOMENT I FELL IN LOVE WITH KONDO-SAN AS WELL.
I KNOW ITO-SENSEI WILL BE A POWERFUL RIGHT-HAND MAN FOR KONDO-SAN!
I REALLY BELIEVE...
...THAT WE NEED TO WORK TO BUILD A SHINSENGUMI THAT'S NOT KNOWN FOR JUST OUR VIOLENCE!
YES!
I'D LIKE TO DO EVERYTHING I CAN DO, AS WELL!
HE REALLY HAS BECOME A MAN.
I HOPE THAT SOMEDAY...
...EVEN HIS PAINFUL-LOOKING SCAR WILL BE SOMETHING HE CAN BRAG ABOUT.
On spy duty. (?)
INTERESTING.

In other words, he's just Kamiya's stalker...

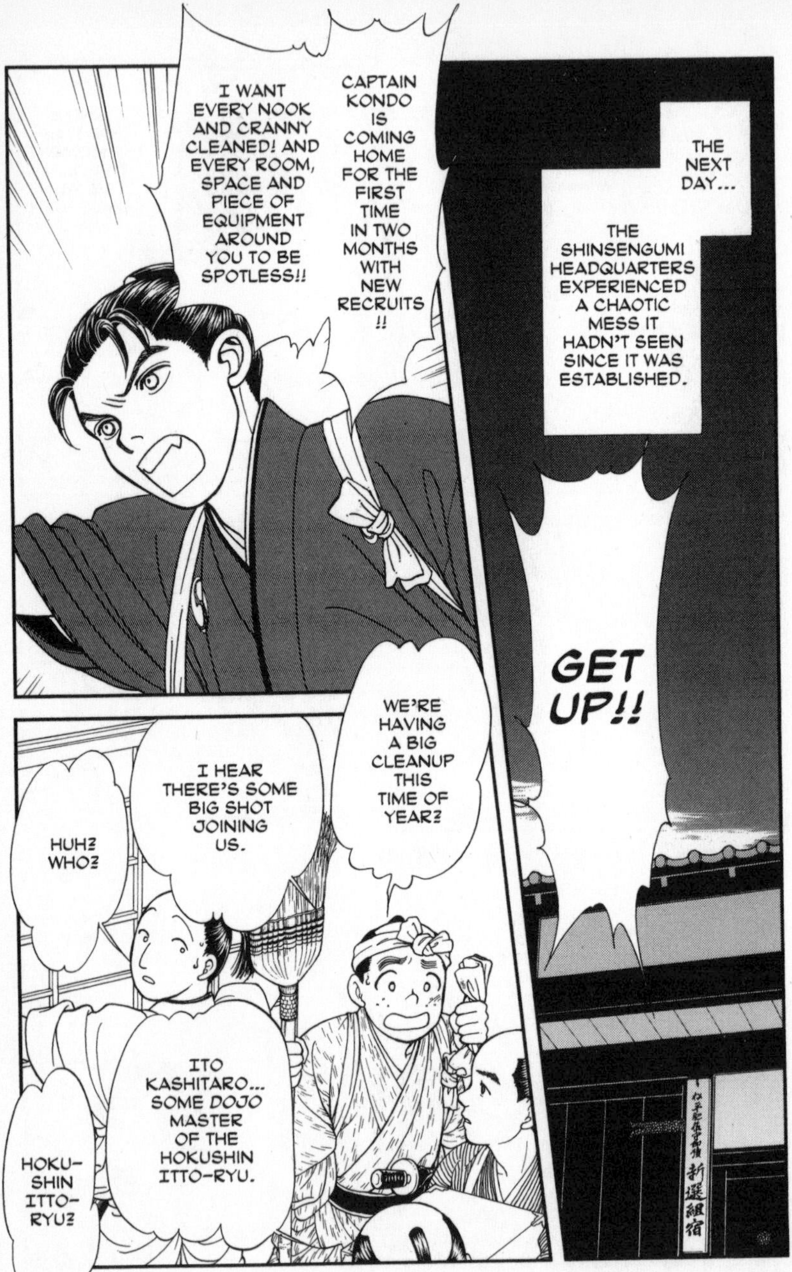
THE NEXT DAY...
THE SHINSENGUMI HEADQUARTERS EXPERIENCED A CHAOTIC MESS IT HADN'T SEEN SINCE IT WAS ESTABLISHED.
新選組宿
GET UP!!
CAPTAIN KONDO IS COMING HOME FOR THE FIRST TIME IN TWO MONTHS WITH NEW RECRUITS!!
I WANT EVERY NOOK AND CRANNY CLEANED! AND EVERY ROOM, SPACE AND PIECE OF EQUIPMENT AROUND YOU TO BE SPOTLESS!!
WE'RE HAVING A BIG CLEANUP THIS TIME OF YEAR?
I HEAR THERE'S SOME BIG SHOT JOINING US.
HUH? WHO?
ITO KASHITARO... SOME *DOJO* MASTER OF THE HOKUSHIN ITTO-RYU.
HOKU-SHIN ITTO-RYU?

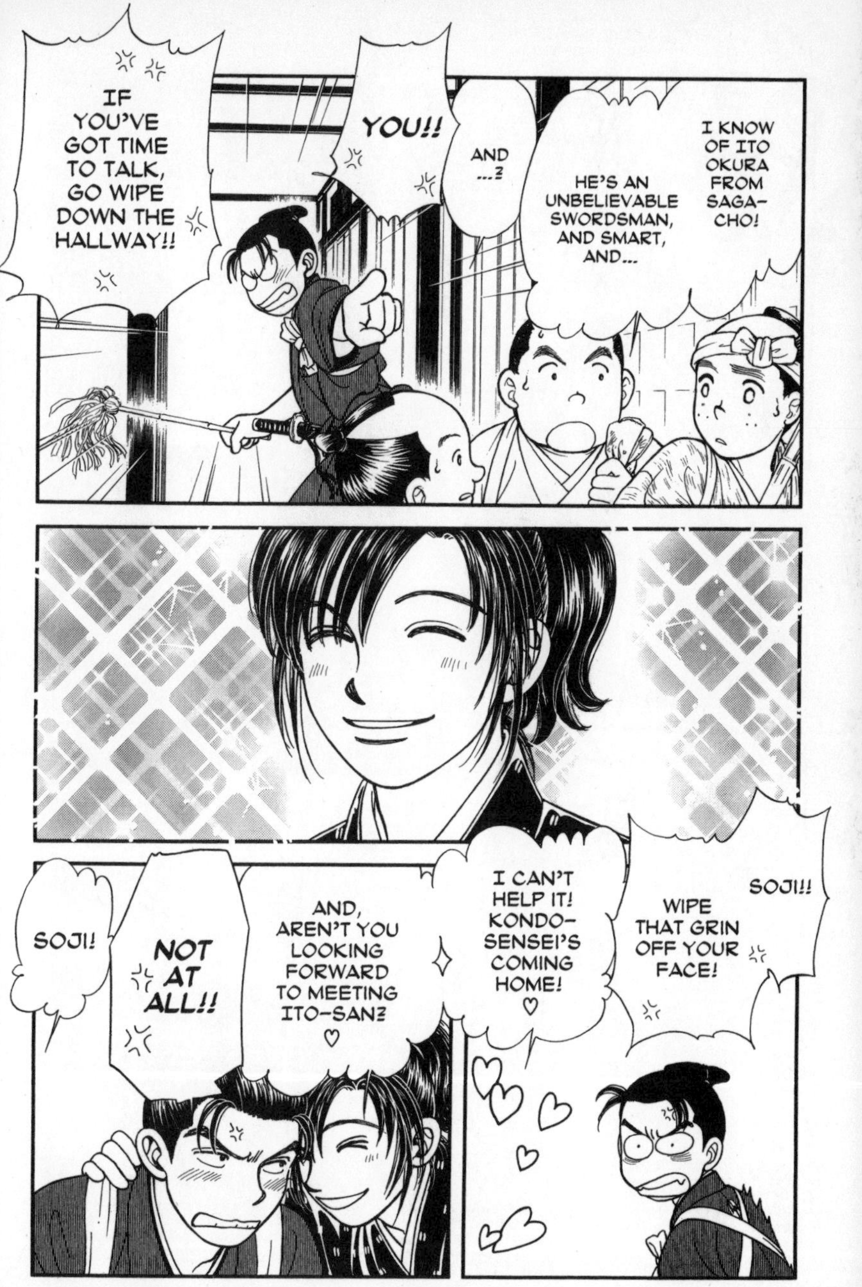
I KNOW OF ITO OKURA FROM SAGA-CHO!
HE'S AN UNBELIEVABLE SWORDSMAN, AND SMART, AND...
AND ...?
YOU!!
IF YOU'VE GOT TIME TO TALK, GO WIPE DOWN THE HALLWAY!!
SOJI!!
WIPE THAT GRIN OFF YOUR FACE!
I CAN'T HELP IT! KONDO-SENSEI'S COMING HOME! ♡
AND, AREN'T YOU LOOKING FORWARD TO MEETING ITO-SAN? ♡
NOT AT ALL!!
SOJI!

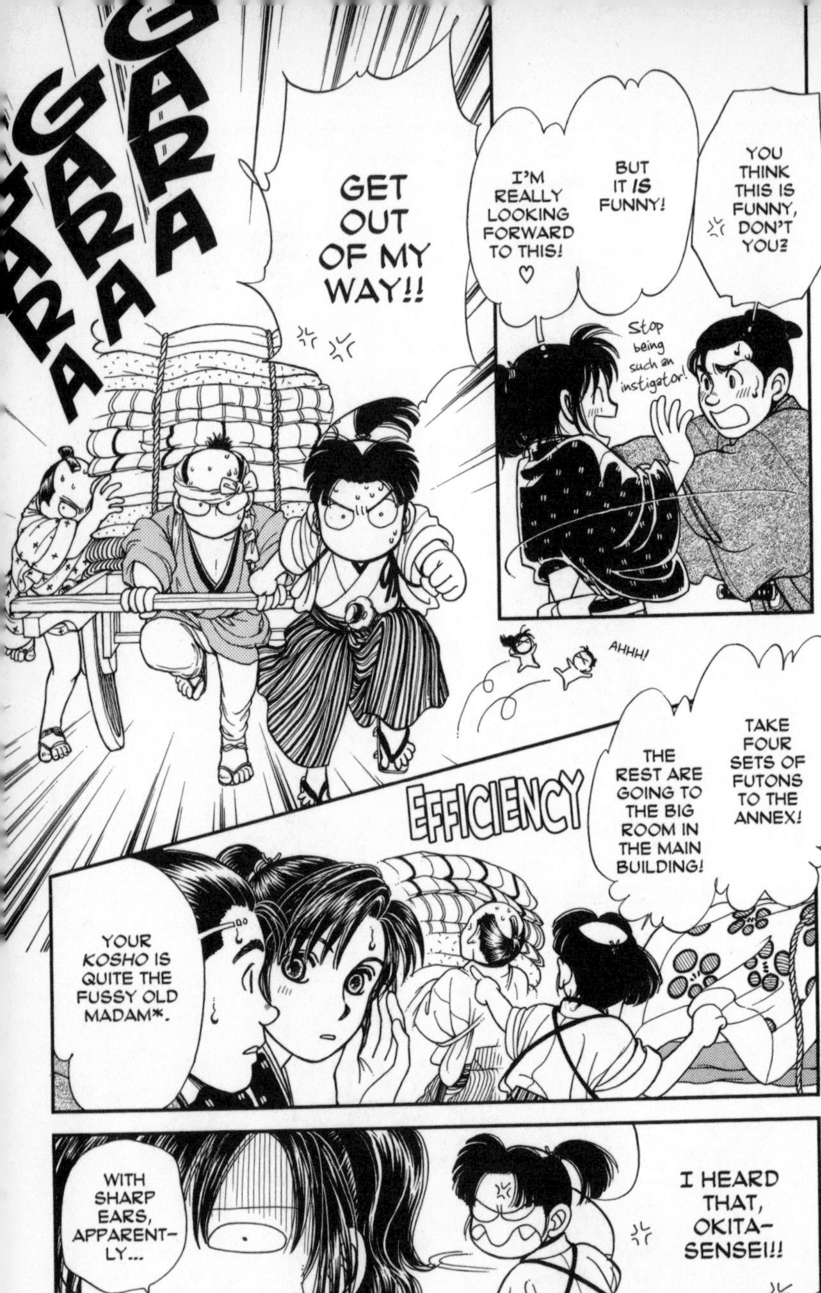
YOU THINK THIS IS FUNNY, DON'T YOU?
BUT IT IS FUNNY!
I'M REALLY LOOKING FORWARD TO THIS! ♡
Stop being such an instigator!
AHHH!
GARA GARA GARA GARA
GET OUT OF MY WAY!!
EFFICIENCY
TAKE FOUR SETS OF FUTONS TO THE ANNEX!
THE REST ARE GOING TO THE BIG ROOM IN THE MAIN BUILDING!
YOUR KOSHO IS QUITE THE FUSSY OLD MADAM*.
I HEARD THAT, OKITA-SENSEI!!!
WITH SHARP EARS, APPARENTLY...

*Okita is hinting that Kamiya resembles a manager at the brothels, who was usually an older woman.

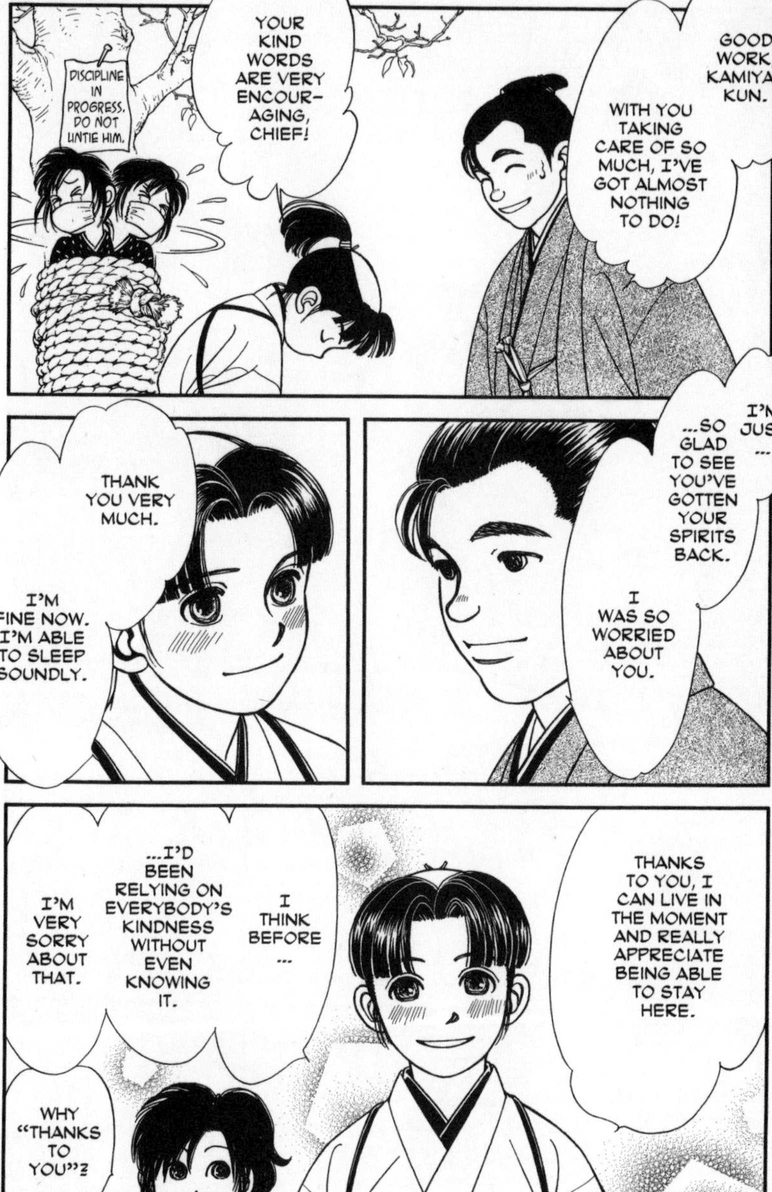
GOOD WORK, KAMIYA-KUN.
WITH YOU TAKING CARE OF SO MUCH, I'VE GOT ALMOST NOTHING TO DO!
YOUR KIND WORDS ARE VERY ENCOURAGING, CHIEF!
DISCIPLINE IN PROGRESS. DO NOT UNTIE HIM.
I'M JUST ...
...SO GLAD TO SEE YOU'VE GOTTEN YOUR SPIRITS BACK.
I WAS SO WORRIED ABOUT YOU.
THANK YOU VERY MUCH.
I'M FINE NOW. I'M ABLE TO SLEEP SOUNDLY.
THANKS TO YOU, I CAN LIVE IN THE MOMENT AND REALLY APPRECIATE BEING ABLE TO STAY HERE.
I THINK BEFORE ...
...I'D BEEN RELYING ON EVERYBODY'S KINDNESS WITHOUT EVEN KNOWING IT.
I'M VERY SORRY ABOUT THAT.
WHY "THANKS TO YOU"?

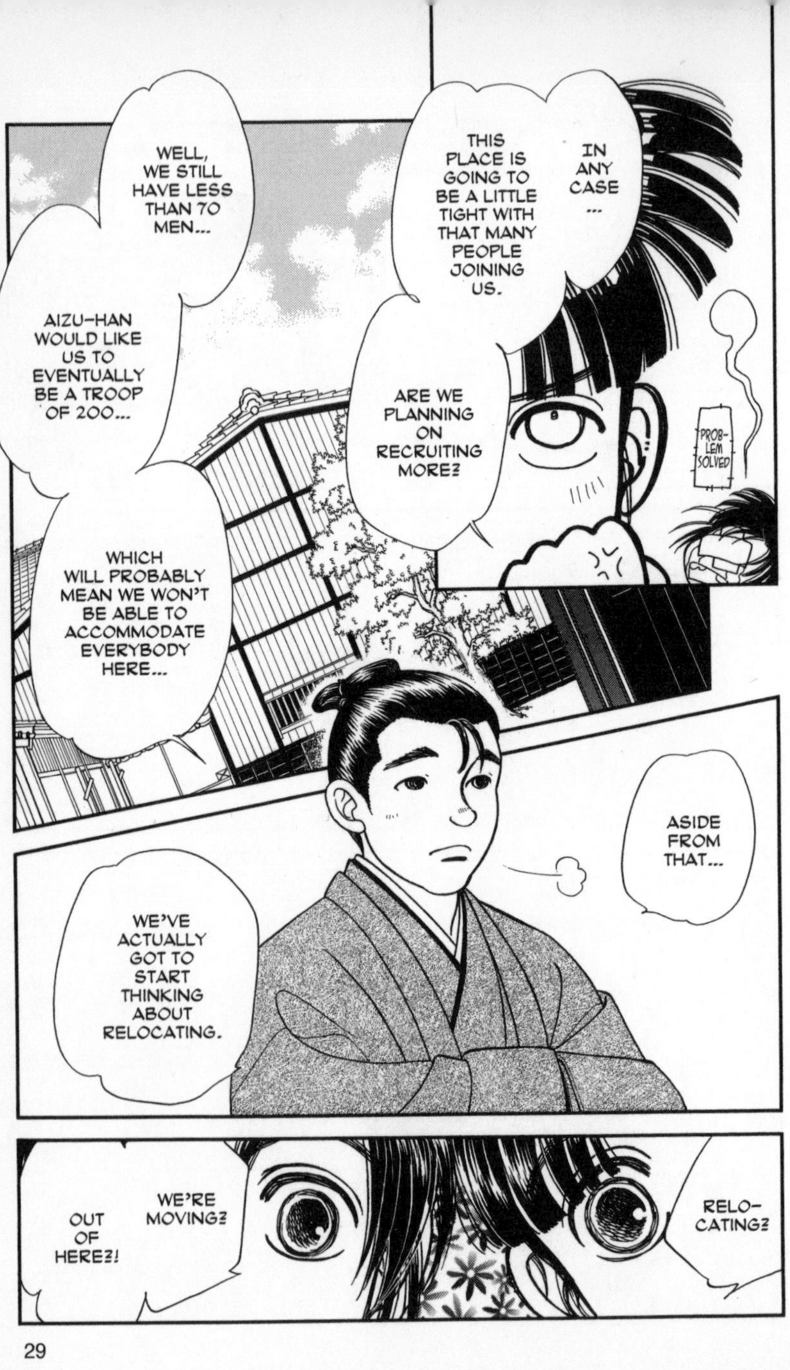
IN ANY CASE ...
THIS PLACE IS GOING TO BE A LITTLE TIGHT WITH THAT MANY PEOPLE JOINING US.
ARE WE PLANNING ON RECRUITING MORE?
PROB-LEM SOLVED
WELL, WE STILL HAVE LESS THAN 70 MEN...
AIZU-HAN WOULD LIKE US TO EVENTUALLY BE A TROOP OF 200...
WHICH WILL PROBABLY MEAN WE WON'T BE ABLE TO ACCOMMODATE EVERYBODY HERE...
ASIDE FROM THAT...
WE'VE ACTUALLY GOT TO START THINKING ABOUT RELOCATING.
RELO-CATING?
WE'RE MOVING?
OUT OF HERE?!

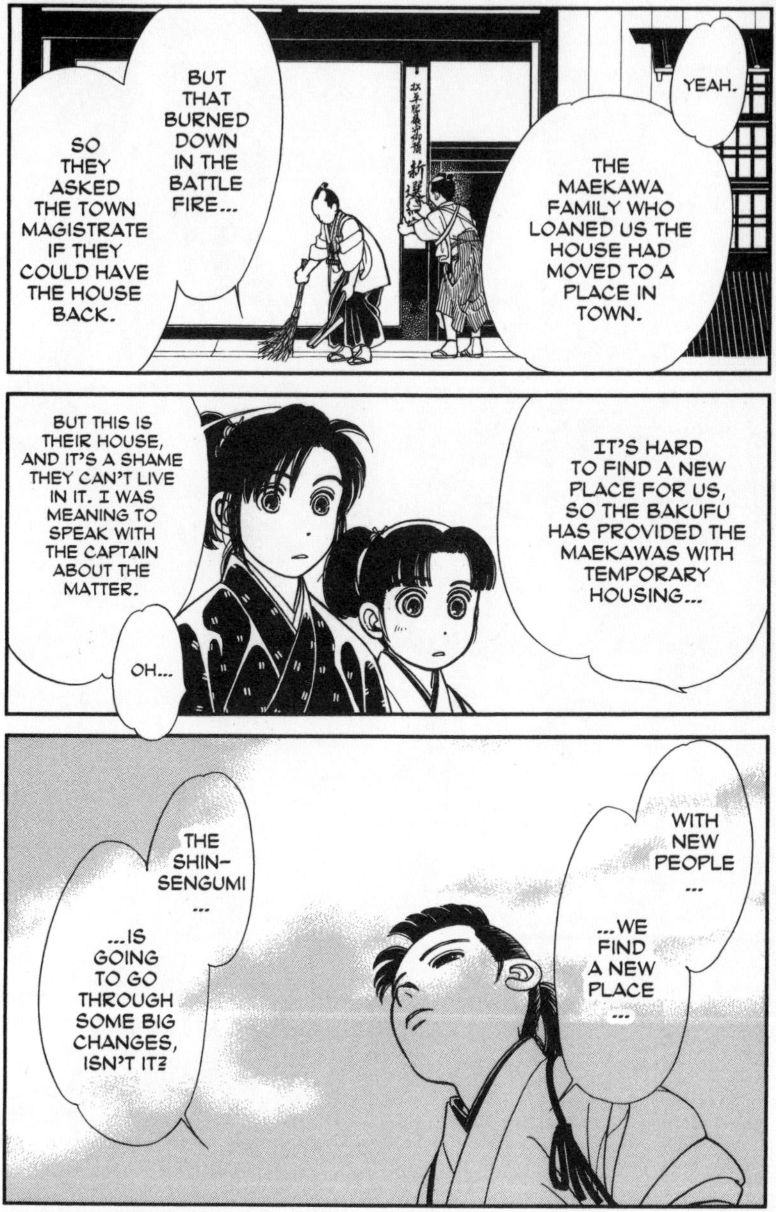

YEAH.
THE MAEKAWA FAMILY WHO LOANED US THE HOUSE HAD MOVED TO A PLACE IN TOWN.
BUT THAT BURNED DOWN IN THE BATTLE FIRE...
SO THEY ASKED THE TOWN MAGISTRATE IF THEY COULD HAVE THE HOUSE BACK.
IT'S HARD TO FIND A NEW PLACE FOR US, SO THE BAKUFU HAS PROVIDED THE MAEKAWAS WITH TEMPORARY HOUSING...
OH...
BUT THIS IS THEIR HOUSE, AND IT'S A SHAME THEY CAN'T LIVE IN IT. I WAS MEANING TO SPEAK WITH THE CAPTAIN ABOUT THE MATTER.
WITH NEW PEOPLE...
...WE FIND A NEW PLACE...
THE SHIN-SENGUMI...
...IS GOING TO GO THROUGH SOME BIG CHANGES, ISN'T IT?

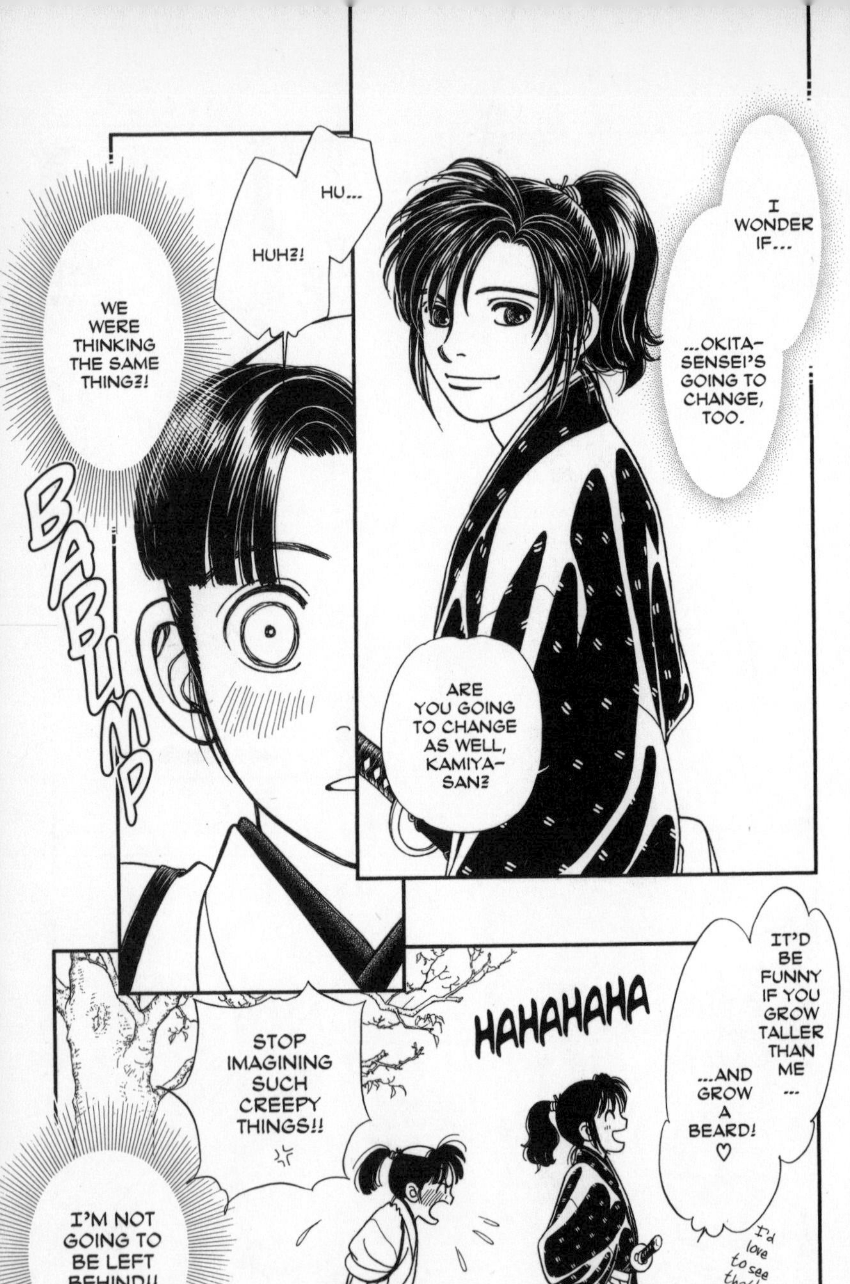
I WONDER IF...
...OKITA-SENSEI'S GOING TO CHANGE, TOO.
ARE YOU GOING TO CHANGE AS WELL, KAMIYA-SAN?
HU...
HUH?!
WE WERE THINKING THE SAME THING?!
BABUMP
IT'D BE FUNNY IF YOU GROW TALLER THAN ME...
...AND GROW A BEARD! ♡
HAHAHAHA
I'd love to see that!
STOP IMAGINING SUCH CREEPY THINGS!!
I'M NOT GOING TO BE LEFT BEHIND!!

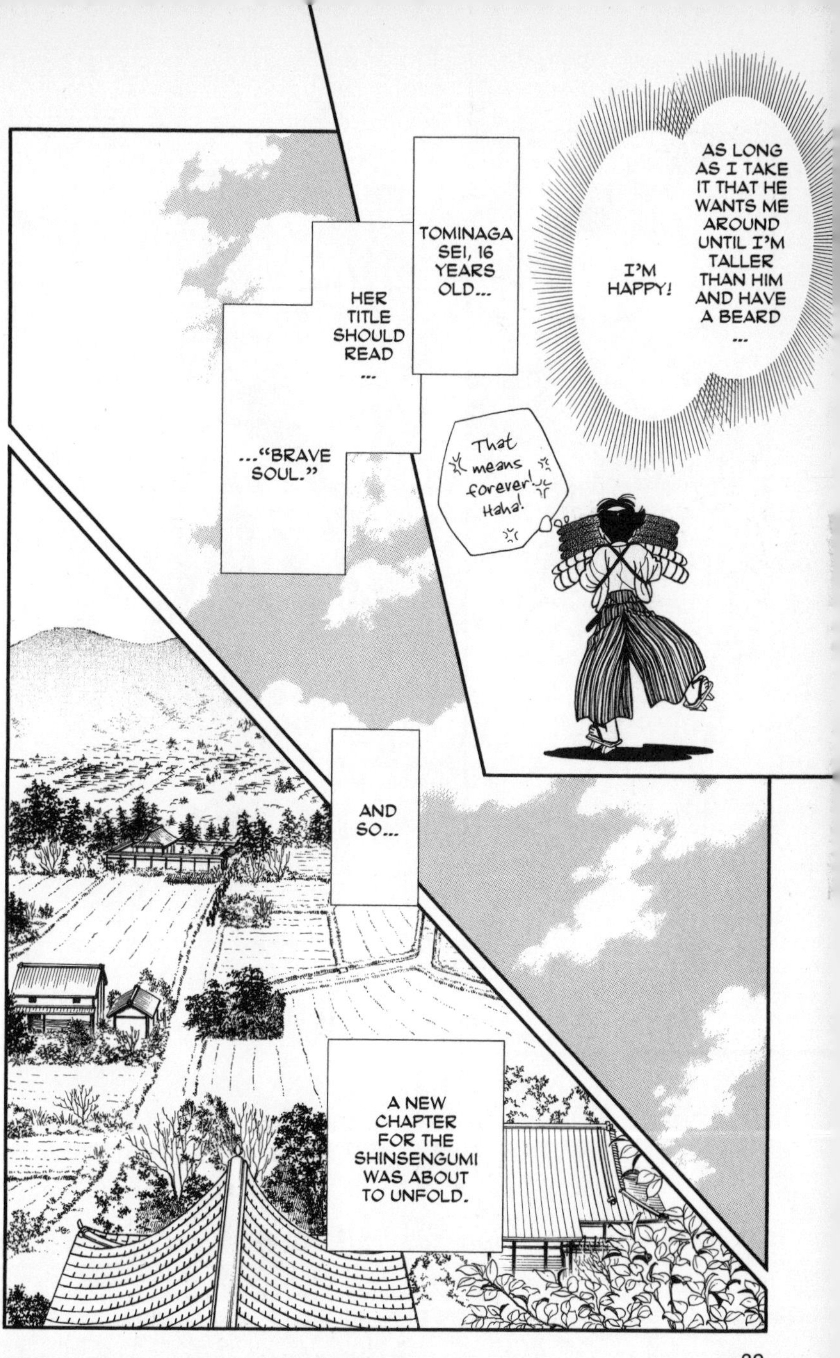
AS LONG AS I TAKE IT THAT HE WANTS ME AROUND UNTIL I'M TALLER THAN HIM AND HAVE A BEARD ...
I'M HAPPY!
That means forever! Haha!
TOMINAGA SEI, 16 YEARS OLD...
HER TITLE SHOULD READ ...
..."BRAVE SOUL."
AND SO...
A NEW CHAPTER FOR THE SHINSENGUMI WAS ABOUT TO UNFOLD.

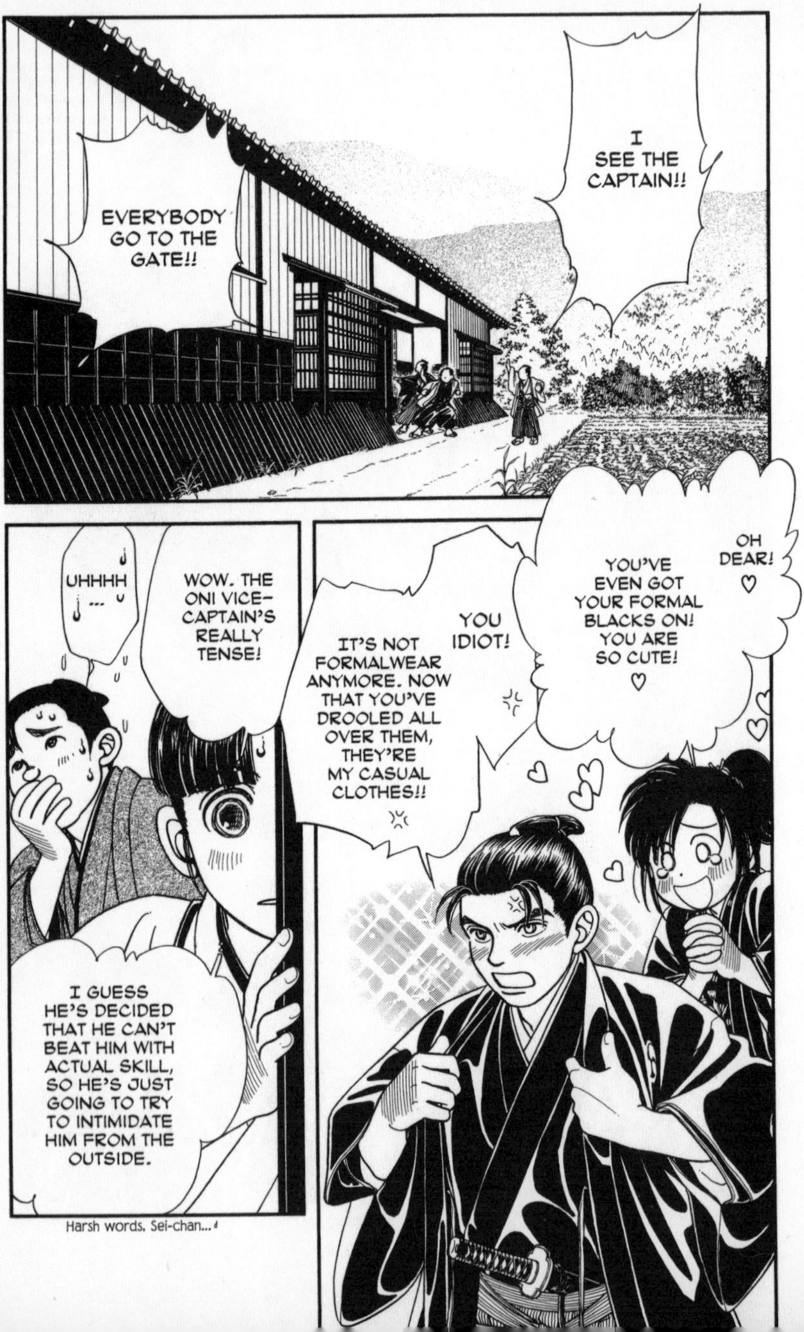
I SEE THE CAPTAIN!!
EVERYBODY GO TO THE GATE!!
OH DEAR! ♡
YOU'VE EVEN GOT YOUR FORMAL BLACKS ON! YOU ARE SO CUTE! ♡
YOU IDIOT!
IT'S NOT FORMALWEAR ANYMORE. NOW THAT YOU'VE DROOLED ALL OVER THEM, THEY'RE MY CASUAL CLOTHES!!
WOW. THE ONI VICE-CAPTAIN'S REALLY TENSE!
UHHHH...
I GUESS HE'S DECIDED THAT HE CAN'T BEAT HIM WITH ACTUAL SKILL, SO HE'S JUST GOING TO TRY TO INTIMIDATE HIM FROM THE OUTSIDE.

Harsh words, Sei-chan...

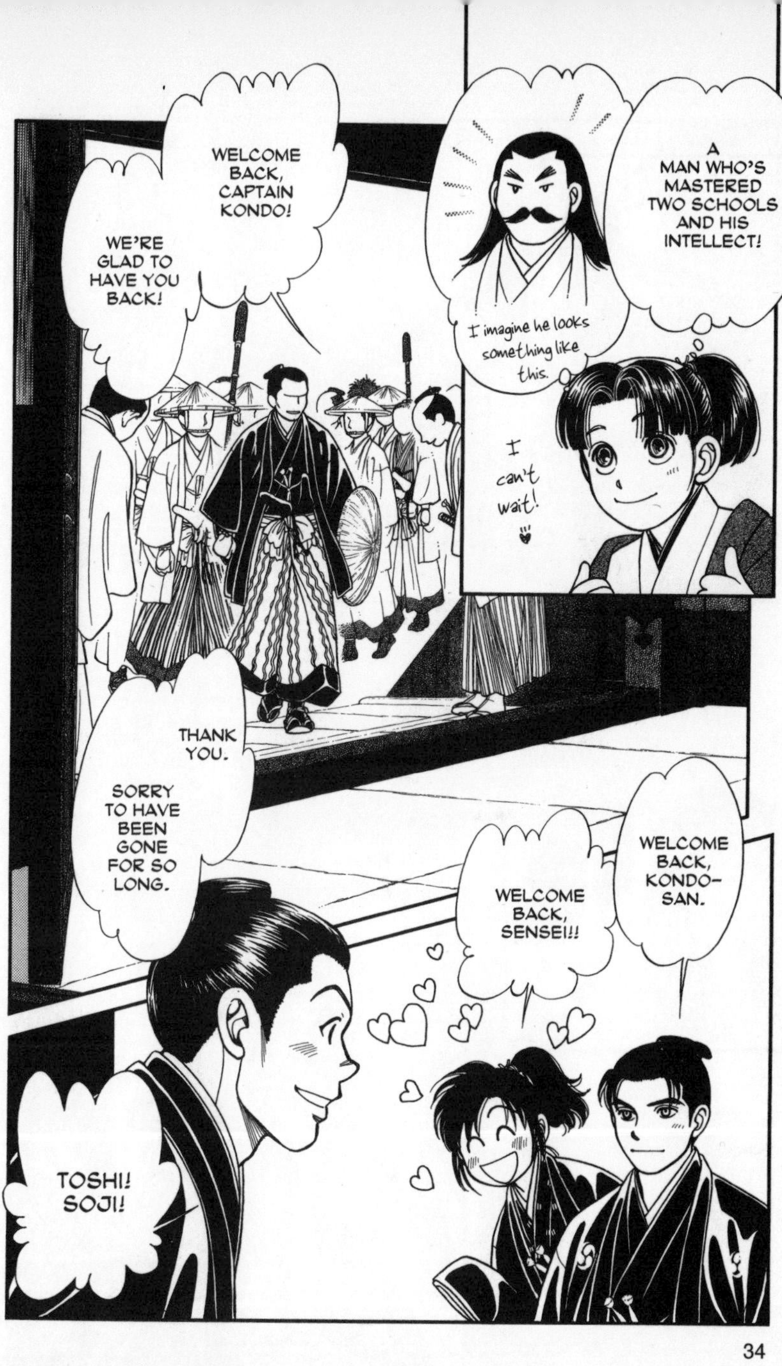
A MAN WHO'S MASTERED TWO SCHOOLS AND HIS INTELLECT!
I imagine he looks something like this.
I can't wait!
WELCOME BACK, CAPTAIN KONDO!
WE'RE GLAD TO HAVE YOU BACK!
THANK YOU.
SORRY TO HAVE BEEN GONE FOR SO LONG.
WELCOME BACK, KONDO-SAN.
WELCOME BACK, SENSEI!!
TOSHI! SOJI!

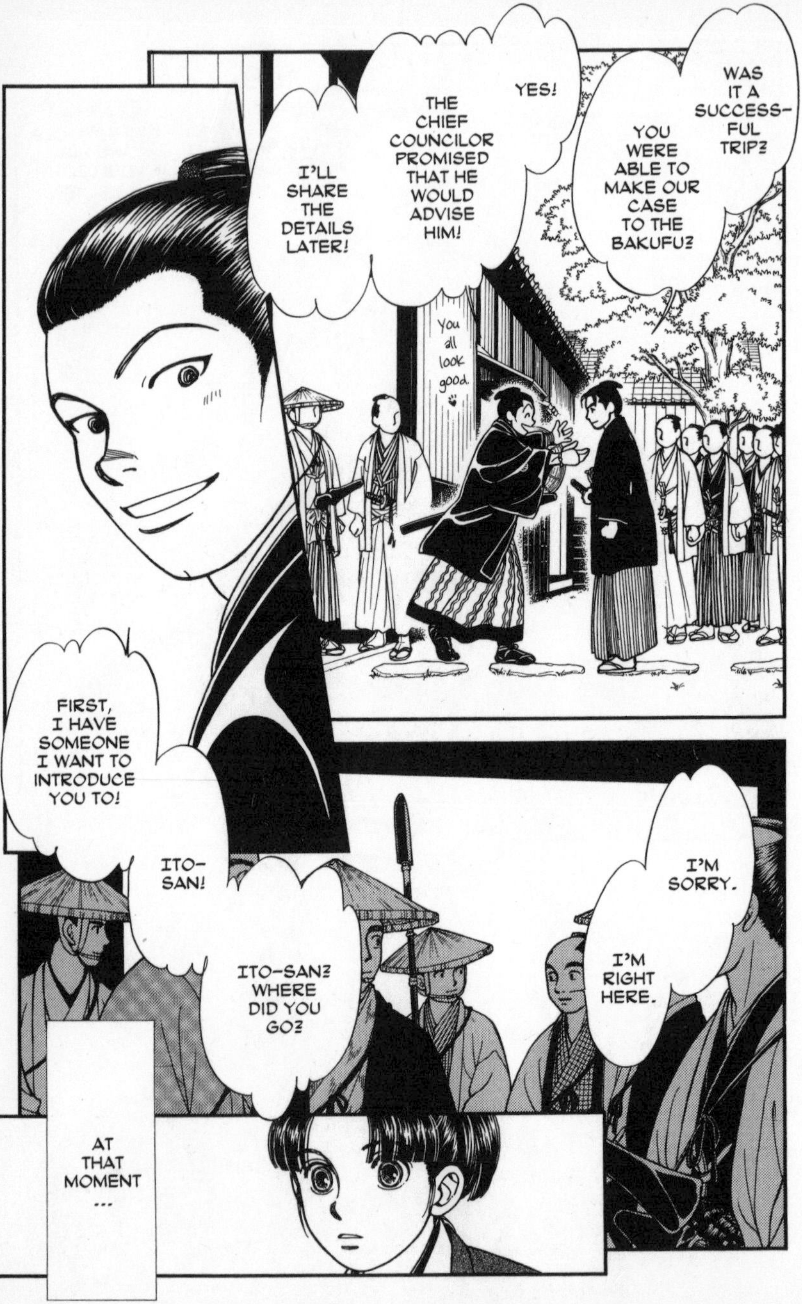
WAS IT A SUCCESSFUL TRIP?
YOU WERE ABLE TO MAKE OUR CASE TO THE BAKUFU?
YES!
THE CHIEF COUNCILOR PROMISED THAT HE WOULD ADVISE HIM!
I'LL SHARE THE DETAILS LATER!
You all look good.
FIRST, I HAVE SOMEONE I WANT TO INTRODUCE YOU TO!
ITO-SAN!
ITO-SAN? WHERE DID YOU GO?
I'M SORRY.
I'M RIGHT HERE.
AT THAT MOMENT ...

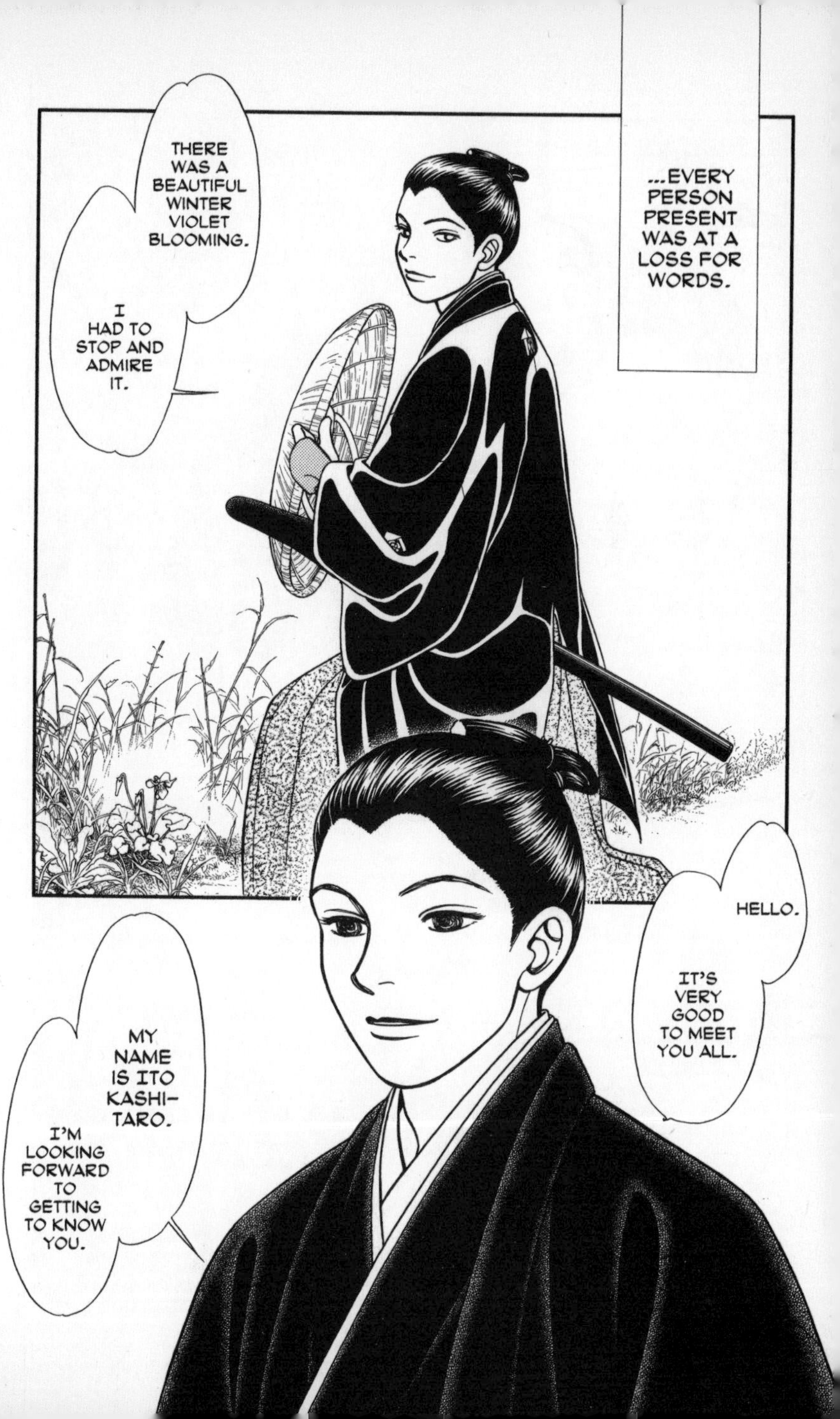
...EVERY PERSON PRESENT WAS AT A LOSS FOR WORDS.
THERE WAS A BEAUTIFUL WINTER VIOLET BLOOMING.
I HAD TO STOP AND ADMIRE IT.
HELLO.
IT'S VERY GOOD TO MEET YOU ALL.
MY NAME IS ITO KASHI-TARO.
I'M LOOKING FORWARD TO GETTING TO KNOW YOU.

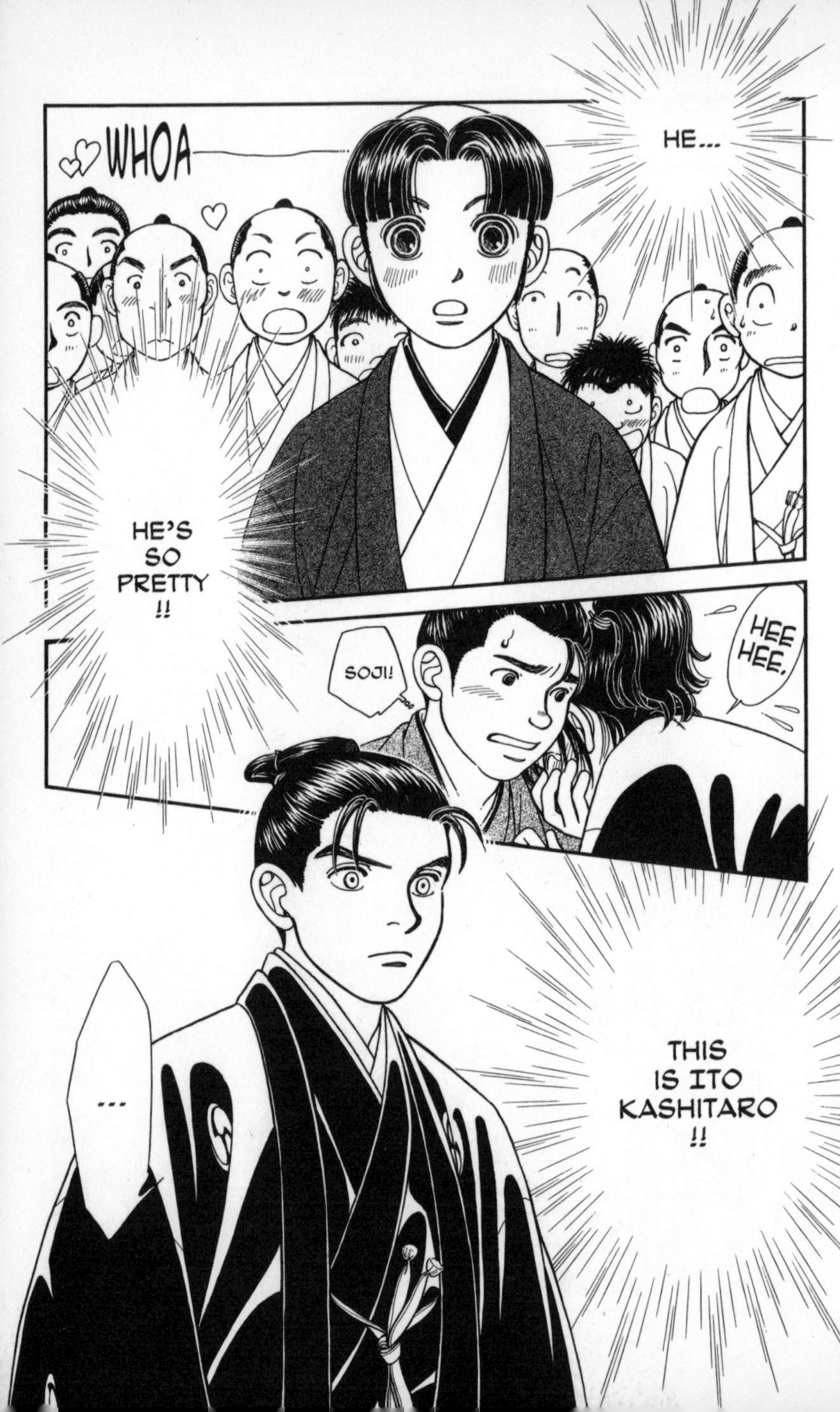
HE...
WHOA
HE'S SO PRETTY !!
HEE HEE.
SOJI!
THIS IS ITO KASHITARO !!
...

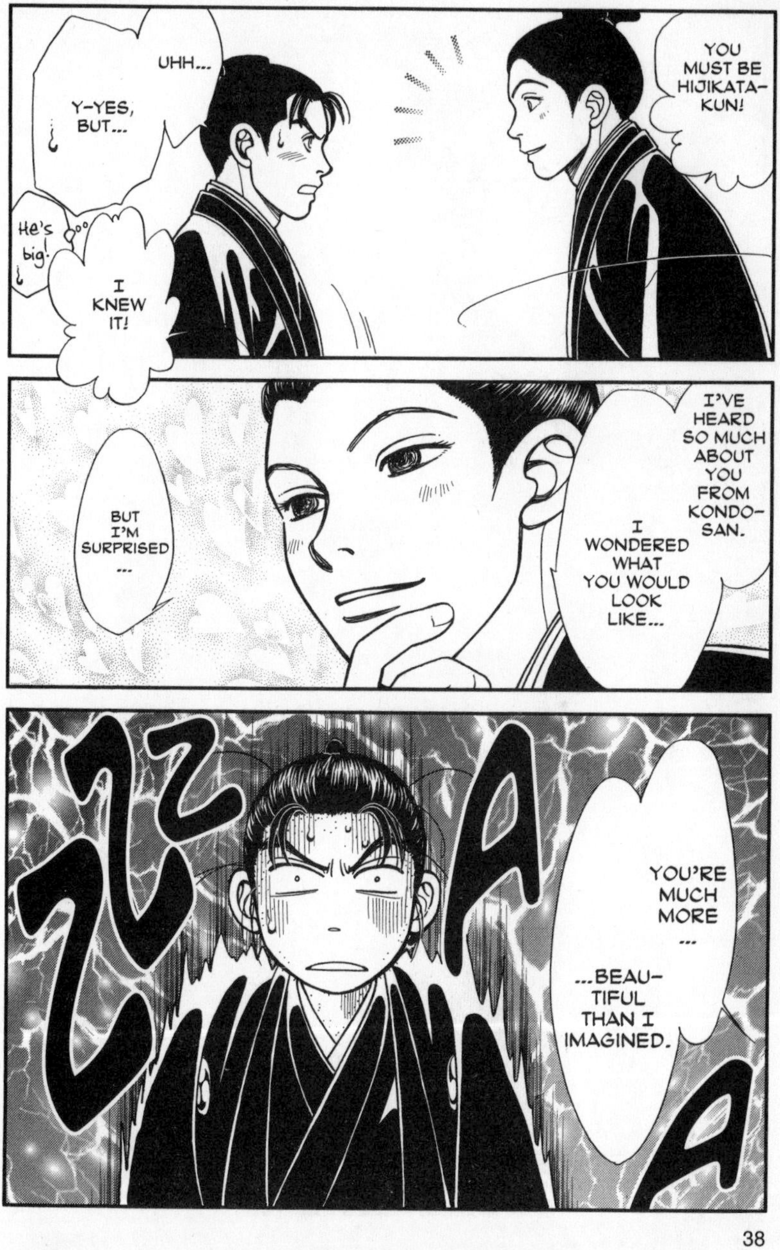
YOU MUST BE HIJIKATA-KUN!
UHH... Y-YES, BUT...
He's big!
I KNEW IT!
I'VE HEARD SO MUCH ABOUT YOU FROM KONDO-SAN.
I WONDERED WHAT YOU WOULD LOOK LIKE...
BUT I'M SURPRISED...
YOU'RE MUCH MORE...
...BEAUTIFUL THAN I IMAGINED.
ZZZAAA

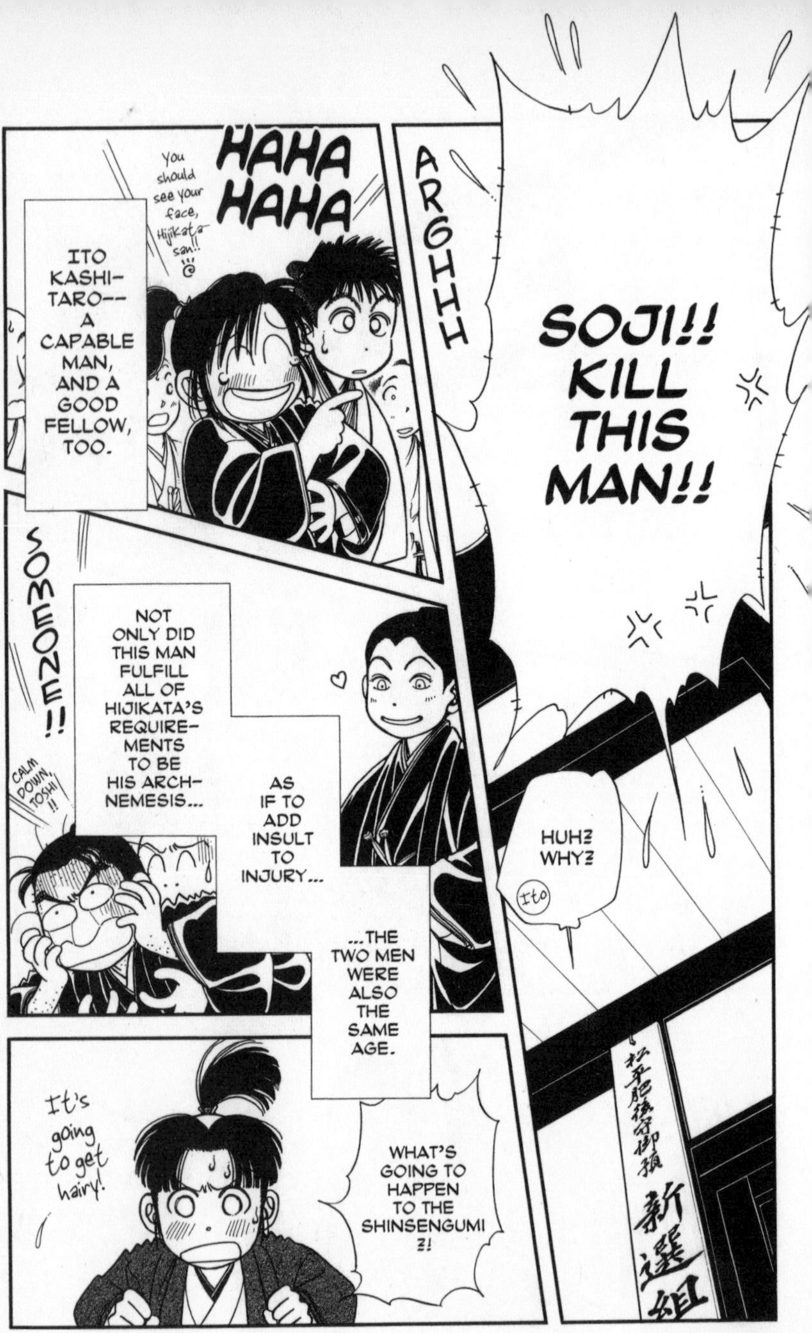

SOJI!! KILL THIS MAN!!
HUH? WHY?
Ito
松平肥後守御預 新選組
ARGHHH
HAHA HAHA
You should see your face, Hijikata-san!!
ITO KASHITARO-- A CAPABLE MAN, AND A GOOD FELLOW, TOO.
NOT ONLY DID THIS MAN FULFILL ALL OF HIJIKATA'S REQUIREMENTS TO BE HIS ARCHNEMESIS...
AS IF TO ADD INSULT TO INJURY...
...THE TWO MEN WERE ALSO THE SAME AGE.
SOMEONE!!
CALM DOWN, TOSHI!!
WHAT'S GOING TO HAPPEN TO THE SHINSENGUMI?!
It's going to get hairy!

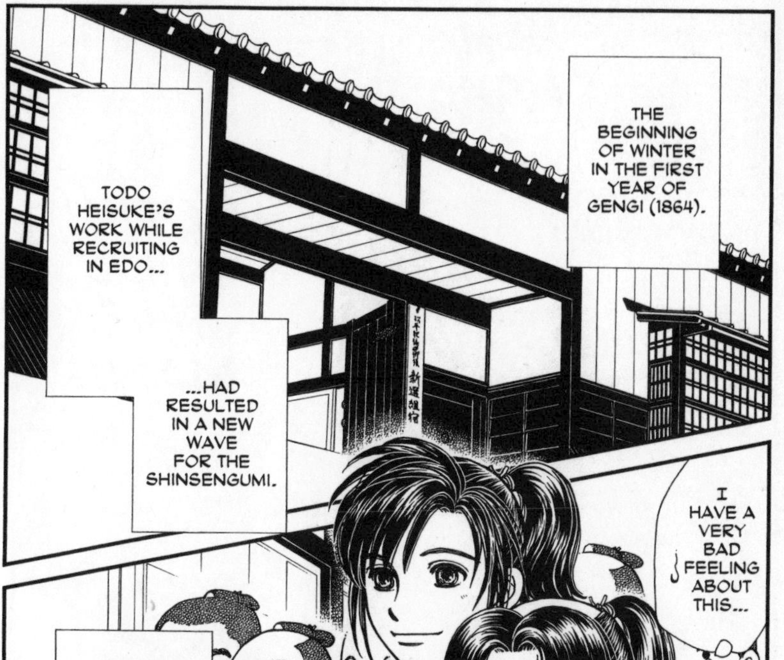
THE BEGINNING OF WINTER IN THE FIRST YEAR OF GENGI (1864).
TODO HEISUKE'S WORK WHILE RECRUITING IN EDO...
...HAD RESULTED IN A NEW WAVE FOR THE SHINSENGUMI.
I HAVE A VERY BAD FEELING ABOUT THIS...
BOTH A MASTER OF THE SWORD AND OF STUDIES, AND A LOYAL SONJO IDEALIST...

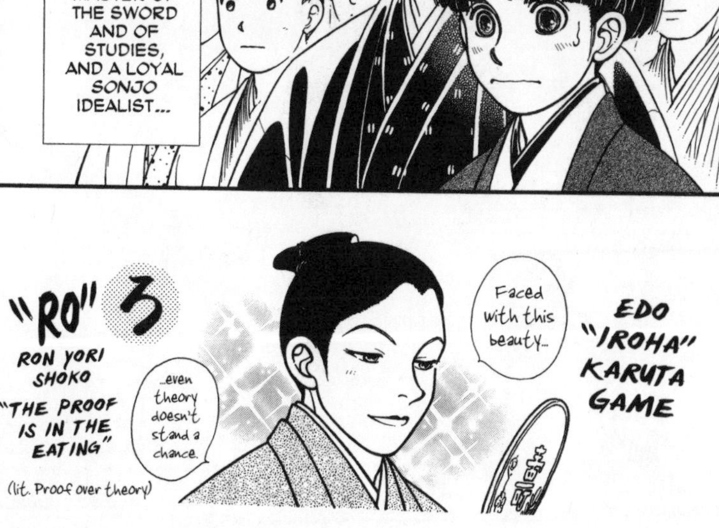
EDO "IROHA" KARUTA GAME
Faced with this beauty...
...even theory doesn't stand a chance.
"RO" ろ
RON YORI SHOKO
"THE PROOF IS IN THE EATING"
(lit. Proof over theory)

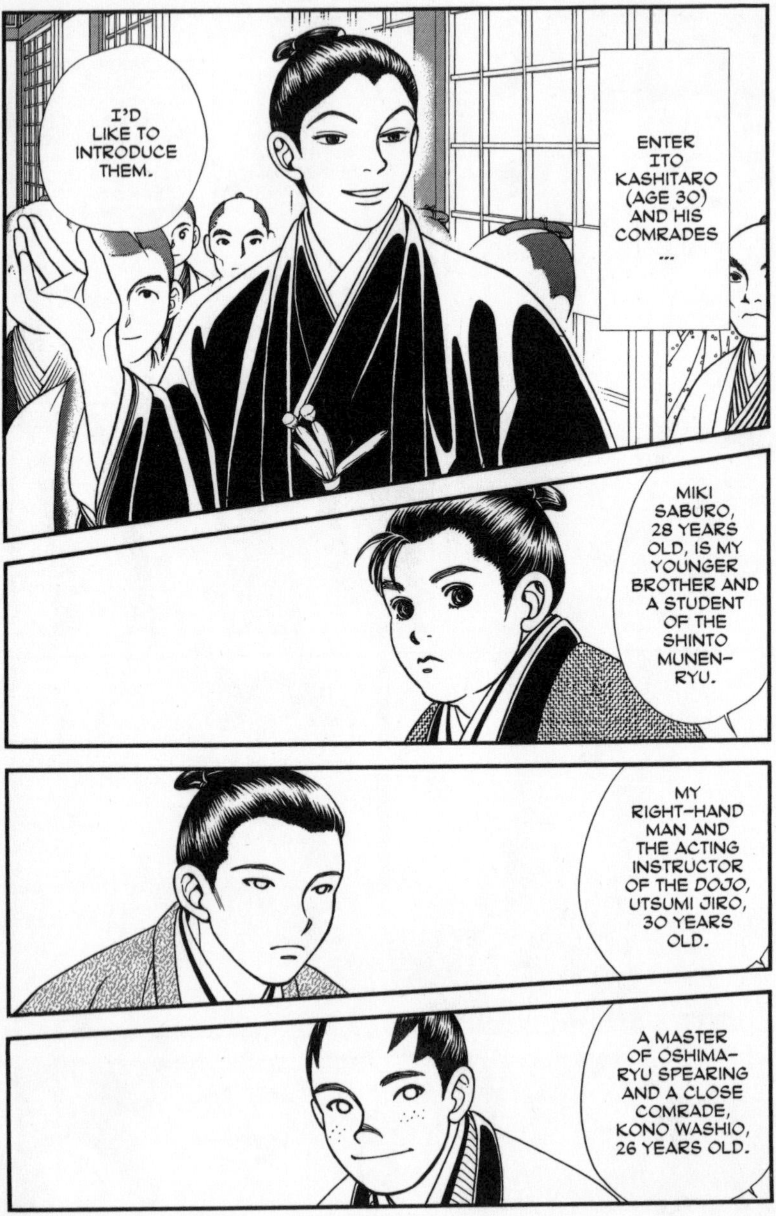
ENTER ITO KASHITARO (AGE 30) AND HIS COMRADES...
I'D LIKE TO INTRODUCE THEM.
MIKI SABURO, 28 YEARS OLD, IS MY YOUNGER BROTHER AND A STUDENT OF THE SHINTO MUNEN-RYU.
MY RIGHT-HAND MAN AND THE ACTING INSTRUCTOR OF THE *DOJO*, UTSUMI JIRO, 30 YEARS OLD.
A MASTER OF OSHIMA-RYU SPEARING AND A CLOSE COMRADE, KONO WASHIO, 26 YEARS OLD.

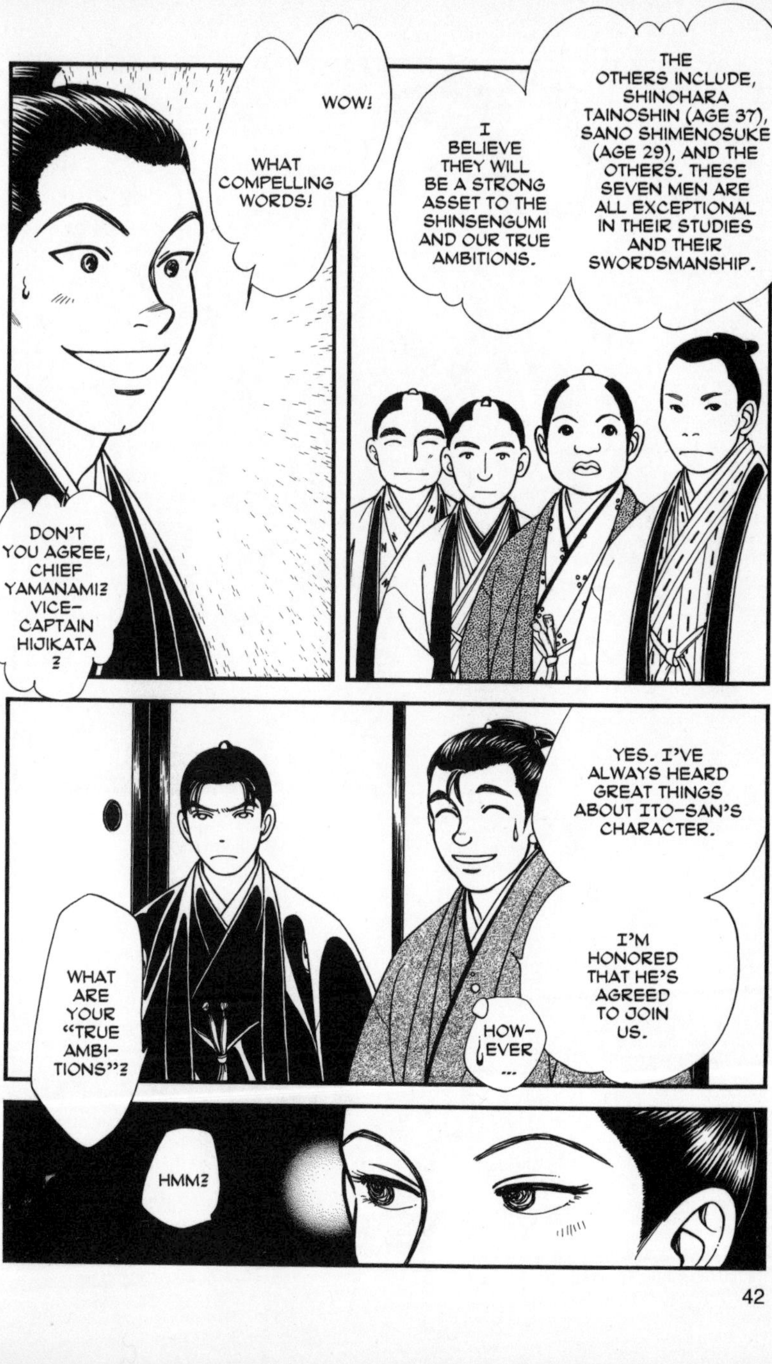
THE OTHERS INCLUDE, SHINOHARA TAINOSHIN (AGE 37), SANO SHIMENOSUKE (AGE 29), AND THE OTHERS. THESE SEVEN MEN ARE ALL EXCEPTIONAL IN THEIR STUDIES AND THEIR SWORDSMANSHIP.
I BELIEVE THEY WILL BE A STRONG ASSET TO THE SHINSENGUMI AND OUR TRUE AMBITIONS.
WOW!
WHAT COMPELLING WORDS!
DON'T YOU AGREE, CHIEF YAMANAMI? VICE-CAPTAIN HIJIKATA?
YES. I'VE ALWAYS HEARD GREAT THINGS ABOUT ITO-SAN'S CHARACTER.
I'M HONORED THAT HE'S AGREED TO JOIN US.
HOW-EVER...
WHAT ARE YOUR "TRUE AMBITIONS"?
HMM?

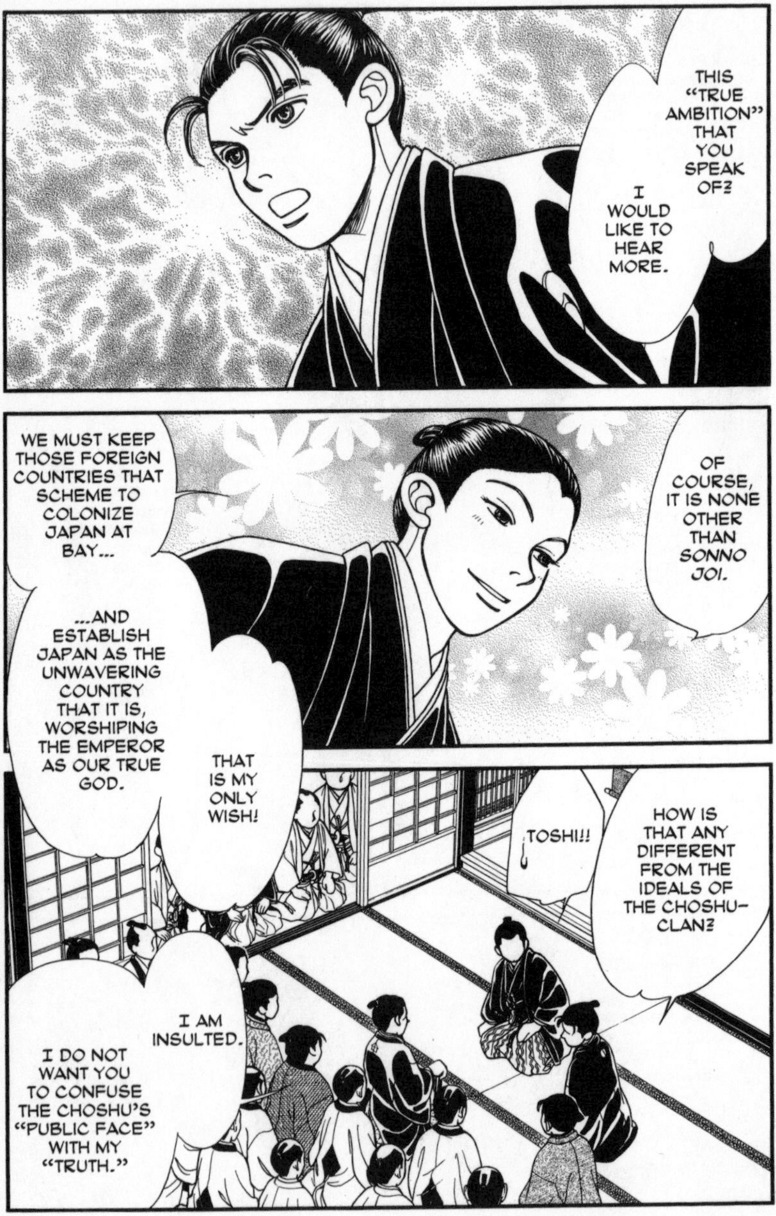
THIS "TRUE AMBITION" THAT YOU SPEAK OF?
I WOULD LIKE TO HEAR MORE.
OF COURSE, IT IS NONE OTHER THAN SONNO JOI.
WE MUST KEEP THOSE FOREIGN COUNTRIES THAT SCHEME TO COLONIZE JAPAN AT BAY...
...AND ESTABLISH JAPAN AS THE UNWAVERING COUNTRY THAT IT IS, WORSHIPING THE EMPEROR AS OUR TRUE GOD.
THAT IS MY ONLY WISH!
HOW IS THAT ANY DIFFERENT FROM THE IDEALS OF THE CHOSHU-CLAN?
TOSHI!!
I AM INSULTED.
I DO NOT WANT YOU TO CONFUSE THE CHOSHU'S "PUBLIC FACE" WITH MY "TRUTH."

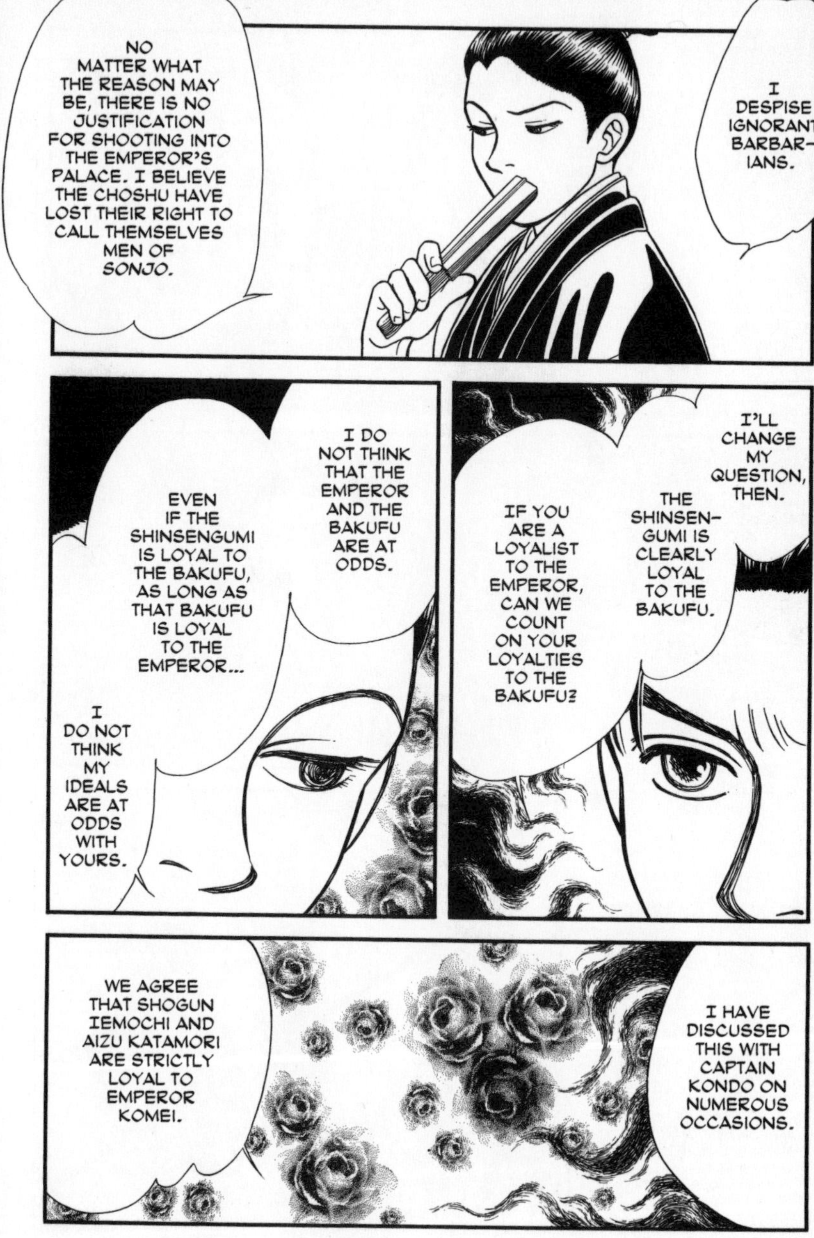
I DESPISE IGNORANT BARBARIANS.
NO MATTER WHAT THE REASON MAY BE, THERE IS NO JUSTIFICATION FOR SHOOTING INTO THE EMPEROR'S PALACE. I BELIEVE THE CHOSHU HAVE LOST THEIR RIGHT TO CALL THEMSELVES MEN OF *SONJO*.
I'LL CHANGE MY QUESTION, THEN.
THE SHINSENGUMI IS CLEARLY LOYAL TO THE BAKUFU.
IF YOU ARE A LOYALIST TO THE EMPEROR, CAN WE COUNT ON YOUR LOYALTIES TO THE BAKUFU?
I DO NOT THINK THAT THE EMPEROR AND THE BAKUFU ARE AT ODDS.
EVEN IF THE SHINSENGUMI IS LOYAL TO THE BAKUFU, AS LONG AS THAT BAKUFU IS LOYAL TO THE EMPEROR...
I DO NOT THINK MY IDEALS ARE AT ODDS WITH YOURS.
I HAVE DISCUSSED THIS WITH CAPTAIN KONDO ON NUMEROUS OCCASIONS.
WE AGREE THAT SHOGUN IEMOCHI AND AIZU KATAMORI ARE STRICTLY LOYAL TO EMPEROR KOMEI.

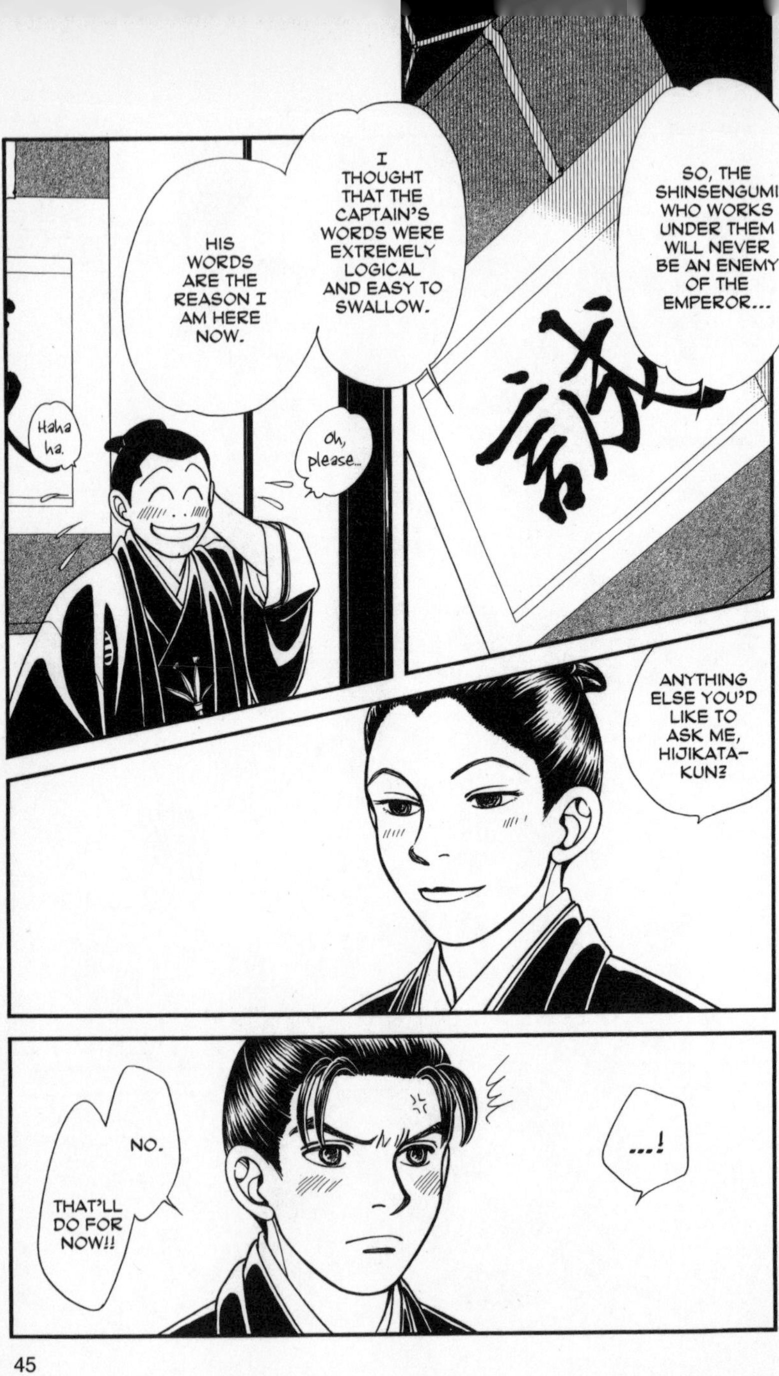
SO, THE SHINSENGUMI WHO WORKS UNDER THEM WILL NEVER BE AN ENEMY OF THE EMPEROR...
誠
I THOUGHT THAT THE CAPTAIN'S WORDS WERE EXTREMELY LOGICAL AND EASY TO SWALLOW.
HIS WORDS ARE THE REASON I AM HERE NOW.
Oh, please...
Haha ha.
ANYTHING ELSE YOU'D LIKE TO ASK ME, HIJIKATA-KUN?
...!
NO.
THAT'LL DO FOR NOW!!

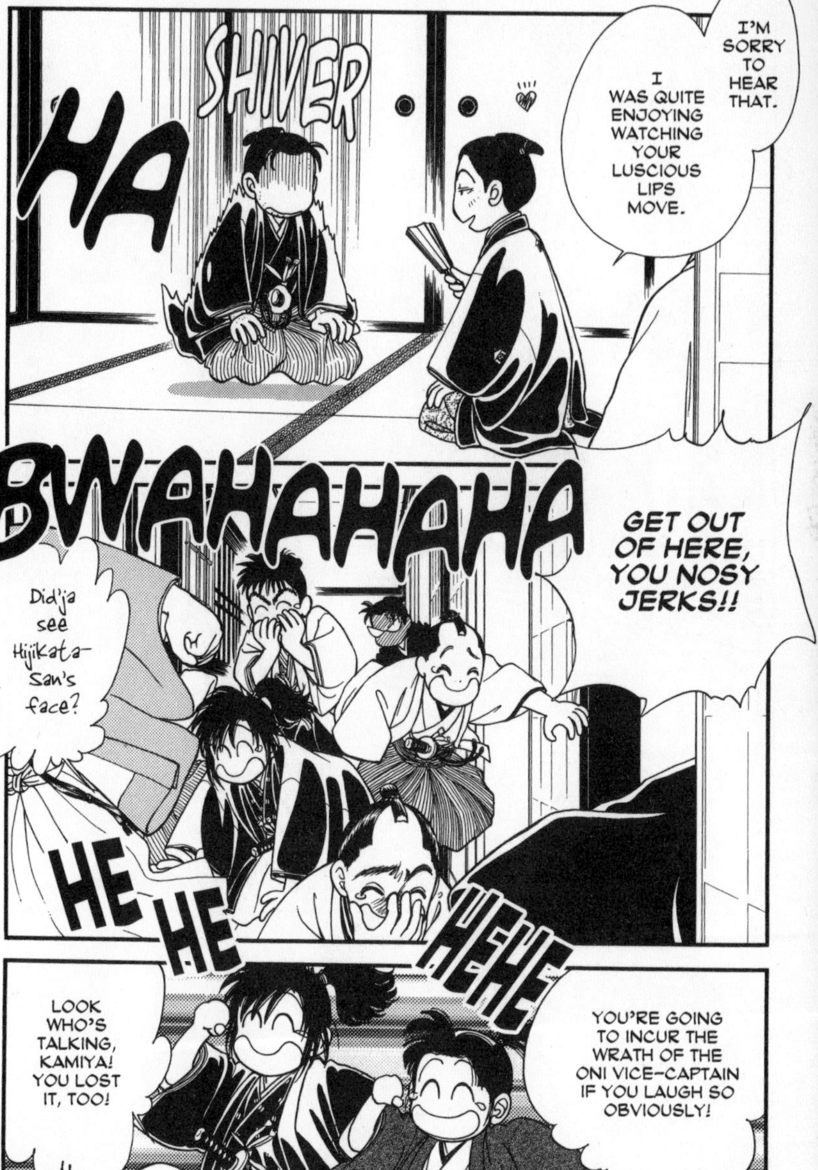
I'M SORRY TO HEAR THAT.
I WAS QUITE ENJOYING WATCHING YOUR LUSCIOUS LIPS MOVE.
SHIVER
HA
GET OUT OF HERE, YOU NOSY JERKS!!
BWAHAHAHA
Did'ja see Hijikata-San's face?
HE HE
HEHE
YOU'RE GOING TO INCUR THE WRATH OF THE ONI VICE-CAPTAIN IF YOU LAUGH SO OBVIOUSLY!
LOOK WHO'S TALKING, KAMIYA! YOU LOST IT, TOO!

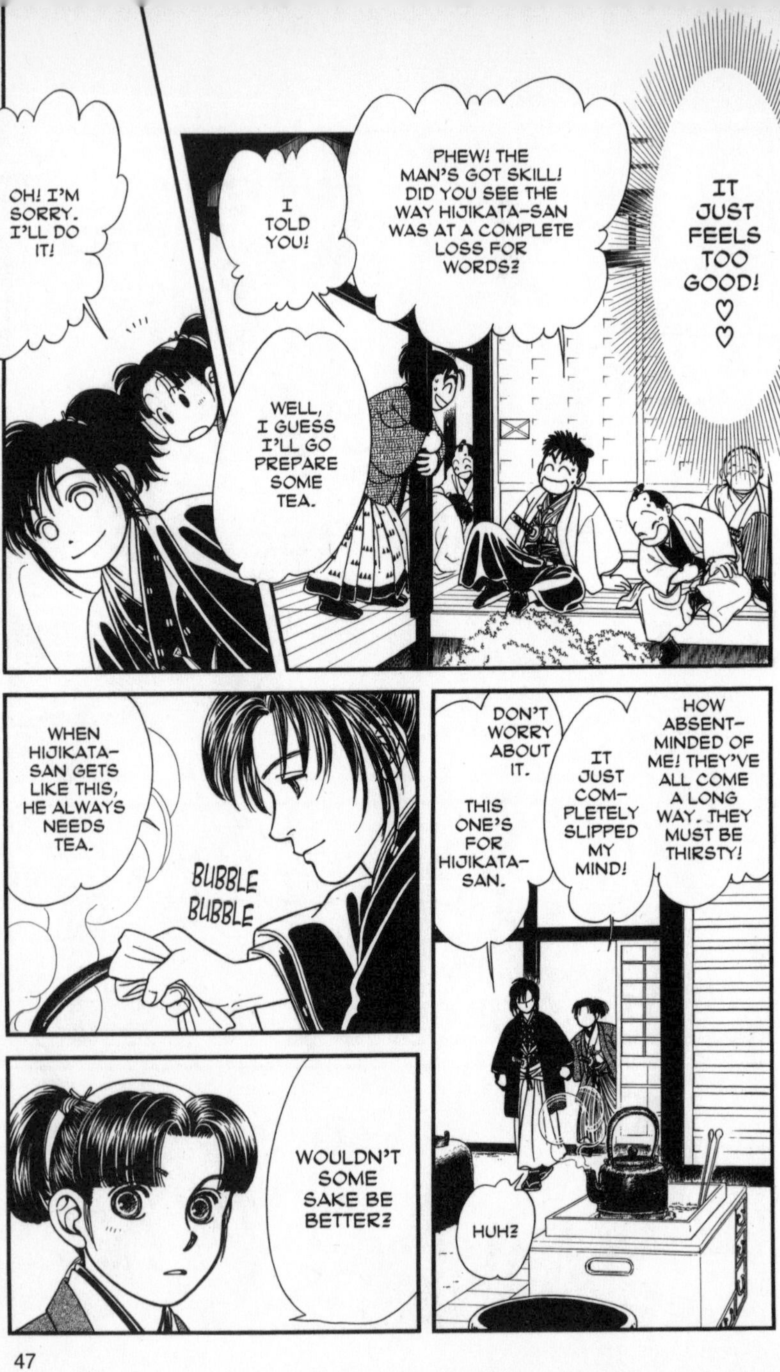
IT JUST FEELS TOO GOOD! ♡ ♡
PHEW! THE MAN'S GOT SKILL! DID YOU SEE THE WAY HIJIKATA-SAN WAS AT A COMPLETE LOSS FOR WORDS?
I TOLD YOU!
WELL, I GUESS I'LL GO PREPARE SOME TEA.
OH! I'M SORRY. I'LL DO IT!
HOW ABSENT-MINDED OF ME! THEY'VE ALL COME A LONG WAY. THEY MUST BE THIRSTY!
IT JUST COM-PLETELY SLIPPED MY MIND!
DON'T WORRY ABOUT IT.
THIS ONE'S FOR HIJIKATA-SAN.
HUH?
WHEN HIJIKATA-SAN GETS LIKE THIS, HE ALWAYS NEEDS TEA.
BUBBLE BUBBLE
WOULDN'T SOME SAKE BE BETTER?

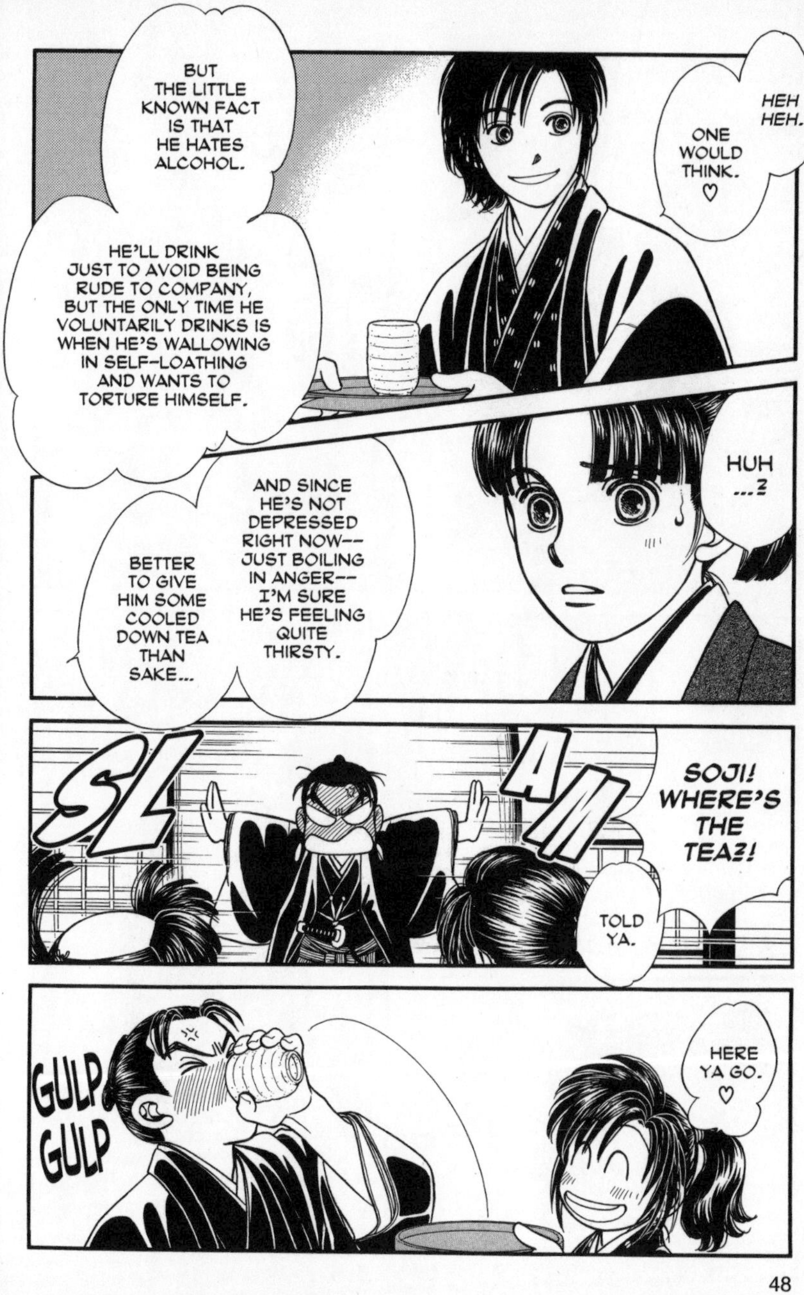
HEH HEH.
ONE WOULD THINK. ♡
BUT THE LITTLE KNOWN FACT IS THAT HE HATES ALCOHOL.
HE'LL DRINK JUST TO AVOID BEING RUDE TO COMPANY, BUT THE ONLY TIME HE VOLUNTARILY DRINKS IS WHEN HE'S WALLOWING IN SELF-LOATHING AND WANTS TO TORTURE HIMSELF.
HUH ...?
AND SINCE HE'S NOT DEPRESSED RIGHT NOW-- JUST BOILING IN ANGER-- I'M SURE HE'S FEELING QUITE THIRSTY.
BETTER TO GIVE HIM SOME COOLED DOWN TEA THAN SAKE...
SOJI! WHERE'S THE TEA?!
SLAM
TOLD YA.
HERE YA GO. ♡
GULP GULP

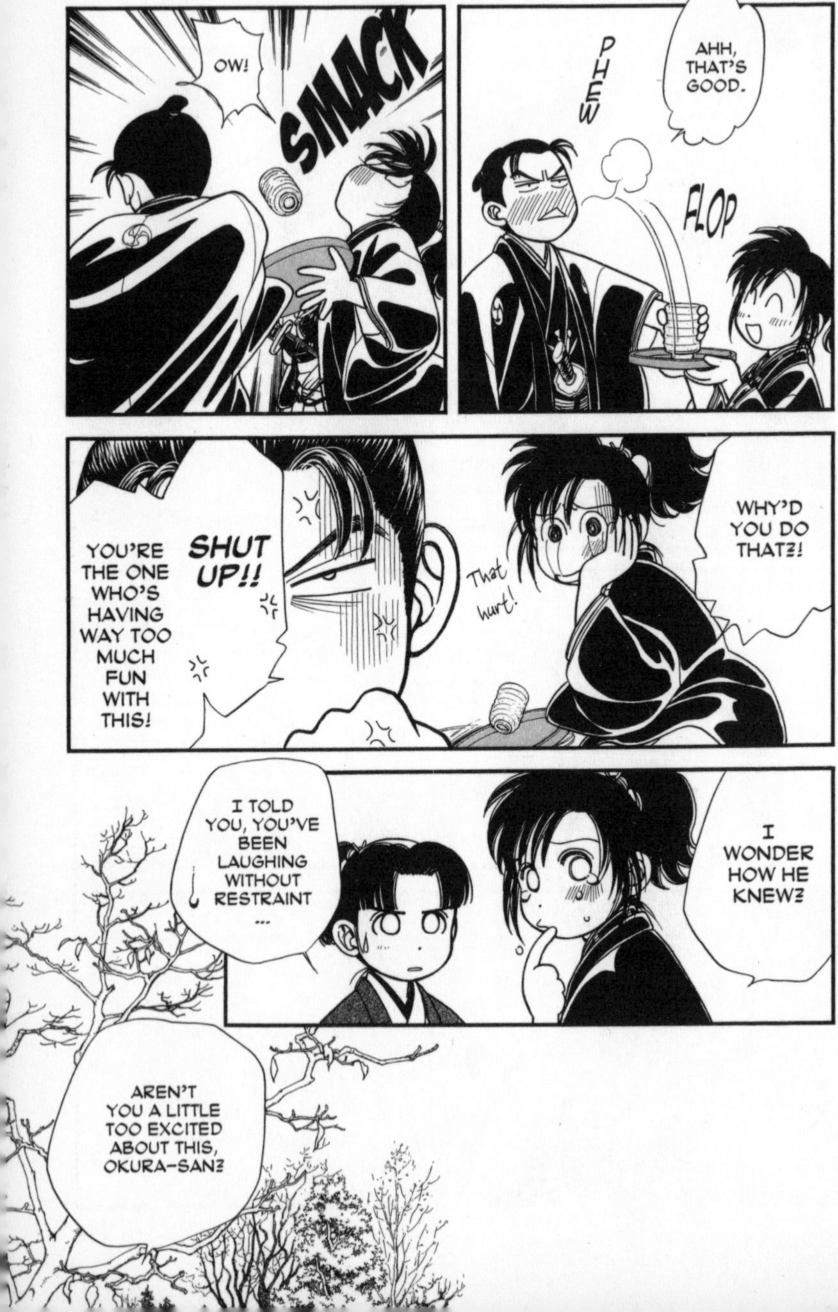
PHEW
AHH, THAT'S GOOD.
FLOP
OW!
SMACK
WHY'D YOU DO THAT?!
That hurt!
SHUT UP!!
YOU'RE THE ONE WHO'S HAVING WAY TOO MUCH FUN WITH THIS!
I WONDER HOW HE KNEW?
I TOLD YOU, YOU'VE BEEN LAUGHING WITHOUT RESTRAINT ...
AREN'T YOU A LITTLE TOO EXCITED ABOUT THIS, OKURA-SAN?

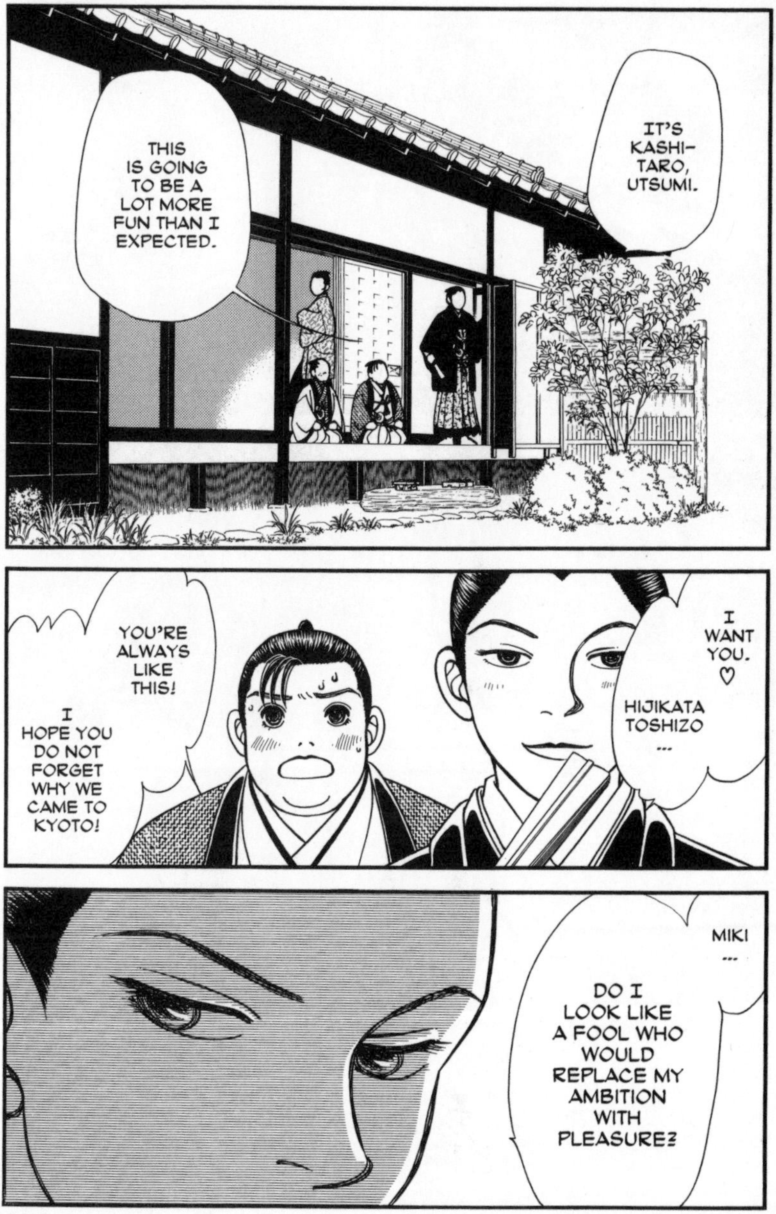
IT'S KASHI-TARO, UTSUMI.
THIS IS GOING TO BE A LOT MORE FUN THAN I EXPECTED.
I WANT YOU. ♡
HIJIKATA TOSHIZO ...
YOU'RE ALWAYS LIKE THIS!
I HOPE YOU DO NOT FORGET WHY WE CAME TO KYOTO!
MIKI ...
DO I LOOK LIKE A FOOL WHO WOULD REPLACE MY AMBITION WITH PLEASURE?

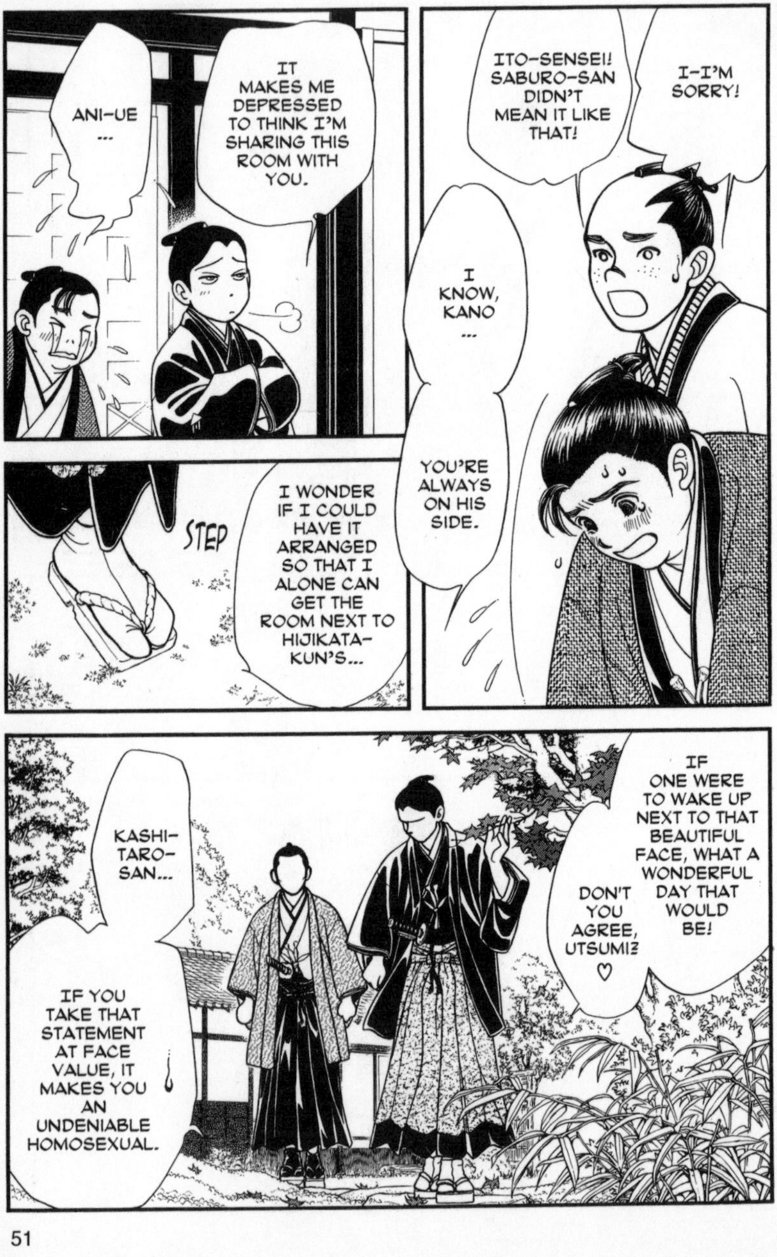
I-I'M SORRY!
ITO-SENSEI! SABURO-SAN DIDN'T MEAN IT LIKE THAT!
I KNOW, KANO ...
YOU'RE ALWAYS ON HIS SIDE.
IT MAKES ME DEPRESSED TO THINK I'M SHARING THIS ROOM WITH YOU.
ANI-UE ...
I WONDER IF I COULD HAVE IT ARRANGED SO THAT I ALONE CAN GET THE ROOM NEXT TO HIJIKATA-KUN'S...
STEP
IF ONE WERE TO WAKE UP NEXT TO THAT BEAUTIFUL FACE, WHAT A WONDERFUL DAY THAT WOULD BE!
DON'T YOU AGREE, UTSUMI? ♡
KASHI-TARO-SAN...
IF YOU TAKE THAT STATEMENT AT FACE VALUE, IT MAKES YOU AN UNDENIABLE HOMOSEXUAL.

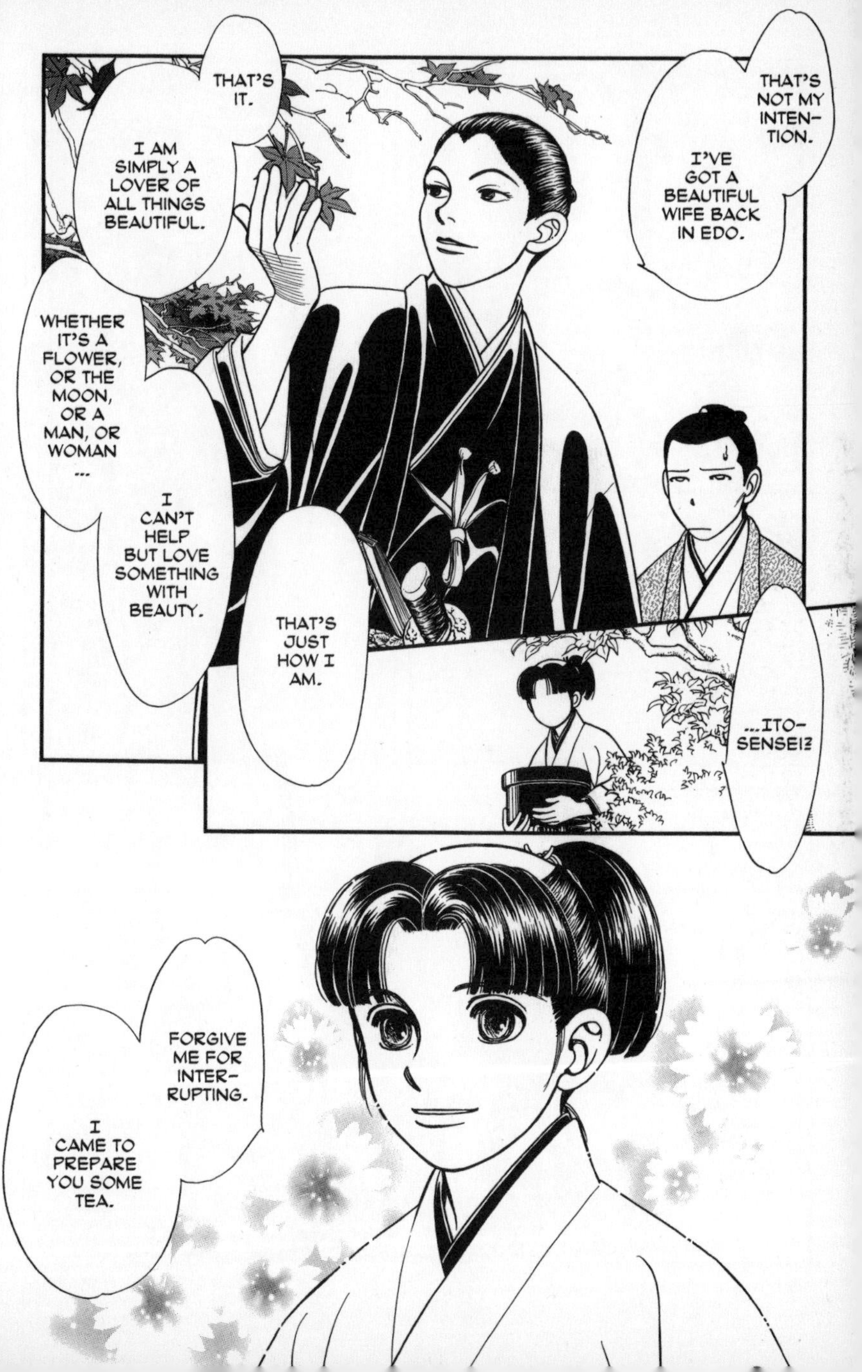
THAT'S NOT MY INTENTION.
I'VE GOT A BEAUTIFUL WIFE BACK IN EDO.
THAT'S IT.
I AM SIMPLY A LOVER OF ALL THINGS BEAUTIFUL.
WHETHER IT'S A FLOWER, OR THE MOON, OR A MAN, OR WOMAN ...
I CAN'T HELP BUT LOVE SOMETHING WITH BEAUTY.
THAT'S JUST HOW I AM.
...ITO-SENSEI!?
FORGIVE ME FOR INTERRUPTING.
I CAME TO PREPARE YOU SOME TEA.

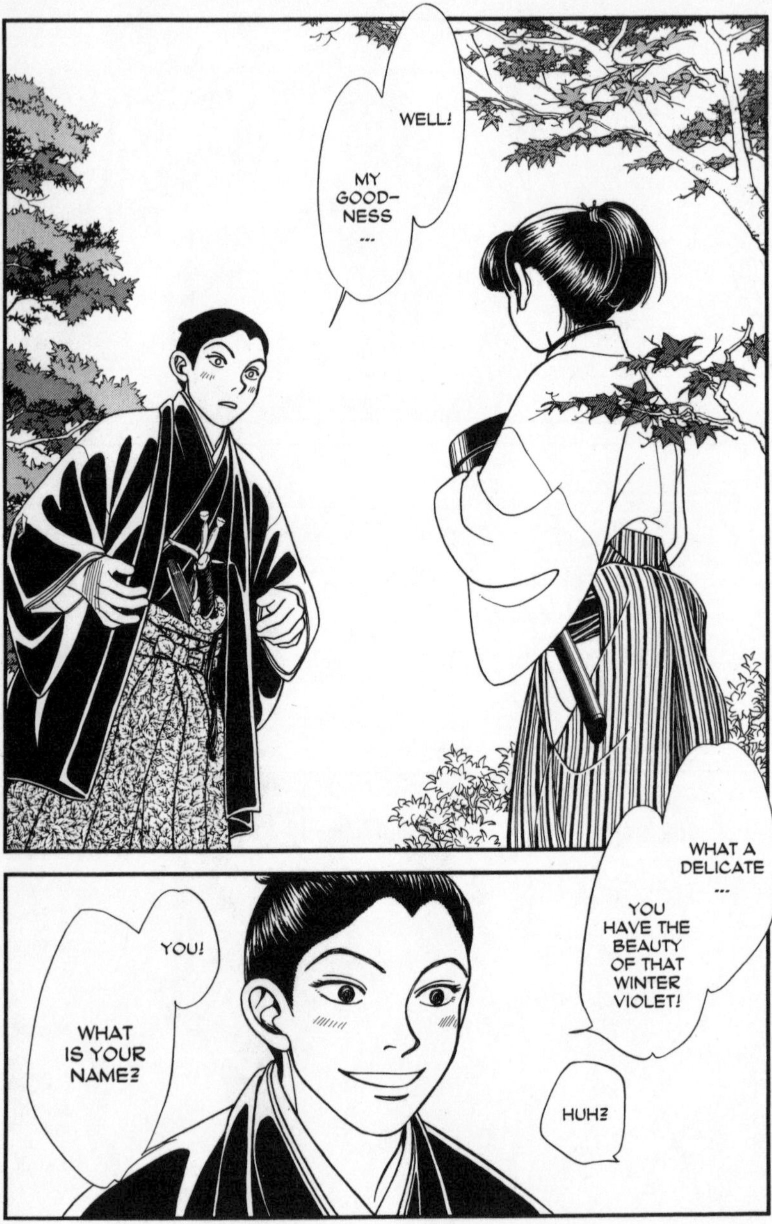
WELL!
MY GOODNESS...
WHAT A DELICATE...
YOU HAVE THE BEAUTY OF THAT WINTER VIOLET!
HUH?
YOU!
WHAT IS YOUR NAME?

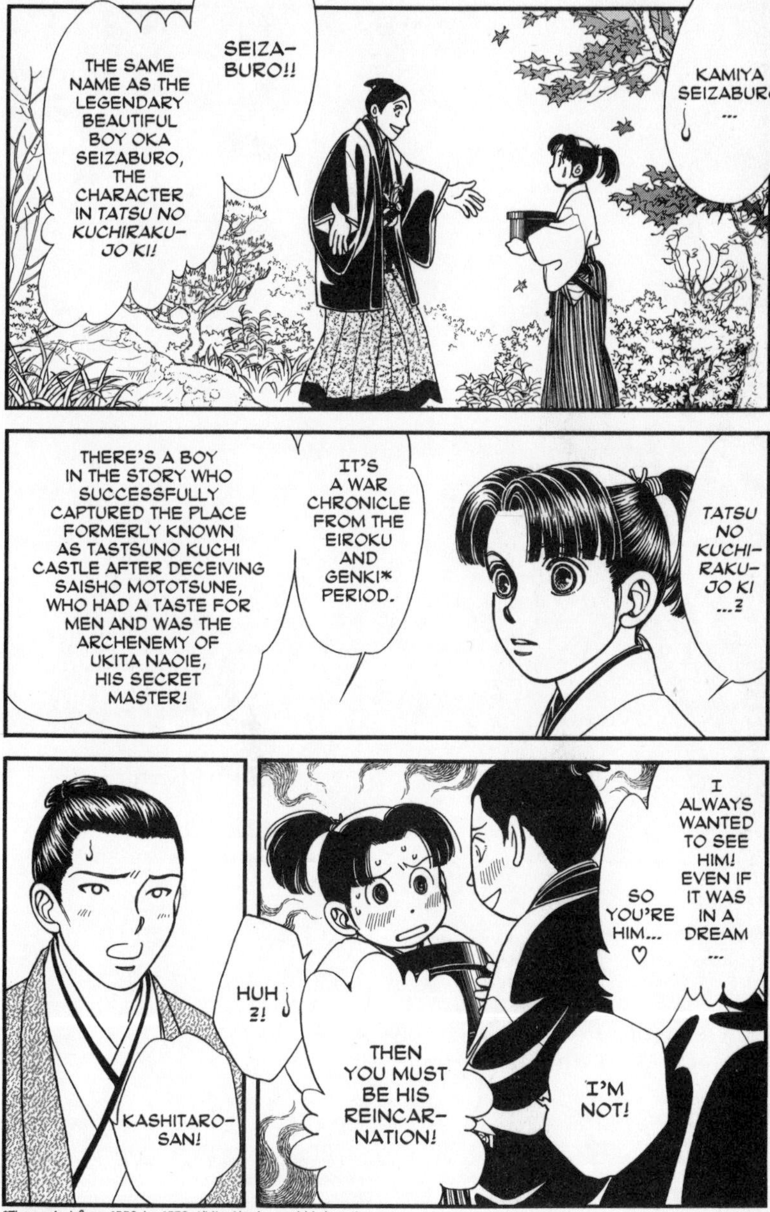
KAMIYA SEIZABURO ...
SEIZA-BURO!!
THE SAME NAME AS THE LEGENDARY BEAUTIFUL BOY OKA SEIZABURO, THE CHARACTER IN *TATSU NO KUCHIRAKU-JO KI!*
TATSU NO KUCHI-RAKU-JO KI ...?
IT'S A WAR CHRONICLE FROM THE EIROKU AND GENKI* PERIOD.
THERE'S A BOY IN THE STORY WHO SUCCESSFULLY CAPTURED THE PLACE FORMERLY KNOWN AS TASTSUNO KUCHI CASTLE AFTER DECEIVING SAISHO MOTOTSUNE, WHO HAD A TASTE FOR MEN AND WAS THE ARCHENEMY OF UKITA NAOIE, HIS SECRET MASTER!
I ALWAYS WANTED TO SEE HIM! EVEN IF IT WAS IN A DREAM ...
SO YOU'RE HIM... ♡
HUH?!
THEN YOU MUST BE HIS REINCARNATION!
I'M NOT!
KASHITARO-SAN!

*The period from 1558 to 1572. Ukita Naoie used his beauty and wit to rise from being a cow herder to a feudal lord.

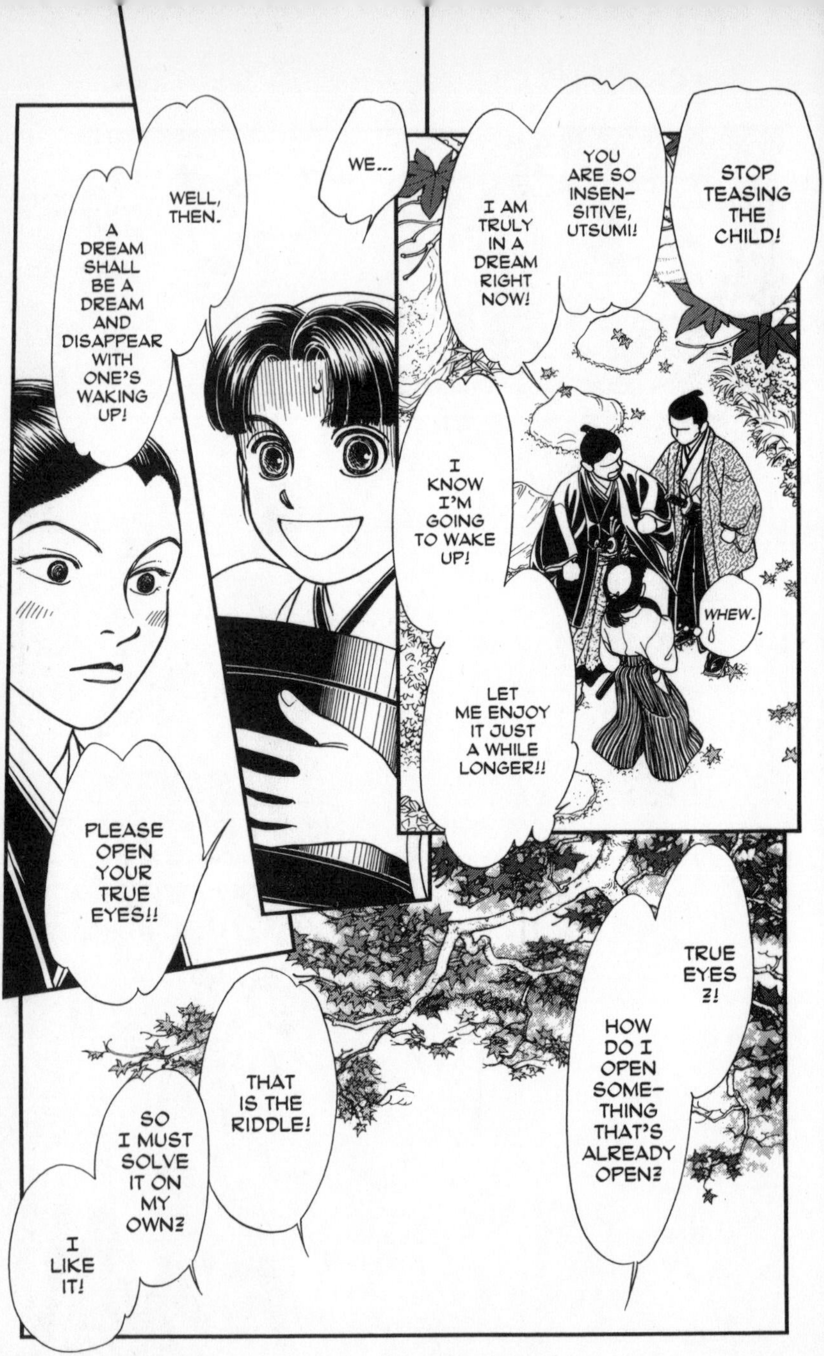

STOP TEASING THE CHILD!
YOU ARE SO INSENSITIVE, UTSUMI!
WHEW.
I AM TRULY IN A DREAM RIGHT NOW!
I KNOW I'M GOING TO WAKE UP!
LET ME ENJOY IT JUST A WHILE LONGER!!
WE...
WELL, THEN.
A DREAM SHALL BE A DREAM AND DISAPPEAR WITH ONE'S WAKING UP!
PLEASE OPEN YOUR TRUE EYES!!
TRUE EYES?!
HOW DO I OPEN SOMETHING THAT'S ALREADY OPEN?
THAT IS THE RIDDLE!
SO I MUST SOLVE IT ON MY OWN?
I LIKE IT!

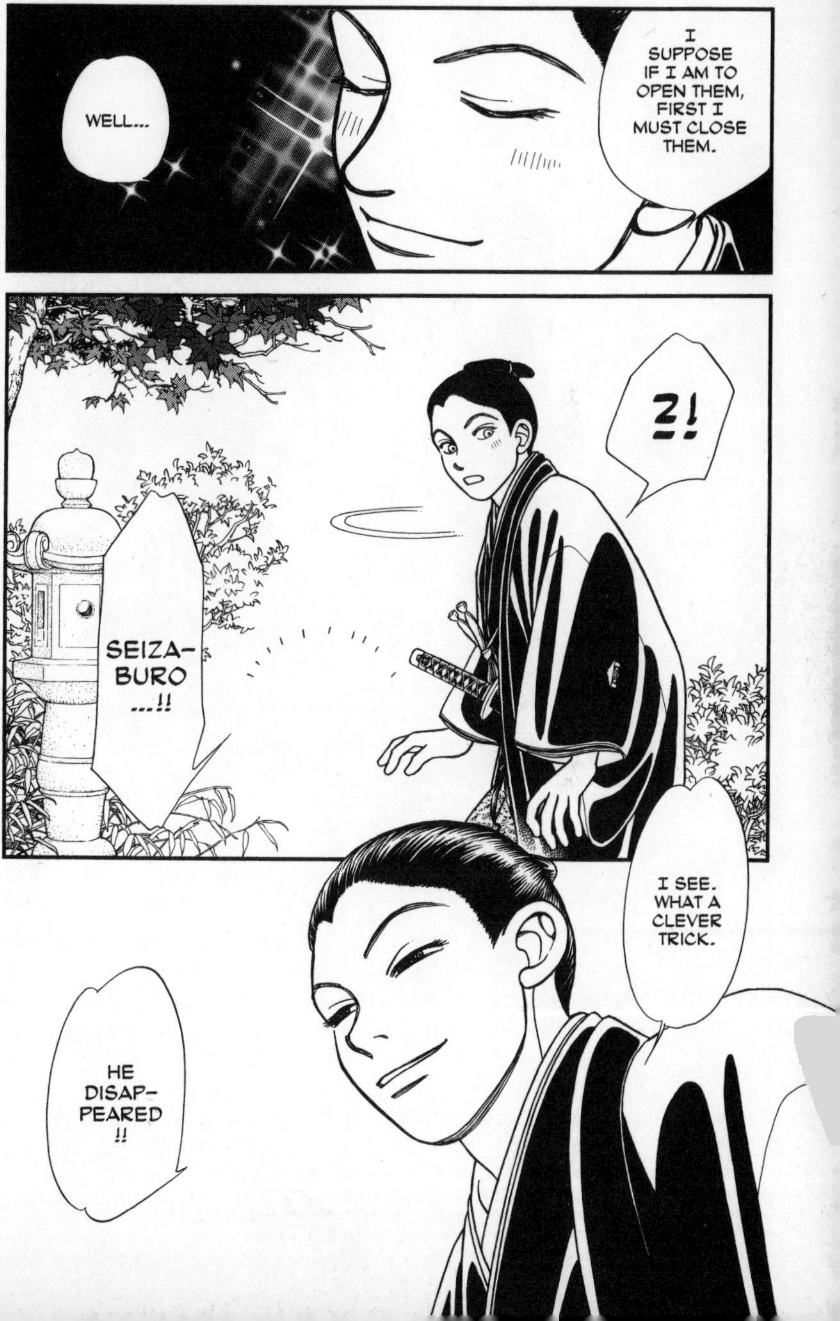
I SUPPOSE IF I AM TO OPEN THEM, FIRST I MUST CLOSE THEM.
WELL...
?!
SEIZA-BURO ...!!
I SEE. WHAT A CLEVER TRICK.
HE DISAP-PEARED !!

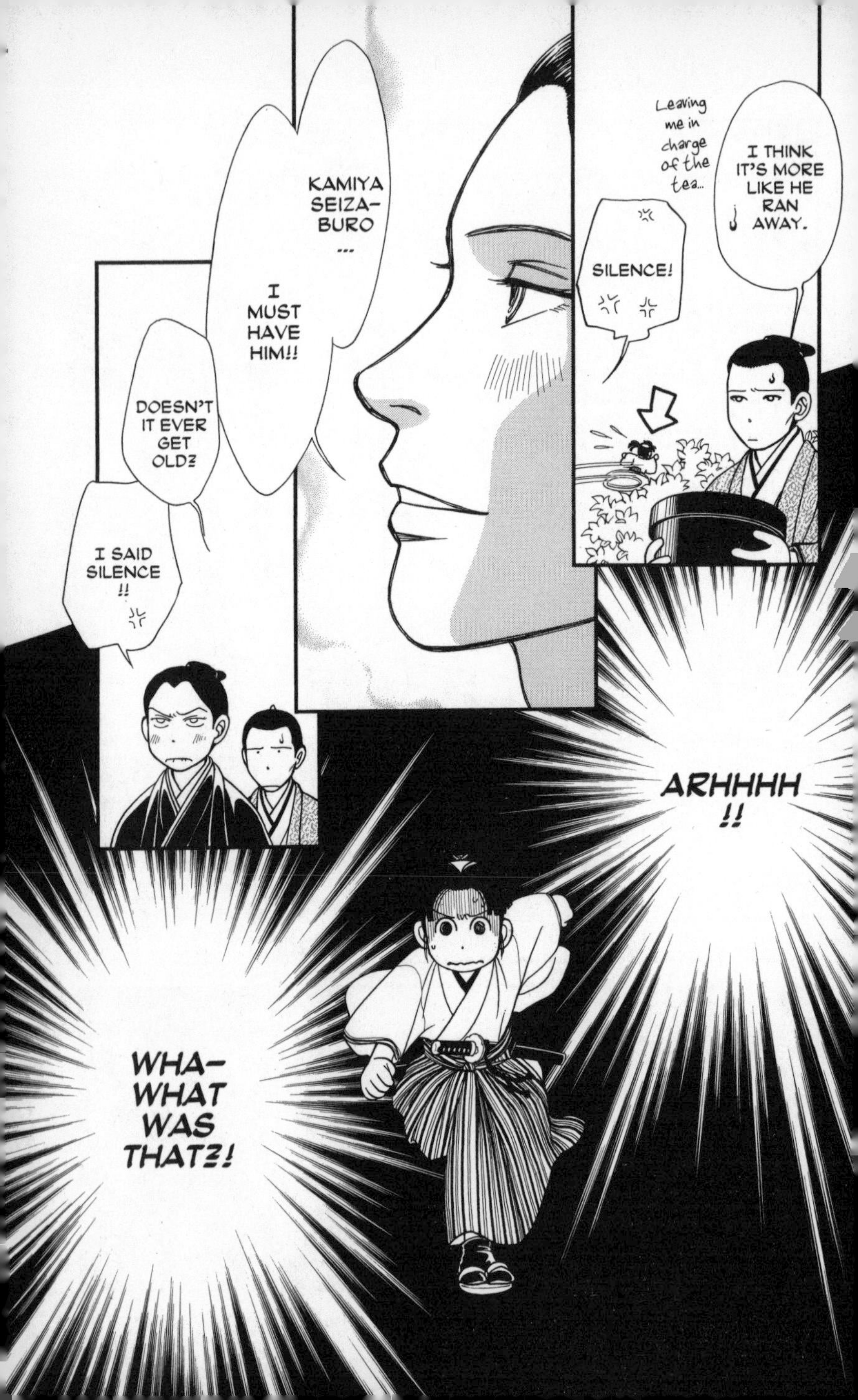
I THINK IT'S MORE LIKE HE RAN AWAY.
Leaving me in charge of the tea...
SILENCE!
KAMIYA SEIZABURO...
I MUST HAVE HIM!!
DOESN'T IT EVER GET OLD?
I SAID SILENCE!!
ARHHHH!!
WHA-WHAT WAS THAT?!

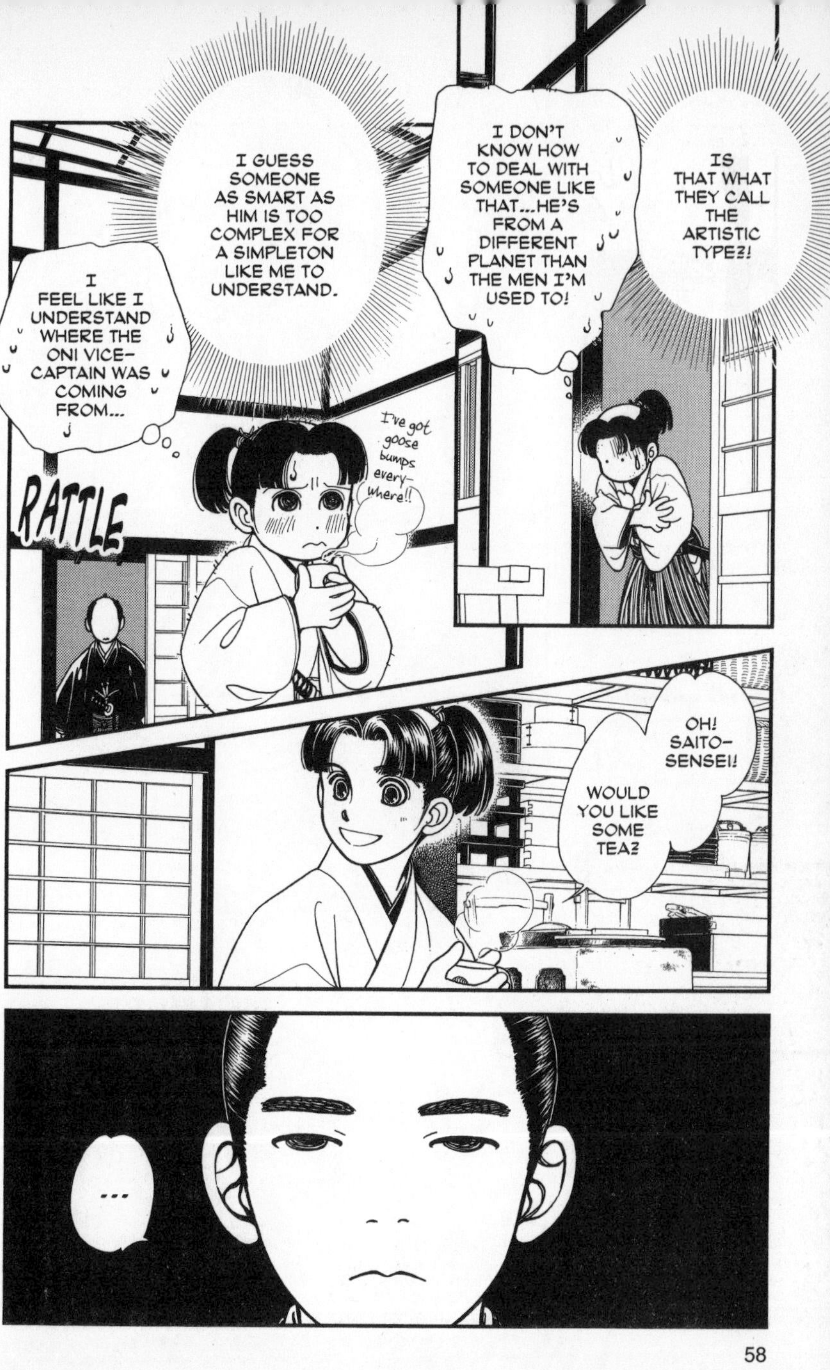
IS THAT WHAT THEY CALL THE ARTISTIC TYPE?!
I DON'T KNOW HOW TO DEAL WITH SOMEONE LIKE THAT...HE'S FROM A DIFFERENT PLANET THAN THE MEN I'M USED TO!
I GUESS SOMEONE AS SMART AS HIM IS TOO COMPLEX FOR A SIMPLETON LIKE ME TO UNDERSTAND.
I FEEL LIKE I UNDERSTAND WHERE THE ONI VICE-CAPTAIN WAS COMING FROM...
I've got goose bumps every-where!!
RATTLE
OH! SAITO-SENSEI!
WOULD YOU LIKE SOME TEA?
...

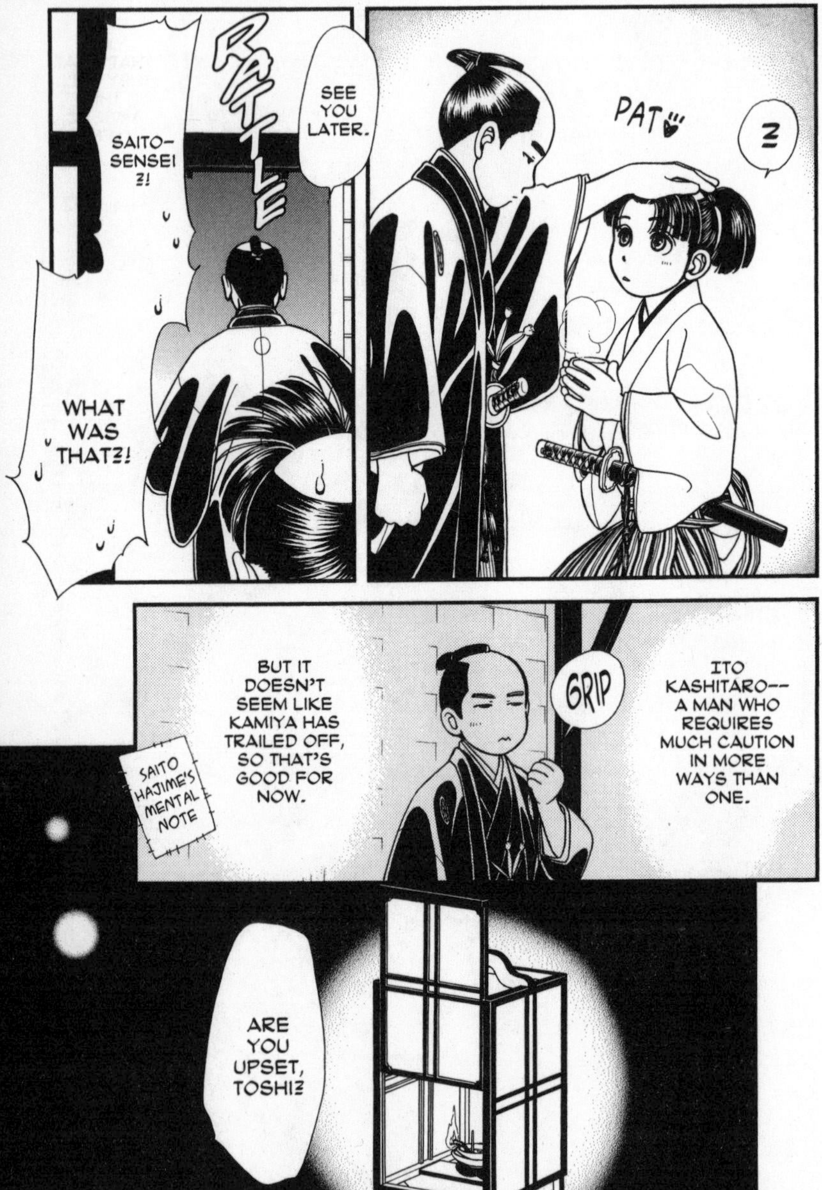
PAT
?
SEE YOU LATER.
RATTLE
SAITO-SENSEI?!
WHAT WAS THAT?!
ITO KASHITARO-- A MAN WHO REQUIRES MUCH CAUTION IN MORE WAYS THAN ONE.
GRIP
BUT IT DOESN'T SEEM LIKE KAMIYA HAS TRAILED OFF, SO THAT'S GOOD FOR NOW.
SAITO HAJIME'S MENTAL NOTE
ARE YOU UPSET, TOSHI?

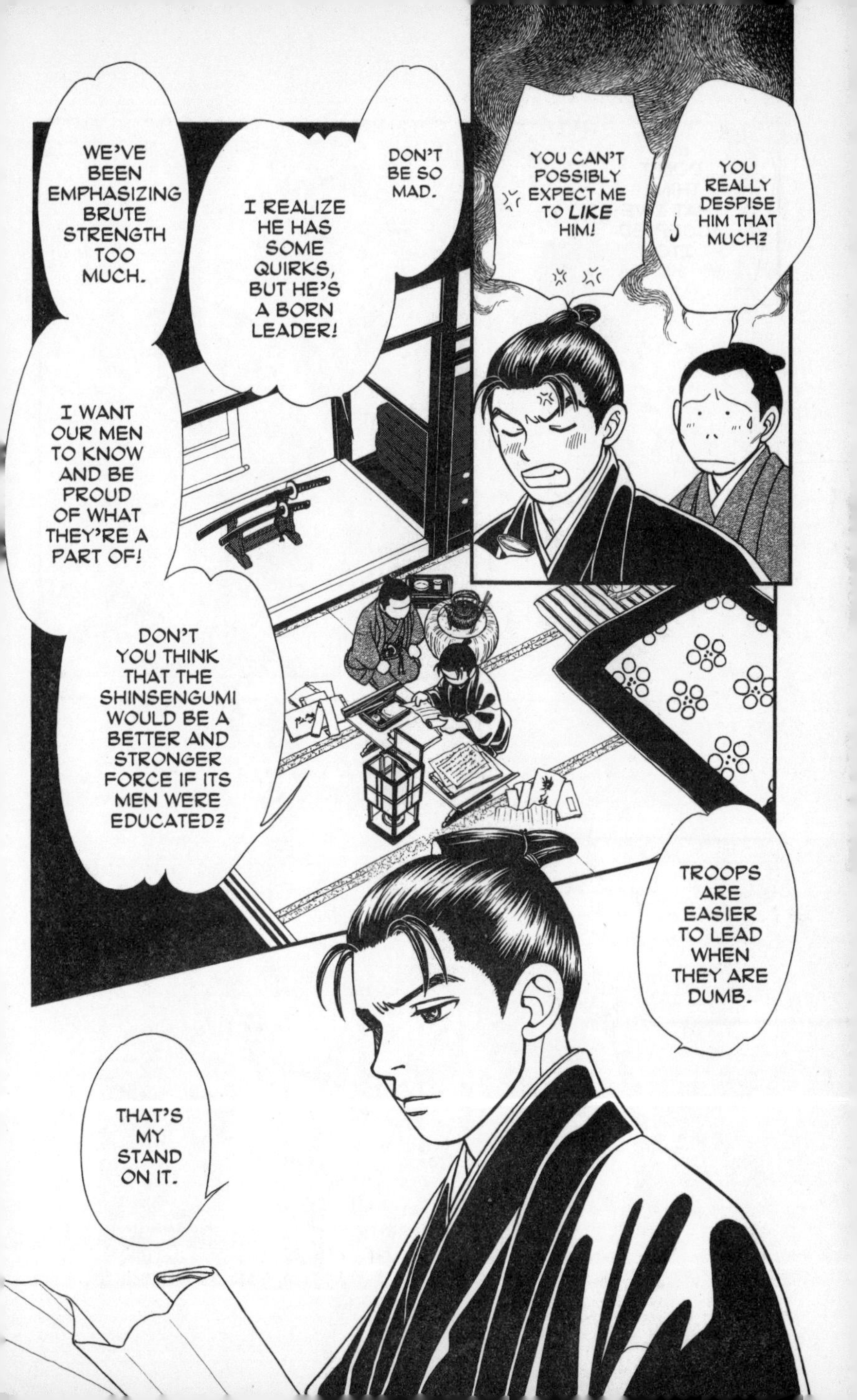
YOU REALLY DESPISE HIM THAT MUCH?
YOU CAN'T POSSIBLY EXPECT ME TO *LIKE* HIM!
DON'T BE SO MAD.
I REALIZE HE HAS SOME QUIRKS, BUT HE'S A BORN LEADER!
WE'VE BEEN EMPHASIZING BRUTE STRENGTH TOO MUCH.
I WANT OUR MEN TO KNOW AND BE PROUD OF WHAT THEY'RE A PART OF!
DON'T YOU THINK THAT THE SHINSENGUMI WOULD BE A BETTER AND STRONGER FORCE IF ITS MEN WERE EDUCATED?
TROOPS ARE EASIER TO LEAD WHEN THEY ARE DUMB.
THAT'S MY STAND ON IT.

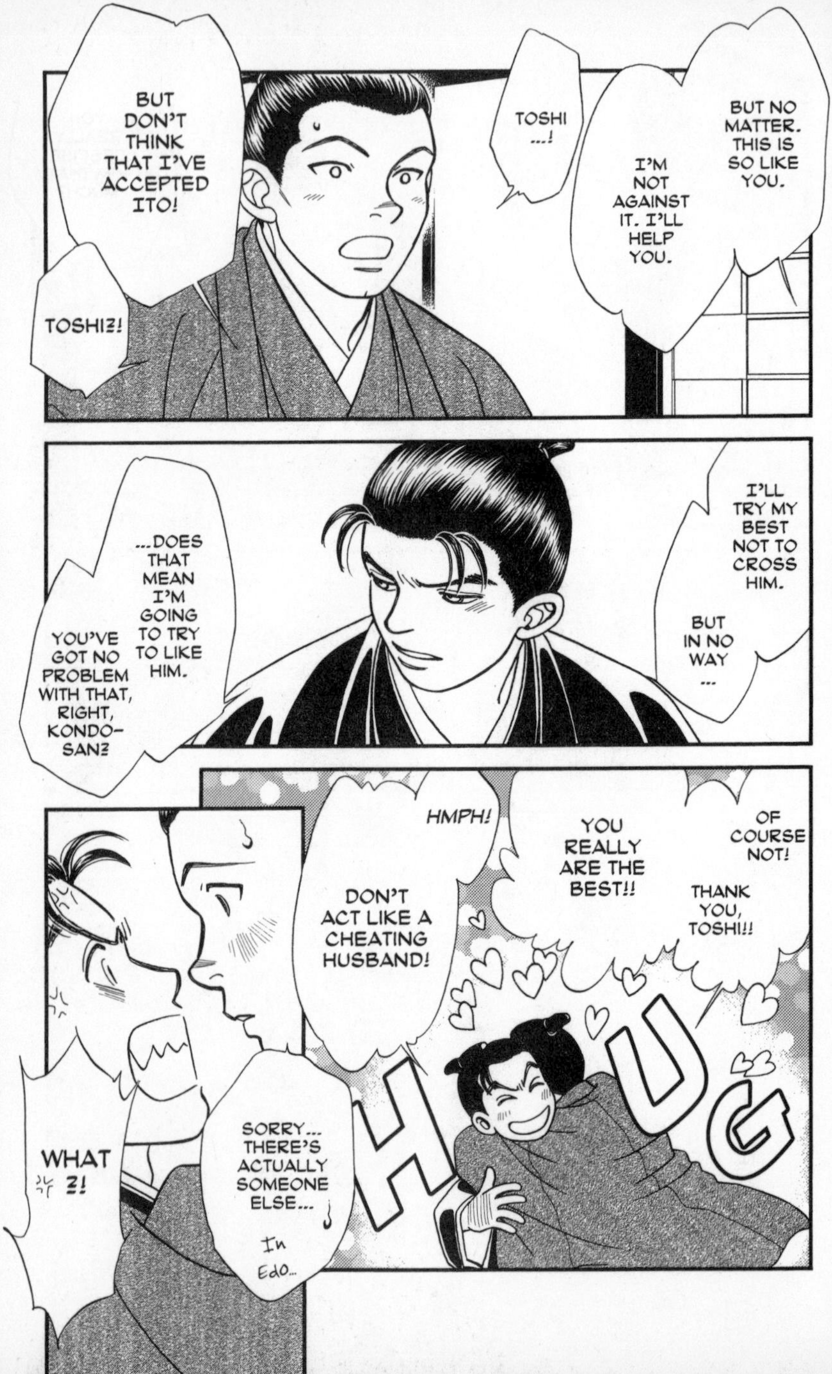
BUT NO MATTER. THIS IS SO LIKE YOU.
I'M NOT AGAINST IT. I'LL HELP YOU.
TOSHI ...!
BUT DON'T THINK THAT I'VE ACCEPTED ITO!
TOSHI?!
I'LL TRY MY BEST NOT TO CROSS HIM.
BUT IN NO WAY ...
...DOES THAT MEAN I'M GOING TO TRY TO LIKE HIM.
YOU'VE GOT NO PROBLEM WITH THAT, RIGHT, KONDO-SAN?
OF COURSE NOT!
THANK YOU, TOSHI!!
YOU REALLY ARE THE BEST!!
HUG
HMPH!
DON'T ACT LIKE A CHEATING HUSBAND!
SORRY... THERE'S ACTUALLY SOMEONE ELSE...
In Edo...
WHAT?!

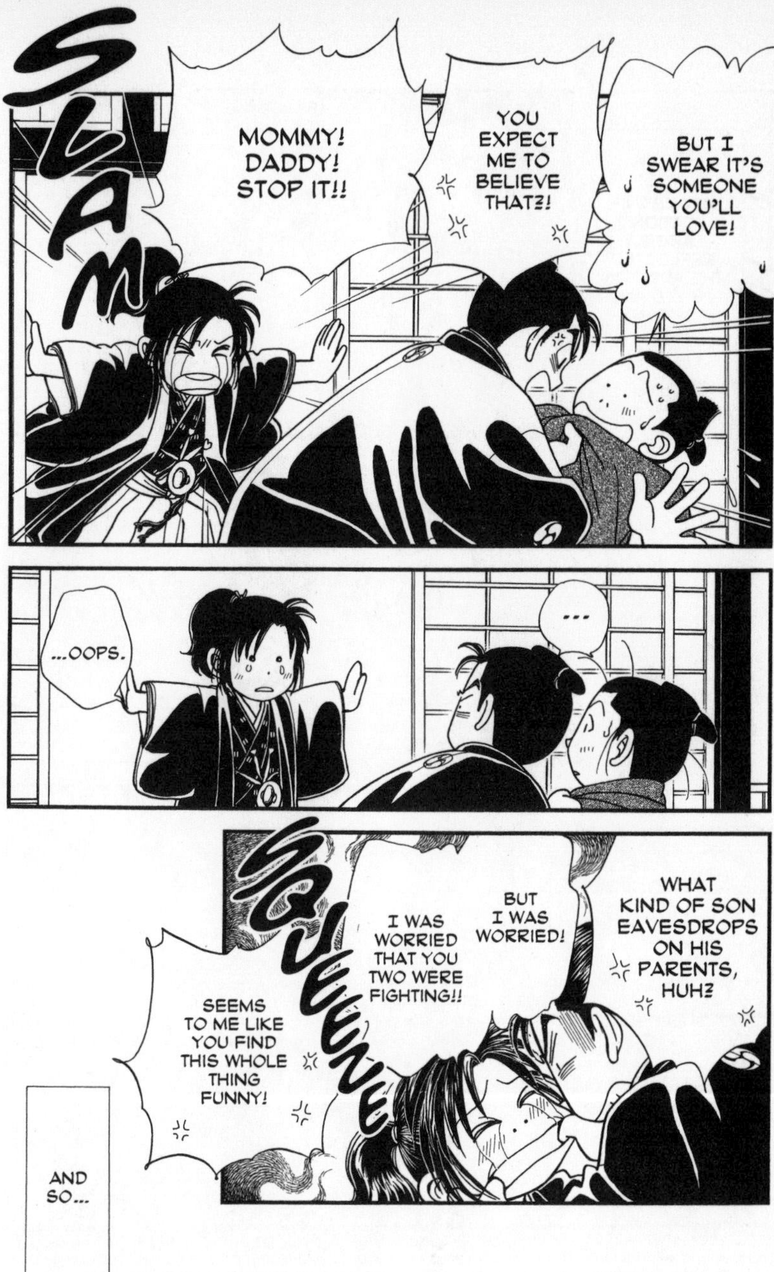
BUT I SWEAR IT'S SOMEONE YOU'LL LOVE!
YOU EXPECT ME TO BELIEVE THAT?!
MOMMY! DADDY! STOP IT!!
SLAM
...
...OOPS.
WHAT KIND OF SON EAVESDROPS ON HIS PARENTS, HUH?
BUT I WAS WORRIED!
I WAS WORRIED THAT YOU TWO WERE FIGHTING!!
SEEMS TO ME LIKE YOU FIND THIS WHOLE THING FUNNY!
AND SO...

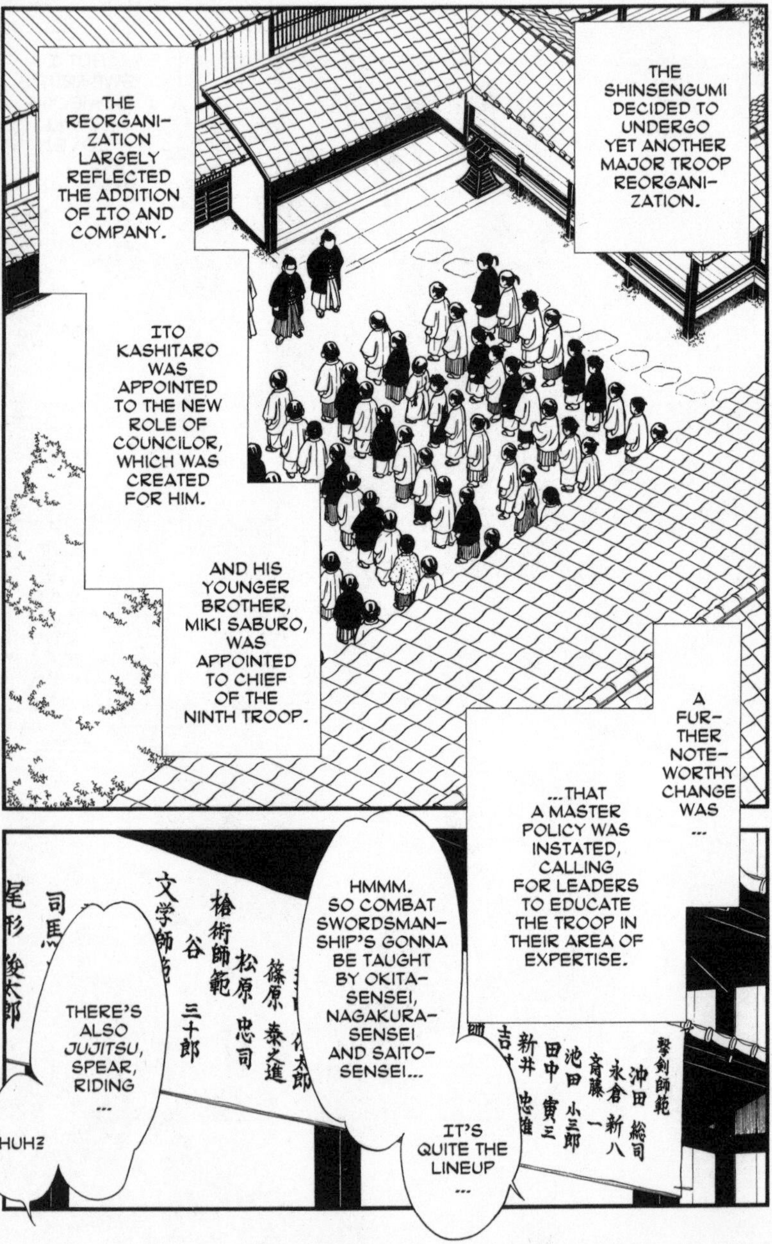
THE SHINSENGUMI DECIDED TO UNDERGO YET ANOTHER MAJOR TROOP REORGANI-ZATION.
THE REORGANI-ZATION LARGELY REFLECTED THE ADDITION OF ITO AND COMPANY.
ITO KASHITARO WAS APPOINTED TO THE NEW ROLE OF COUNCILOR, WHICH WAS CREATED FOR HIM.
AND HIS YOUNGER BROTHER, MIKI SABURO, WAS APPOINTED TO CHIEF OF THE NINTH TROOP.
A FUR-THER NOTE-WORTHY CHANGE WAS ...
...THAT A MASTER POLICY WAS INSTATED, CALLING FOR LEADERS TO EDUCATE THE TROOP IN THEIR AREA OF EXPERTISE.
撃剣師範
沖田 総司
永倉 新八
斎藤 一
池田 小三郎
田中 寅三
新井 忠雄
HMMM. SO COMBAT SWORDSMAN-SHIP'S GONNA BE TAUGHT BY OKITA-SENSEI, NAGAKURA-SENSEI AND SAITO-SENSEI...
IT'S QUITE THE LINEUP ...
篠原 泰之進
松原 忠司
槍術師範
谷 三十郎
尾形 俊太郎
THERE'S ALSO JUJITSU, SPEAR, RIDING ...
HUH?

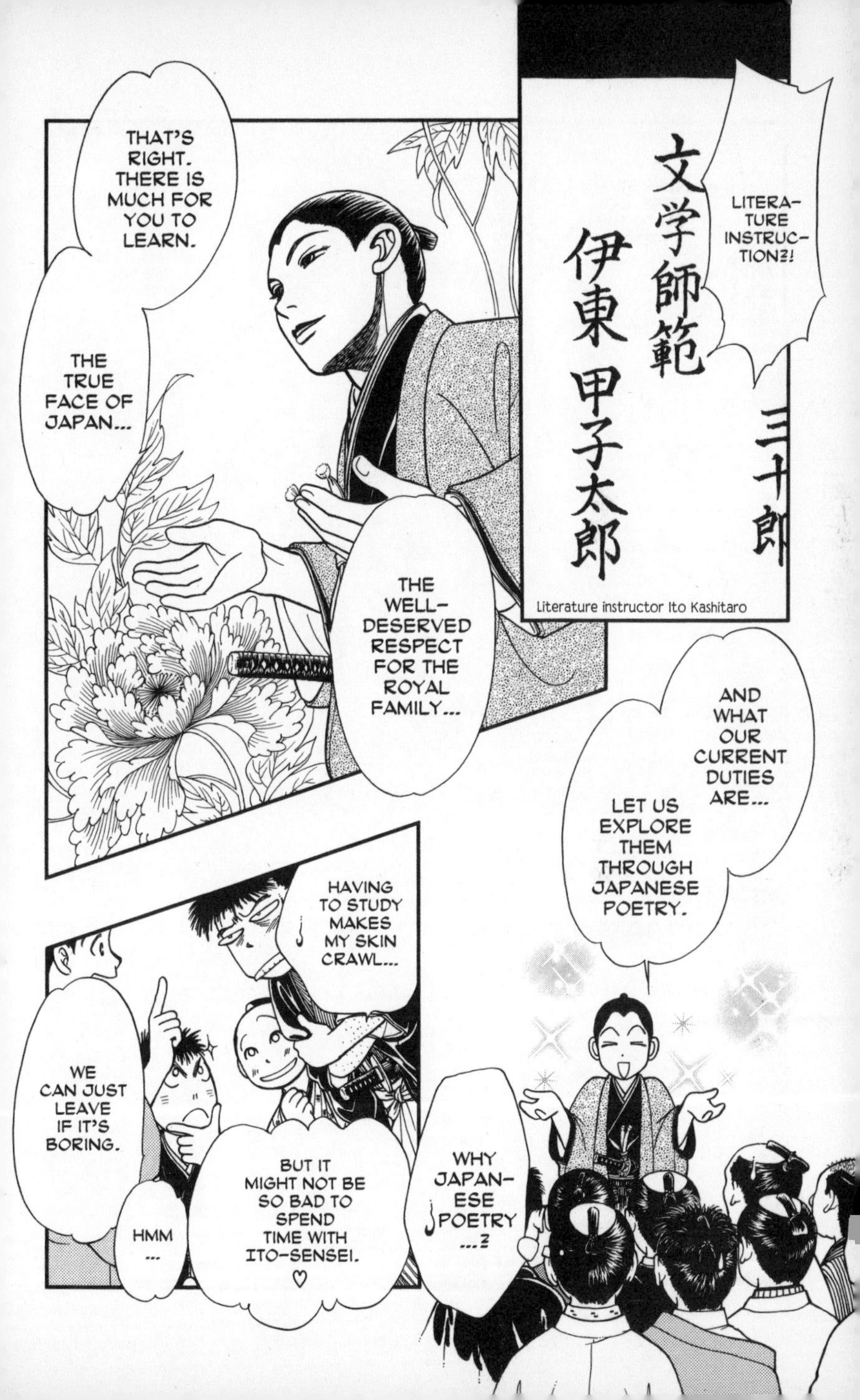
LITERATURE INSTRUCTION?!
三十郎
文学師範
伊東甲子太郎
Literature instructor Ito Kashitaro
THAT'S RIGHT. THERE IS MUCH FOR YOU TO LEARN.
THE TRUE FACE OF JAPAN...
THE WELL-DESERVED RESPECT FOR THE ROYAL FAMILY...
AND WHAT OUR CURRENT DUTIES ARE...
LET US EXPLORE THEM THROUGH JAPANESE POETRY.
WHY JAPANESE POETRY...?
HAVING TO STUDY MAKES MY SKIN CRAWL...
WE CAN JUST LEAVE IF IT'S BORING.
BUT IT MIGHT NOT BE SO BAD TO SPEND TIME WITH ITO-SENSEI. ♡
HMM...

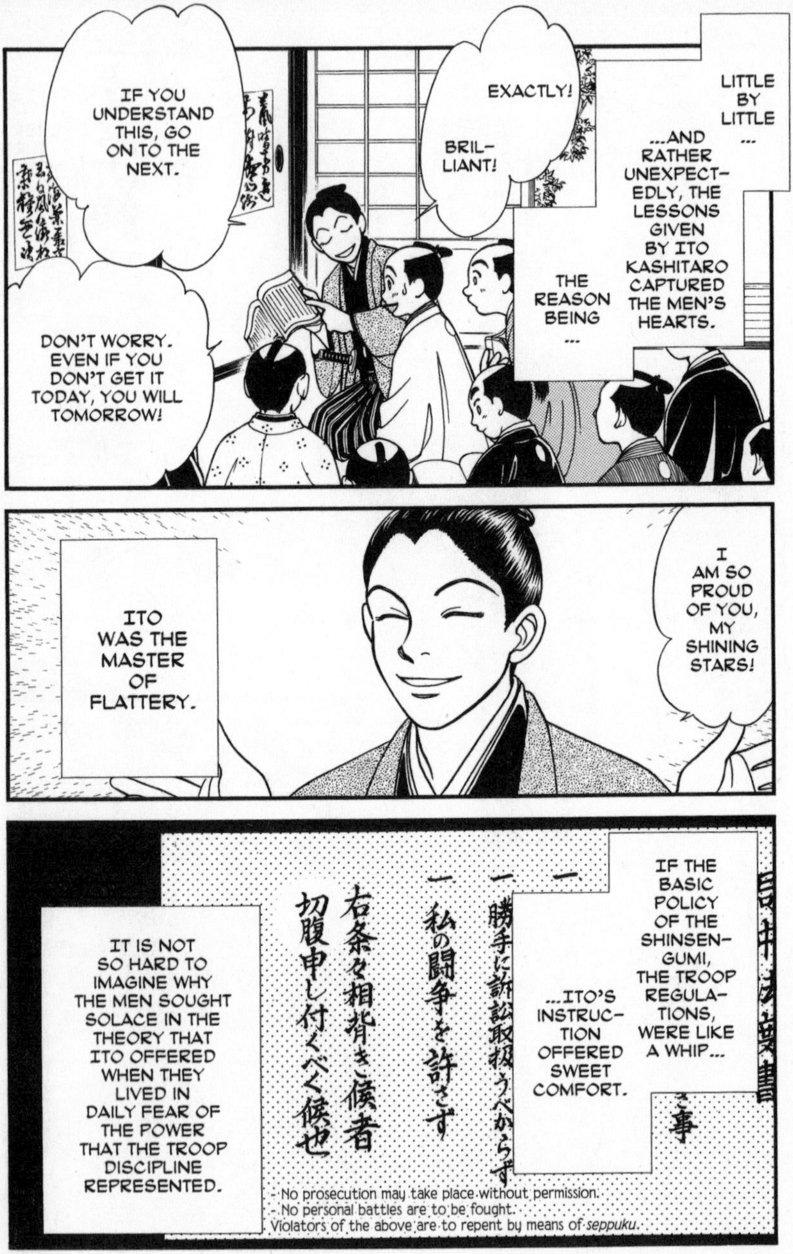
LITTLE BY LITTLE ...
...AND RATHER UNEXPECTEDLY, THE LESSONS GIVEN BY ITO KASHITARO CAPTURED THE MEN'S HEARTS.
THE REASON BEING ...
EXACTLY!
BRILLIANT!
IF YOU UNDERSTAND THIS, GO ON TO THE NEXT.
DON'T WORRY. EVEN IF YOU DON'T GET IT TODAY, YOU WILL TOMORROW!
I AM SO PROUD OF YOU, MY SHINING STARS!
ITO WAS THE MASTER OF FLATTERY.
IF THE BASIC POLICY OF THE SHINSENGUMI, THE TROOP REGULATIONS, WERE LIKE A WHIP...
...ITO'S INSTRUCTION OFFERED SWEET COMFORT.
一 勝手に訴訟取扱うべからず
一 私の闘争を許さず
一 右条々相背き候者切腹申し付くべく候也
- No prosecution may take place without permission.
- No personal battles are to be fought.
Violators of the above are to repent by means of *seppuku*.
IT IS NOT SO HARD TO IMAGINE WHY THE MEN SOUGHT SOLACE IN THE THEORY THAT ITO OFFERED WHEN THEY LIVED IN DAILY FEAR OF THE POWER THAT THE TROOP DISCIPLINE REPRESENTED.

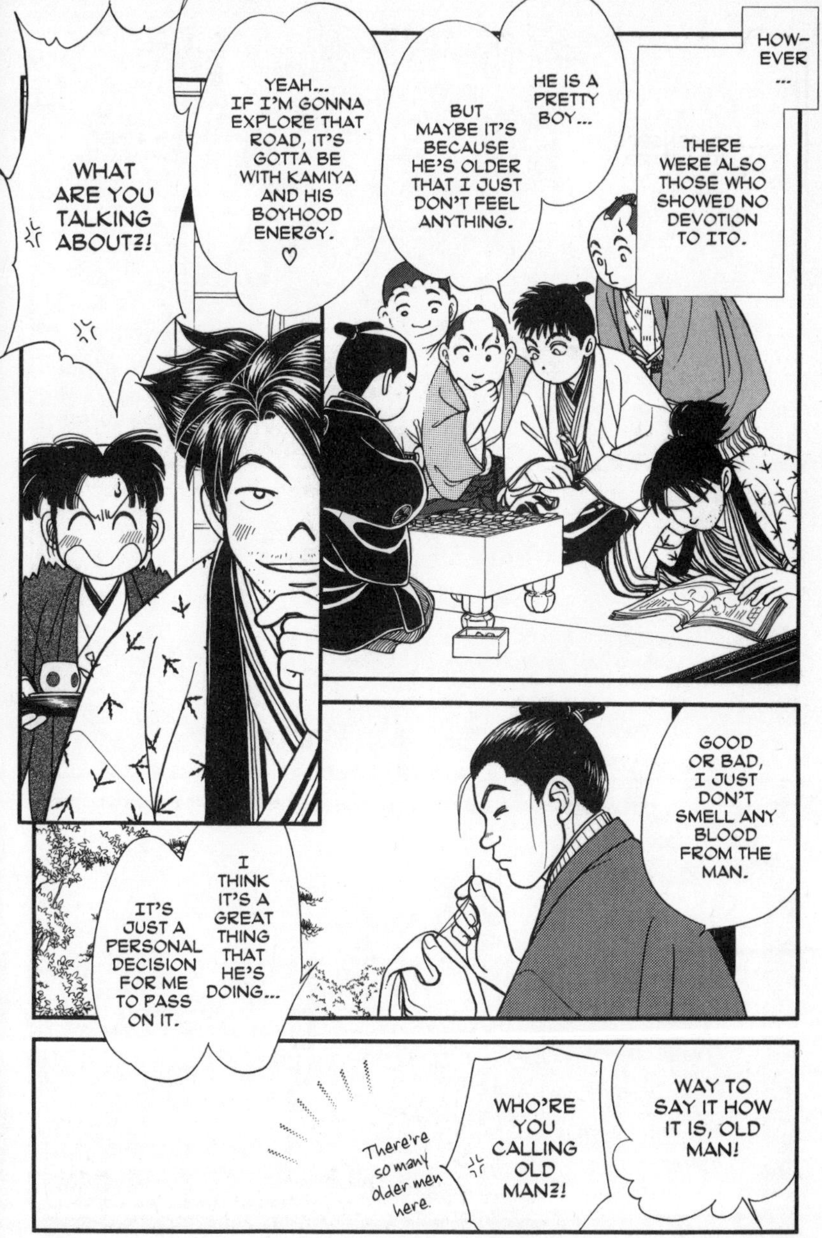
HOW-EVER...
THERE WERE ALSO THOSE WHO SHOWED NO DEVOTION TO ITO.
HE IS A PRETTY BOY...
BUT MAYBE IT'S BECAUSE HE'S OLDER THAT I JUST DON'T FEEL ANYTHING.
YEAH... IF I'M GONNA EXPLORE THAT ROAD, IT'S GOTTA BE WITH KAMIYA AND HIS BOYHOOD ENERGY. ♡
WHAT ARE YOU TALKING ABOUT?!
GOOD OR BAD, I JUST DON'T SMELL ANY BLOOD FROM THE MAN.
I THINK IT'S A GREAT THING THAT HE'S DOING...
IT'S JUST A PERSONAL DECISION FOR ME TO PASS ON IT.
WAY TO SAY IT HOW IT IS, OLD MAN!
WHO'RE YOU CALLING OLD MAN?!
There're so many older men here.

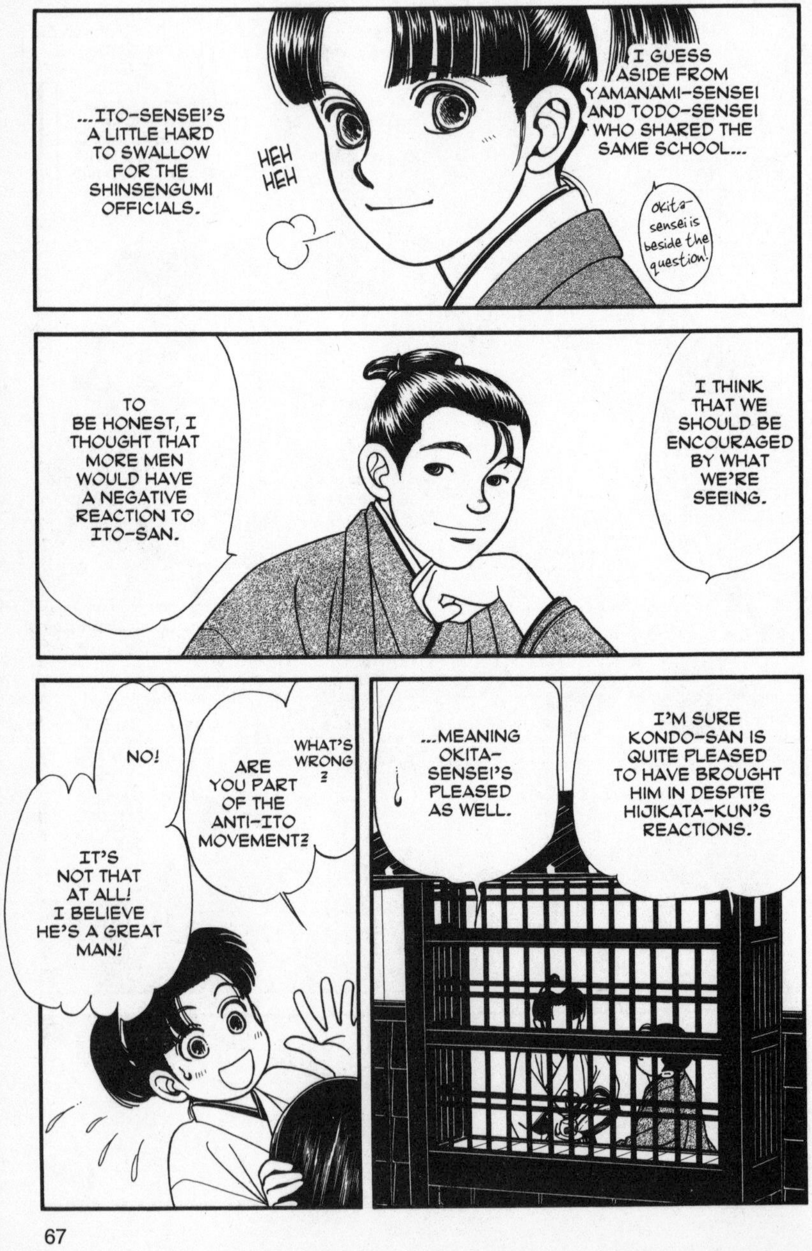
I GUESS ASIDE FROM YAMANAMI-SENSEI AND TODO-SENSEI WHO SHARED THE SAME SCHOOL...
Okita-sensei is beside the question!
HEH HEH
...ITO-SENSEI'S A LITTLE HARD TO SWALLOW FOR THE SHINSENGUMI OFFICIALS.
I THINK THAT WE SHOULD BE ENCOURAGED BY WHAT WE'RE SEEING.
TO BE HONEST, I THOUGHT THAT MORE MEN WOULD HAVE A NEGATIVE REACTION TO ITO-SAN.
I'M SURE KONDO-SAN IS QUITE PLEASED TO HAVE BROUGHT HIM IN DESPITE HIJIKATA-KUN'S REACTIONS.
...MEANING OKITA-SENSEI'S PLEASED AS WELL.
WHAT'S WRONG?
ARE YOU PART OF THE ANTI-ITO MOVEMENT?
NO!
IT'S NOT THAT AT ALL! I BELIEVE HE'S A GREAT MAN!

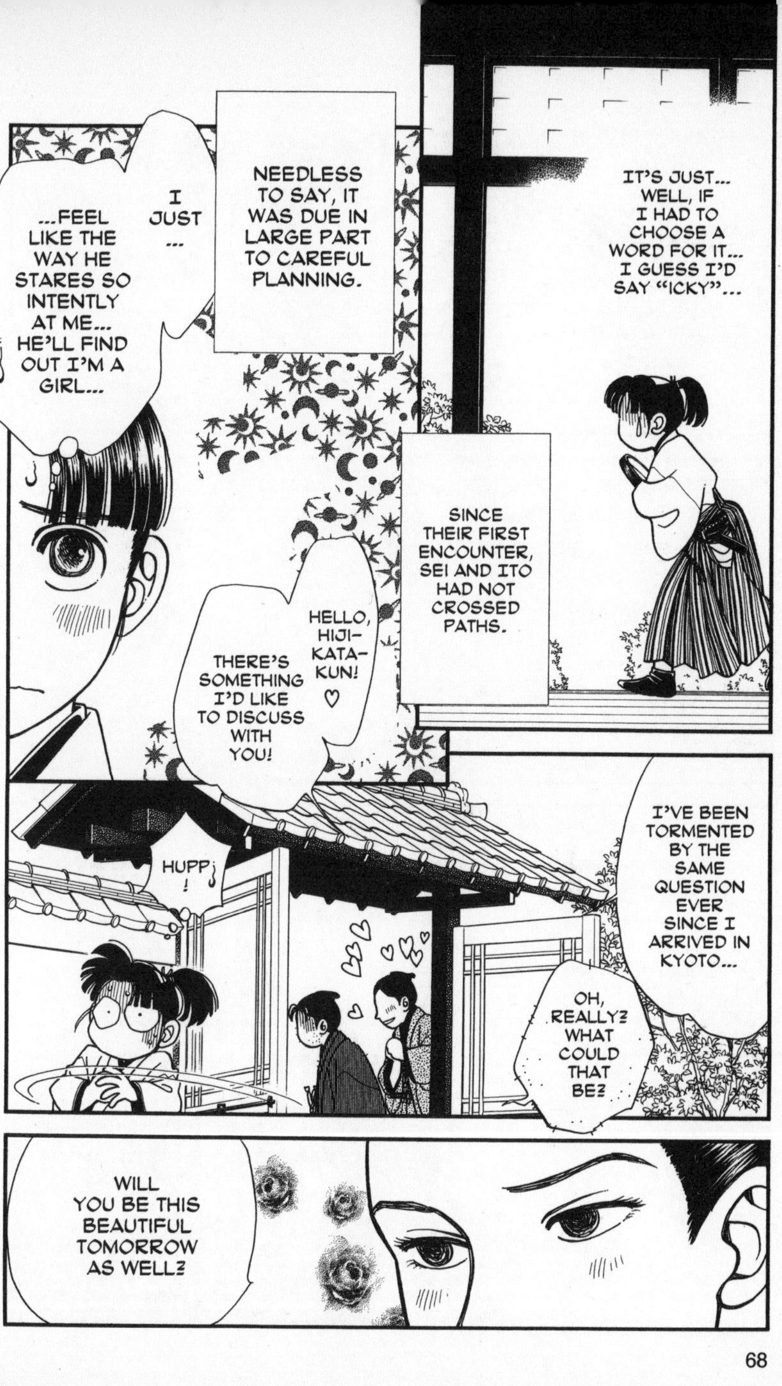
IT'S JUST... WELL, IF I HAD TO CHOOSE A WORD FOR IT... I GUESS I'D SAY "ICKY"...
SINCE THEIR FIRST ENCOUNTER, SEI AND ITO HAD NOT CROSSED PATHS.
NEEDLESS TO SAY, IT WAS DUE IN LARGE PART TO CAREFUL PLANNING.
I JUST ...
...FEEL LIKE THE WAY HE STARES SO INTENTLY AT ME... HE'LL FIND OUT I'M A GIRL...
HELLO, HIJI-KATA-KUN! ♡
THERE'S SOMETHING I'D LIKE TO DISCUSS WITH YOU!
I'VE BEEN TORMENTED BY THE SAME QUESTION EVER SINCE I ARRIVED IN KYOTO...
OH, REALLY? WHAT COULD THAT BE?
HUPP!
WILL YOU BE THIS BEAUTIFUL TOMORROW AS WELL?

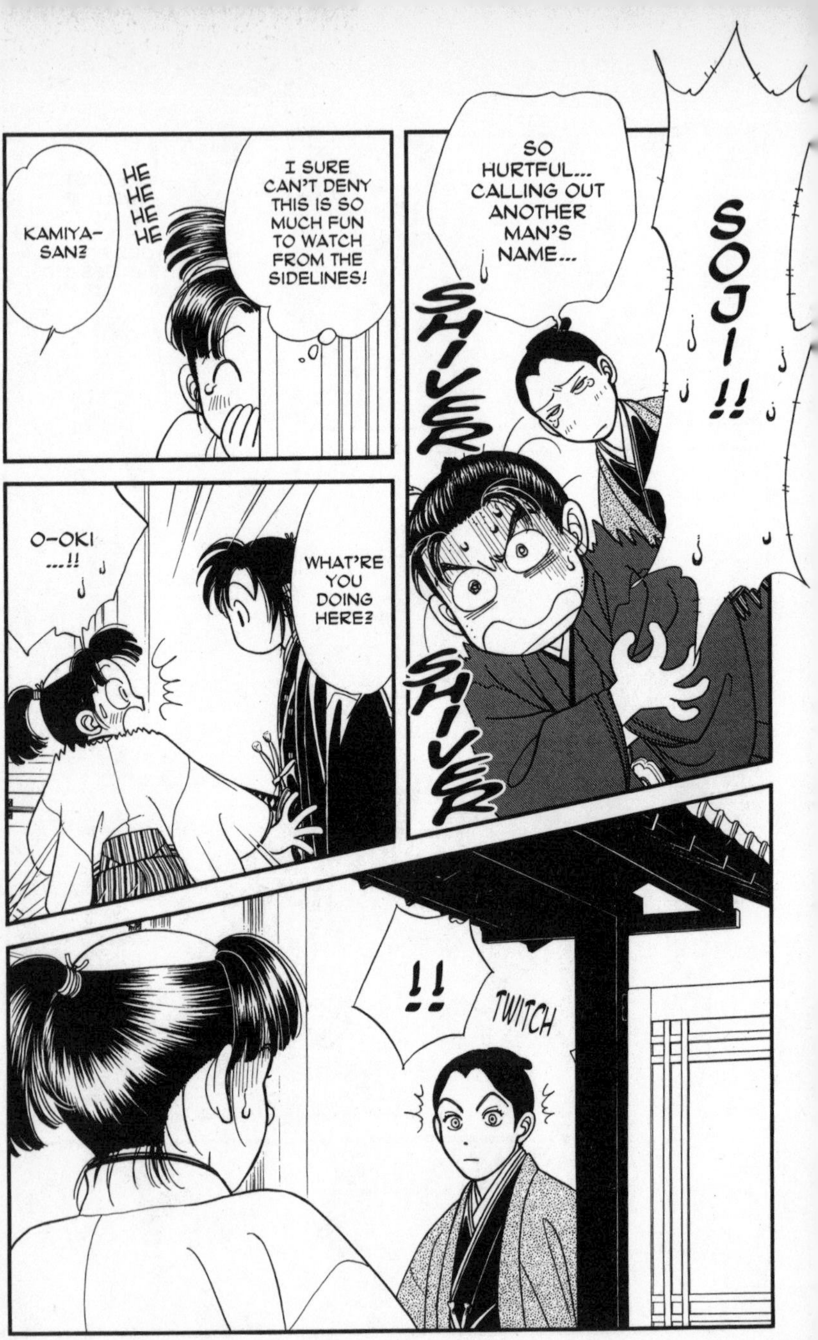
SOJI!!
SO HURTFUL... CALLING OUT ANOTHER MAN'S NAME...
SHIVER
SHIVER
I SURE CAN'T DENY THIS IS SO MUCH FUN TO WATCH FROM THE SIDELINES!
HE HE HE HE
KAMIYA-SAN?
WHAT'RE YOU DOING HERE?
O-OKI ...!!
!!
TWITCH

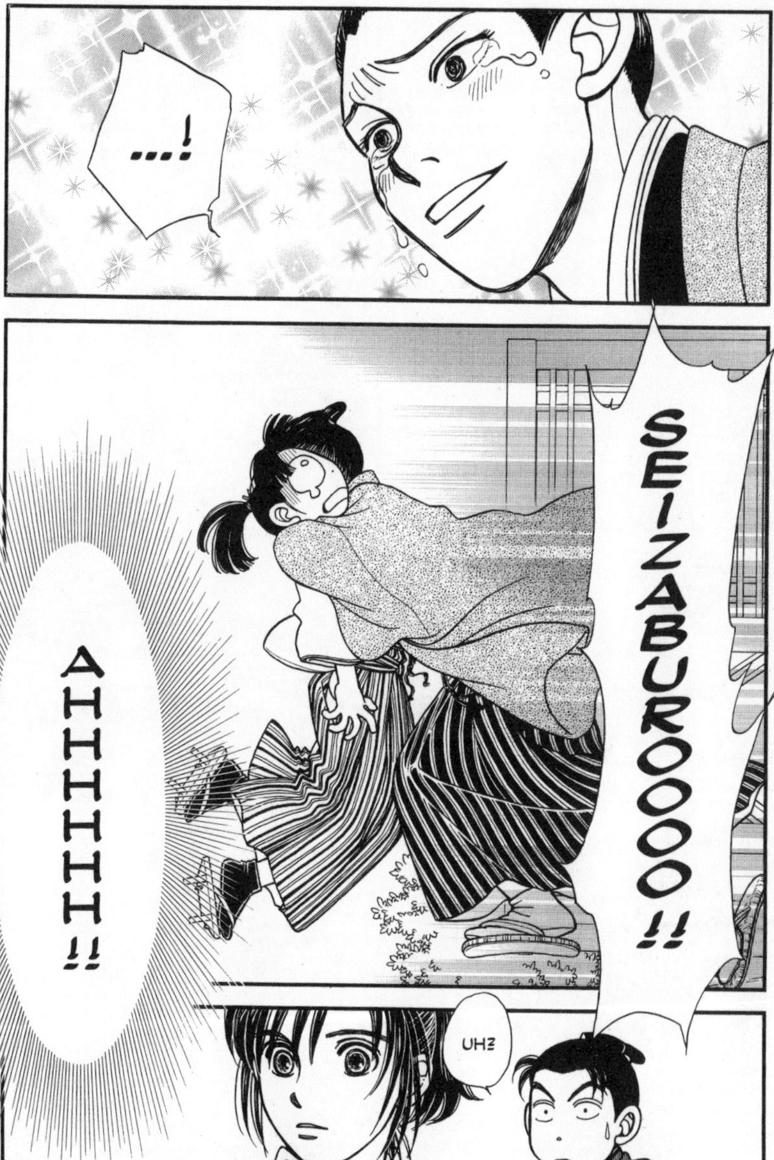
...!
SEIZABUROOOOO!!
AHHHHHH!!
UH?

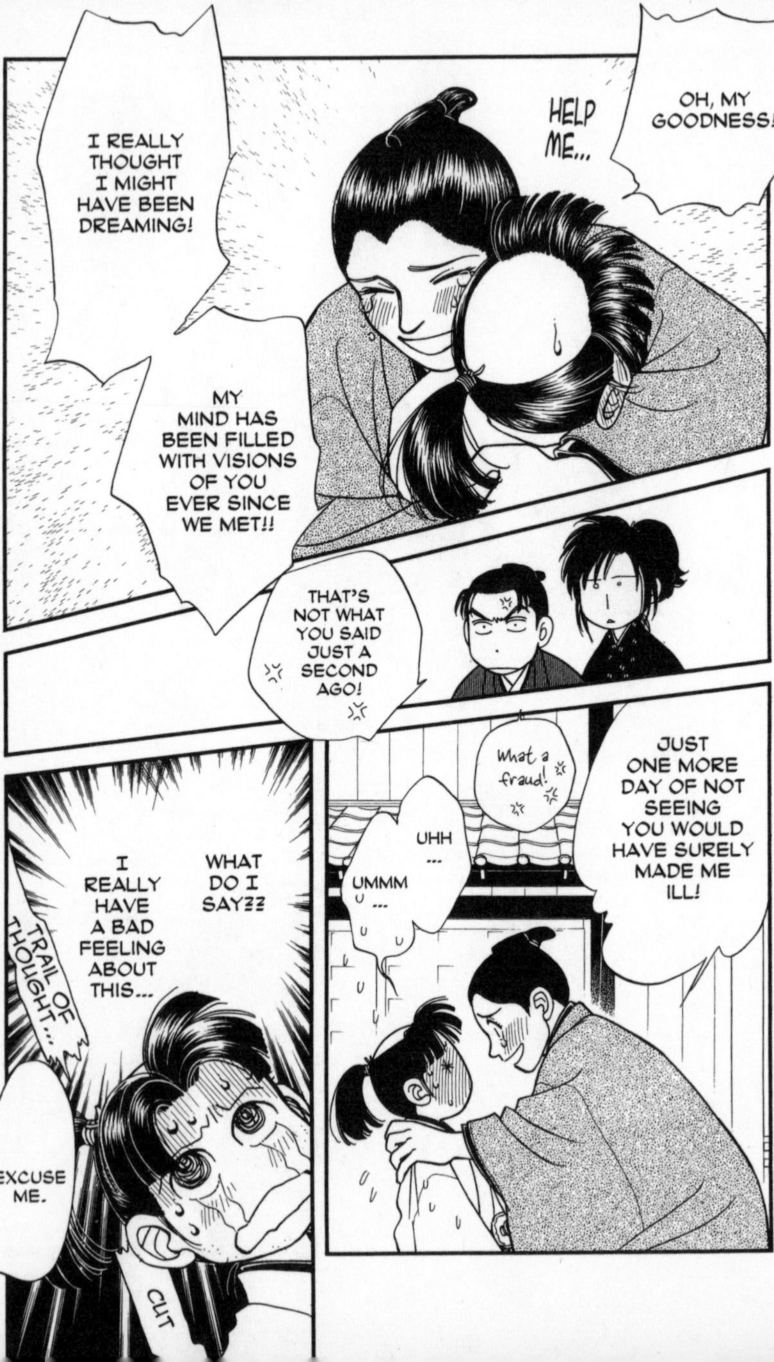
OH, MY GOODNESS!
HELP ME...
I REALLY THOUGHT I MIGHT HAVE BEEN DREAMING!
MY MIND HAS BEEN FILLED WITH VISIONS OF YOU EVER SINCE WE MET!!
THAT'S NOT WHAT YOU SAID JUST A SECOND AGO!
JUST ONE MORE DAY OF NOT SEEING YOU WOULD HAVE SURELY MADE ME ILL!
What a fraud!
UHH ...
UMMM ...
WHAT DO I SAY??
I REALLY HAVE A BAD FEELING ABOUT THIS...
TRAIL OF THOUGHT...
EXCUSE ME.
CUT

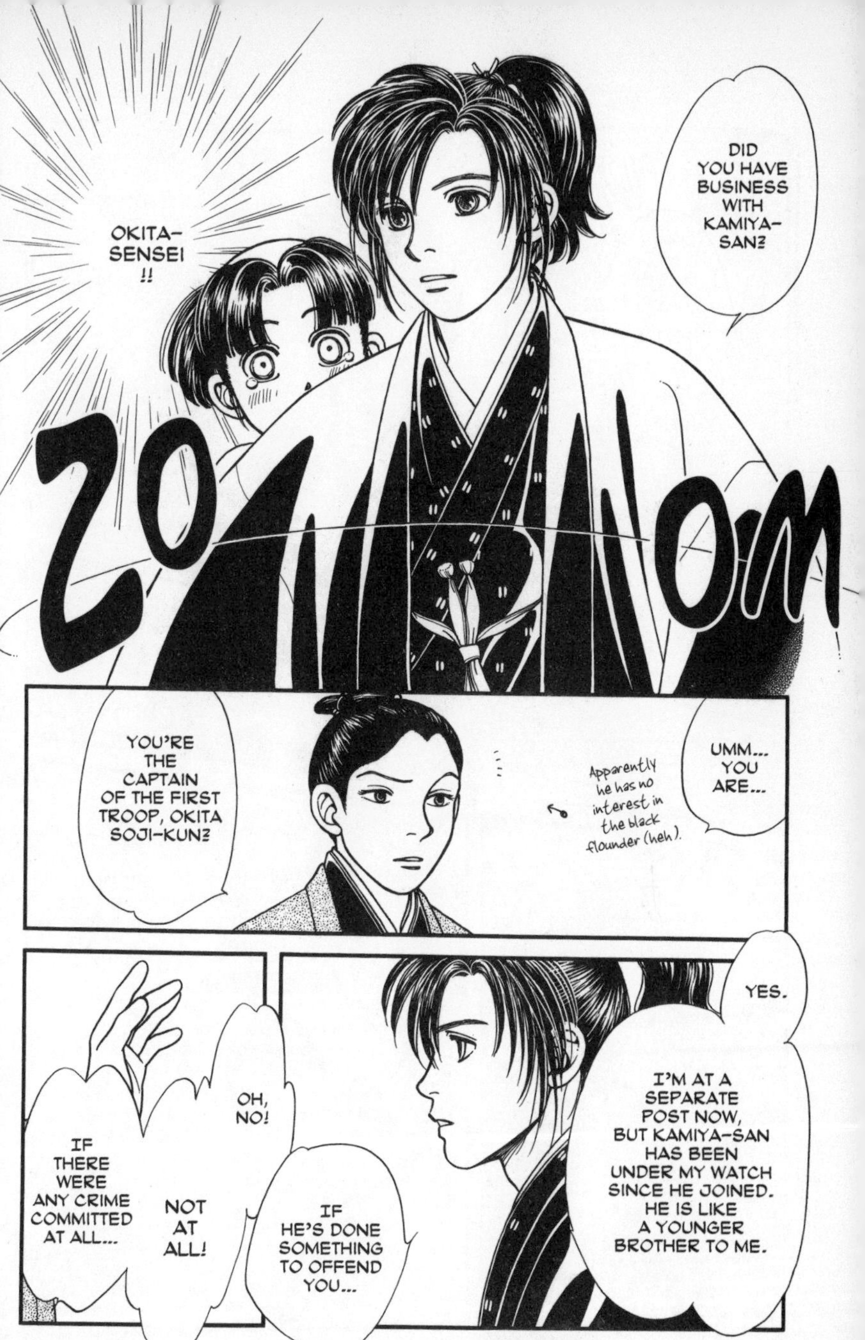
DID YOU HAVE BUSINESS WITH KAMIYA-SAN?
OKITA-SENSEI!!
UMM... YOU ARE...
Apparently he has no interest in the black flounder (heh).
YOU'RE THE CAPTAIN OF THE FIRST TROOP, OKITA SOJI-KUN?
YES.
I'M AT A SEPARATE POST NOW, BUT KAMIYA-SAN HAS BEEN UNDER MY WATCH SINCE HE JOINED. HE IS LIKE A YOUNGER BROTHER TO ME.
IF HE'S DONE SOMETHING TO OFFEND YOU...
OH, NO!
NOT AT ALL!
IF THERE WERE ANY CRIME COMMITTED AT ALL...

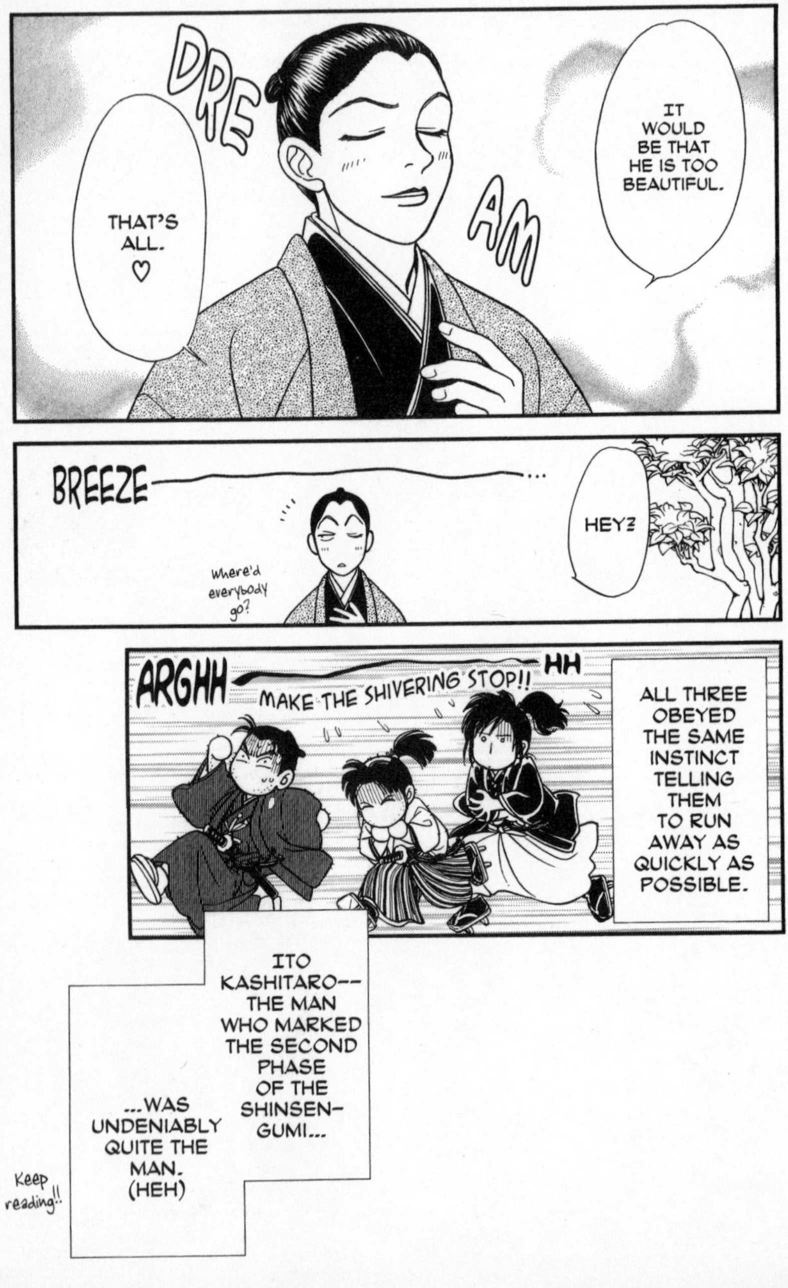
IT WOULD BE THAT HE IS TOO BEAUTIFUL.
DREAM
THAT'S ALL. ♡
HEY?
BREEZE——...
Where'd everybody go?
ALL THREE OBEYED THE SAME INSTINCT TELLING THEM TO RUN AWAY AS QUICKLY AS POSSIBLE.
ARGHH——HH
MAKE THE SHIVERING STOP!!
ITO KASHITARO-- THE MAN WHO MARKED THE SECOND PHASE OF THE SHINSEN-GUMI...
...WAS UNDENIABLY QUITE THE MAN. (HEH)
Keep reading!!

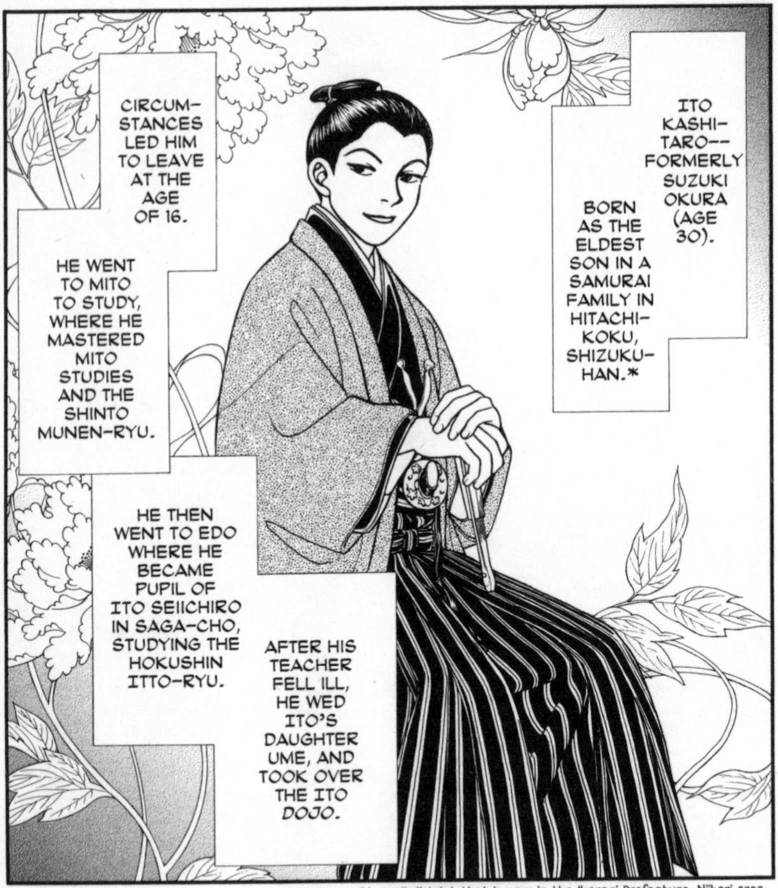
ITO KASHITARO--FORMERLY SUZUKI OKURA (AGE 30).
BORN AS THE ELDEST SON IN A SAMURAI FAMILY IN HITACHI-KOKU, SHIZUKU-HAN.*
CIRCUMSTANCES LED HIM TO LEAVE AT THE AGE OF 16.
HE WENT TO MITO TO STUDY, WHERE HE MASTERED MITO STUDIES AND THE SHINTO MUNEN-RYU.
HE THEN WENT TO EDO WHERE HE BECAME PUPIL OF ITO SEIICHIRO IN SAGA-CHO, STUDYING THE HOKUSHIN ITTO-RYU.
AFTER HIS TEACHER FELL ILL, HE WED ITO'S DAUGHTER UME, AND TOOK OVER THE ITO *DOJO*.

*A small district that is now in the Ibaragi Prefecture, Niihari area.

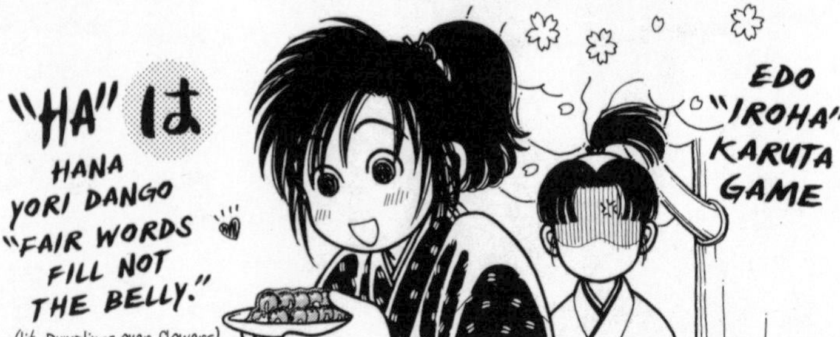
EDO "IROHA" KARUTA GAME
"HA" は
HANA YORI DANGO
"FAIR WORDS FILL NOT THE BELLY."
(lit. Dumplings over flowers)

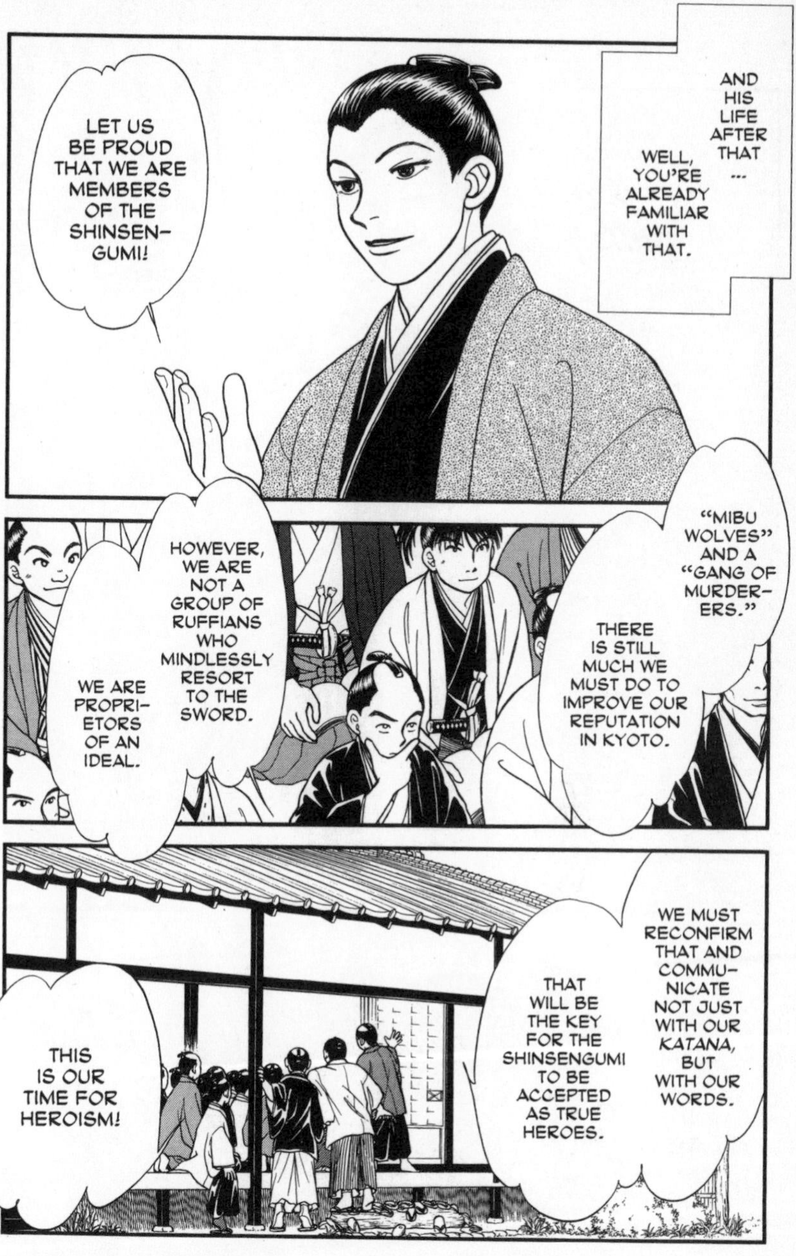
AND HIS LIFE AFTER THAT ---
WELL, YOU'RE ALREADY FAMILIAR WITH THAT.
LET US BE PROUD THAT WE ARE MEMBERS OF THE SHINSENGUMI!
"MIBU WOLVES" AND A "GANG OF MURDERERS."
THERE IS STILL MUCH WE MUST DO TO IMPROVE OUR REPUTATION IN KYOTO.
HOWEVER, WE ARE NOT A GROUP OF RUFFIANS WHO MINDLESSLY RESORT TO THE SWORD.
WE ARE PROPRIETORS OF AN IDEAL.
WE MUST RECONFIRM THAT AND COMMUNICATE NOT JUST WITH OUR *KATANA*, BUT WITH OUR WORDS.
THAT WILL BE THE KEY FOR THE SHINSENGUMI TO BE ACCEPTED AS TRUE HEROES.
THIS IS OUR TIME FOR HEROISM!

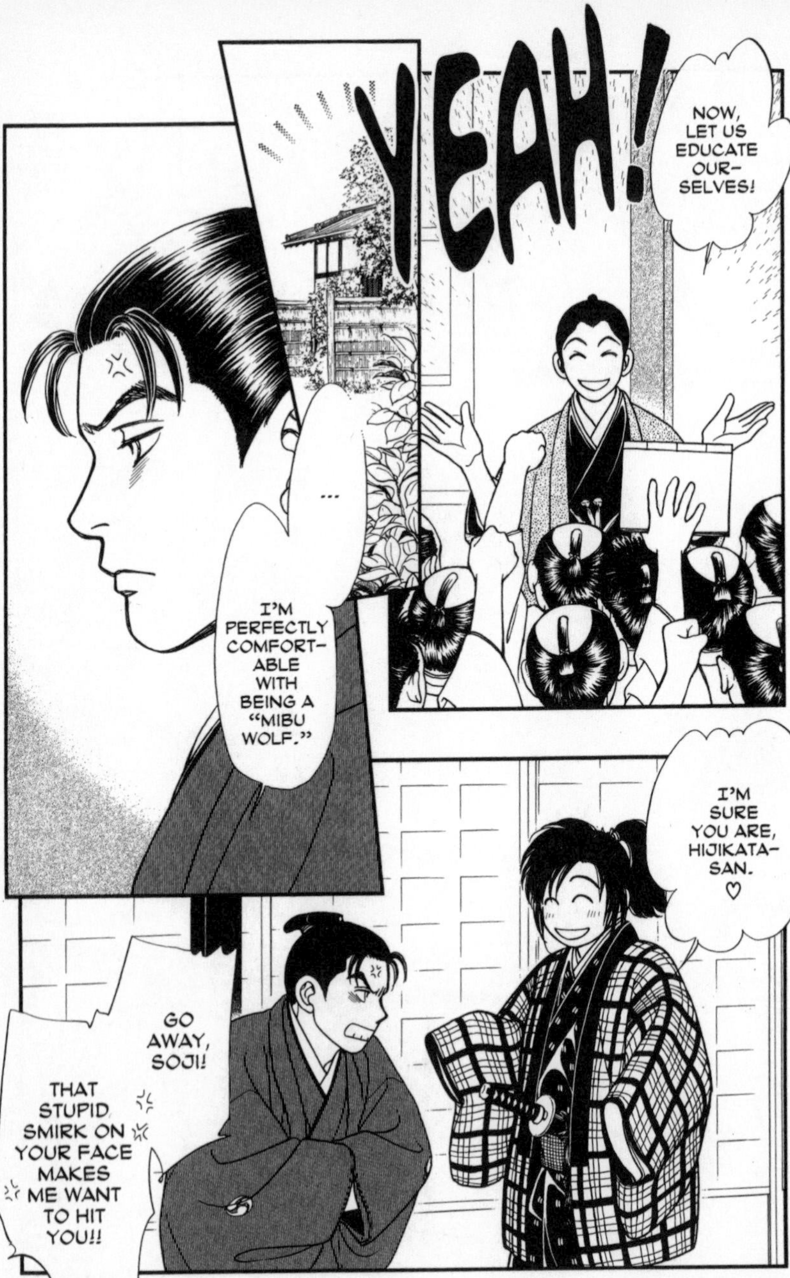
NOW, LET US EDUCATE OUR-SELVES!
YEAH!
...
I'M PERFECTLY COMFORT-ABLE WITH BEING A "MIBU WOLF."
I'M SURE YOU ARE, HIJIKATA-SAN. ♡
GO AWAY, SOJI!
THAT STUPID SMIRK ON YOUR FACE MAKES ME WANT TO HIT YOU!!

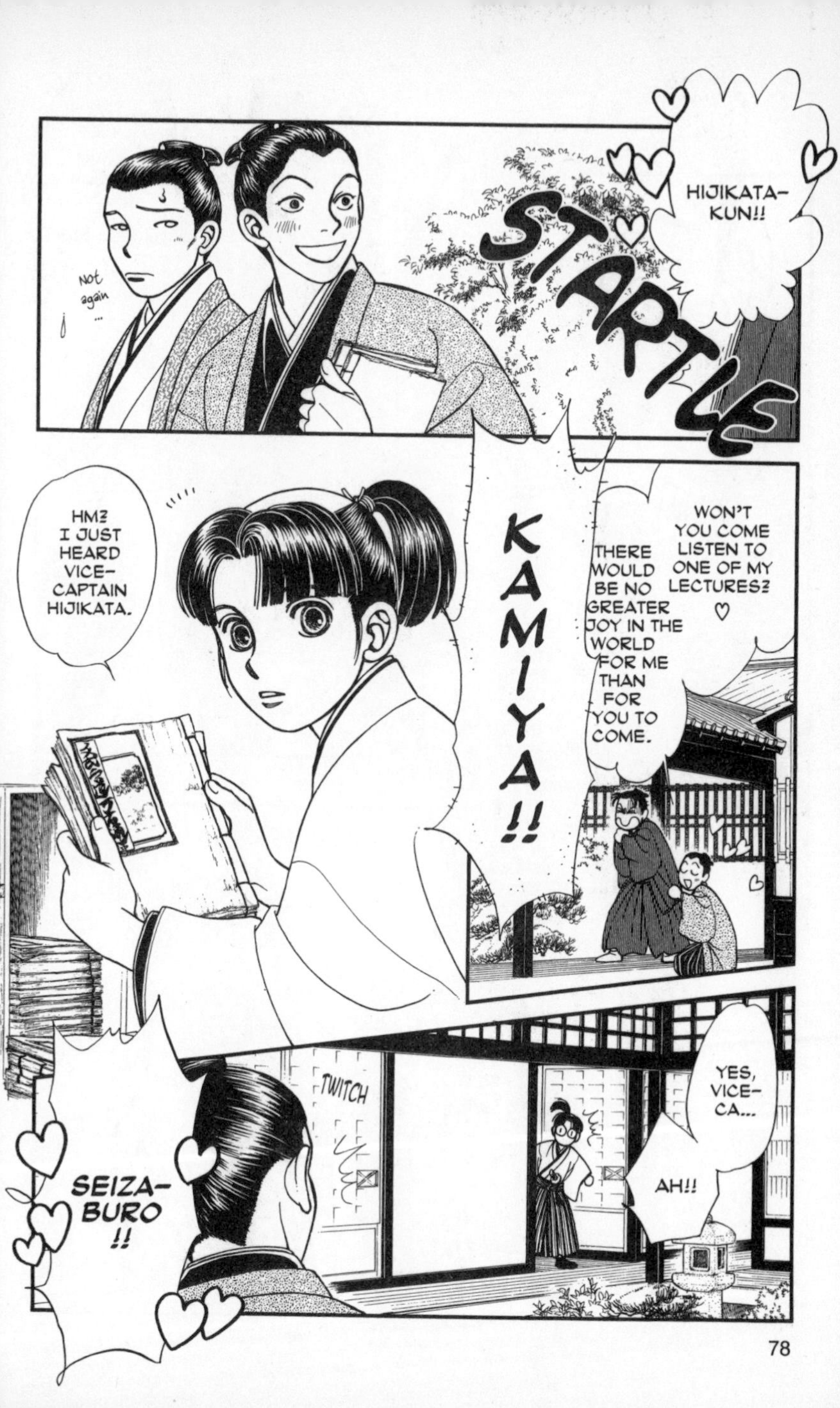
HIJIKATA-KUN!!
STARTLE
Not again ...
WON'T YOU COME LISTEN TO ONE OF MY LECTURES? ♡
THERE WOULD BE NO GREATER JOY IN THE WORLD FOR ME THAN FOR YOU TO COME.
KAMIYA!!
HM? I JUST HEARD VICE-CAPTAIN HIJIKATA.
YES, VICE-CA...
AH!!
TWITCH
SEIZABURO!!

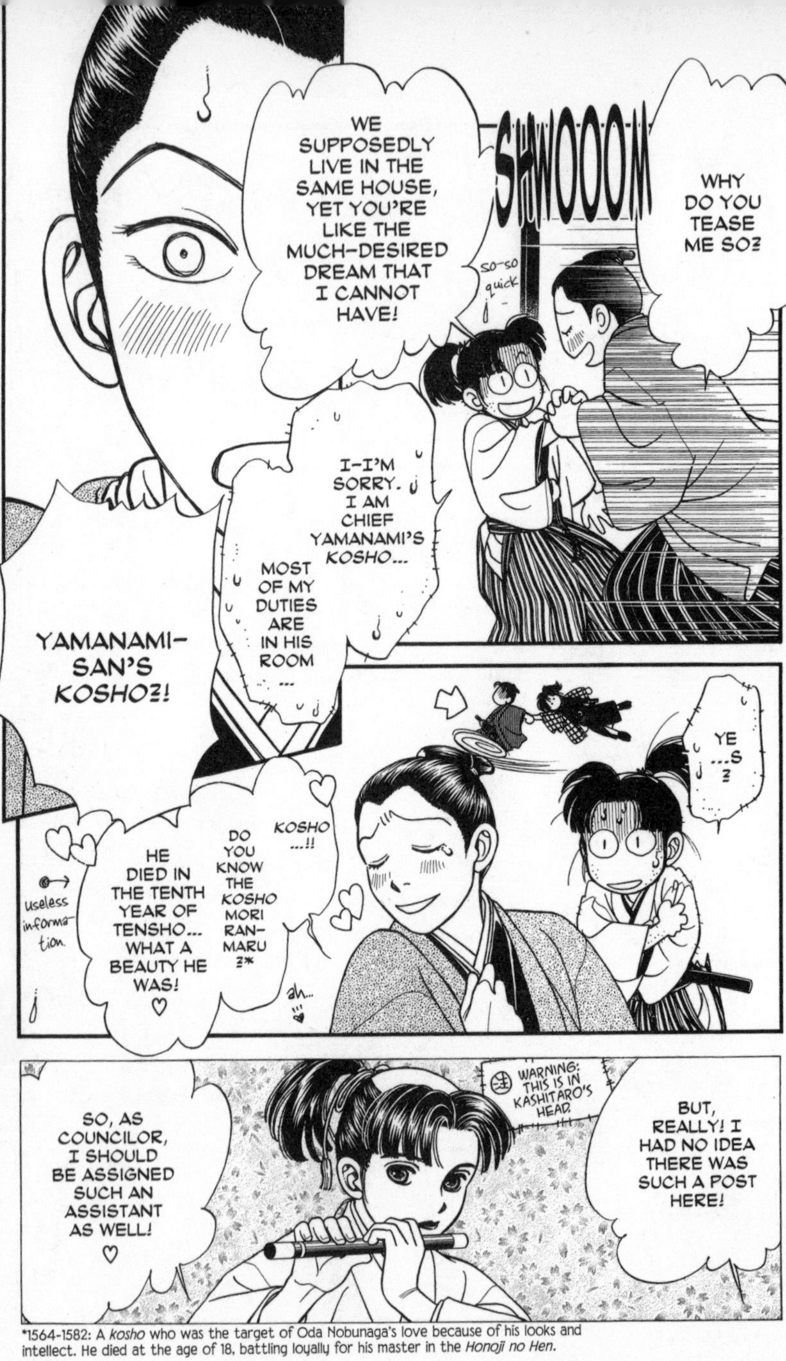
WE SUPPOSEDLY LIVE IN THE SAME HOUSE, YET YOU'RE LIKE THE MUCH-DESIRED DREAM THAT I CANNOT HAVE!
WHY DO YOU TEASE ME SO?
SHWOOOM
so-so quick
I-I'M SORRY. I AM CHIEF YAMANAMI'S KOSHO...
MOST OF MY DUTIES ARE IN HIS ROOM ...
YAMANAMI-SAN'S KOSHO?!
YE ...S ?
KOSHO ...!!
DO YOU KNOW THE KOSHO MORI RANMARU?*
HE DIED IN THE TENTH YEAR OF TENSHO... WHAT A BEAUTY HE WAS! ♡
useless information.
ah...
WARNING: THIS IS IN KASHITARO'S HEAD
BUT, REALLY! I HAD NO IDEA THERE WAS SUCH A POST HERE!
SO, AS COUNCILOR, I SHOULD BE ASSIGNED SUCH AN ASSISTANT AS WELL! ♡

*1564-1582: A *kosho* who was the target of Oda Nobunaga's love because of his looks and intellect. He died at the age of 18, battling loyally for his master in the *Honoji no Hen*.

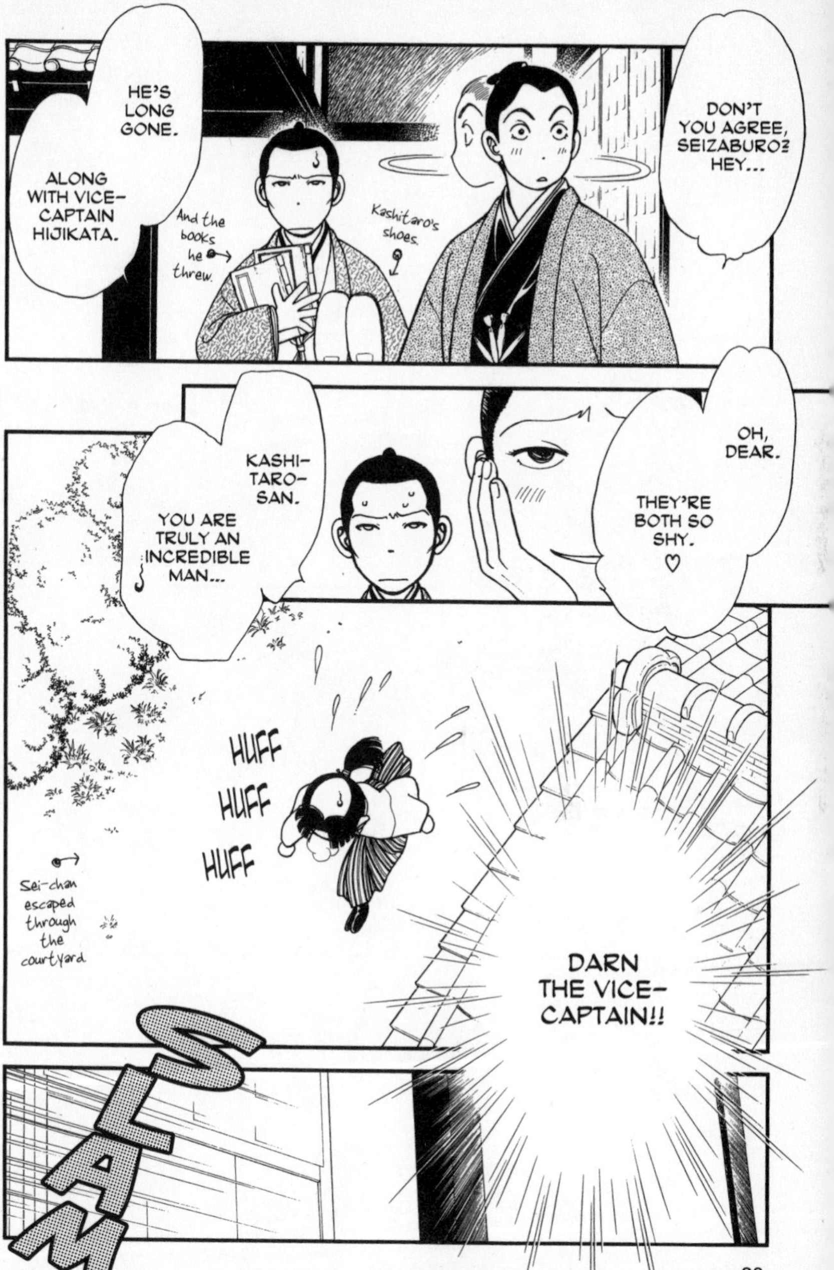
DON'T YOU AGREE, SEIZABURO? HEY...
Kashitaro's shoes.
And the books he threw.
HE'S LONG GONE.
ALONG WITH VICE-CAPTAIN HIJIKATA.
OH, DEAR.
THEY'RE BOTH SO SHY. ♡
KASHITARO-SAN.
YOU ARE TRULY AN INCREDIBLE MAN...
DARN THE VICE-CAPTAIN!!
HUFF
HUFF
HUFF
Sei-chan escaped through the courtyard
SLAM

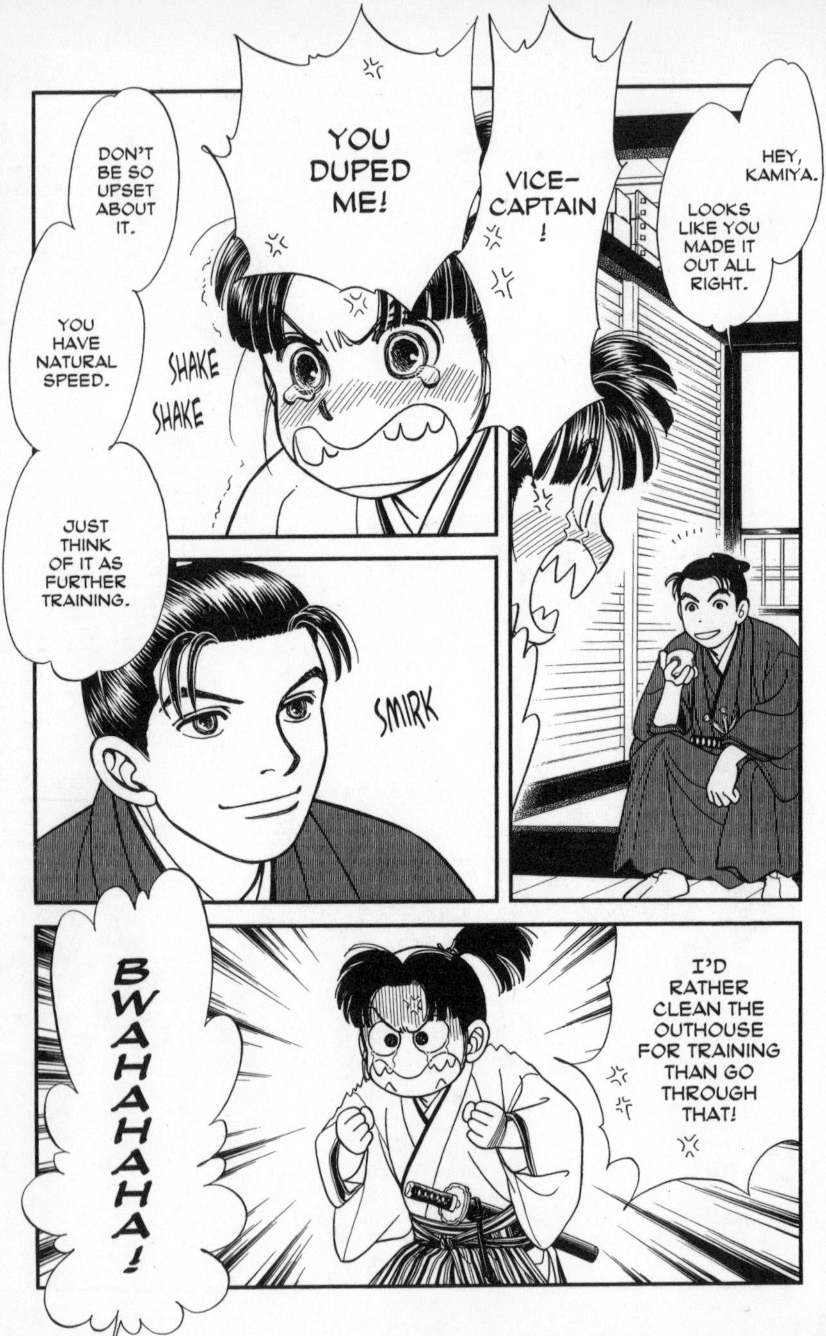
HEY, KAMIYA.
LOOKS LIKE YOU MADE IT OUT ALL RIGHT.
VICE-CAPTAIN!
YOU DUPED ME!
SHAKE
SHAKE
DON'T BE SO UPSET ABOUT IT.
YOU HAVE NATURAL SPEED.
JUST THINK OF IT AS FURTHER TRAINING.
SMIRK
I'D RATHER CLEAN THE OUTHOUSE FOR TRAINING THAN GO THROUGH THAT!
BWAHAHAHAHA!

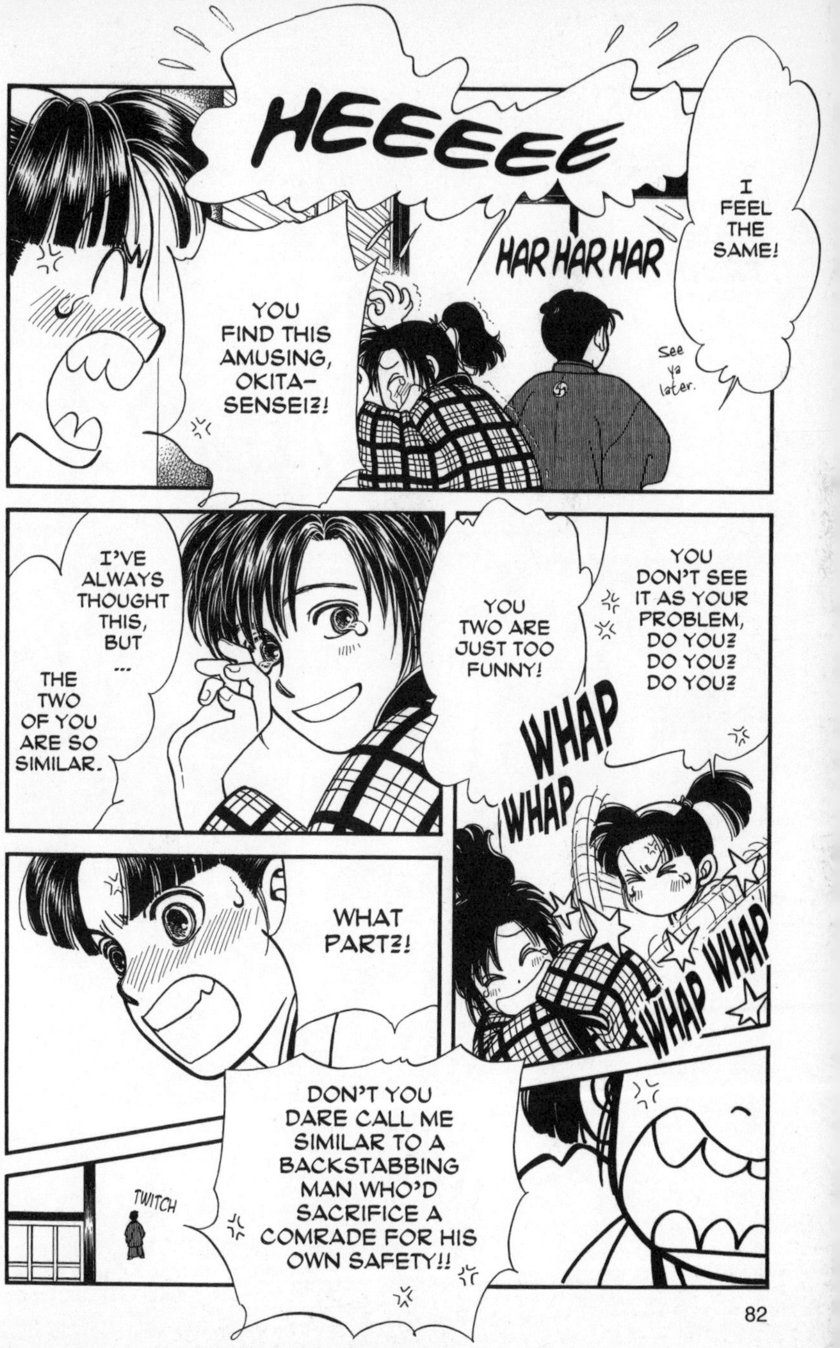
HEEEEEE
I FEEL THE SAME!
See ya later.
HAR HAR HAR
YOU FIND THIS AMUSING, OKITA-SENSEI!?
YOU DON'T SEE IT AS YOUR PROBLEM, DO YOU? DO YOU? DO YOU?
YOU TWO ARE JUST TOO FUNNY!
WHAP
WHAP
WHAP
WHAP
I'VE ALWAYS THOUGHT THIS, BUT...
THE TWO OF YOU ARE SO SIMILAR.
WHAT PART?!
DON'T YOU DARE CALL ME SIMILAR TO A BACKSTABBING MAN WHO'D SACRIFICE A COMRADE FOR HIS OWN SAFETY!!
TWITCH

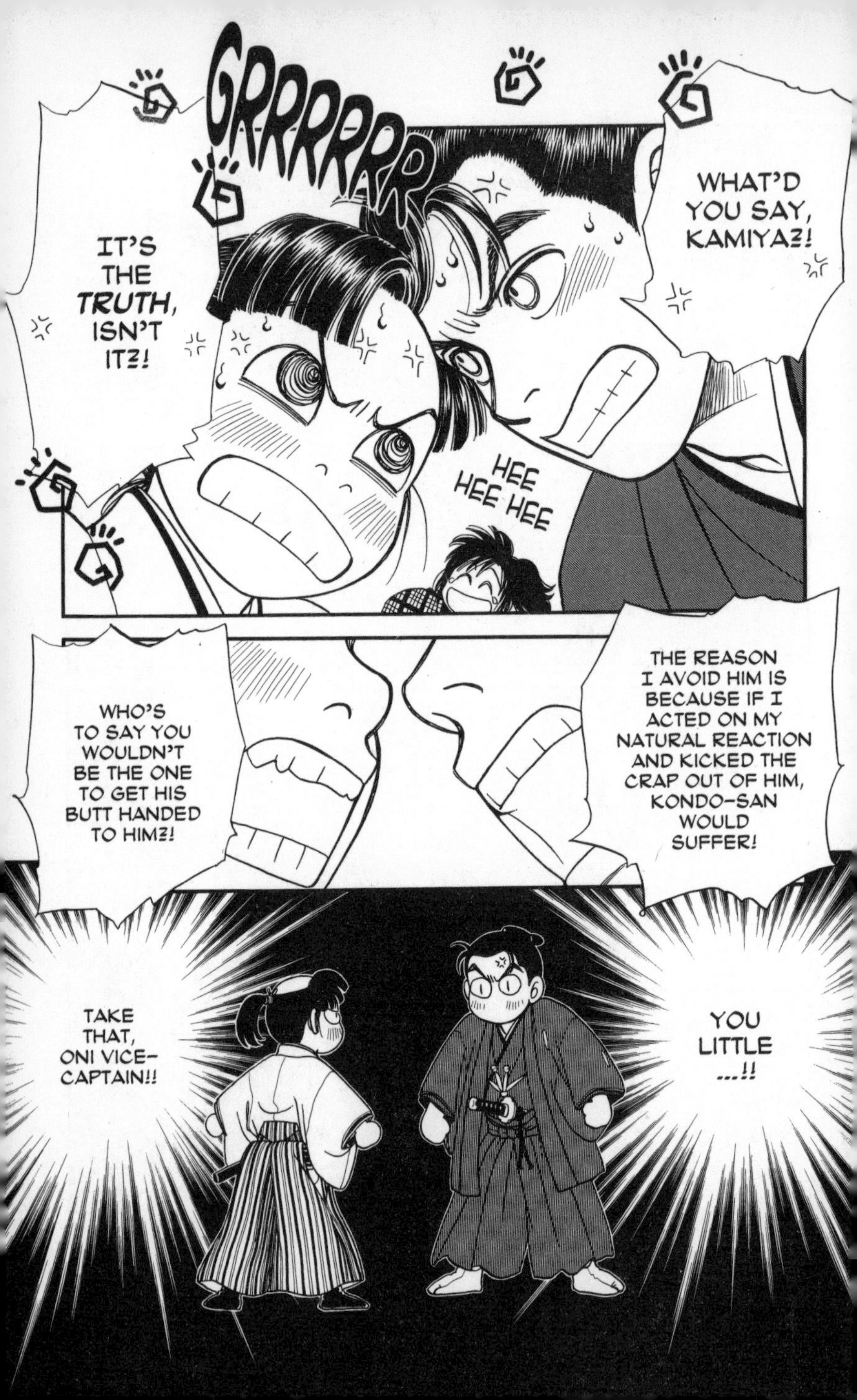
WHAT'D YOU SAY, KAMIYA?!
GRRRRRRR
IT'S THE *TRUTH*, ISN'T IT?!
HEE HEE HEE
THE REASON I AVOID HIM IS BECAUSE IF I ACTED ON MY NATURAL REACTION AND KICKED THE CRAP OUT OF HIM, KONDO-SAN WOULD SUFFER!
WHO'S TO SAY YOU WOULDN'T BE THE ONE TO GET HIS BUTT HANDED TO HIM?!
YOU LITTLE ...!!
TAKE THAT, ONI VICE-CAPTAIN!!

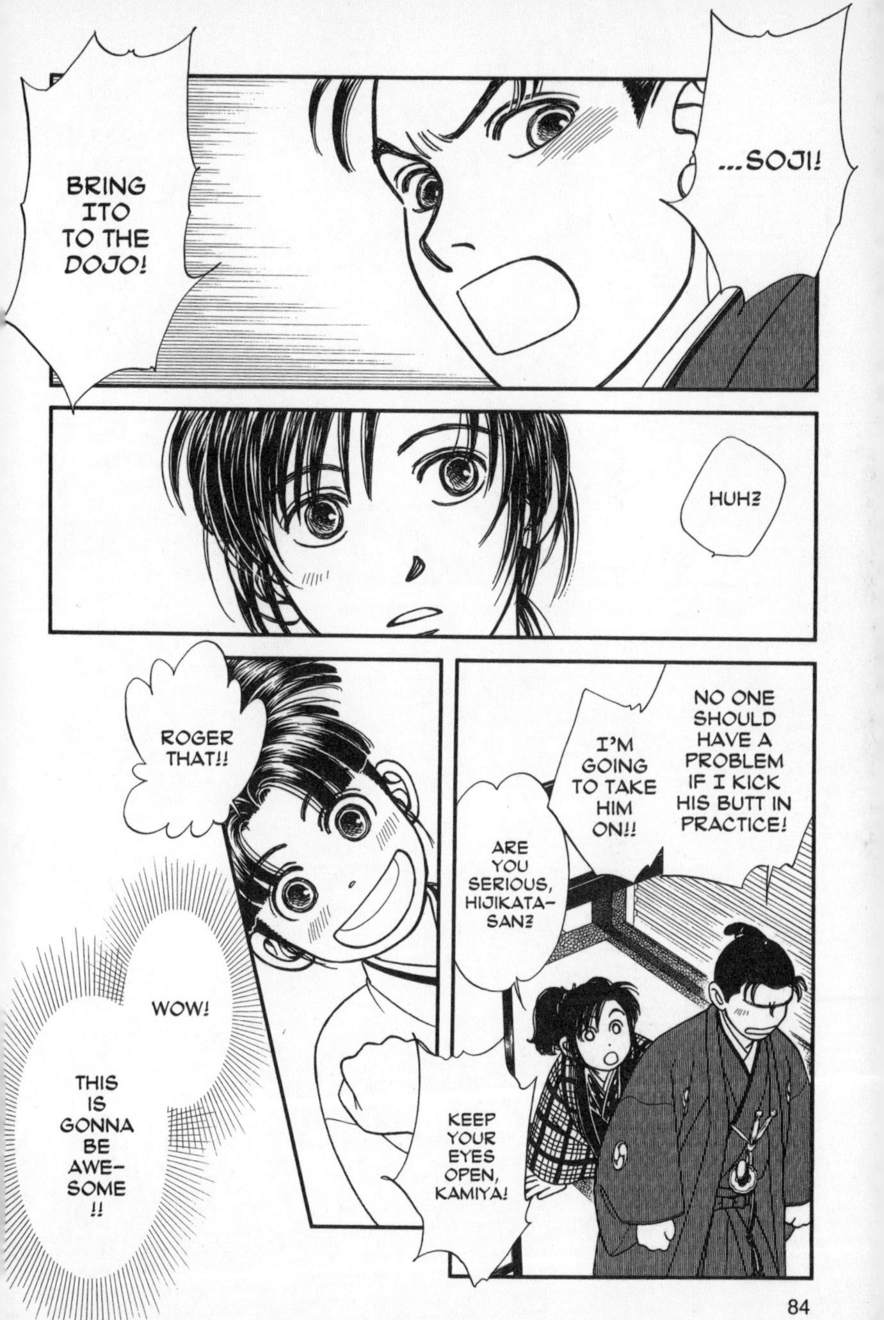
...SOJI!
BRING ITO TO THE DOJO!
HUH?
NO ONE SHOULD HAVE A PROBLEM IF I KICK HIS BUTT IN PRACTICE!
I'M GOING TO TAKE HIM ON!!
ARE YOU SERIOUS, HIJIKATA-SAN?
KEEP YOUR EYES OPEN, KAMIYA!
ROGER THAT!!
WOW!
THIS IS GONNA BE AWE-SOME!!

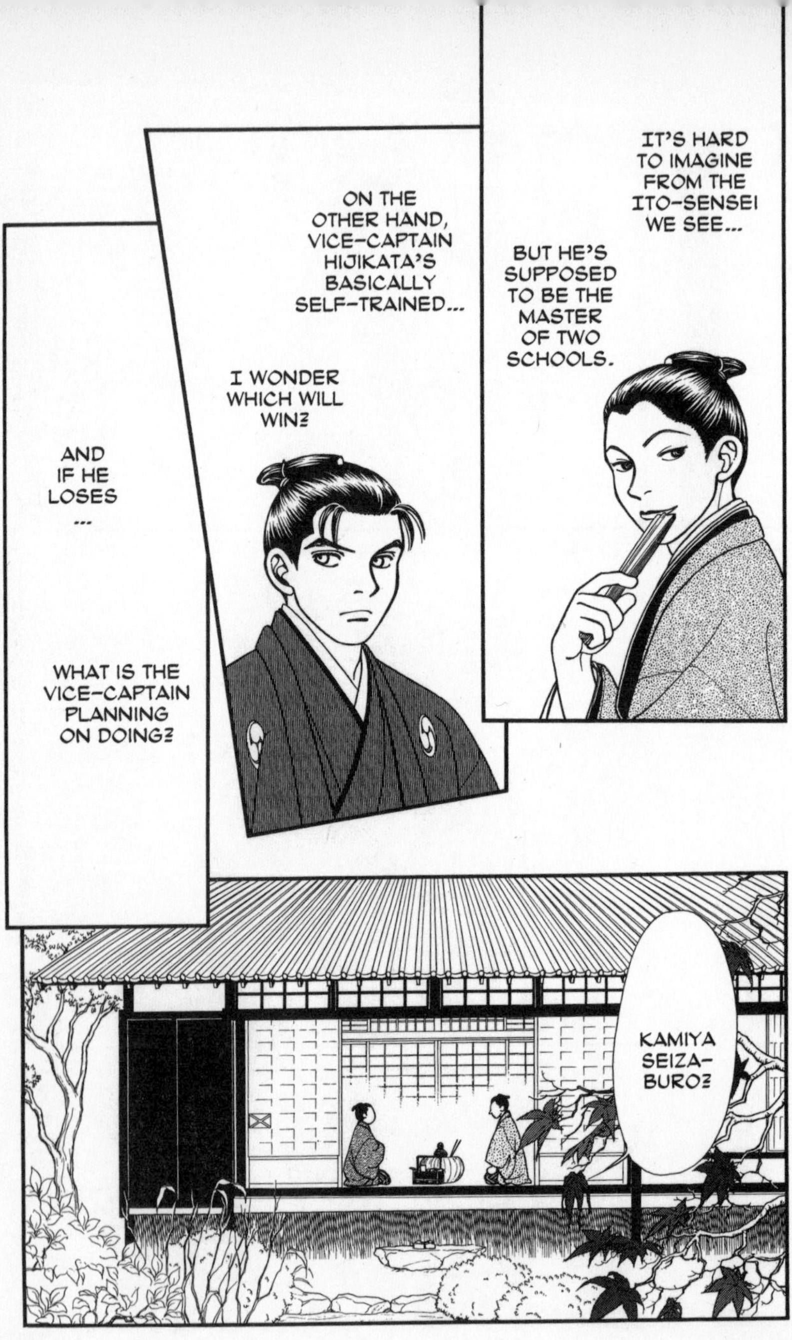
IT'S HARD TO IMAGINE FROM THE ITO-SENSEI WE SEE...
BUT HE'S SUPPOSED TO BE THE MASTER OF TWO SCHOOLS.
ON THE OTHER HAND, VICE-CAPTAIN HIJIKATA'S BASICALLY SELF-TRAINED...
I WONDER WHICH WILL WIN?
AND IF HE LOSES ...
WHAT IS THE VICE-CAPTAIN PLANNING ON DOING?
KAMIYA SEIZA-BURO?

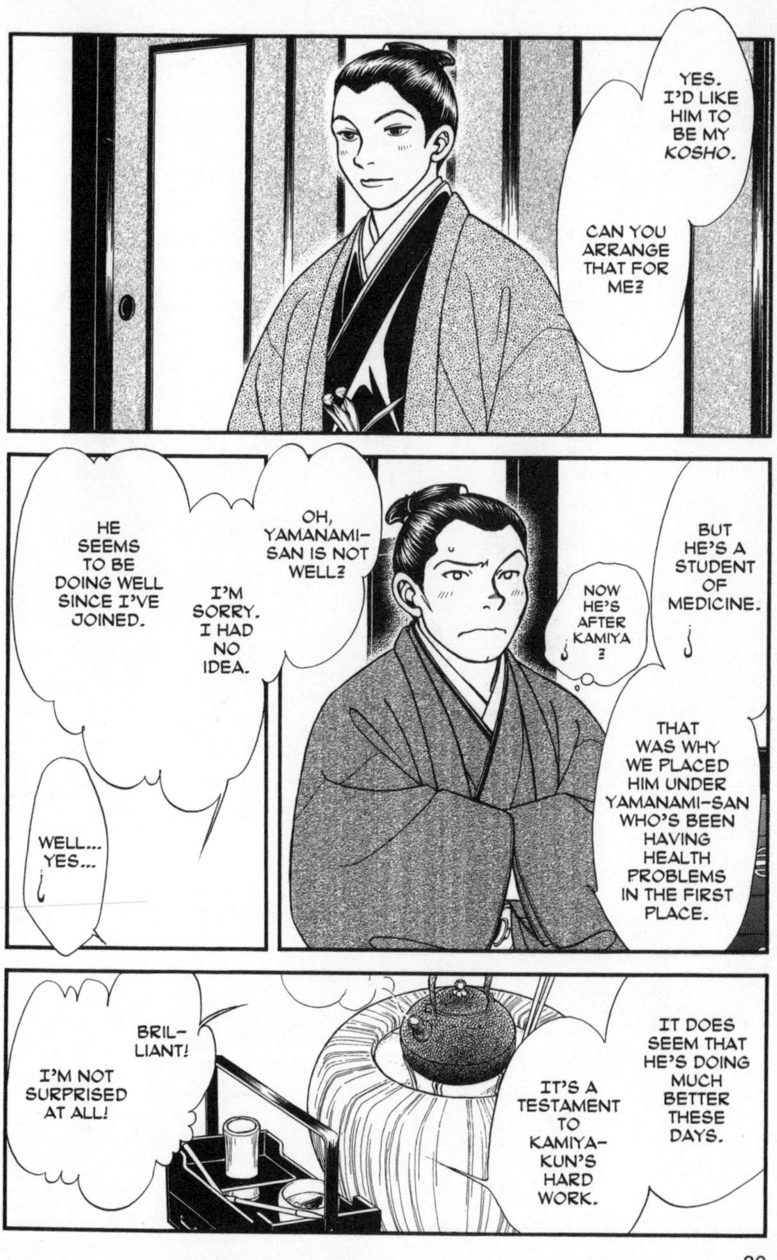
YES. I'D LIKE HIM TO BE MY *KOSHO*.
CAN YOU ARRANGE THAT FOR ME?
BUT HE'S A STUDENT OF MEDICINE.
NOW HE'S AFTER KAMIYA?
THAT WAS WHY WE PLACED HIM UNDER YAMANAMI-SAN WHO'S BEEN HAVING HEALTH PROBLEMS IN THE FIRST PLACE.
OH, YAMANAMI-SAN IS NOT WELL?
I'M SORRY. I HAD NO IDEA.
HE SEEMS TO BE DOING WELL SINCE I'VE JOINED.
WELL... YES...
IT DOES SEEM THAT HE'S DOING MUCH BETTER THESE DAYS.
IT'S A TESTAMENT TO KAMIYA-KUN'S HARD WORK.
BRIL-LIANT!
I'M NOT SURPRISED AT ALL!

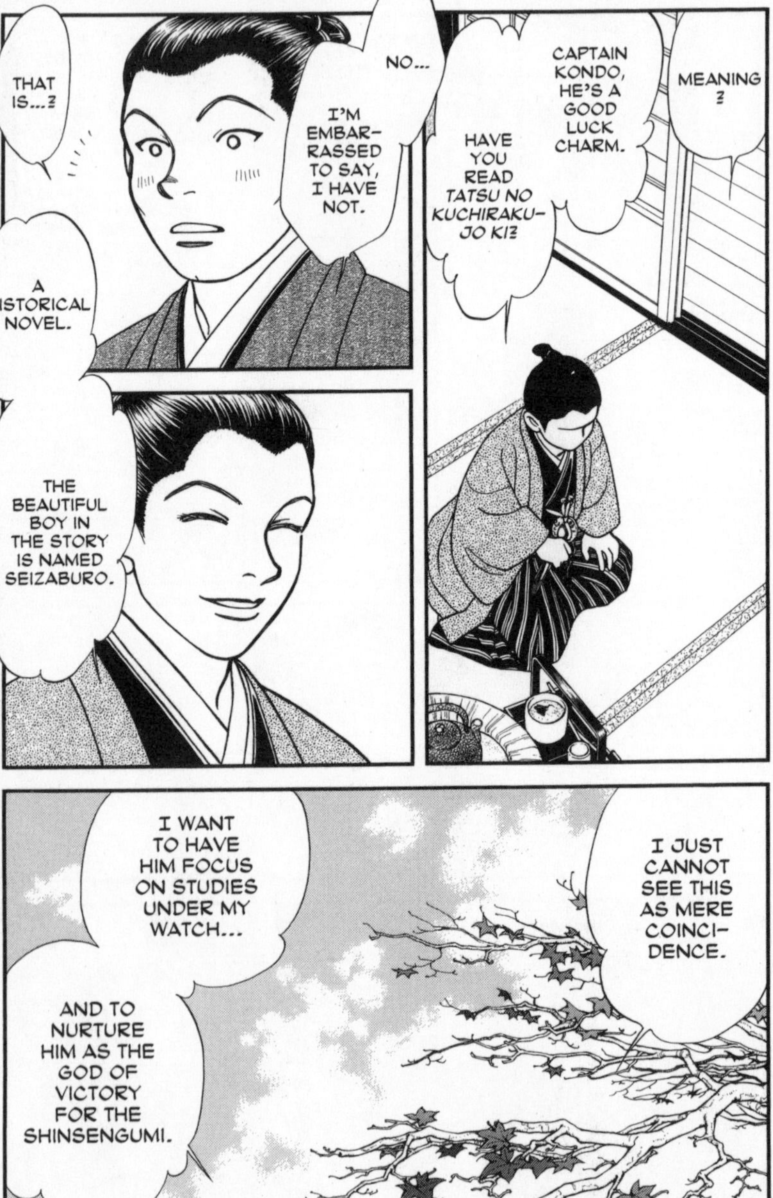
MEANING?
CAPTAIN KONDO, HE'S A GOOD LUCK CHARM.
HAVE YOU READ *TATSU NO KUCHIRAKUJO KI*?
NO...
I'M EMBARRASSED TO SAY, I HAVE NOT.
THAT IS...?
A HISTORICAL NOVEL.
THE BEAUTIFUL BOY IN THE STORY IS NAMED SEIZABURO.
I JUST CANNOT SEE THIS AS MERE COINCIDENCE.
I WANT TO HAVE HIM FOCUS ON STUDIES UNDER MY WATCH...
AND TO NURTURE HIM AS THE GOD OF VICTORY FOR THE SHINSENGUMI.

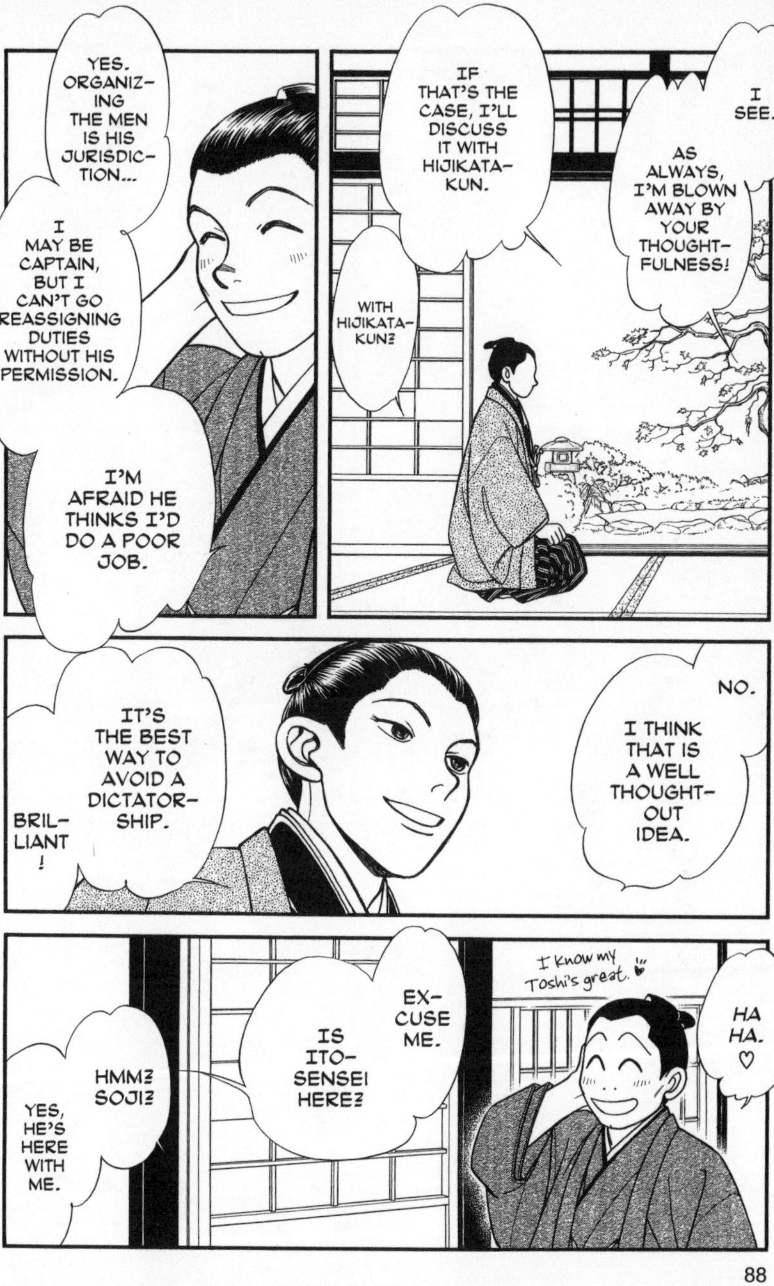
I SEE. AS ALWAYS, I'M BLOWN AWAY BY YOUR THOUGHTFULNESS!
IF THAT'S THE CASE, I'LL DISCUSS IT WITH HIJIKATA-KUN.
WITH HIJIKATA-KUN?
YES. ORGANIZING THE MEN IS HIS JURISDICTION...
I MAY BE CAPTAIN, BUT I CAN'T GO REASSIGNING DUTIES WITHOUT HIS PERMISSION.
I'M AFRAID HE THINKS I'D DO A POOR JOB.
NO.
I THINK THAT IS A WELL THOUGHT-OUT IDEA.
IT'S THE BEST WAY TO AVOID A DICTATORSHIP.
BRILLIANT!
HA HA. ♡
I know my Toshi's great.
EXCUSE ME.
IS ITO-SENSEI HERE?
HMM? SOJI?
YES, HE'S HERE WITH ME.

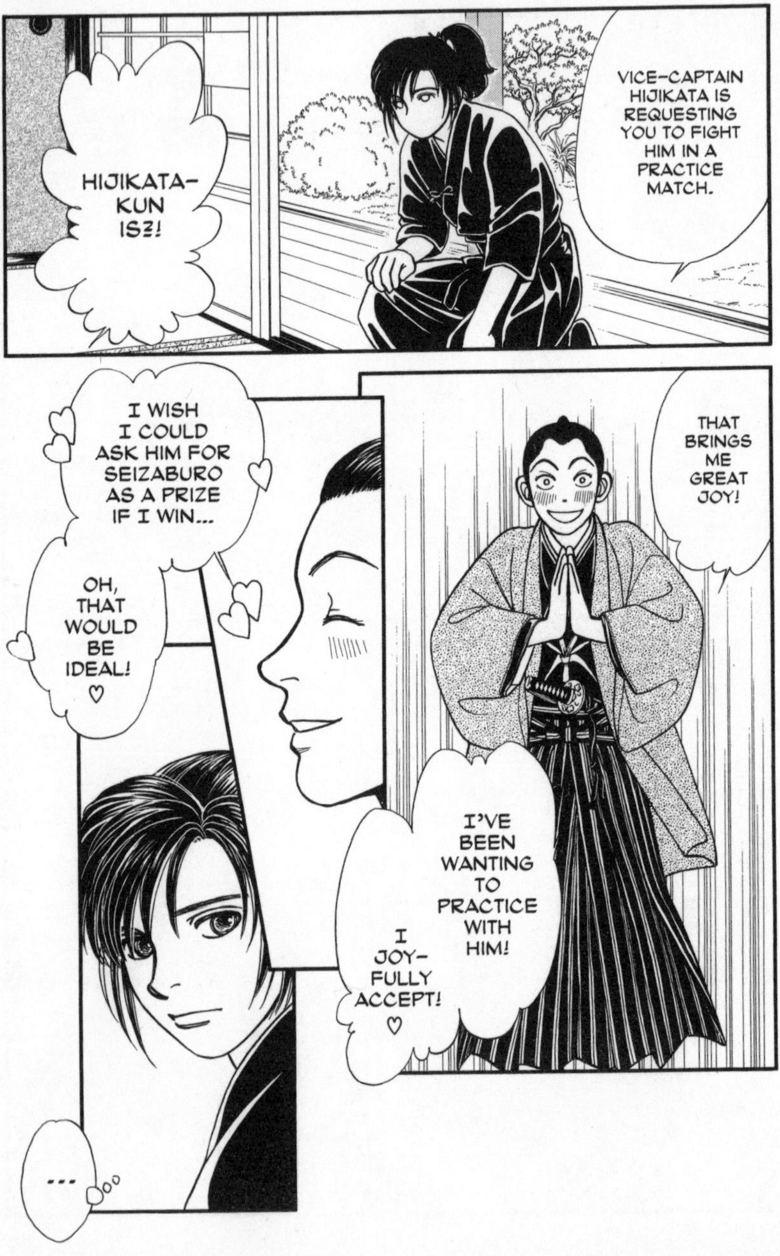
VICE-CAPTAIN HIJIKATA IS REQUESTING YOU TO FIGHT HIM IN A PRACTICE MATCH.
HIJIKATA-KUN IS?!
THAT BRINGS ME GREAT JOY!
I'VE BEEN WANTING TO PRACTICE WITH HIM!
I JOY-FULLY ACCEPT! ♡
I WISH I COULD ASK HIM FOR SEIZABURO AS A PRIZE IF I WIN...
OH, THAT WOULD BE IDEAL! ♡
...

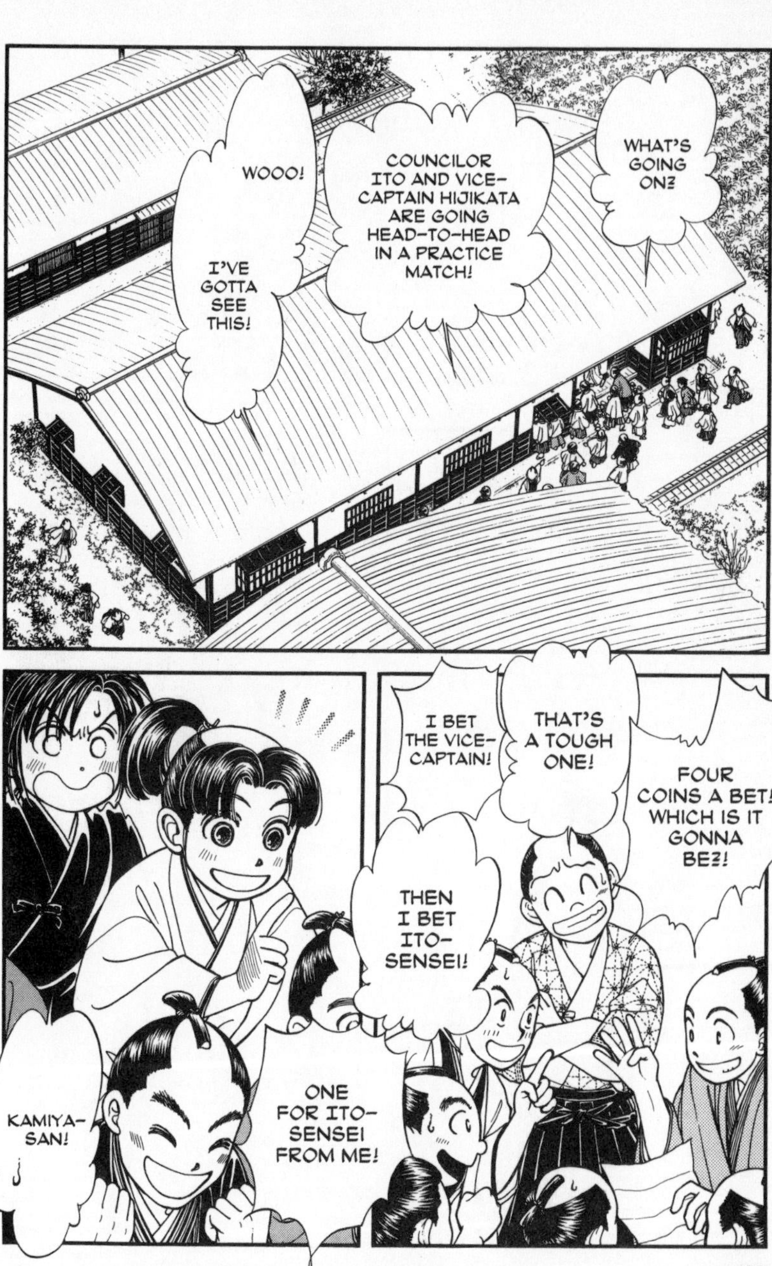
WHAT'S GOING ON?
COUNCILOR ITO AND VICE-CAPTAIN HIJIKATA ARE GOING HEAD-TO-HEAD IN A PRACTICE MATCH!
WOOO!
I'VE GOTTA SEE THIS!
FOUR COINS A BET! WHICH IS IT GONNA BE?!
THAT'S A TOUGH ONE!
I BET THE VICE-CAPTAIN!
THEN I BET ITO-SENSEI!
ONE FOR ITO-SENSEI FROM ME!
KAMIYA-SAN!

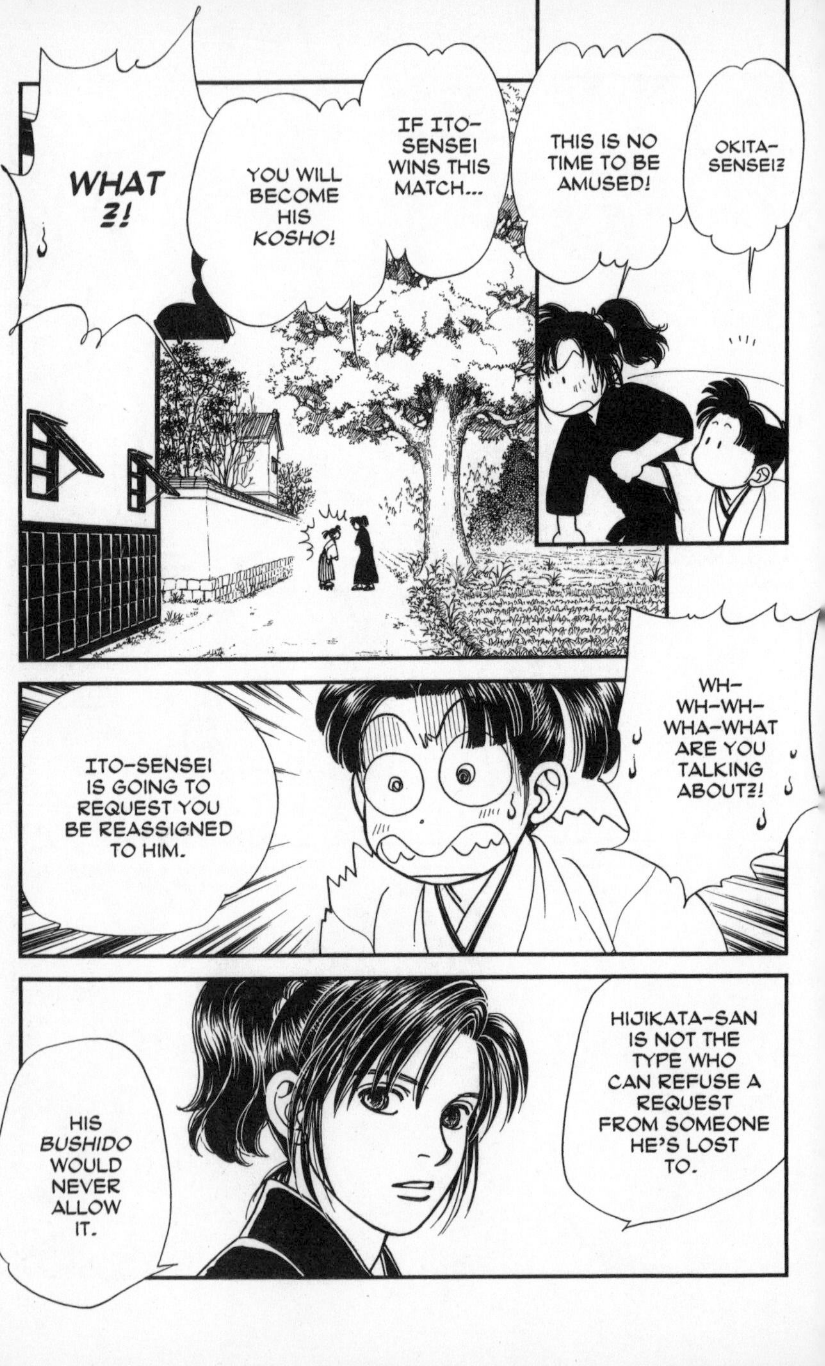
OKITA-SENSEI!?
THIS IS NO TIME TO BE AMUSED!
IF ITO-SENSEI WINS THIS MATCH...
YOU WILL BECOME HIS KOSHO!
WHAT ?!
WH-WH-WH-WHA-WHAT ARE YOU TALKING ABOUT?!
ITO-SENSEI IS GOING TO REQUEST YOU BE REASSIGNED TO HIM.
HIJIKATA-SAN IS NOT THE TYPE WHO CAN REFUSE A REQUEST FROM SOMEONE HE'S LOST TO.
HIS BUSHIDO WOULD NEVER ALLOW IT.

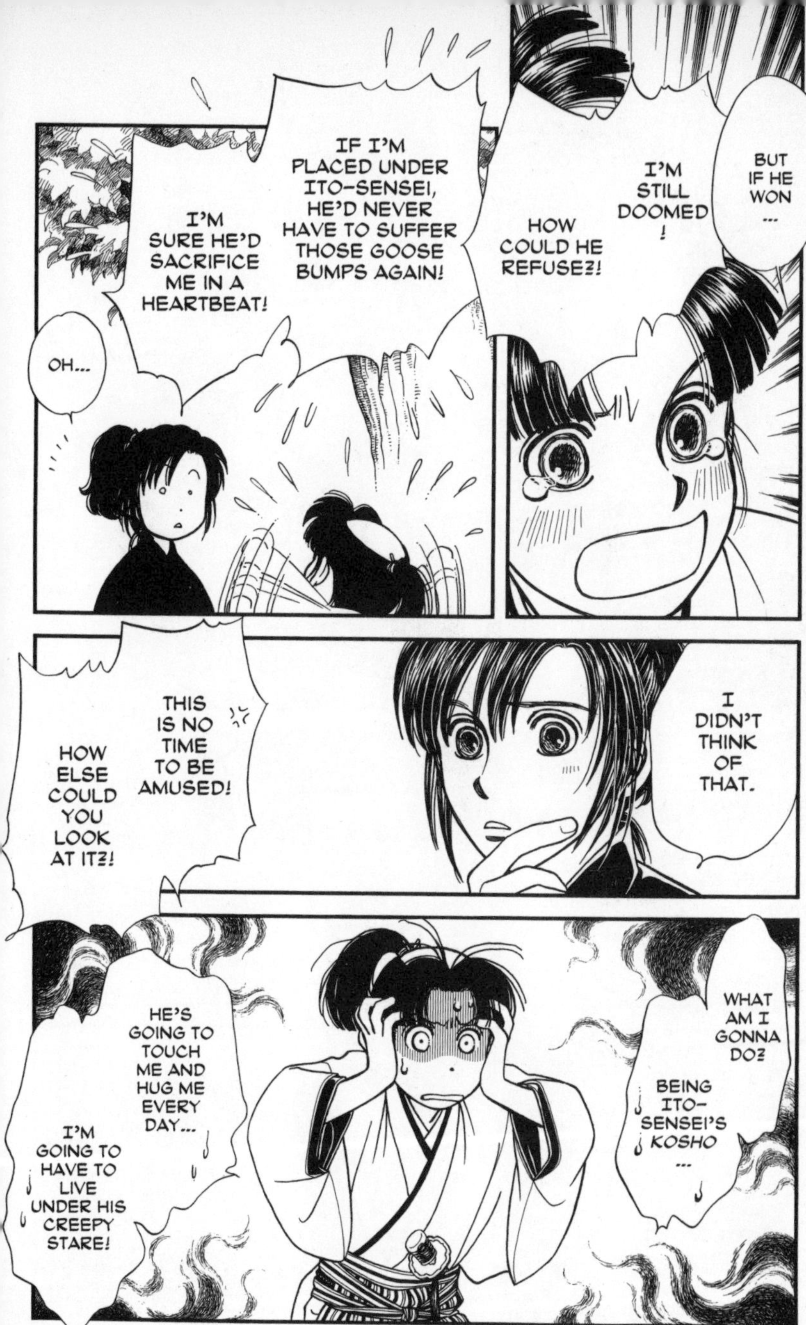

BUT IF HE WON...
I'M STILL DOOMED!
HOW COULD HE REFUSE?!
IF I'M PLACED UNDER ITO-SENSEI, HE'D NEVER HAVE TO SUFFER THOSE GOOSE BUMPS AGAIN!
I'M SURE HE'D SACRIFICE ME IN A HEARTBEAT!
OH...
I DIDN'T THINK OF THAT.
THIS IS NO TIME TO BE AMUSED!
HOW ELSE COULD YOU LOOK AT IT?!
WHAT AM I GONNA DO?
BEING ITO-SENSEI'S KOSHO...
HE'S GOING TO TOUCH ME AND HUG ME EVERY DAY...
I'M GOING TO HAVE TO LIVE UNDER HIS CREEPY STARE!

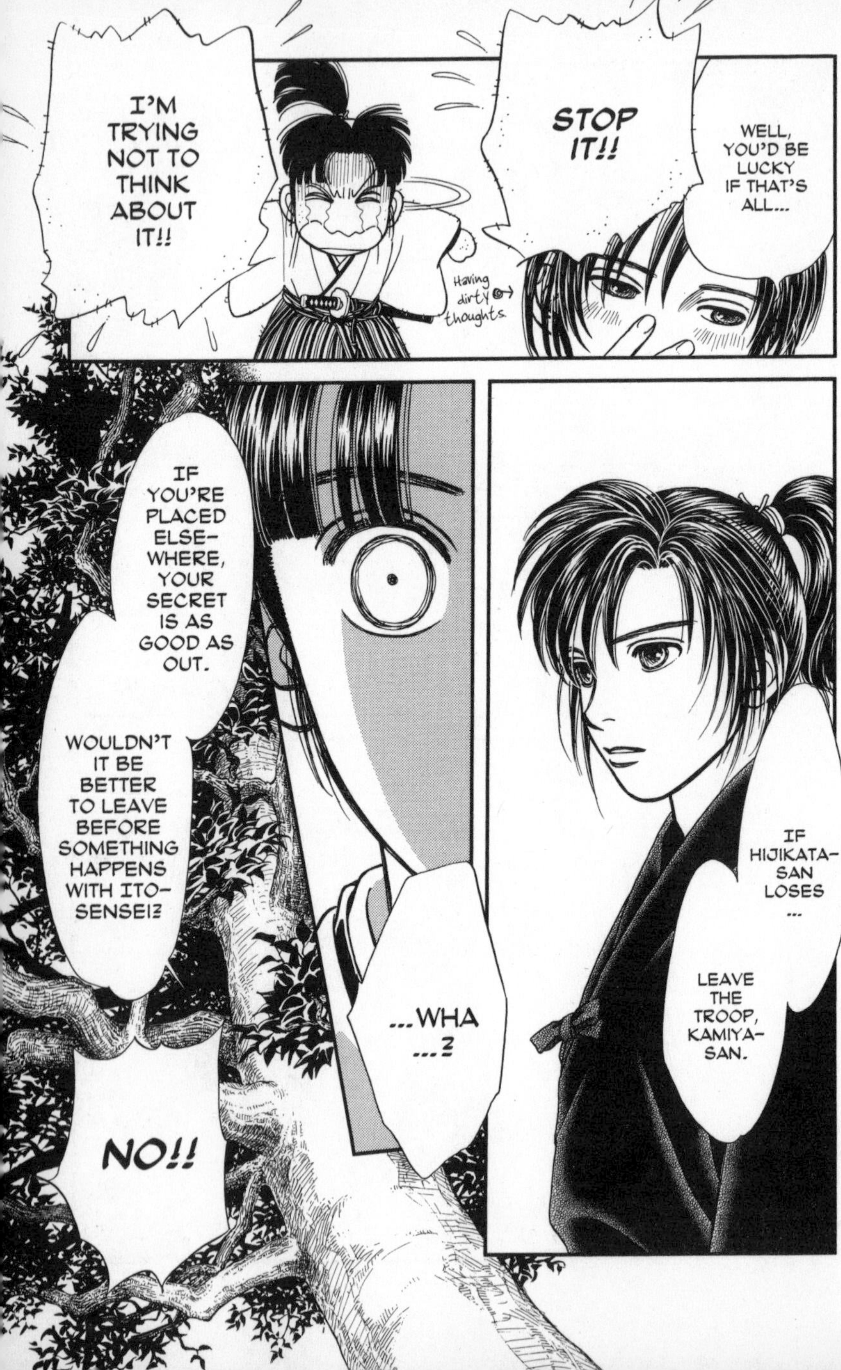
WELL, YOU'D BE LUCKY IF THAT'S ALL...
STOP IT!!
Having dirty thoughts
I'M TRYING NOT TO THINK ABOUT IT!!
IF HIJIKATA-SAN LOSES ...
LEAVE THE TROOP, KAMIYA-SAN.
...WHA ...?
IF YOU'RE PLACED ELSE-WHERE, YOUR SECRET IS AS GOOD AS OUT.
WOULDN'T IT BE BETTER TO LEAVE BEFORE SOMETHING HAPPENS WITH ITO-SENSEI?
NO!!

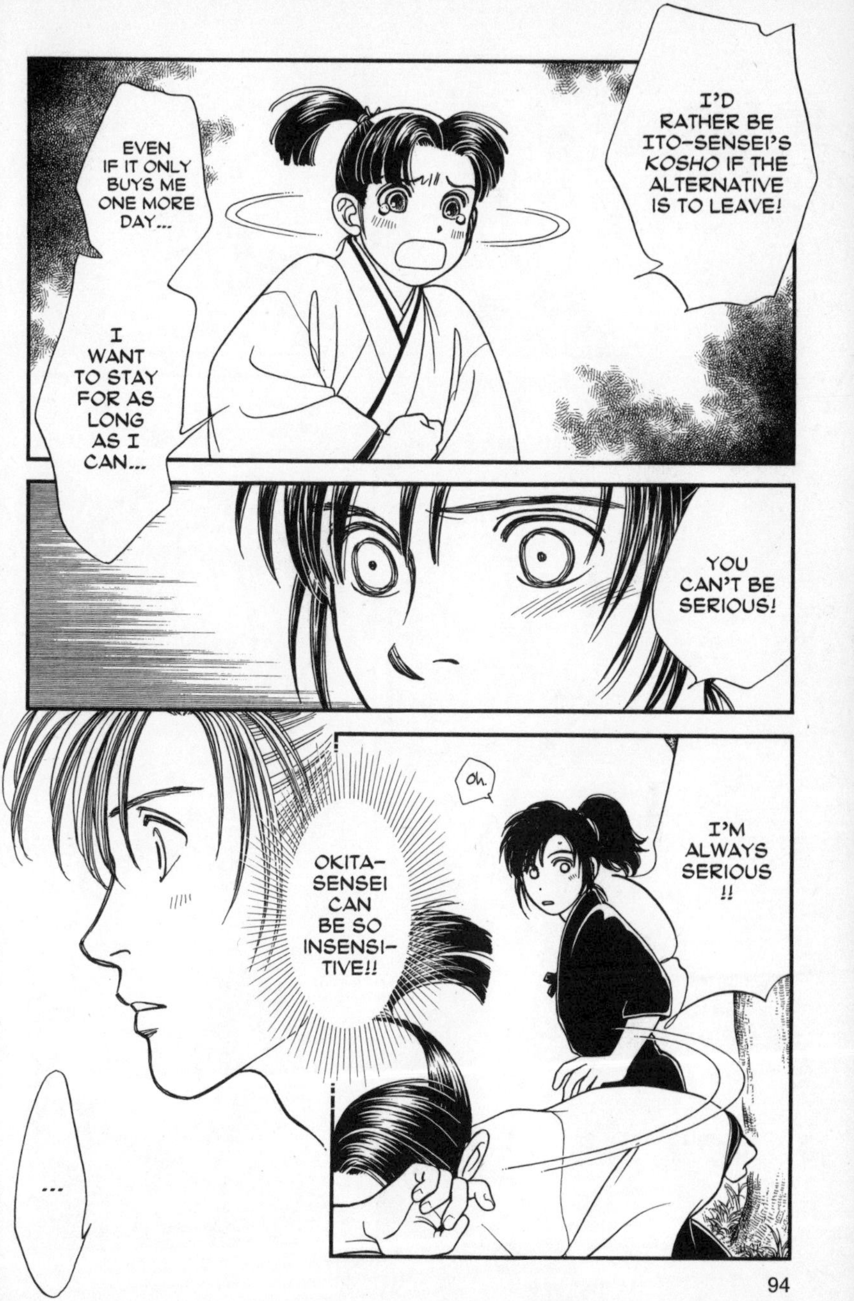
I'D RATHER BE ITO-SENSEI'S *KOSHO* IF THE ALTERNATIVE IS TO LEAVE!
EVEN IF IT ONLY BUYS ME ONE MORE DAY...
I WANT TO STAY FOR AS LONG AS I CAN...
YOU CAN'T BE SERIOUS!
I'M ALWAYS SERIOUS !!
Oh.
OKITA-SENSEI CAN BE SO INSENSITIVE!!
...

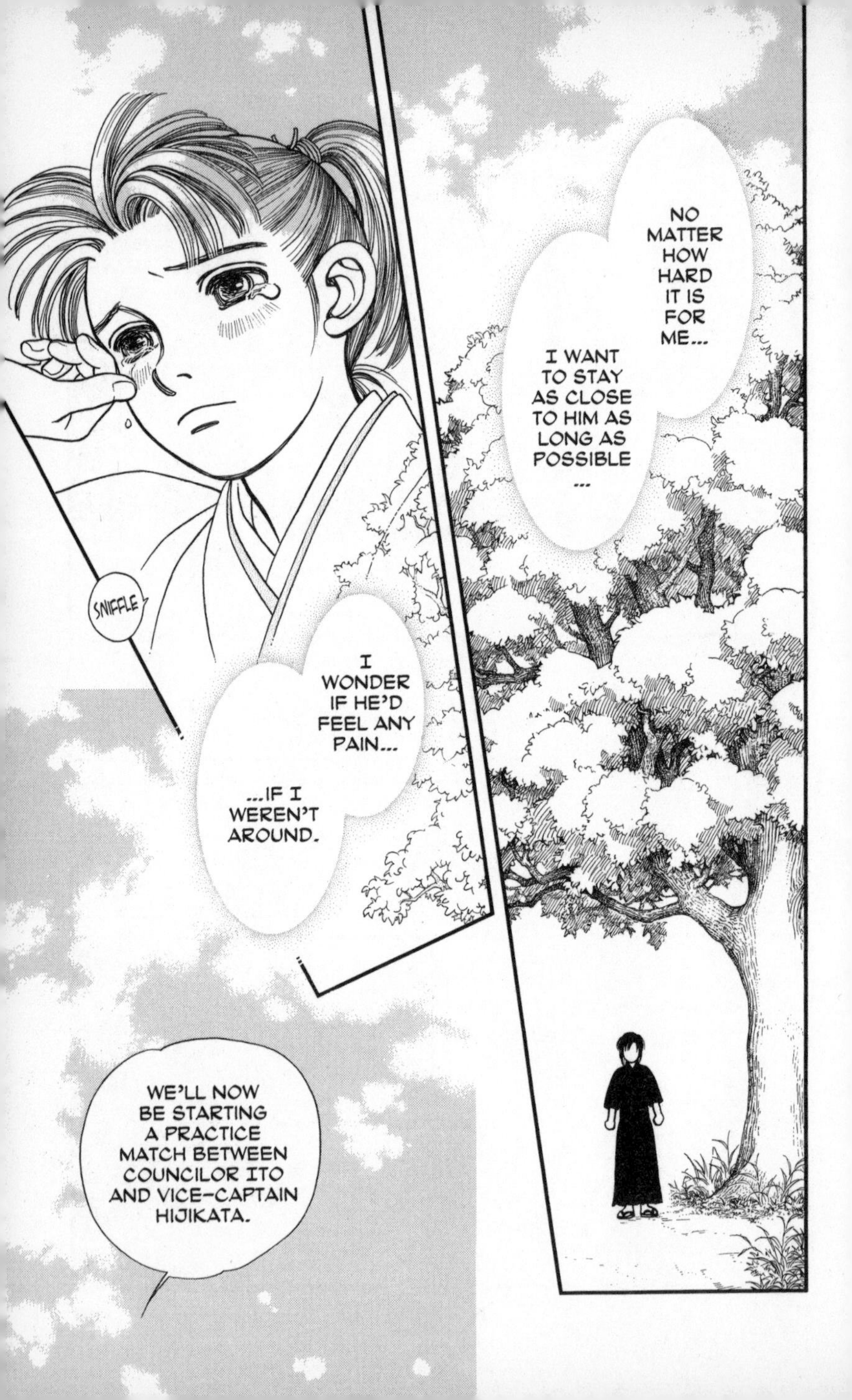
NO MATTER HOW HARD IT IS FOR ME...
I WANT TO STAY AS CLOSE TO HIM AS LONG AS POSSIBLE...
SNIFFLE
I WONDER IF HE'D FEEL ANY PAIN...
...IF I WEREN'T AROUND.
WE'LL NOW BE STARTING A PRACTICE MATCH BETWEEN COUNCILOR ITO AND VICE-CAPTAIN HIJIKATA.

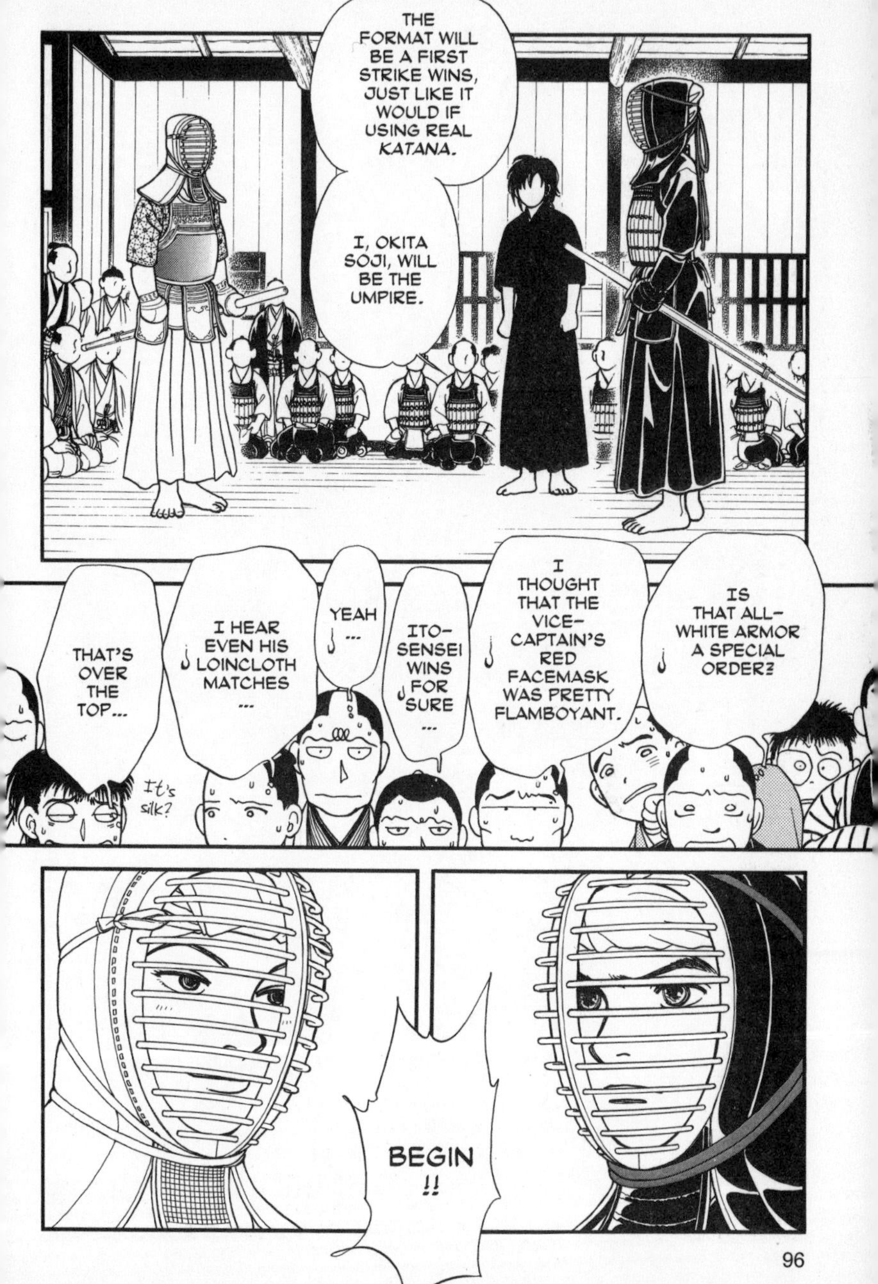

THE FORMAT WILL BE A FIRST STRIKE WINS, JUST LIKE IT WOULD IF USING REAL *KATANA*.
I, OKITA SOJI, WILL BE THE UMPIRE.
IS THAT ALL-WHITE ARMOR A SPECIAL ORDER?
I THOUGHT THAT THE VICE-CAPTAIN'S RED FACEMASK WAS PRETTY FLAMBOYANT.
ITO-SENSEI WINS FOR SURE...
YEAH...
I HEAR EVEN HIS LOINCLOTH MATCHES...
THAT'S OVER THE TOP...
It's silk?
BEGIN!!

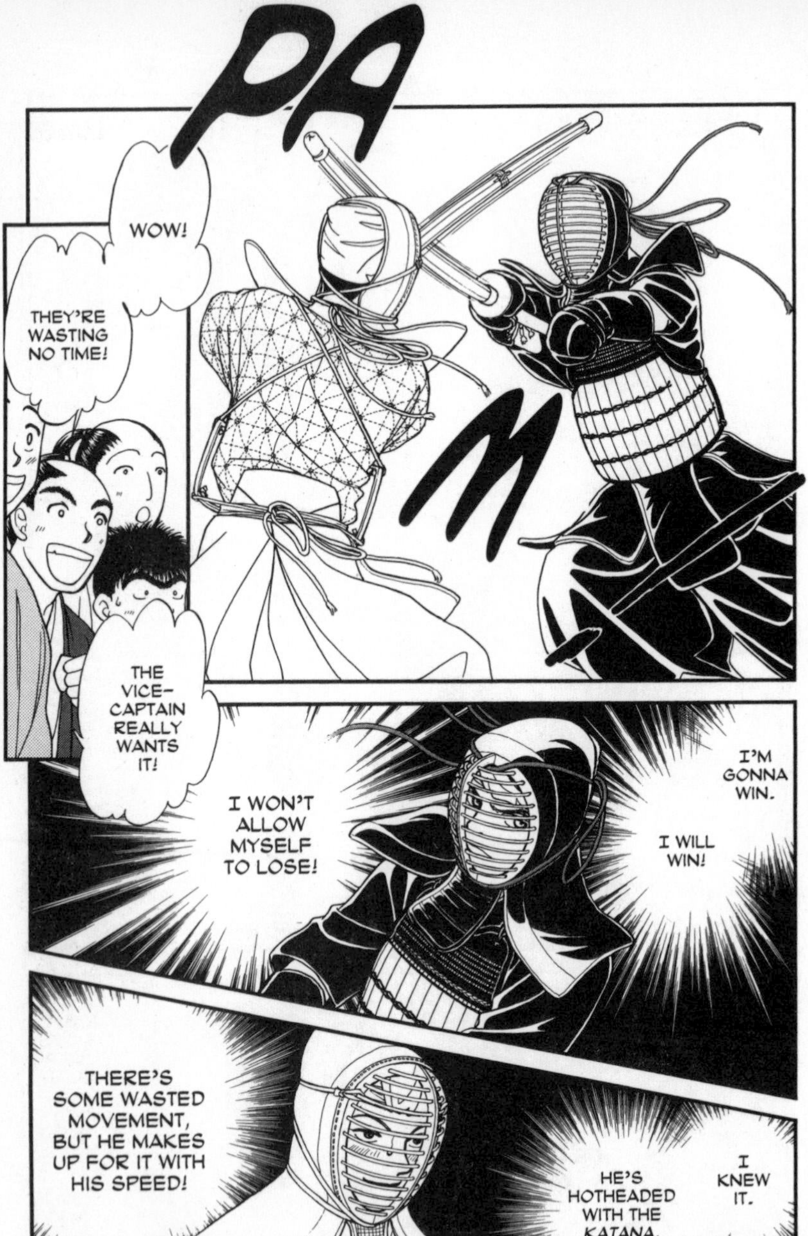
PA
M
WOW!
THEY'RE WASTING NO TIME!
THE VICE-CAPTAIN REALLY WANTS IT!
I'M GONNA WIN.
I WILL WIN!
I WON'T ALLOW MYSELF TO LOSE!
I KNEW IT.
HE'S HOTHEADED WITH THE KATANA, AS WELL.
THERE'S SOME WASTED MOVEMENT, BUT HE MAKES UP FOR IT WITH HIS SPEED!

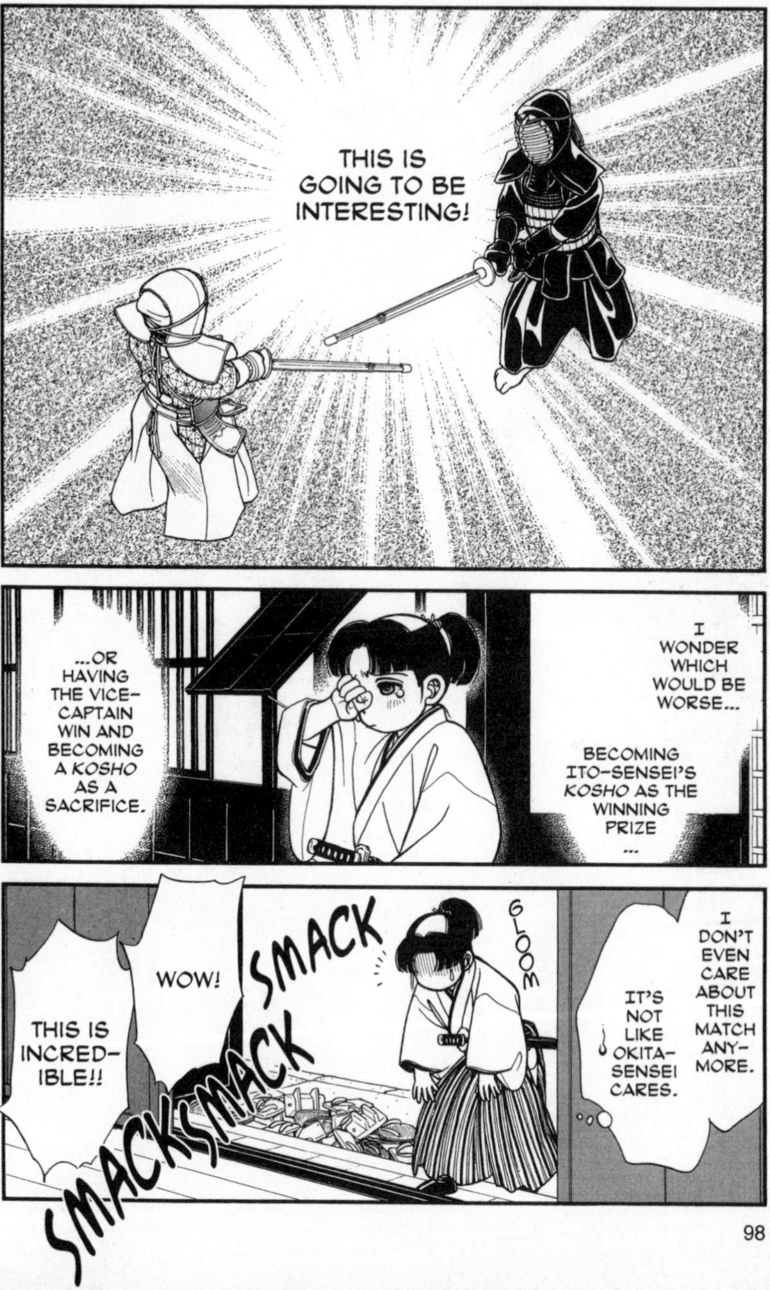
THIS IS GOING TO BE INTERESTING!
I WONDER WHICH WOULD BE WORSE...
BECOMING ITO-SENSEI'S *KOSHO* AS THE WINNING PRIZE...
...OR HAVING THE VICE-CAPTAIN WIN AND BECOMING A *KOSHO* AS A SACRIFICE.
I DON'T EVEN CARE ABOUT THIS MATCH ANYMORE.
IT'S NOT LIKE OKITA-SENSEI CARES.
GLOOM
SMACK
WOW!
THIS IS INCREDIBLE!!
SMACKSMACK

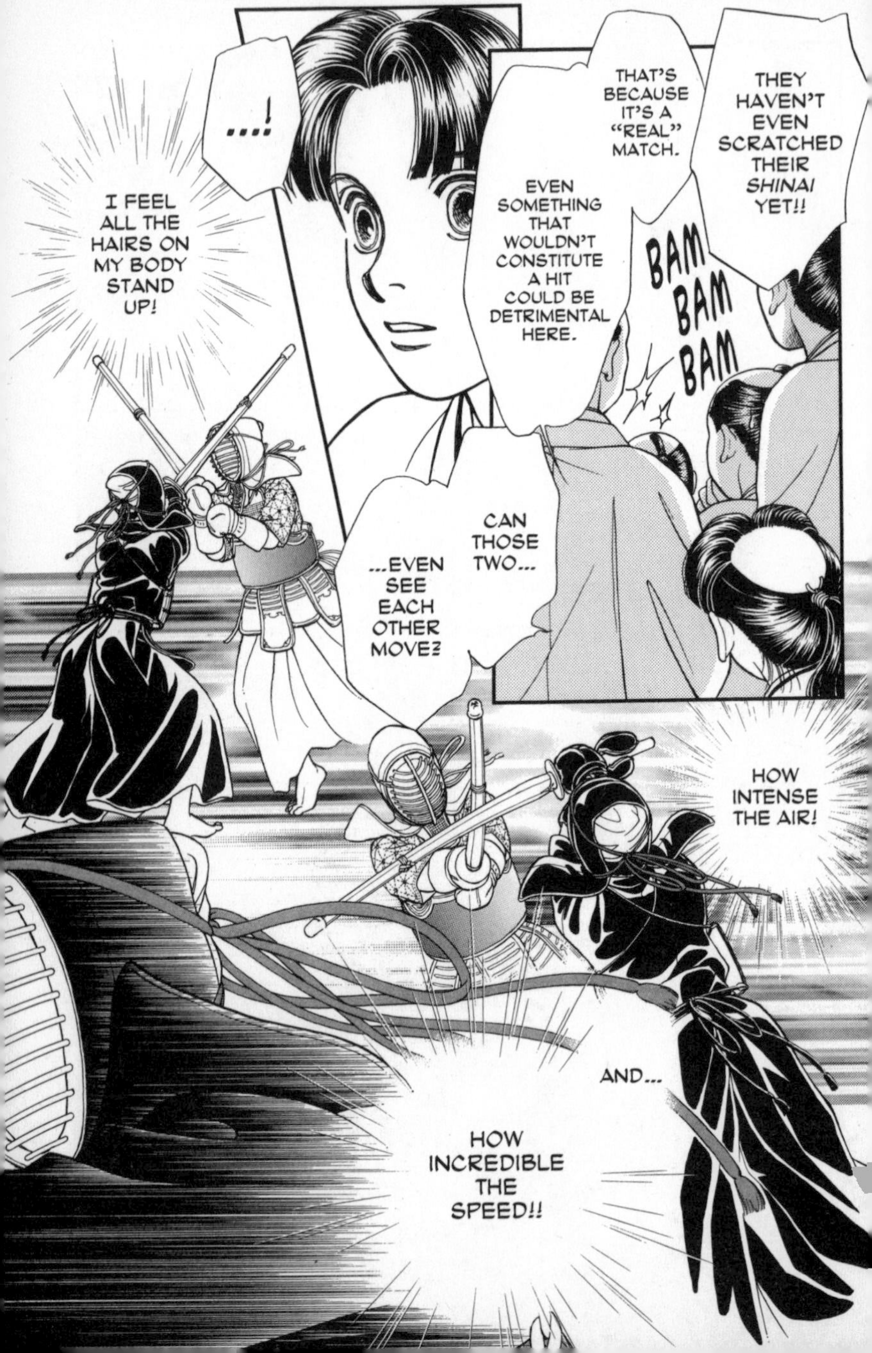
THEY HAVEN'T EVEN SCRATCHED THEIR *SHINAI* YET!!
THAT'S BECAUSE IT'S A "REAL" MATCH.
EVEN SOMETHING THAT WOULDN'T CONSTITUTE A HIT COULD BE DETRIMENTAL HERE.
BAM BAM BAM
CAN THOSE TWO...
...EVEN SEE EACH OTHER MOVE?
...!
I FEEL ALL THE HAIRS ON MY BODY STAND UP!
HOW INTENSE THE AIR!
AND...
HOW INCREDIBLE THE SPEED!!

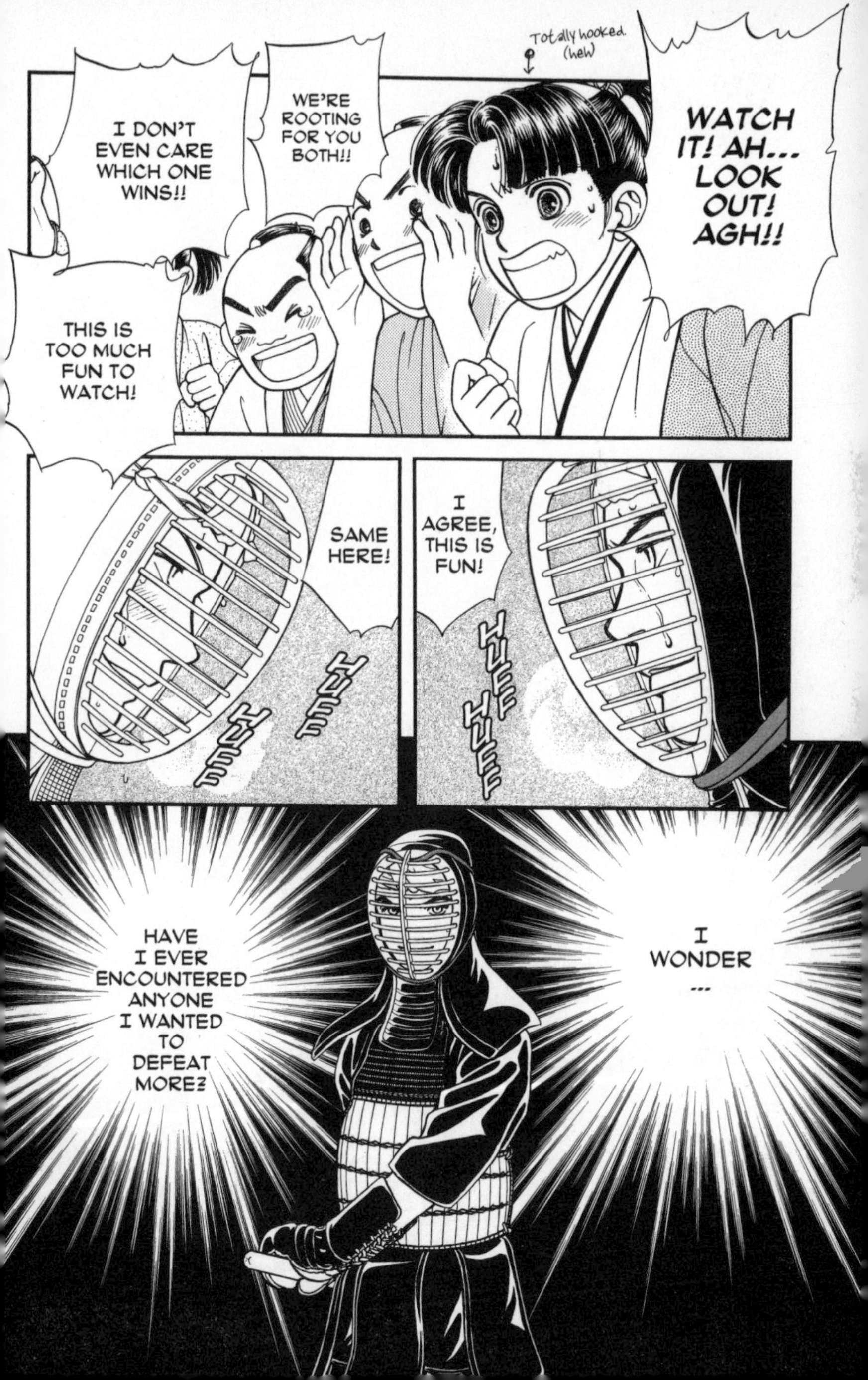
WATCH IT! AH... LOOK OUT! AGH!!
Totally hooked. (heh)
WE'RE ROOTING FOR YOU BOTH!!
I DON'T EVEN CARE WHICH ONE WINS!!
THIS IS TOO MUCH FUN TO WATCH!
I AGREE, THIS IS FUN!
HUFF HUFF
SAME HERE!
HUFF HUFF
I WONDER ...
HAVE I EVER ENCOUNTERED ANYONE I WANTED TO DEFEAT MORE?

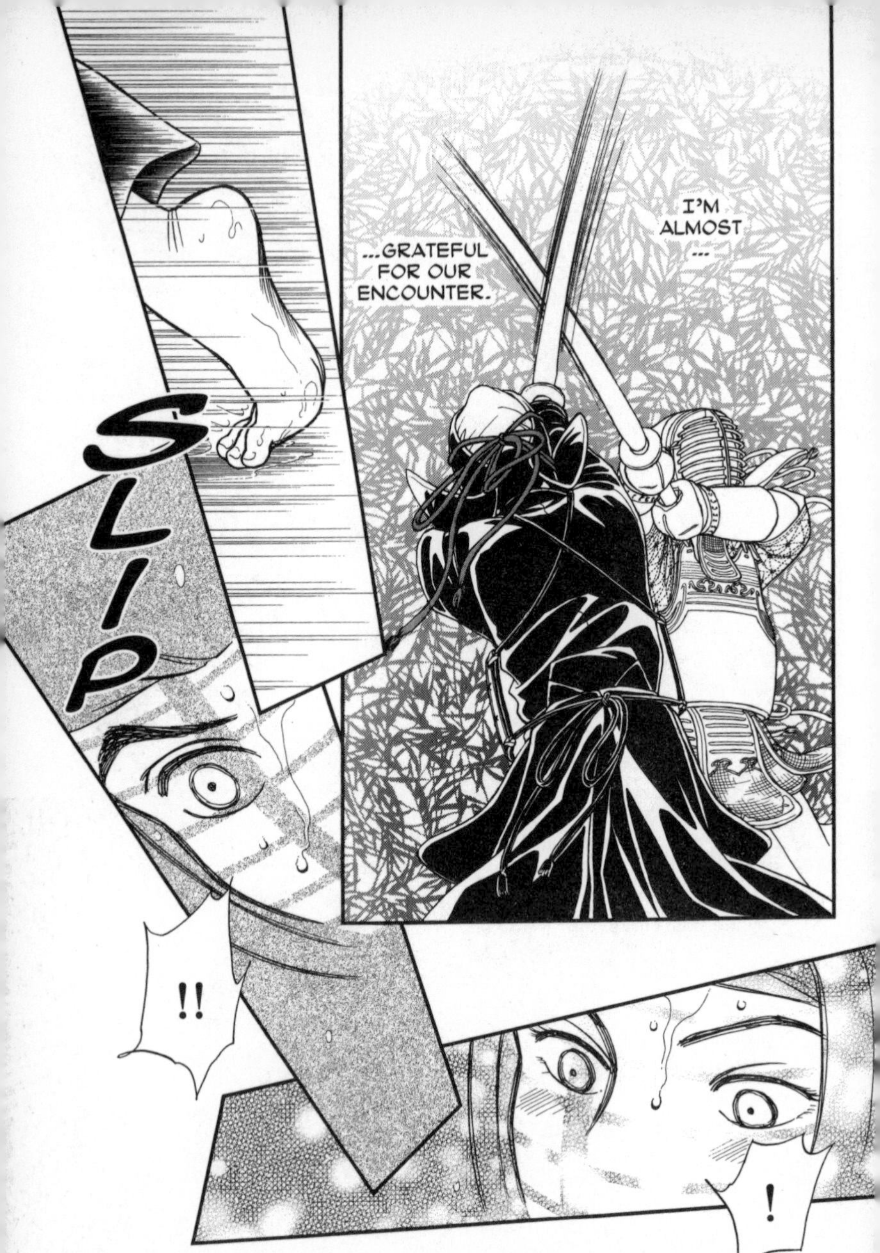
I'M ALMOST ---
...GRATEFUL FOR OUR ENCOUNTER.
SLIP
!!
!

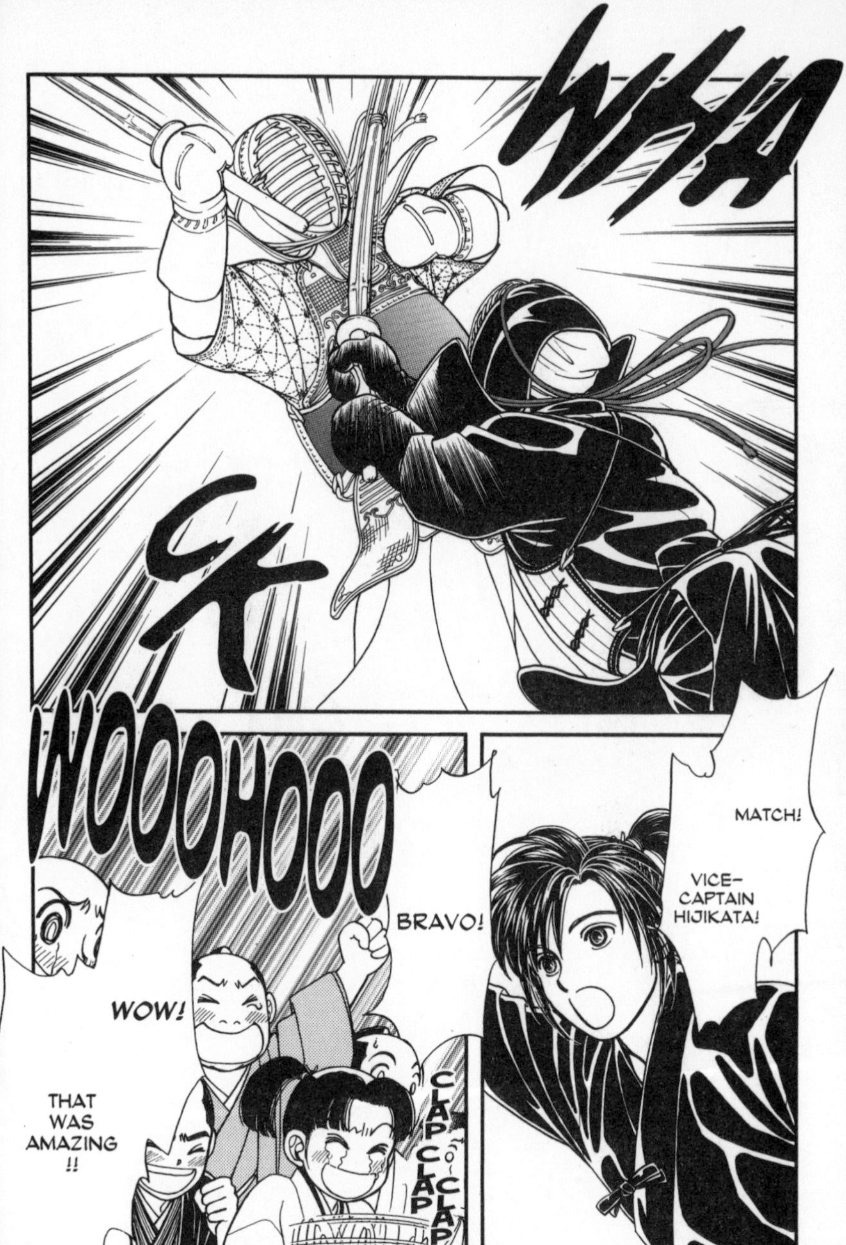
WHA
CK
MATCH!
VICE-CAPTAIN HIJIKATA!
WOOHOOO
BRAVO!
WOW!
THAT WAS AMAZING!!
CLAP CLAP
CLAP CLAP

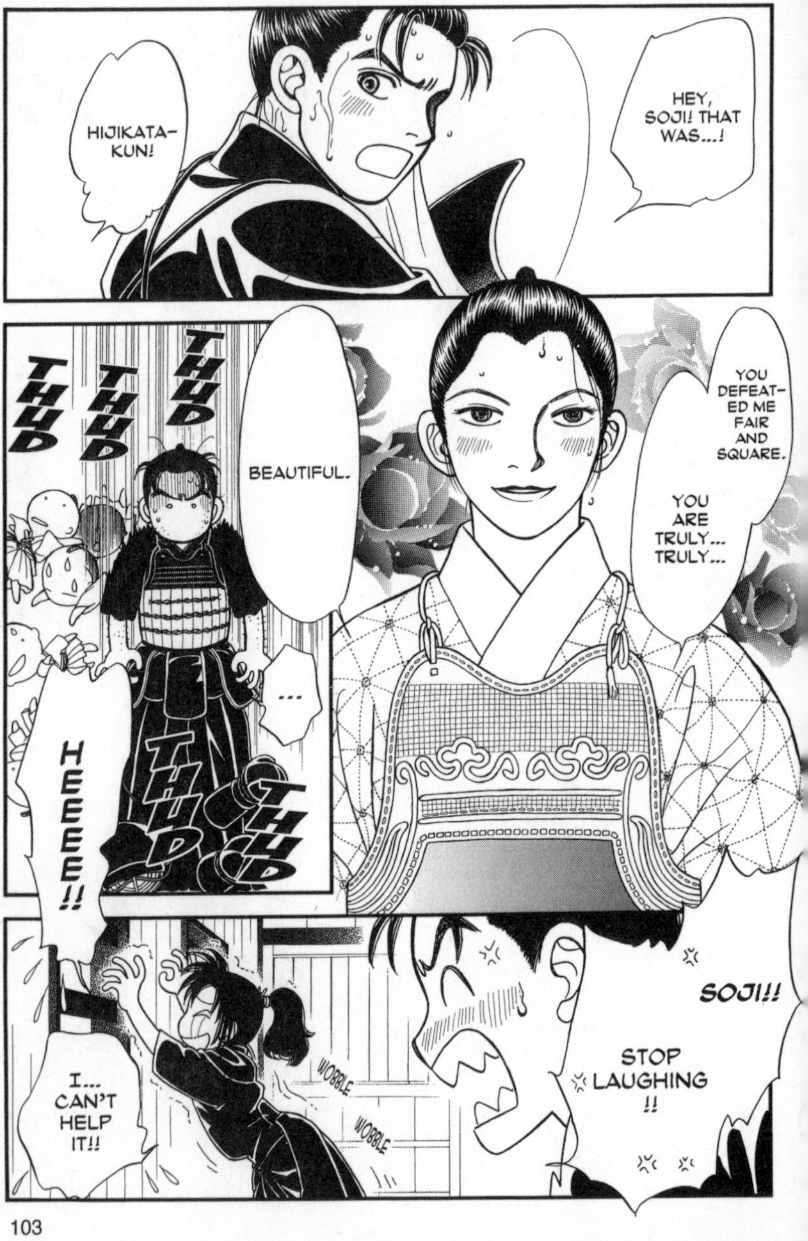
HEY, SOJI! THAT WAS...!
HIJIKATA-KUN!
YOU DEFEATED ME FAIR AND SQUARE.
YOU ARE TRULY... TRULY...
BEAUTIFUL.
THUD THUD THUD
...
HEEEEE!!
THUD THUD
SOJI!!
STOP LAUGHING!!
WOBBLE WOBBLE
I... CAN'T HELP IT!!

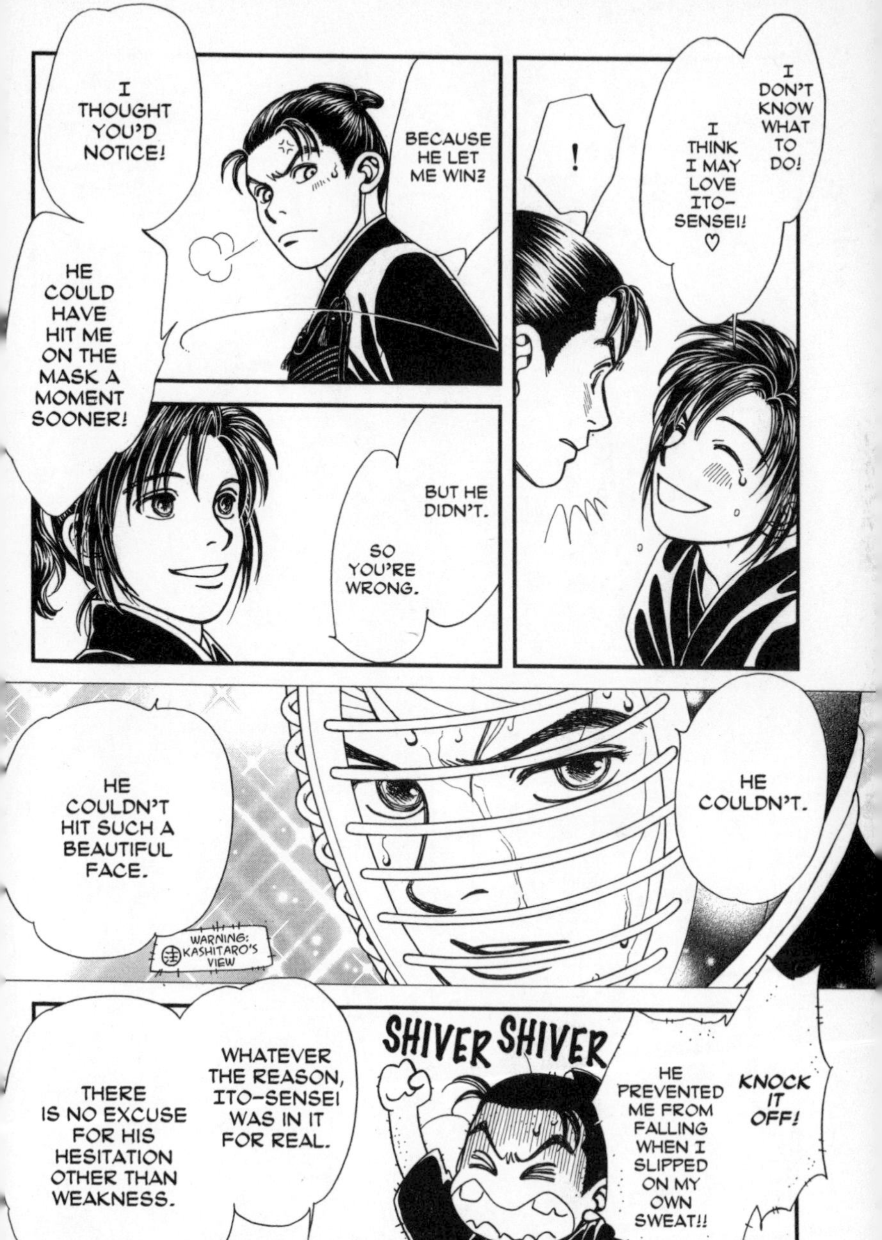
I DON'T KNOW WHAT TO DO!
I THINK I MAY LOVE ITO-SENSEI! ♡
!
BECAUSE HE LET ME WIN?
I THOUGHT YOU'D NOTICE!
HE COULD HAVE HIT ME ON THE MASK A MOMENT SOONER!
BUT HE DIDN'T.
SO YOU'RE WRONG.
HE COULDN'T.
HE COULDN'T HIT SUCH A BEAUTIFUL FACE.
WARNING: KASHITARO'S VIEW
KNOCK IT OFF!
HE PREVENTED ME FROM FALLING WHEN I SLIPPED ON MY OWN SWEAT!!
SHIVER SHIVER
WHATEVER THE REASON, ITO-SENSEI WAS IN IT FOR REAL.
THERE IS NO EXCUSE FOR HIS HESITATION OTHER THAN WEAKNESS.

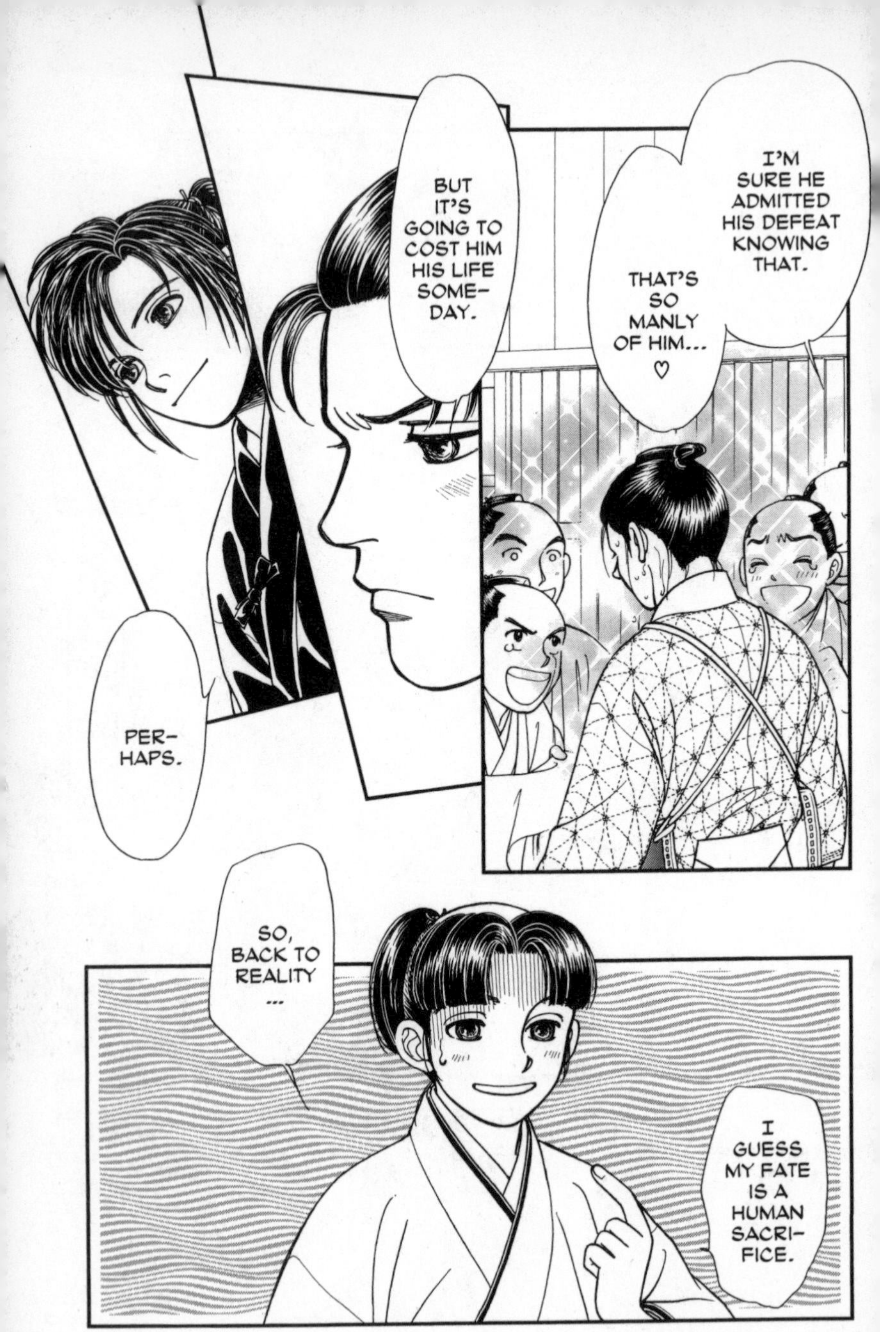
I'M SURE HE ADMITTED HIS DEFEAT KNOWING THAT.
THAT'S SO MANLY OF HIM... ♡
BUT IT'S GOING TO COST HIM HIS LIFE SOME-DAY.
PER-HAPS.
SO, BACK TO REALITY ...
I GUESS MY FATE IS A HUMAN SACRI-FICE.

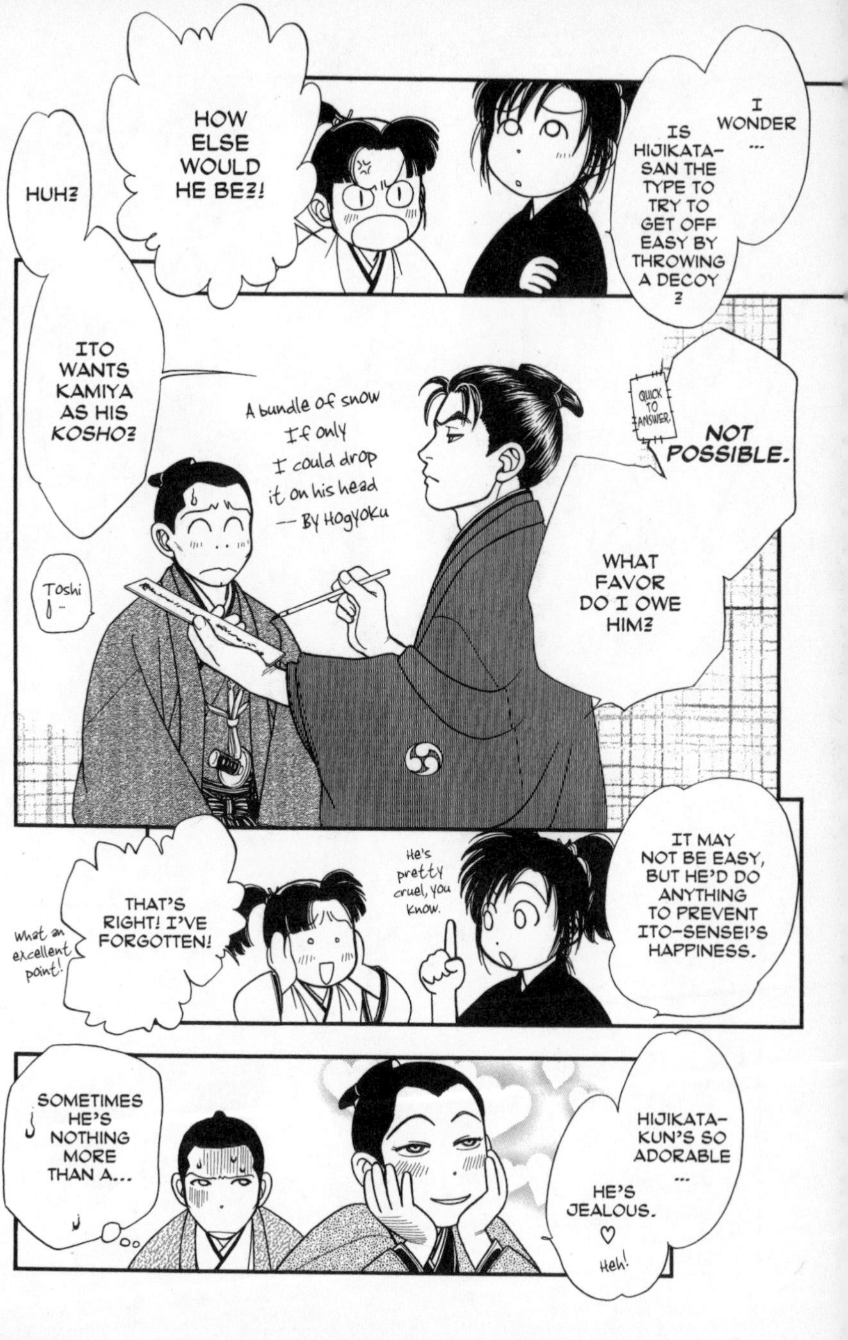
I WONDER... IS HIJIKATA-SAN THE TYPE TO TRY TO GET OFF EASY BY THROWING A DECOY?
HOW ELSE WOULD HE BE?!
HUH? ITO WANTS KAMIYA AS HIS KOSHO?
QUICK TO ANSWER.
NOT POSSIBLE.
WHAT FAVOR DO I OWE HIM?
A bundle of snow If only I could drop it on his head -- By Hogyoku
Toshi...
IT MAY NOT BE EASY, BUT HE'D DO ANYTHING TO PREVENT ITO-SENSEI'S HAPPINESS.
He's pretty cruel, you know.
THAT'S RIGHT! I'VE FORGOTTEN!
What an excellent point!
HIJIKATA-KUN'S SO ADORABLE... HE'S JEALOUS. ♡
Heh!
SOMETIMES HE'S NOTHING MORE THAN A...

"NI" に

NIKUMAREKO
YO NI
HABAKARU
"THE DEVIL LOOKS
AFTER HIS OWN"

(Lit. A hated child
should be held back)

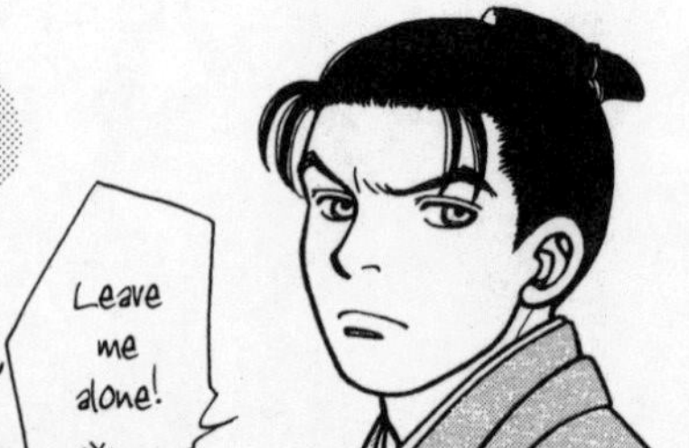
Leave me alone!

EDO
"IROHA"
KARUTA
GAME

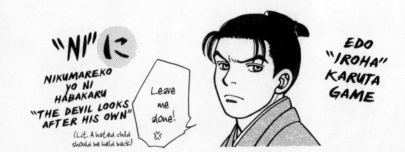

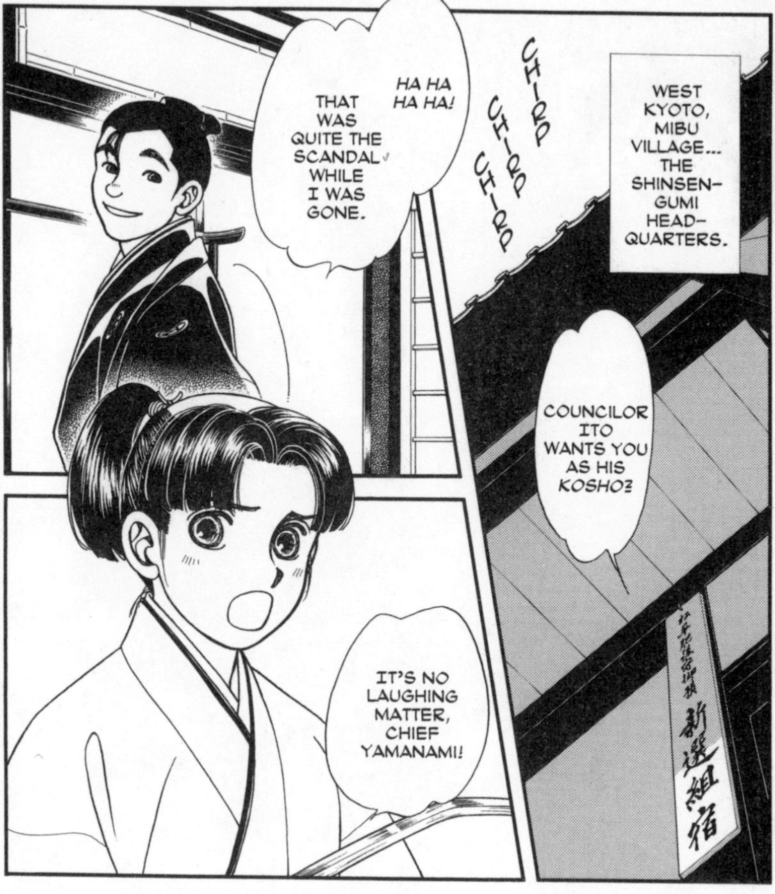
WEST KYOTO, MIBU VILLAGE... THE SHINSEN-GUMI HEAD-QUARTERS.
CHIRP CHIRP CHIRP
COUNCILOR ITO WANTS YOU AS HIS KOSHO?!
新選組宿
HA HA HA HA!
THAT WAS QUITE THE SCANDAL WHILE I WAS GONE.
IT'S NO LAUGHING MATTER, CHIEF YAMANAMI!

EDO "IROHA" KARUTA GAME

"HO" ほ

HONE ORI ZON NO KUTABIRE MOUKE "ALL TROUBLE FOR NOTHING"

(Lit. Broken bones for a fool's errand)

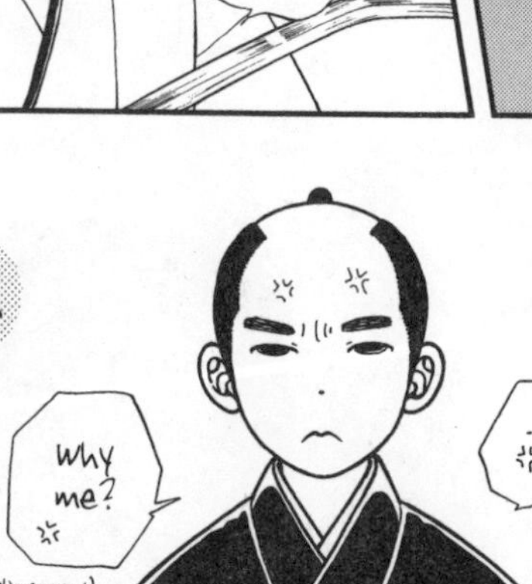
...
Why me?

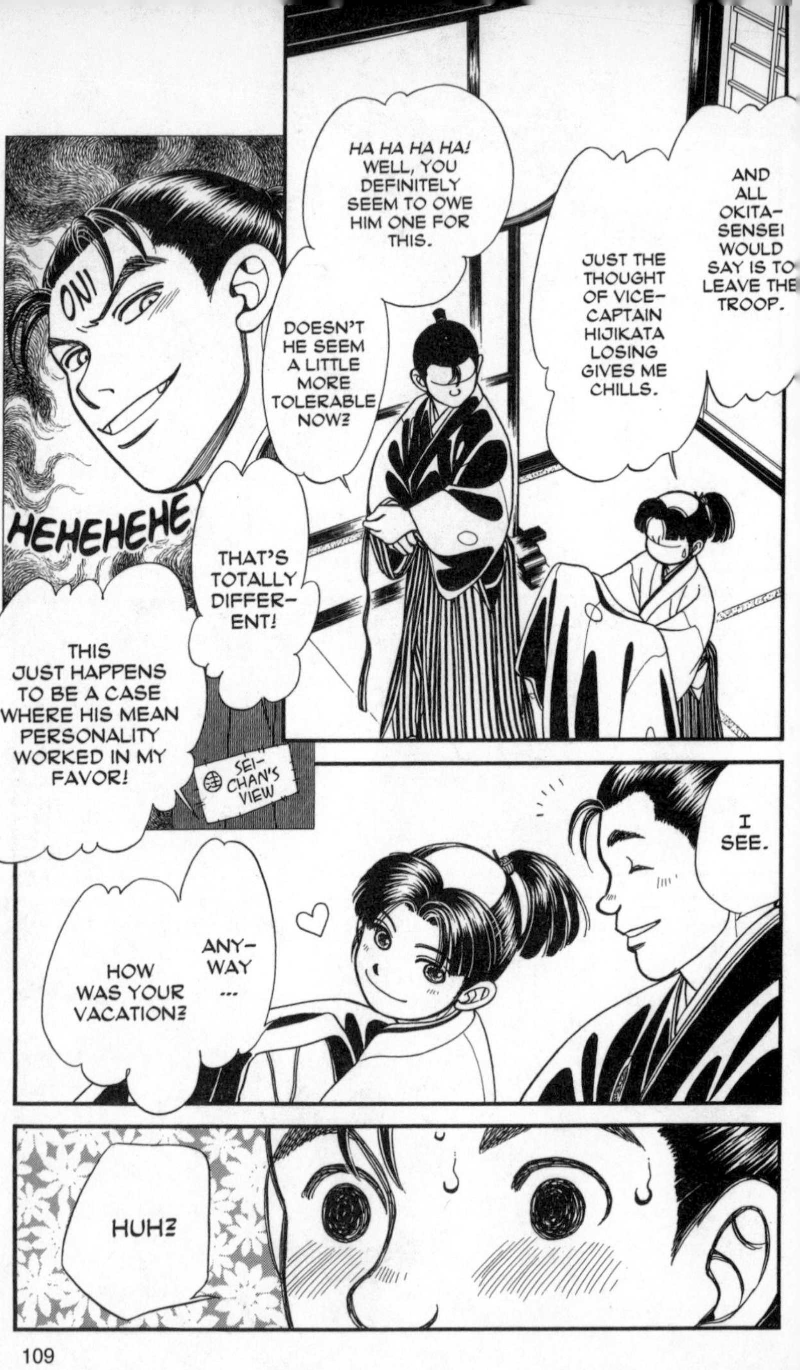
AND ALL OKITA-SENSEI WOULD SAY IS TO LEAVE THE TROOP.
JUST THE THOUGHT OF VICE-CAPTAIN HIJIKATA LOSING GIVES ME CHILLS.
HA HA HA HA! WELL, YOU DEFINITELY SEEM TO OWE HIM ONE FOR THIS.
DOESN'T HE SEEM A LITTLE MORE TOLERABLE NOW?
THAT'S TOTALLY DIFFER-ENT!
ONI
HEHEHEHE
THIS JUST HAPPENS TO BE A CASE WHERE HIS MEAN PERSONALITY WORKED IN MY FAVOR!
SEI-CHAN'S VIEW
I SEE.
ANY-WAY---
HOW WAS YOUR VACATION?
HUH?

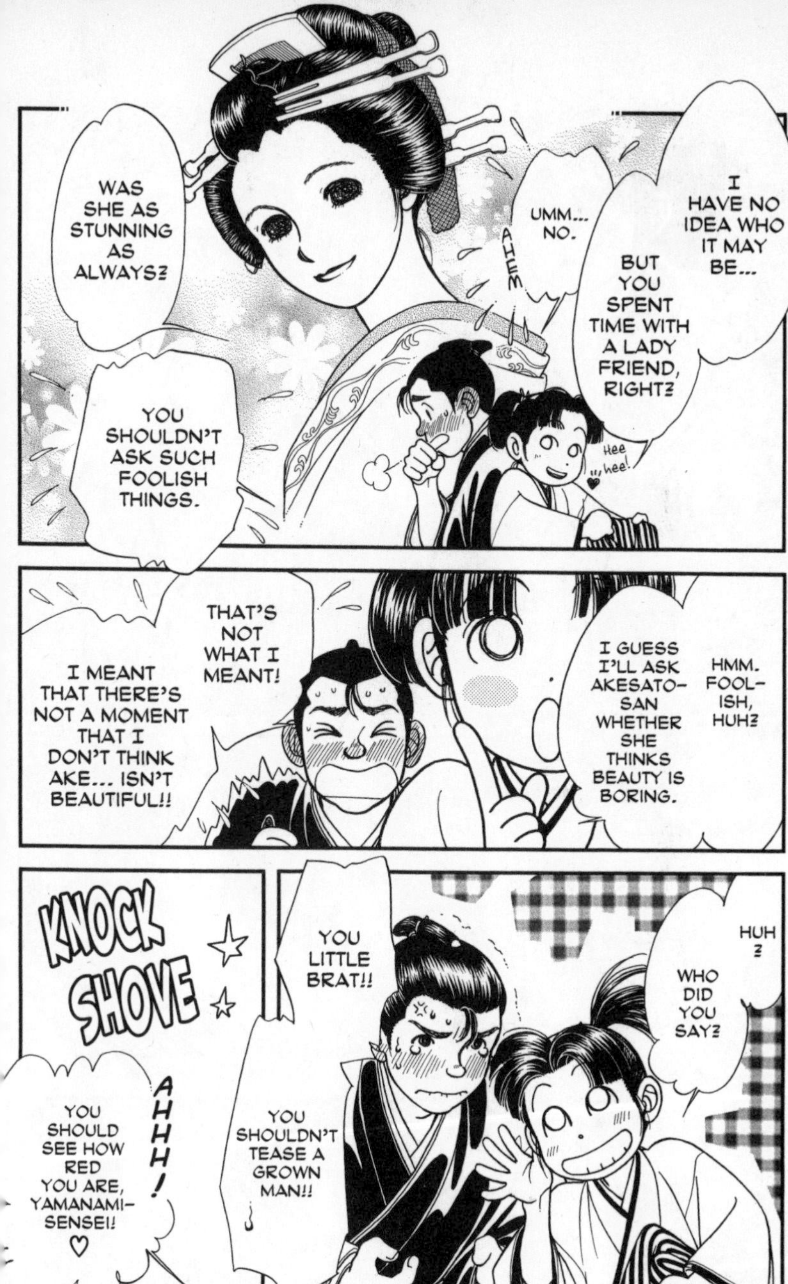
I HAVE NO IDEA WHO IT MAY BE...
BUT YOU SPENT TIME WITH A LADY FRIEND, RIGHT?
UMM... NO.
AHEM
Hee hee!
WAS SHE AS STUNNING AS ALWAYS?
YOU SHOULDN'T ASK SUCH FOOLISH THINGS.
HMM. FOOLISH, HUH?
I GUESS I'LL ASK AKESATO-SAN WHETHER SHE THINKS BEAUTY IS BORING.
THAT'S NOT WHAT I MEANT!
I MEANT THAT THERE'S NOT A MOMENT THAT I DON'T THINK AKE... ISN'T BEAUTIFUL!!
HUH?
WHO DID YOU SAY?
YOU LITTLE BRAT!!
YOU SHOULDN'T TEASE A GROWN MAN!!
KNOCK
SHOVE
AHHH!
YOU SHOULD SEE HOW RED YOU ARE, YAMANAMI-SENSEI! ♡

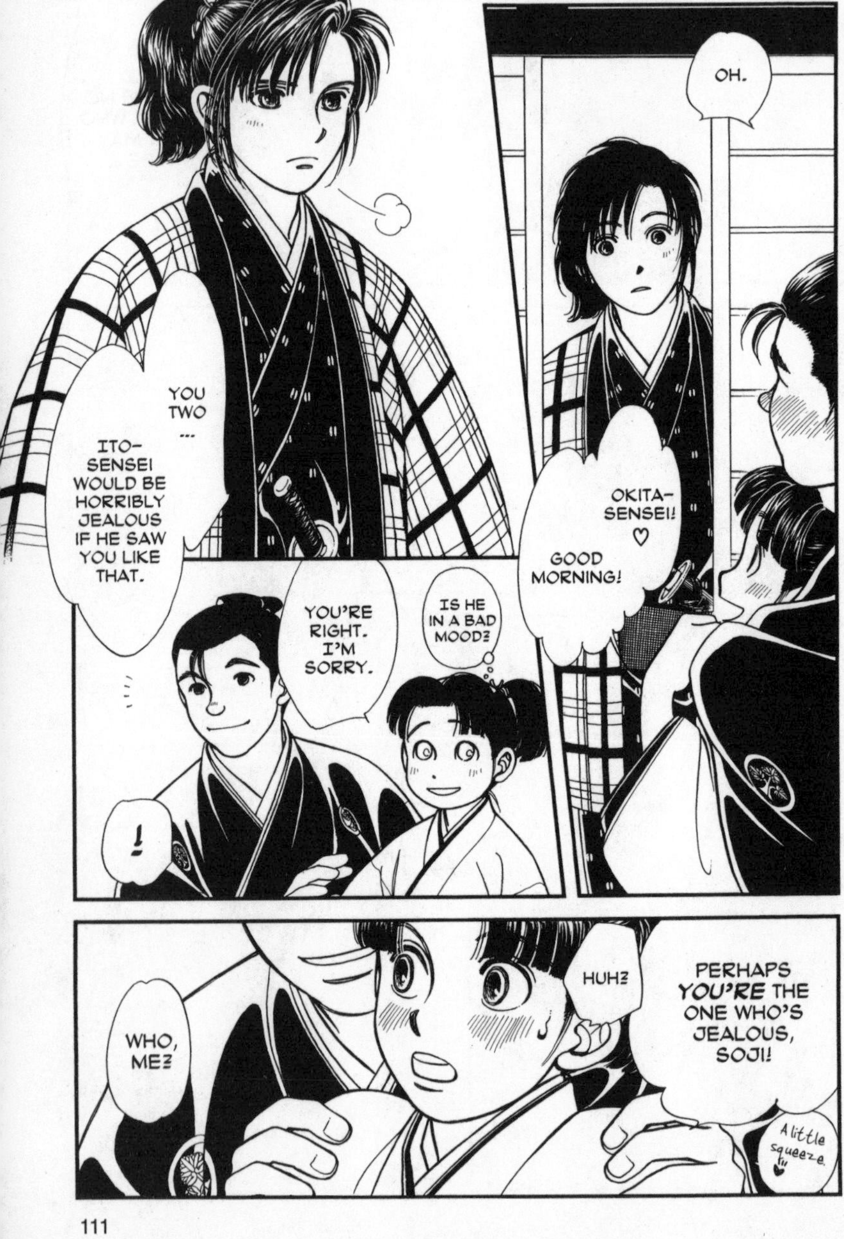
OH.
OKITA-SENSEI! ♡ GOOD MORNING!
YOU TWO... ITO-SENSEI WOULD BE HORRIBLY JEALOUS IF HE SAW YOU LIKE THAT.
YOU'RE RIGHT. I'M SORRY.
IS HE IN A BAD MOOD?
!
PERHAPS *YOU'RE* THE ONE WHO'S JEALOUS, SOJI!
A little squeeze
HUH?
WHO, ME?

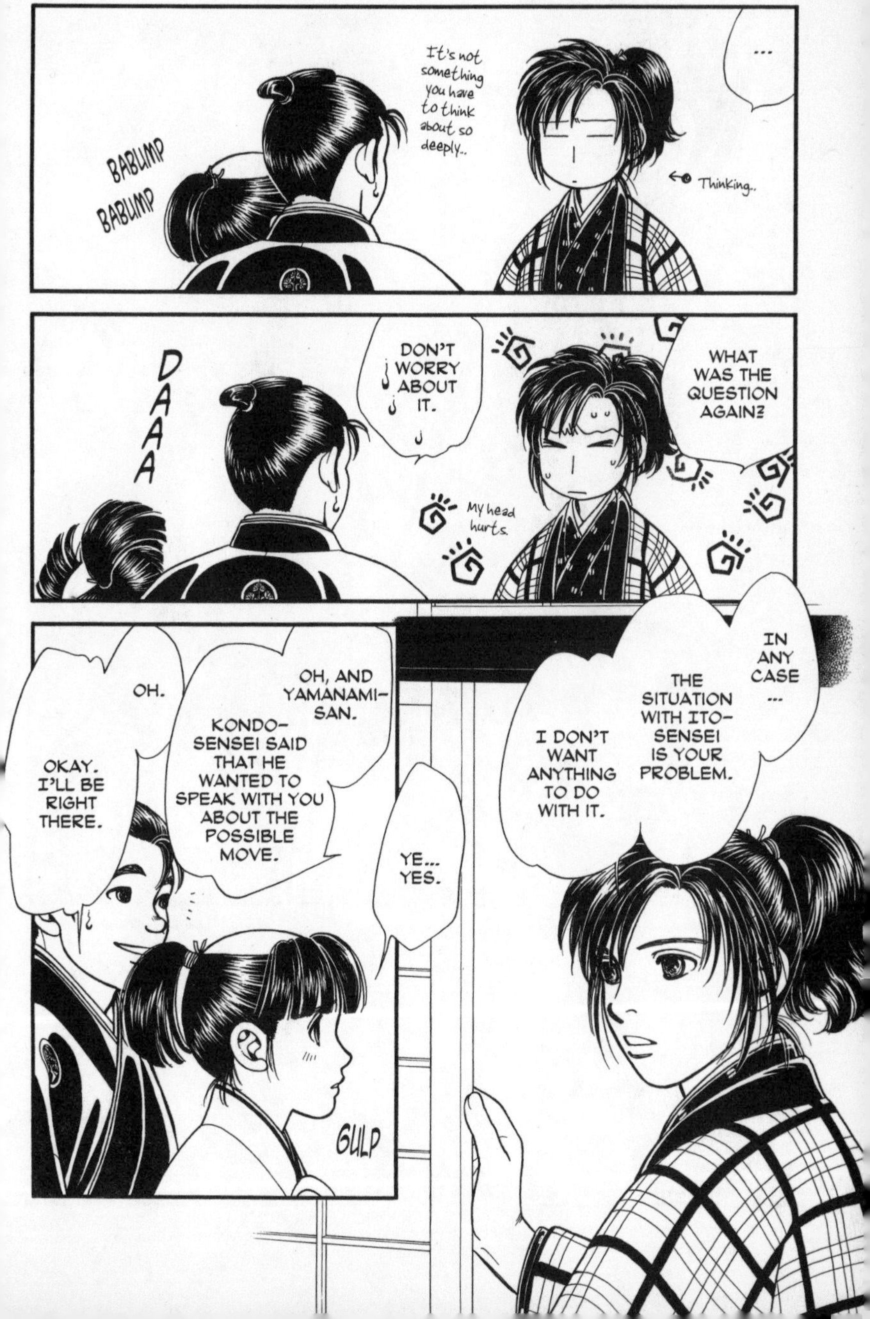
...
← Thinking..
It's not something you have to think about so deeply..
BABUMP
BABUMP
WHAT WAS THE QUESTION AGAIN?
My head hurts.
DON'T WORRY ABOUT IT.
DAAAA
IN ANY CASE...
THE SITUATION WITH ITO-SENSEI IS YOUR PROBLEM.
I DON'T WANT ANYTHING TO DO WITH IT.
YE... YES.
OH, AND YAMANAMI-SAN.
KONDO-SENSEI SAID THAT HE WANTED TO SPEAK WITH YOU ABOUT THE POSSIBLE MOVE.
OH.
OKAY. I'LL BE RIGHT THERE.
GULP

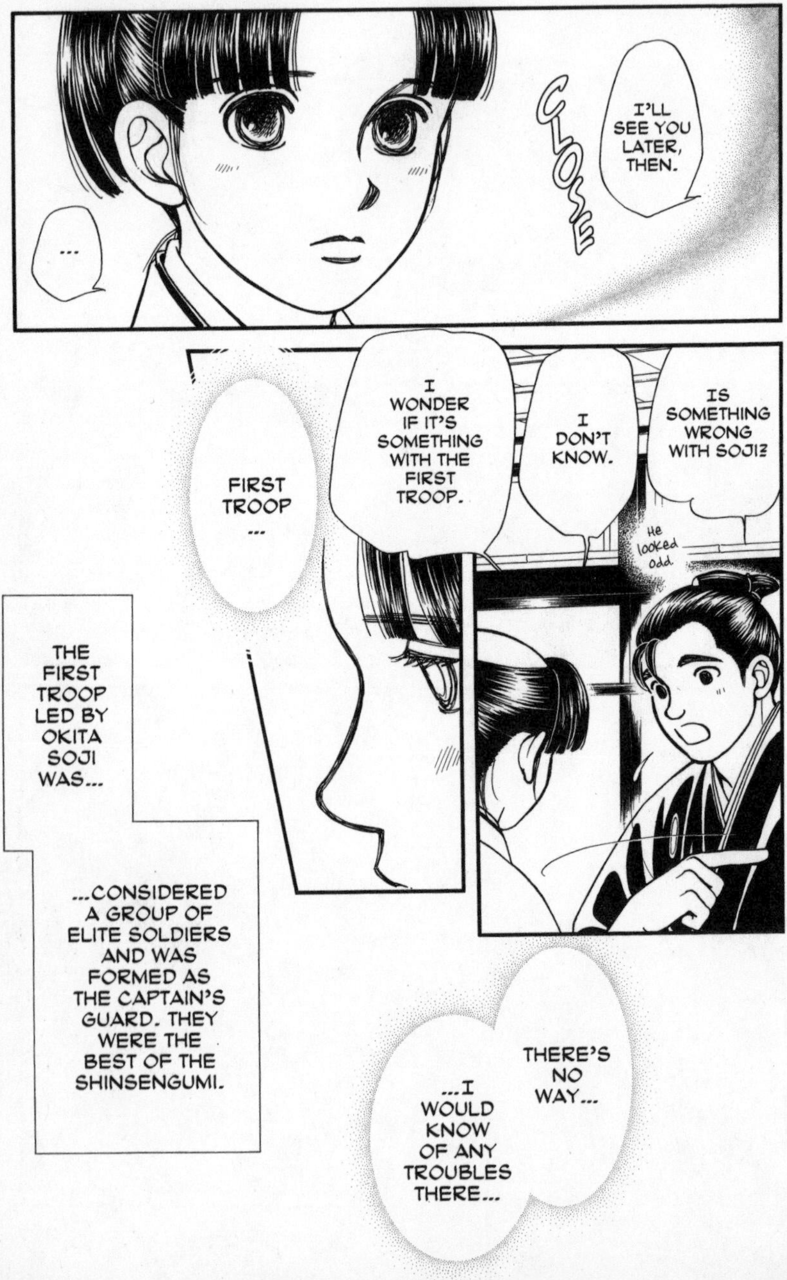
I'LL SEE YOU LATER, THEN.
CLOSE
...
IS SOMETHING WRONG WITH SOJI?
He looked odd.
I DON'T KNOW.
I WONDER IF IT'S SOMETHING WITH THE FIRST TROOP.
FIRST TROOP ...
THE FIRST TROOP LED BY OKITA SOJI WAS...
...CONSIDERED A GROUP OF ELITE SOLDIERS AND WAS FORMED AS THE CAPTAIN'S GUARD. THEY WERE THE BEST OF THE SHINSENGUMI.
THERE'S NO WAY...
...I WOULD KNOW OF ANY TROUBLES THERE...

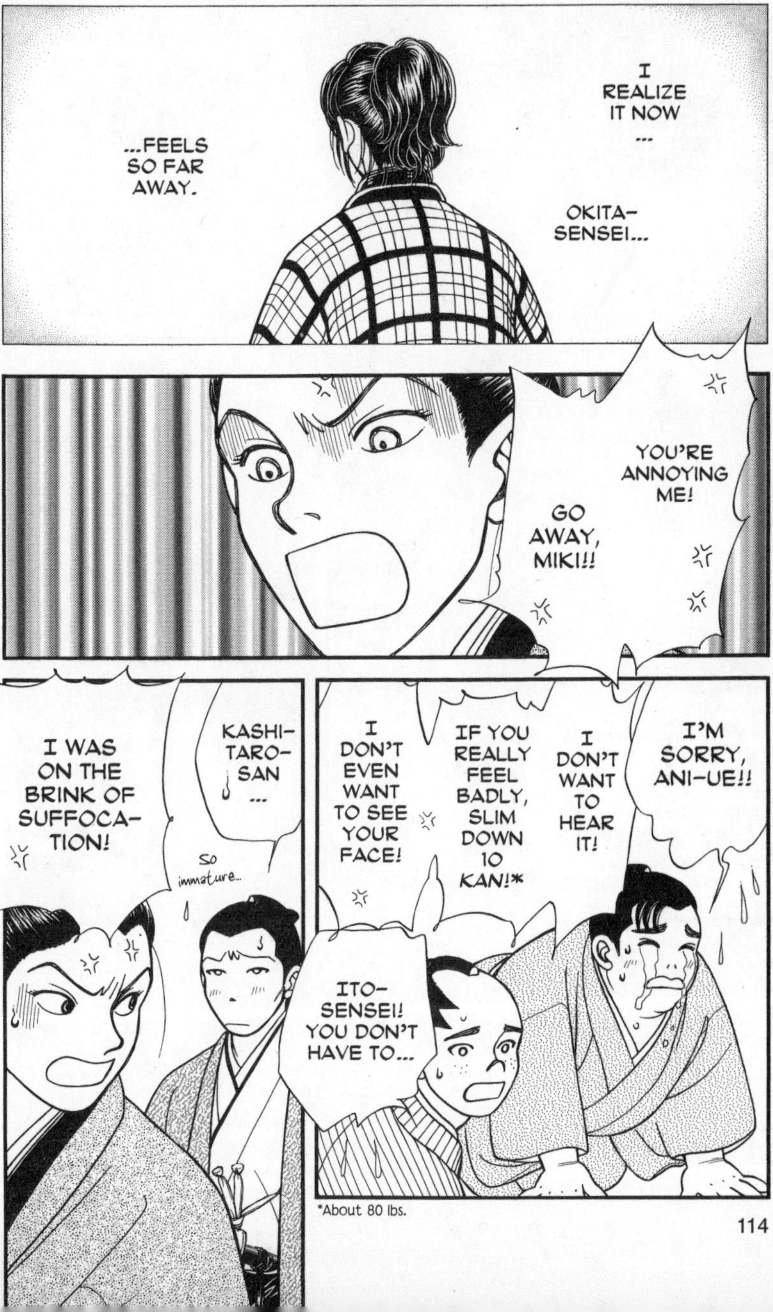
I REALIZE IT NOW...
OKITA-SENSEI...
...FEELS SO FAR AWAY.
YOU'RE ANNOYING ME!
GO AWAY, MIKI!!
I'M SORRY, ANI-UE!!
I DON'T WANT TO HEAR IT!
IF YOU REALLY FEEL BADLY, SLIM DOWN 10 KAN!*
I DON'T EVEN WANT TO SEE YOUR FACE!
ITO-SENSEI! YOU DON'T HAVE TO...
KASHI-TARO-SAN...
I WAS ON THE BRINK OF SUFFOCA-TION!
So immature...

*About 80 lbs.

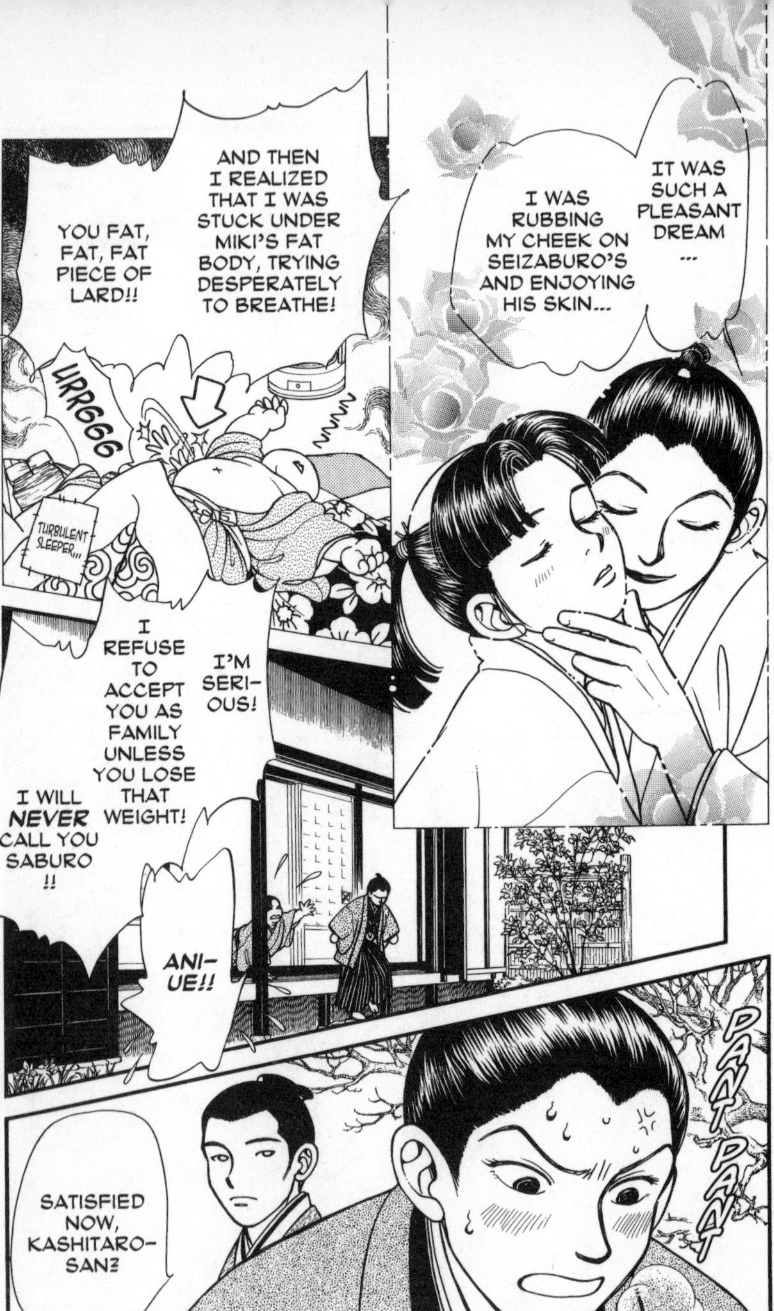
IT WAS SUCH A PLEASANT DREAM ...
I WAS RUBBING MY CHEEK ON SEIZABURO'S AND ENJOYING HIS SKIN...
AND THEN I REALIZED THAT I WAS STUCK UNDER MIKI'S FAT BODY, TRYING DESPERATELY TO BREATHE!
YOU FAT, FAT, FAT PIECE OF LARD!!
URRGGG
TURBULENT SLEEPER...
I'M SERI- OUS!
I REFUSE TO ACCEPT YOU AS FAMILY UNLESS YOU LOSE THAT WEIGHT!
I WILL **NEVER** CALL YOU SABURO !!
ANI- UE!!
PANT PANT
SATISFIED NOW, KASHITARO- SAN?

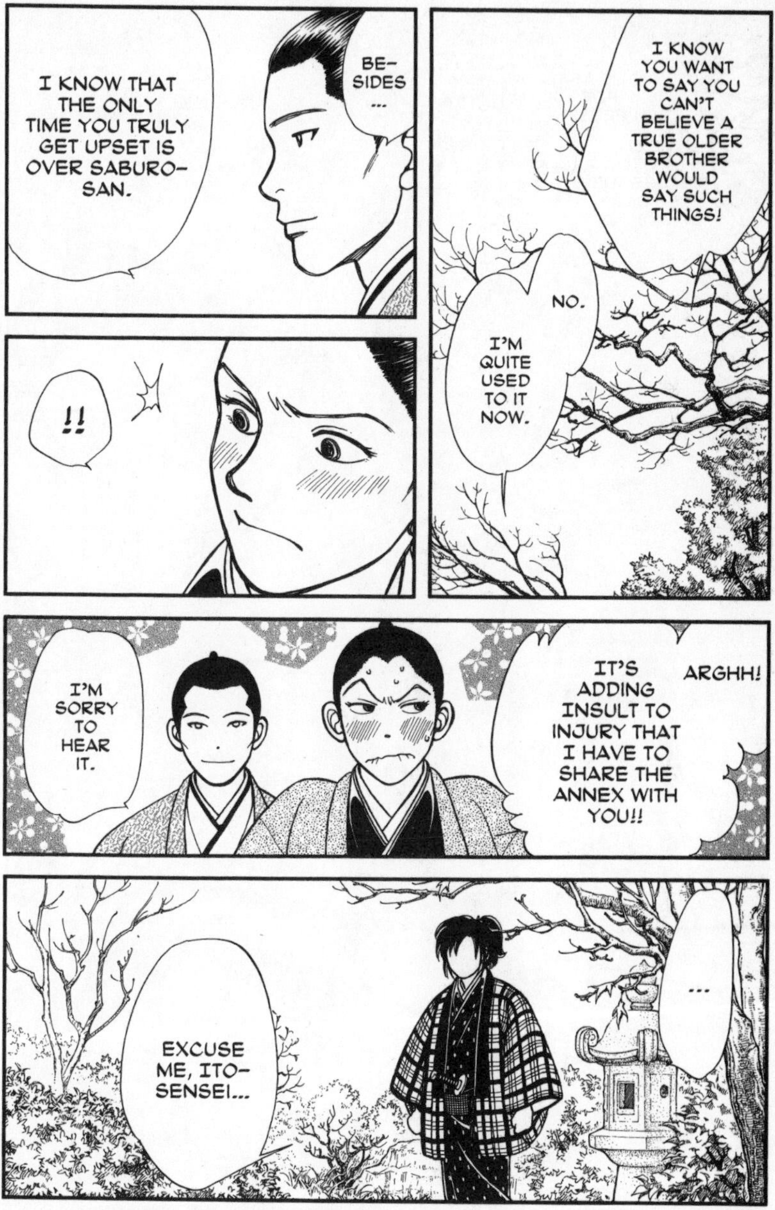
I KNOW YOU WANT TO SAY YOU CAN'T BELIEVE A TRUE OLDER BROTHER WOULD SAY SUCH THINGS!
NO.
I'M QUITE USED TO IT NOW.
BE-SIDES...
I KNOW THAT THE ONLY TIME YOU TRULY GET UPSET IS OVER SABURO-SAN.
!!
ARGHH!
IT'S ADDING INSULT TO INJURY THAT I HAVE TO SHARE THE ANNEX WITH YOU!!
I'M SORRY TO HEAR IT.
...
EXCUSE ME, ITO-SENSEI...

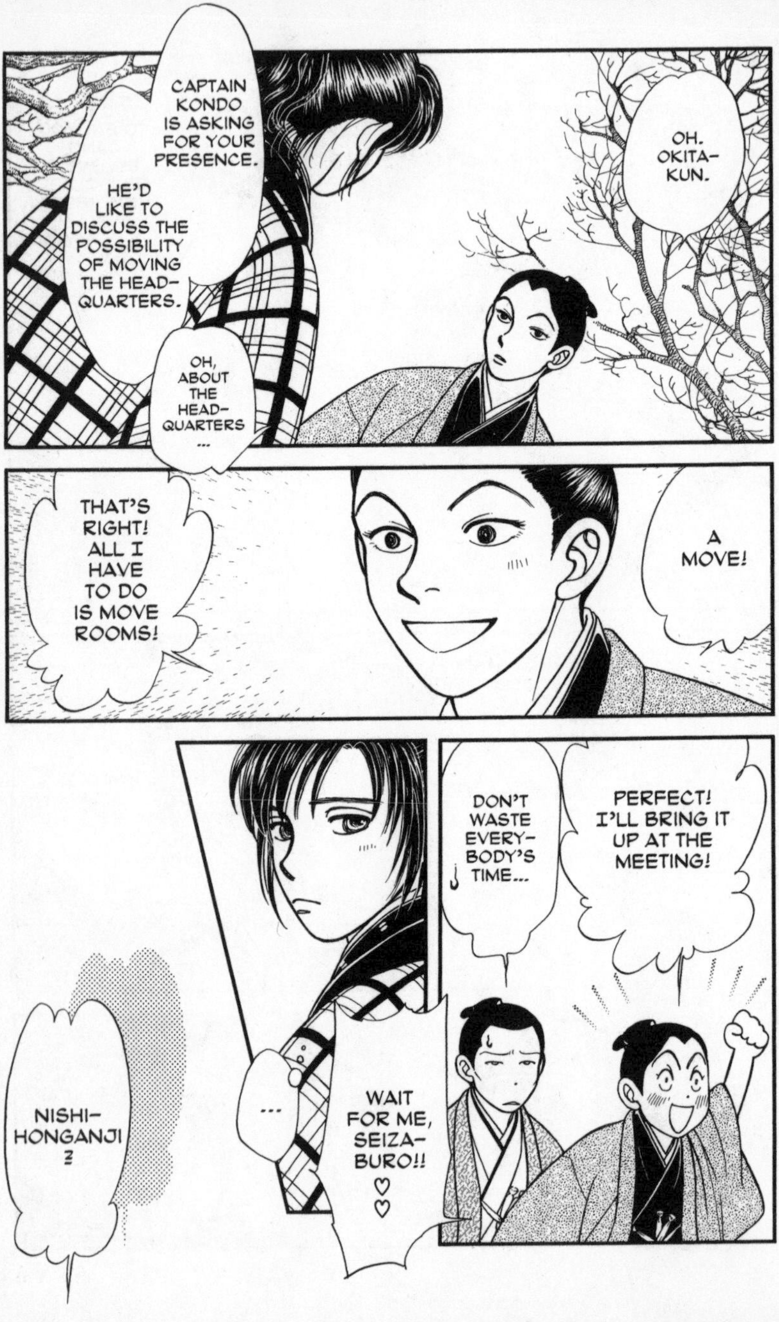
OH. OKITA-KUN.
CAPTAIN KONDO IS ASKING FOR YOUR PRESENCE.
HE'D LIKE TO DISCUSS THE POSSIBILITY OF MOVING THE HEADQUARTERS.
OH, ABOUT THE HEADQUARTERS...
A MOVE!
THAT'S RIGHT! ALL I HAVE TO DO IS MOVE ROOMS!
PERFECT! I'LL BRING IT UP AT THE MEETING!
DON'T WASTE EVERYBODY'S TIME...
WAIT FOR ME, SEIZABURO!! ♡♡
...
NISHI-HONGANJI?

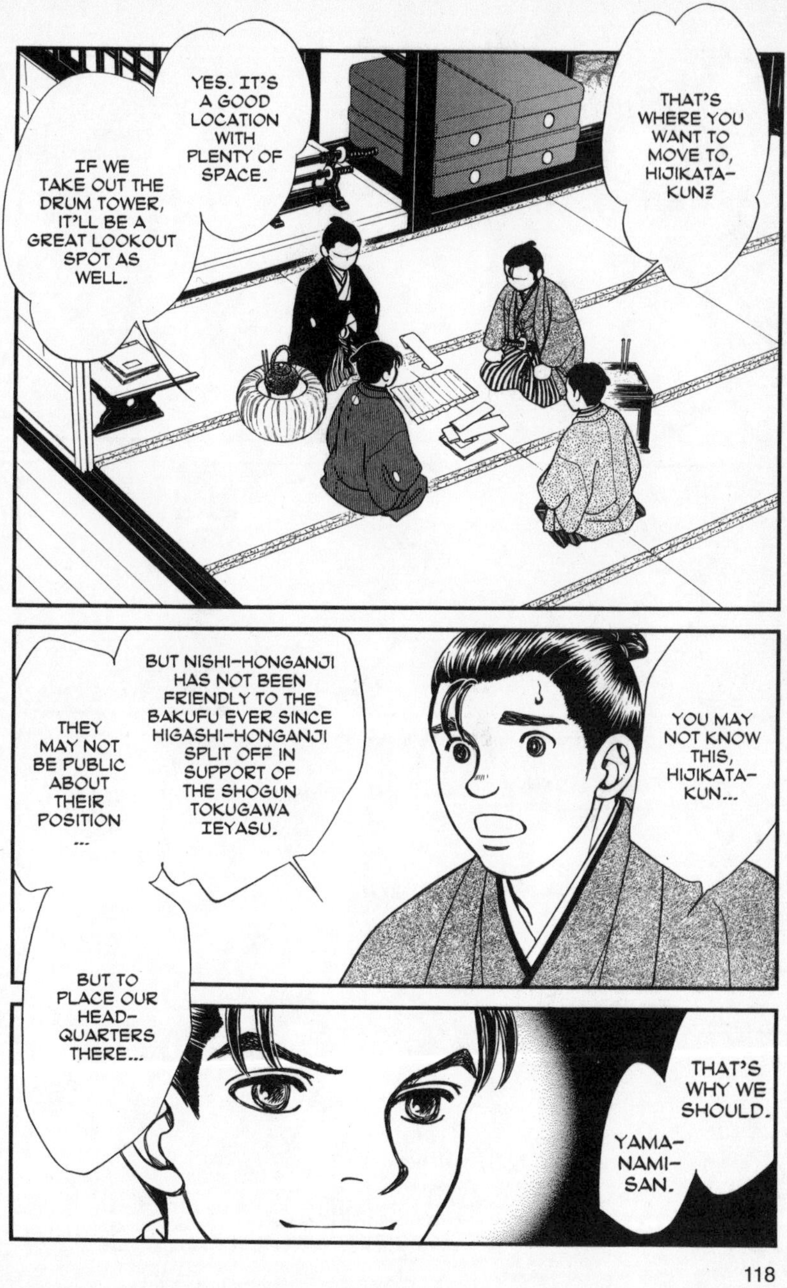
THAT'S WHERE YOU WANT TO MOVE TO, HIJIKATA-KUN?
YES. IT'S A GOOD LOCATION WITH PLENTY OF SPACE.
IF WE TAKE OUT THE DRUM TOWER, IT'LL BE A GREAT LOOKOUT SPOT AS WELL.
YOU MAY NOT KNOW THIS, HIJIKATA-KUN...
BUT NISHI-HONGANJI HAS NOT BEEN FRIENDLY TO THE BAKUFU EVER SINCE HIGASHI-HONGANJI SPLIT OFF IN SUPPORT OF THE SHOGUN TOKUGAWA IEYASU.
THEY MAY NOT BE PUBLIC ABOUT THEIR POSITION...
BUT TO PLACE OUR HEAD-QUARTERS THERE...
THAT'S WHY WE SHOULD.
YAMA-NAMI-SAN.

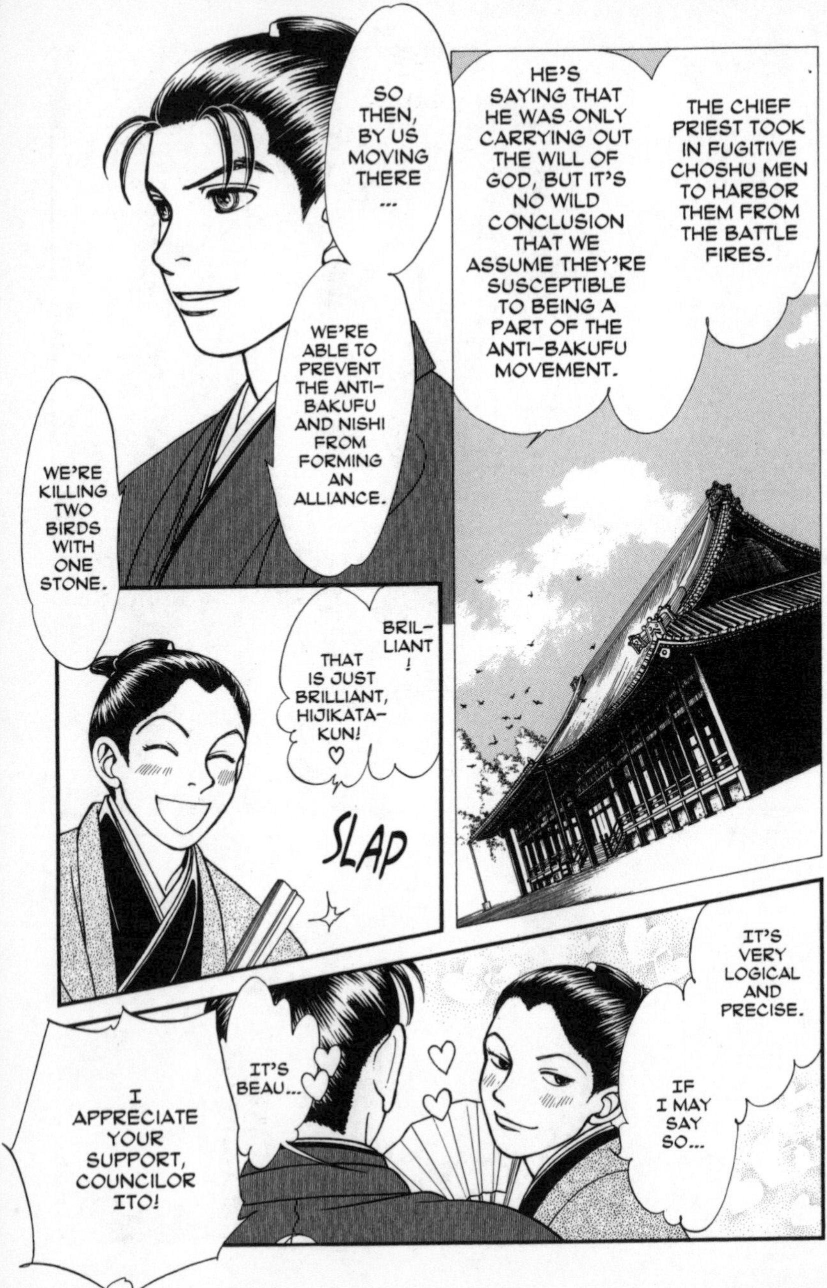
THE CHIEF PRIEST TOOK IN FUGITIVE CHOSHU MEN TO HARBOR THEM FROM THE BATTLE FIRES.
HE'S SAYING THAT HE WAS ONLY CARRYING OUT THE WILL OF GOD, BUT IT'S NO WILD CONCLUSION THAT WE ASSUME THEY'RE SUSCEPTIBLE TO BEING A PART OF THE ANTI-BAKUFU MOVEMENT.
SO THEN, BY US MOVING THERE ...
WE'RE ABLE TO PREVENT THE ANTI-BAKUFU AND NISHI FROM FORMING AN ALLIANCE.
WE'RE KILLING TWO BIRDS WITH ONE STONE.
BRIL-LIANT!
THAT IS JUST BRILLIANT, HIJIKATA-KUN! ♡
SLAP
IT'S VERY LOGICAL AND PRECISE.
IF I MAY SAY SO...
IT'S BEAU...
I APPRECIATE YOUR SUPPORT, COUNCILOR ITO!

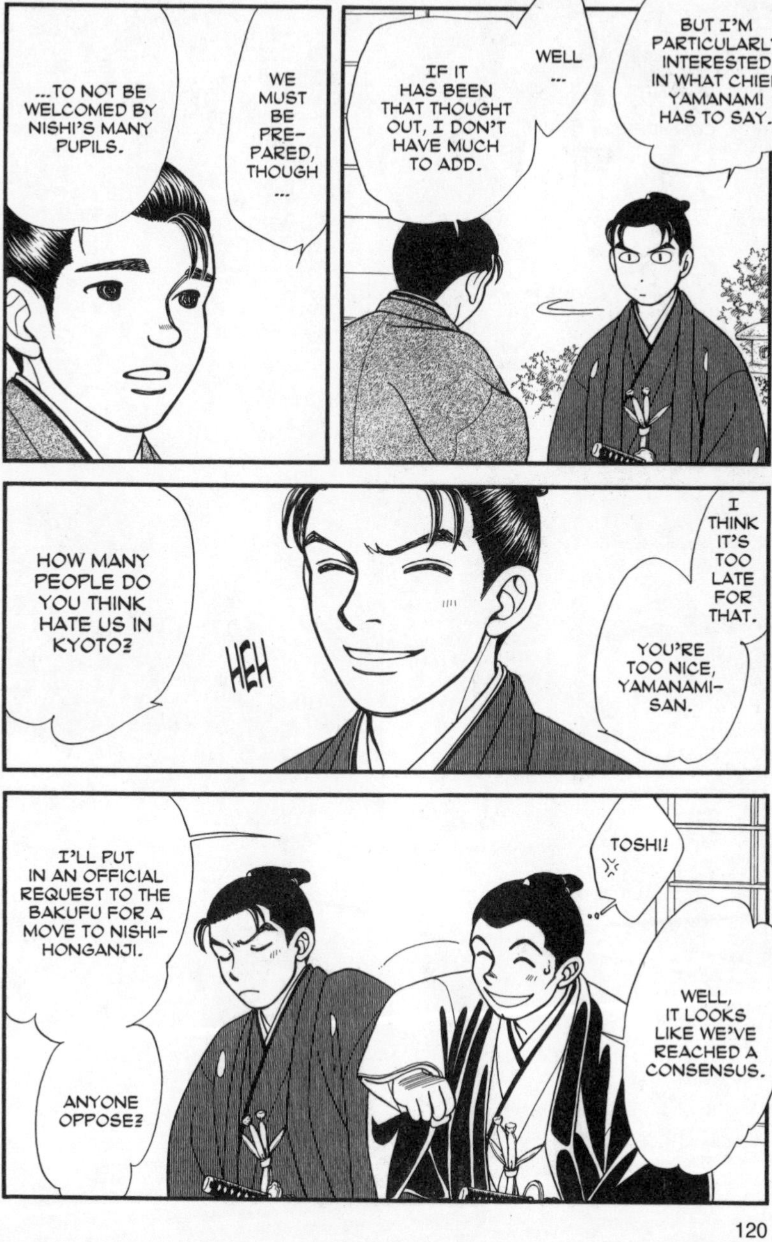
BUT I'M PARTICULARLY INTERESTED IN WHAT CHIEF YAMANAMI HAS TO SAY.
WELL...
IF IT HAS BEEN THAT THOUGHT OUT, I DON'T HAVE MUCH TO ADD.
WE MUST BE PRE-PARED, THOUGH...
...TO NOT BE WELCOMED BY NISHI'S MANY PUPILS.
I THINK IT'S TOO LATE FOR THAT.
YOU'RE TOO NICE, YAMANAMI-SAN.
HEH
HOW MANY PEOPLE DO YOU THINK HATE US IN KYOTO?
TOSHI!
WELL, IT LOOKS LIKE WE'VE REACHED A CONSENSUS.
I'LL PUT IN AN OFFICIAL REQUEST TO THE BAKUFU FOR A MOVE TO NISHI-HONGANJI.
ANYONE OPPOSE?

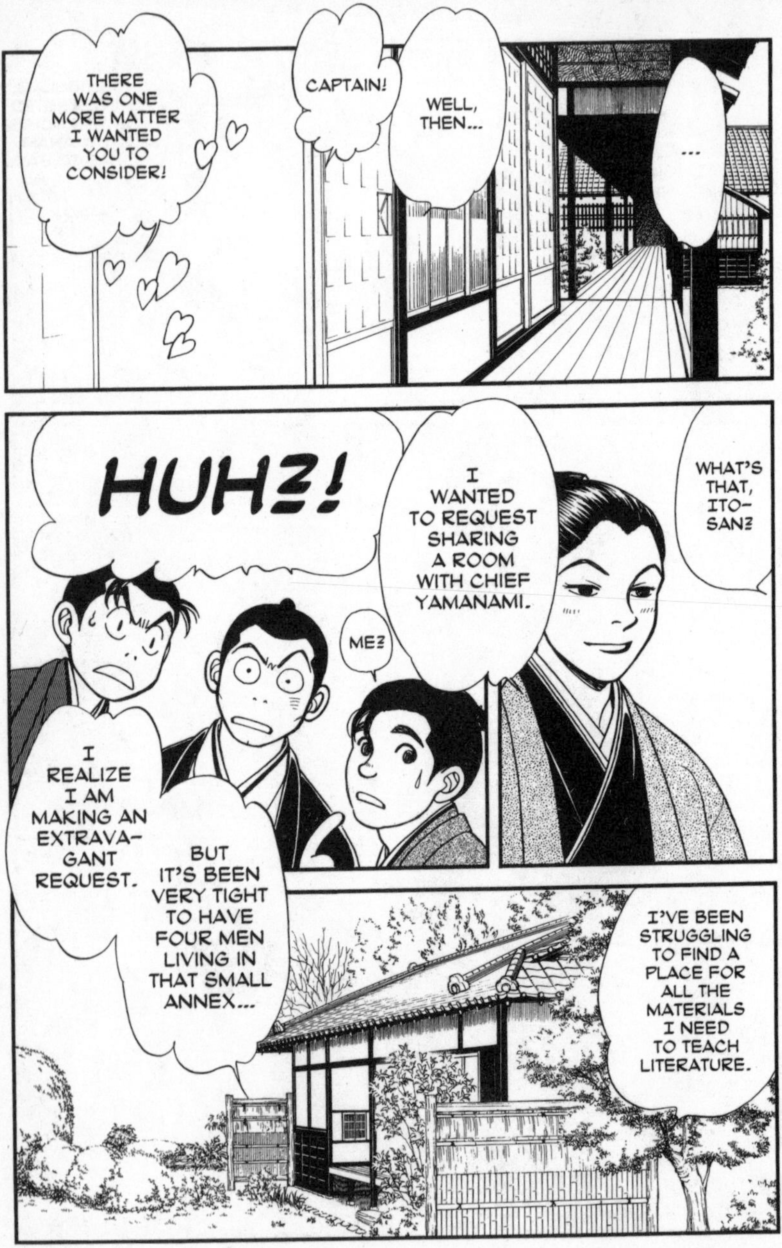
...
WELL, THEN...
CAPTAIN!
THERE WAS ONE MORE MATTER I WANTED YOU TO CONSIDER!
WHAT'S THAT, ITO-SAN?
I WANTED TO REQUEST SHARING A ROOM WITH CHIEF YAMANAMI.
HUH?!
ME?
I REALIZE I AM MAKING AN EXTRAVA-GANT REQUEST.
I'VE BEEN STRUGGLING TO FIND A PLACE FOR ALL THE MATERIALS I NEED TO TEACH LITERATURE.
BUT IT'S BEEN VERY TIGHT TO HAVE FOUR MEN LIVING IN THAT SMALL ANNEX...

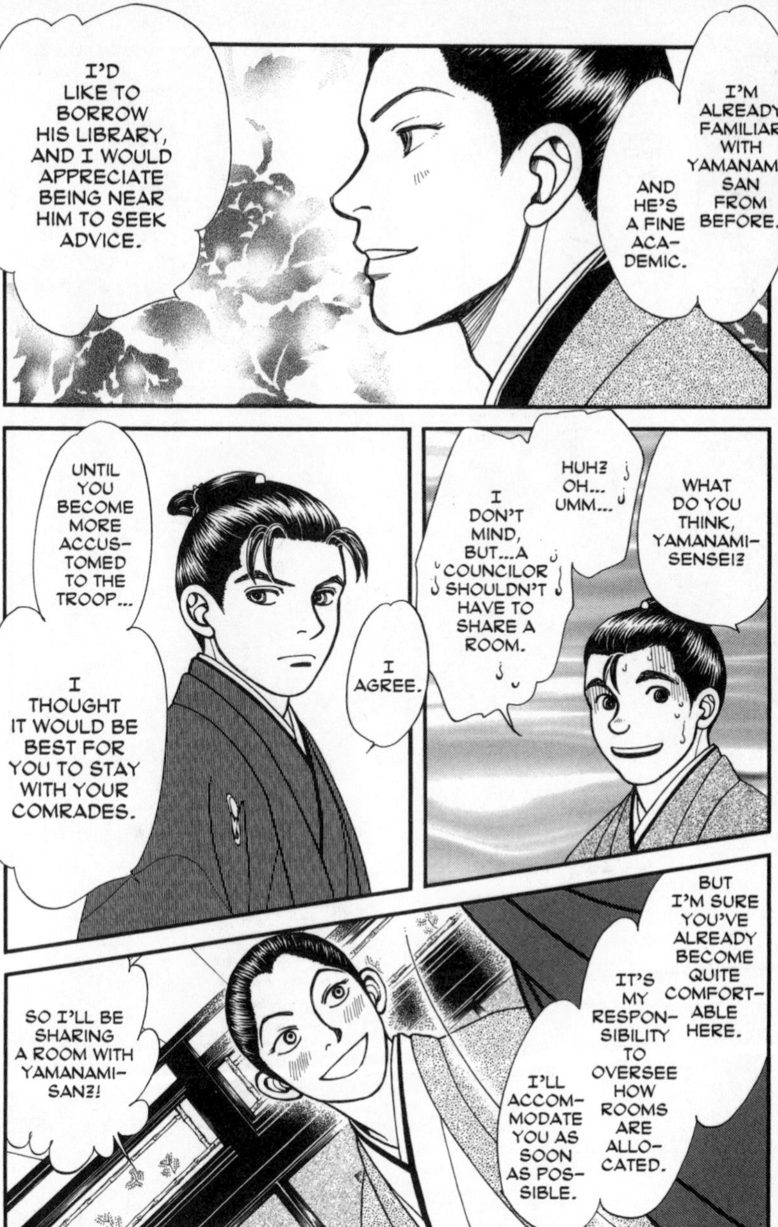
I'M ALREADY FAMILIAR WITH YAMANAMI-SAN FROM BEFORE.
AND HE'S A FINE ACADEMIC.
I'D LIKE TO BORROW HIS LIBRARY, AND I WOULD APPRECIATE BEING NEAR HIM TO SEEK ADVICE.
WHAT DO YOU THINK, YAMANAMI-SENSEI!?
HUH!? OH... UMM...
I DON'T MIND, BUT...A COUNCILOR SHOULDN'T HAVE TO SHARE A ROOM.
I AGREE.
UNTIL YOU BECOME MORE ACCUSTOMED TO THE TROOP...
I THOUGHT IT WOULD BE BEST FOR YOU TO STAY WITH YOUR COMRADES.
BUT I'M SURE YOU'VE ALREADY BECOME QUITE COMFORTABLE HERE.
IT'S MY RESPONSIBILITY TO OVERSEE HOW ROOMS ARE ALLOCATED.
I'LL ACCOMMODATE YOU AS SOON AS POSSIBLE.
SO I'LL BE SHARING A ROOM WITH YAMANAMI-SAN!?!

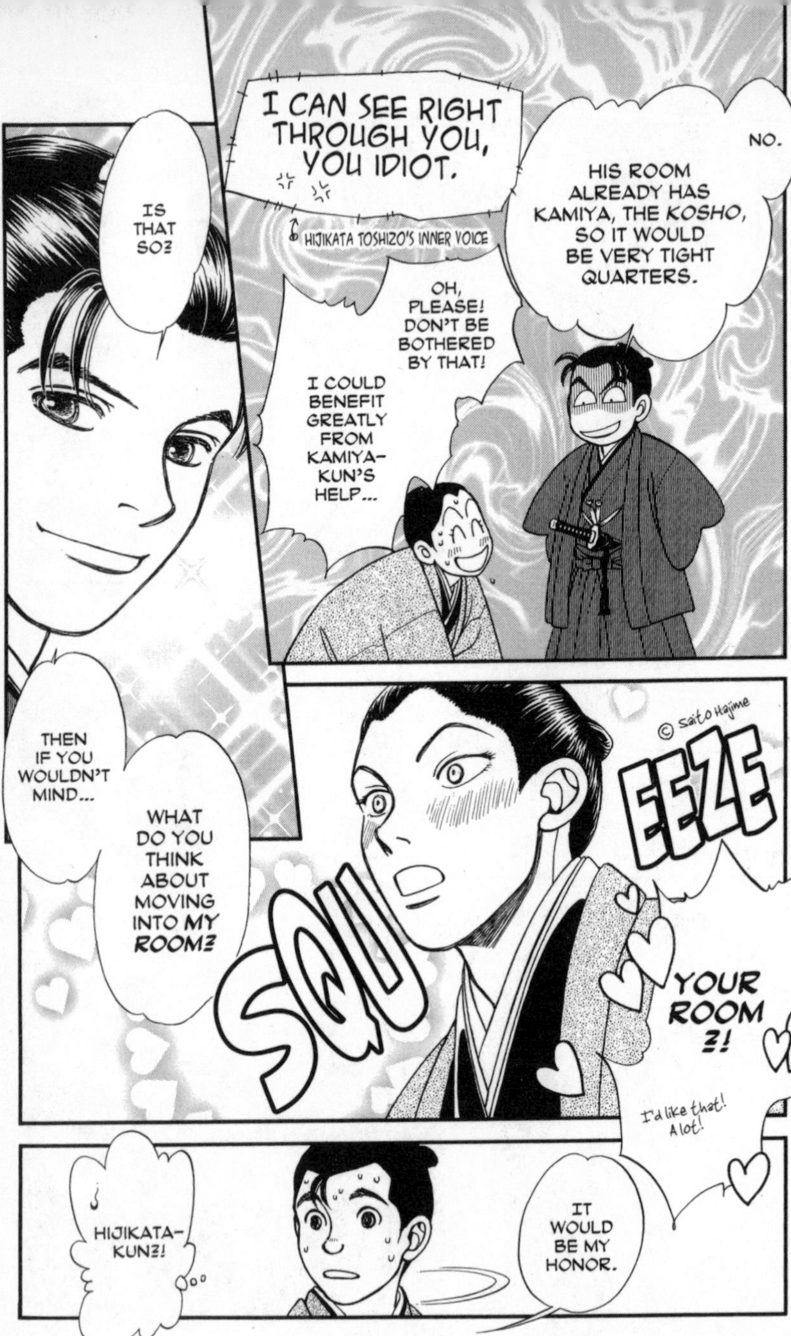

NO.
HIS ROOM ALREADY HAS KAMIYA, THE *KOSHO*, SO IT WOULD BE VERY TIGHT QUARTERS.
I CAN SEE RIGHT THROUGH YOU, YOU IDIOT.
HIJIKATA TOSHIZO'S INNER VOICE
OH, PLEASE! DON'T BE BOTHERED BY THAT!
I COULD BENEFIT GREATLY FROM KAMIYA-KUN'S HELP...
IS THAT SO?
THEN IF YOU WOULDN'T MIND...
WHAT DO YOU THINK ABOUT MOVING INTO **MY *ROOM*?**
© Saito Hajime
SQUEEZE
YOUR ROOM?!
I'd like that! A lot!
IT WOULD BE MY HONOR.
HIJIKATA-KUN?!

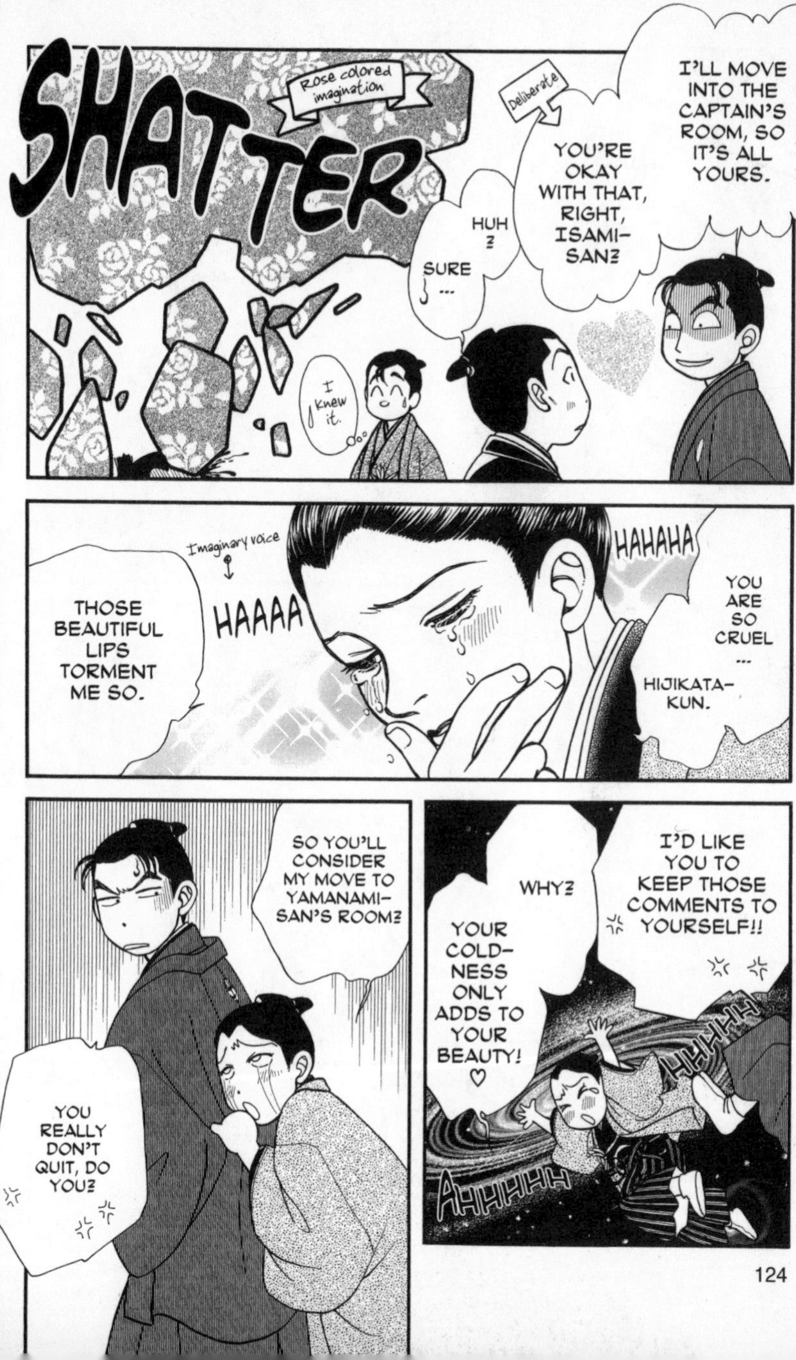
I'LL MOVE INTO THE CAPTAIN'S ROOM, SO IT'S ALL YOURS.
Deliberate
YOU'RE OKAY WITH THAT, RIGHT, ISAMI-SAN?
HUH? SURE ...
I knew it.
Rose colored imagination
SHATTER
HAHAHA
YOU ARE SO CRUEL ... HIJIKATA-KUN.
HAAAA
Imaginary voice
THOSE BEAUTIFUL LIPS TORMENT ME SO.
I'D LIKE YOU TO KEEP THOSE COMMENTS TO YOURSELF!!
WHY?
YOUR COLDNESS ONLY ADDS TO YOUR BEAUTY! ♡
HHHHH
AHHHHHH
SO YOU'LL CONSIDER MY MOVE TO YAMANAMI-SAN'S ROOM?
YOU REALLY DON'T QUIT, DO YOU?

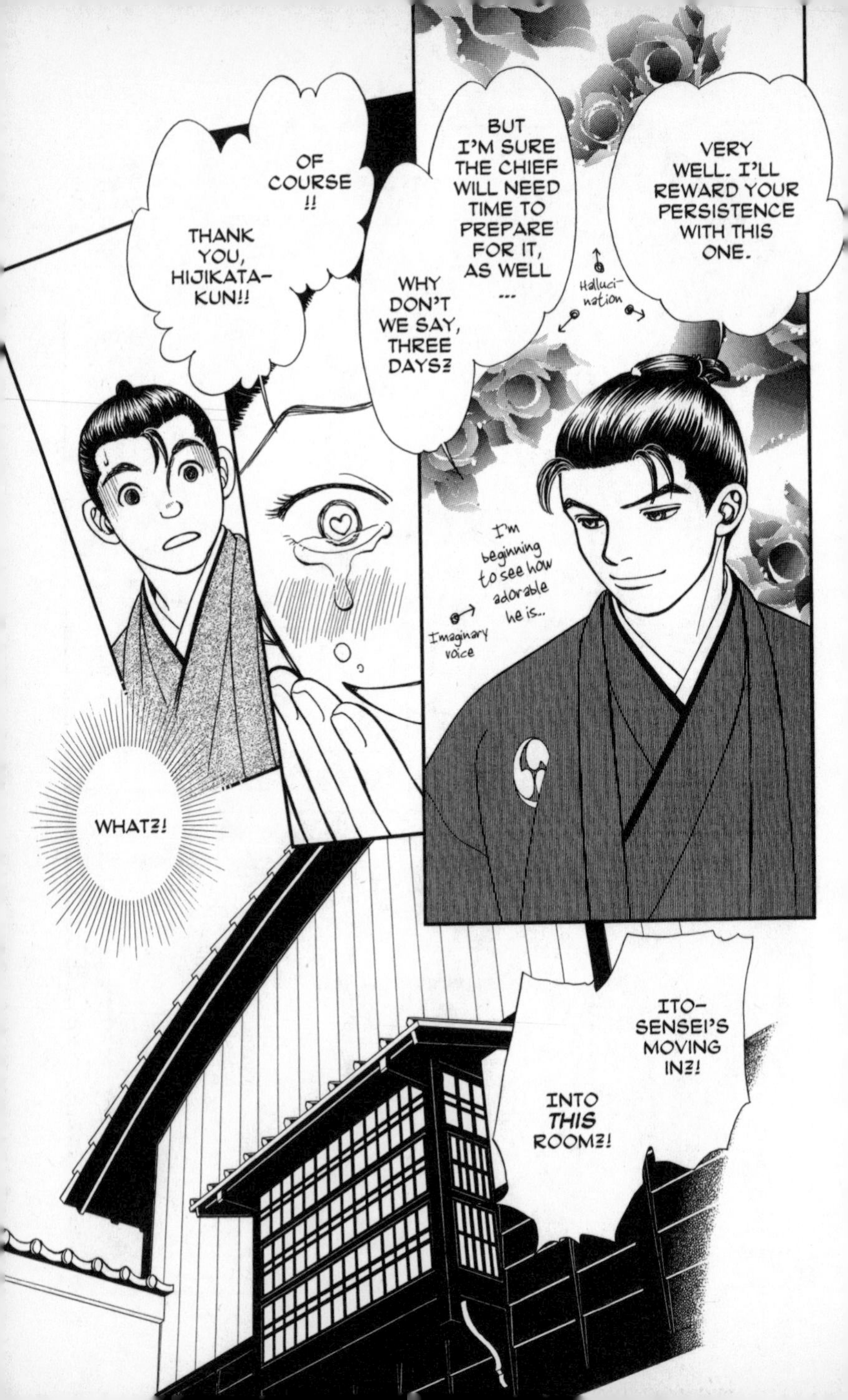
VERY WELL. I'LL REWARD YOUR PERSISTENCE WITH THIS ONE.
BUT I'M SURE THE CHIEF WILL NEED TIME TO PREPARE FOR IT, AS WELL ...
Hallucination
WHY DON'T WE SAY, THREE DAYS?
I'm beginning to see how adorable he is..
Imaginary voice
OF COURSE !!
THANK YOU, HIJIKATA-KUN!!
WHAT?!
ITO-SENSEI'S MOVING IN?!
INTO THIS ROOM?!

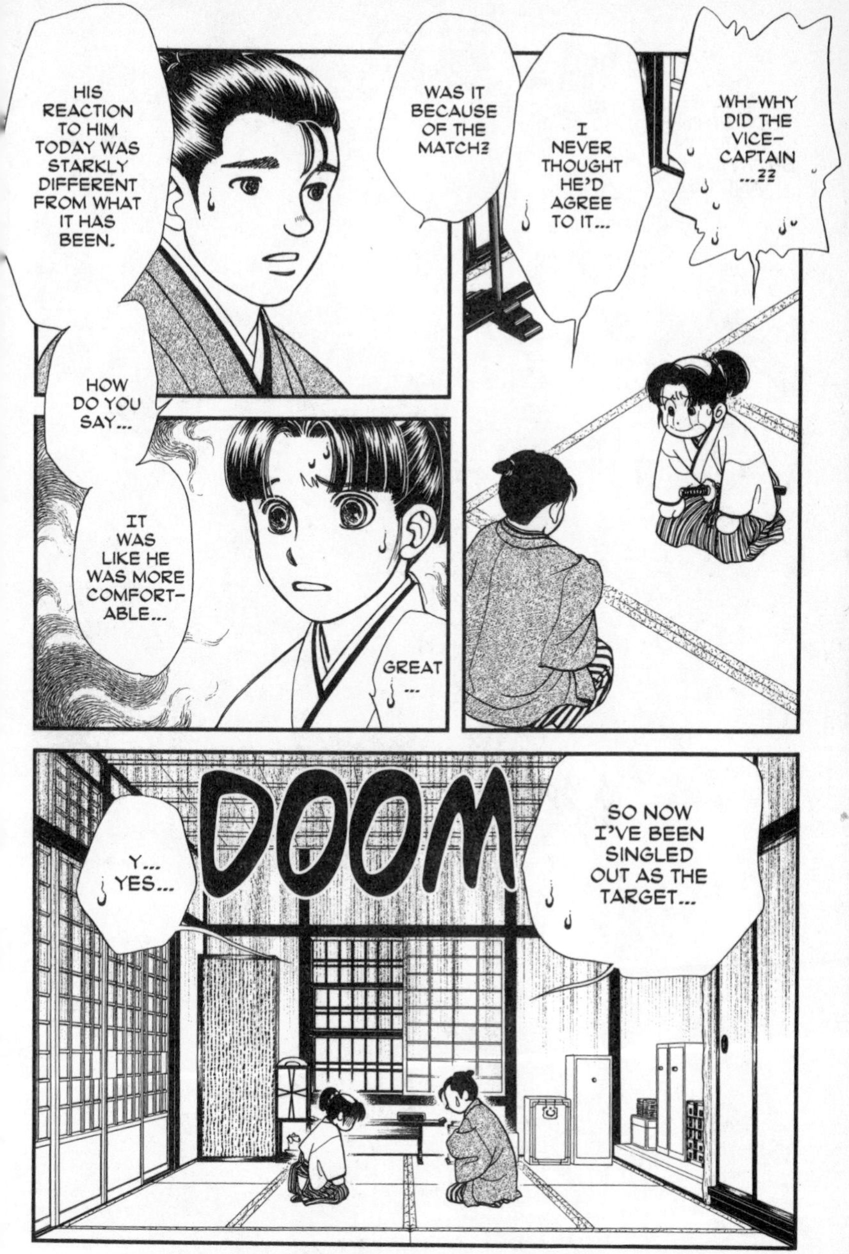
WH-WHY DID THE VICE-CAPTAIN ...??
I NEVER THOUGHT HE'D AGREE TO IT...
WAS IT BECAUSE OF THE MATCH?
HIS REACTION TO HIM TODAY WAS STARKLY DIFFERENT FROM WHAT IT HAS BEEN.
HOW DO YOU SAY...
IT WAS LIKE HE WAS MORE COMFORTABLE...
GREAT...
SO NOW I'VE BEEN SINGLED OUT AS THE TARGET...
DOOM
Y... YES...

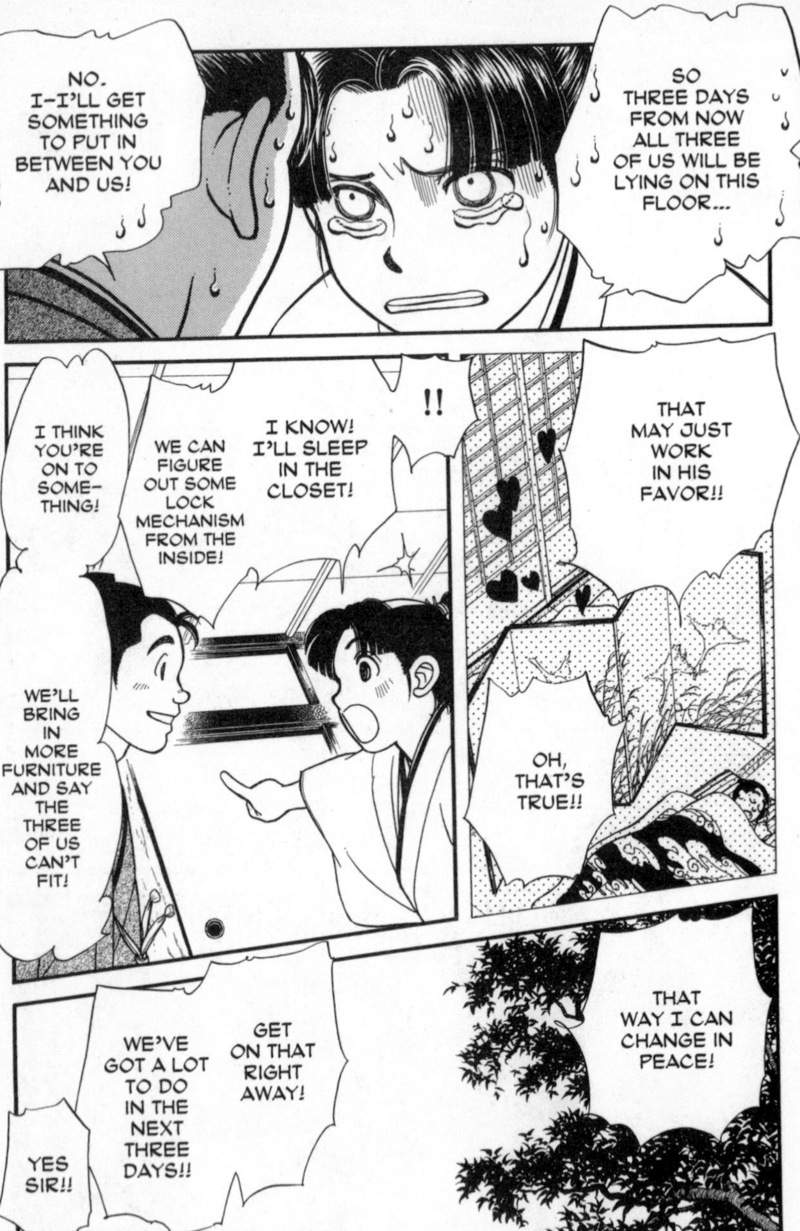

SO THREE DAYS FROM NOW ALL THREE OF US WILL BE LYING ON THIS FLOOR...
NO. I-I'LL GET SOMETHING TO PUT IN BETWEEN YOU AND US!
THAT MAY JUST WORK IN HIS FAVOR!!
OH, THAT'S TRUE!!
!!
I KNOW! I'LL SLEEP IN THE CLOSET!
WE CAN FIGURE OUT SOME LOCK MECHANISM FROM THE INSIDE!
I THINK YOU'RE ON TO SOME-THING!
WE'LL BRING IN MORE FURNITURE AND SAY THE THREE OF US CAN'T FIT!
THAT WAY I CAN CHANGE IN PEACE!
GET ON THAT RIGHT AWAY!
WE'VE GOT A LOT TO DO IN THE NEXT THREE DAYS!!
YES SIR!!

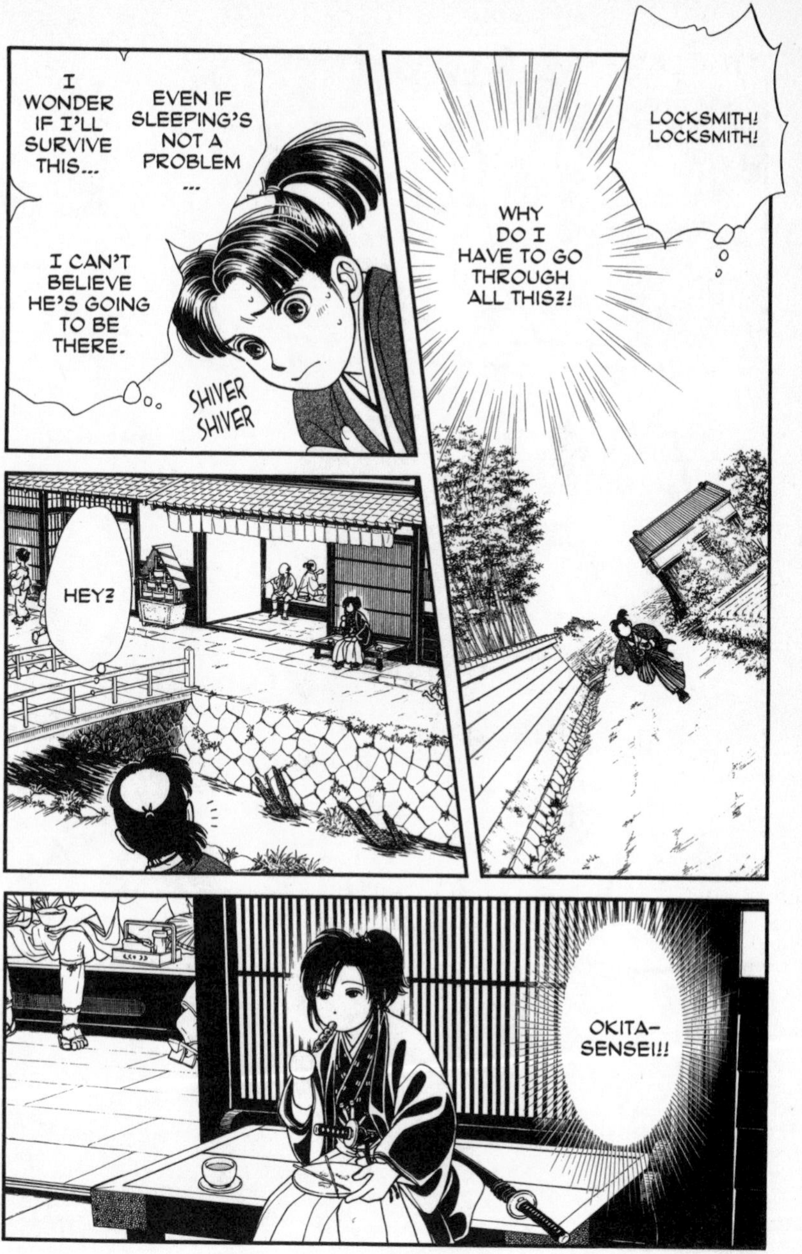
LOCKSMITH! LOCKSMITH!
WHY DO I HAVE TO GO THROUGH ALL THIS?!
EVEN IF SLEEPING'S NOT A PROBLEM ...
I WONDER IF I'LL SURVIVE THIS...
I CAN'T BELIEVE HE'S GOING TO BE THERE.
SHIVER SHIVER
HEY?
OKITA-SENSEI!!!

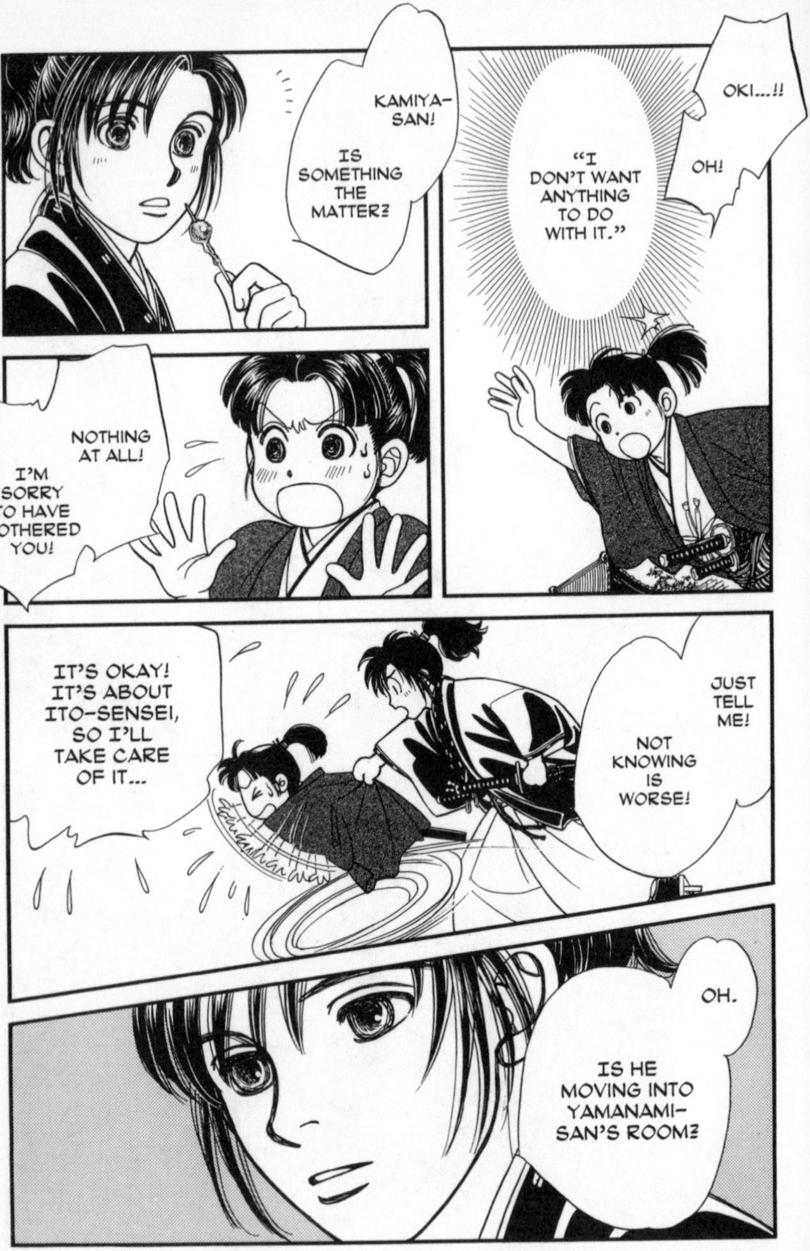
OKI...!!
OH!
"I DON'T WANT ANYTHING TO DO WITH IT."
KAMIYA-SAN!
IS SOMETHING THE MATTER?
NOTHING AT ALL!
I'M SORRY TO HAVE BOTHERED YOU!
JUST TELL ME!
NOT KNOWING IS WORSE!
IT'S OKAY! IT'S ABOUT ITO-SENSEI, SO I'LL TAKE CARE OF IT...
OH.
IS HE MOVING INTO YAMANAMI-SAN'S ROOM?

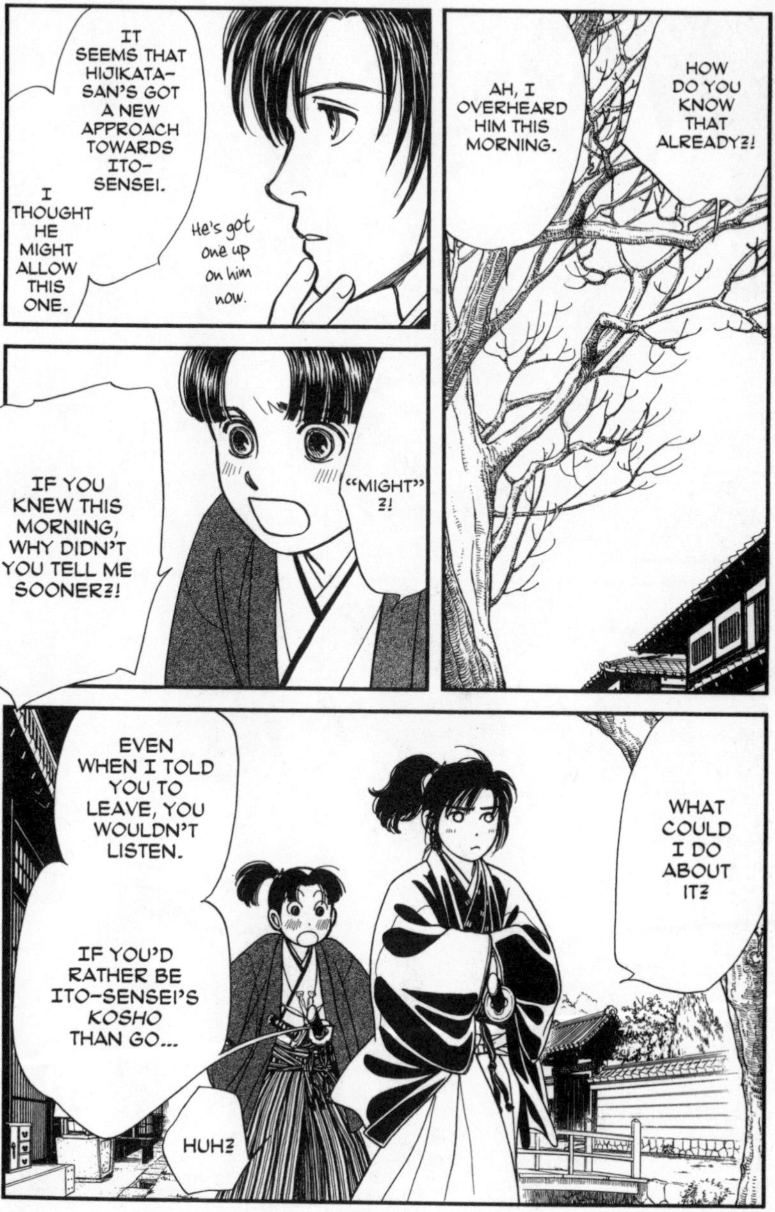
HOW DO YOU KNOW THAT ALREADY?!
AH, I OVERHEARD HIM THIS MORNING.
IT SEEMS THAT HIJIKATA-SAN'S GOT A NEW APPROACH TOWARDS ITO-SENSEI.
He's got one up on him now.
I THOUGHT HE MIGHT ALLOW THIS ONE.
"MIGHT"?!
IF YOU KNEW THIS MORNING, WHY DIDN'T YOU TELL ME SOONER?!
WHAT COULD I DO ABOUT IT?
EVEN WHEN I TOLD YOU TO LEAVE, YOU WOULDN'T LISTEN.
IF YOU'D RATHER BE ITO-SENSEI'S *KOSHO* THAN GO...
HUH?

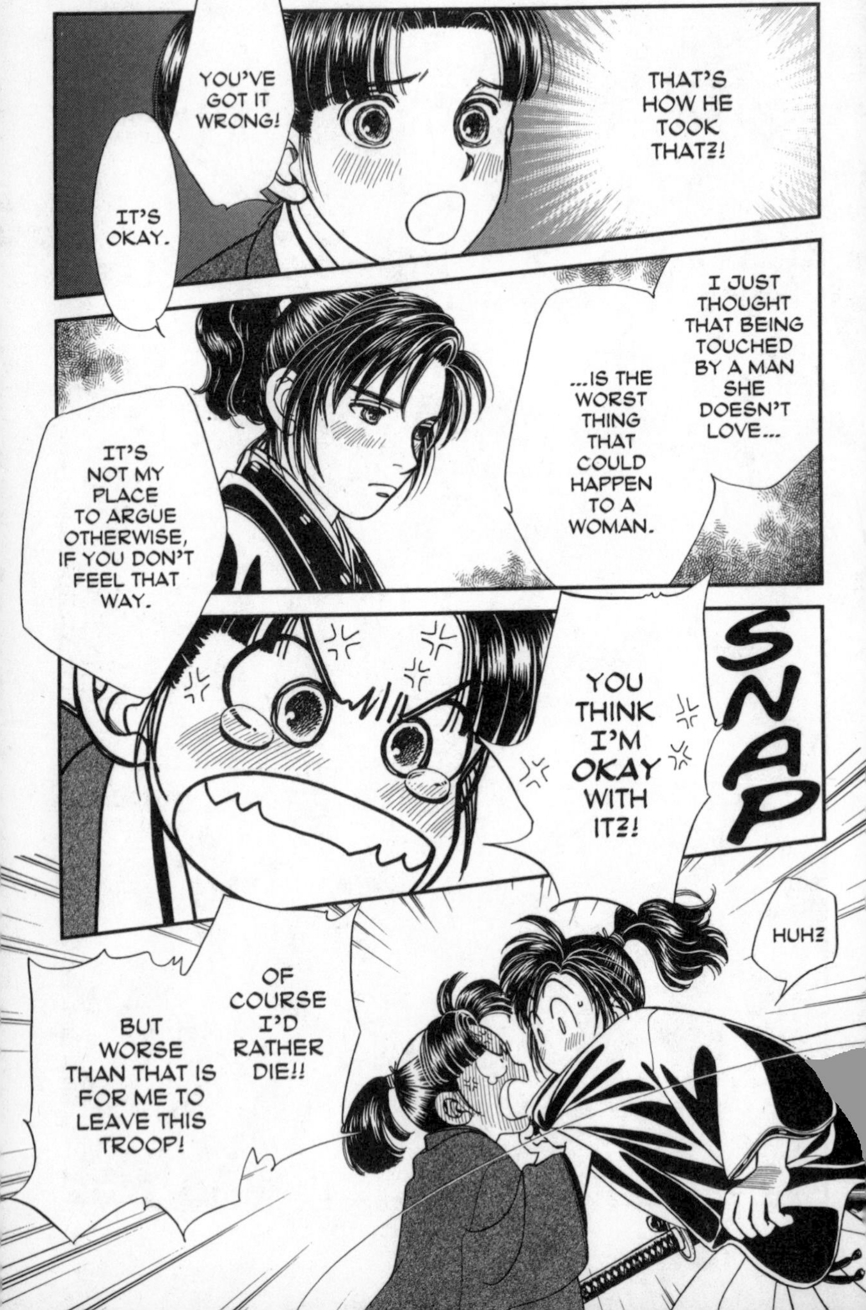
THAT'S HOW HE TOOK THAT?!
YOU'VE GOT IT WRONG!
IT'S OKAY.
I JUST THOUGHT THAT BEING TOUCHED BY A MAN SHE DOESN'T LOVE...
...IS THE WORST THING THAT COULD HAPPEN TO A WOMAN.
IT'S NOT MY PLACE TO ARGUE OTHERWISE, IF YOU DON'T FEEL THAT WAY.
SNAP
YOU THINK I'M OKAY WITH IT?!
HUH?
OF COURSE I'D RATHER DIE!!
BUT WORSE THAN THAT IS FOR ME TO LEAVE THIS TROOP!

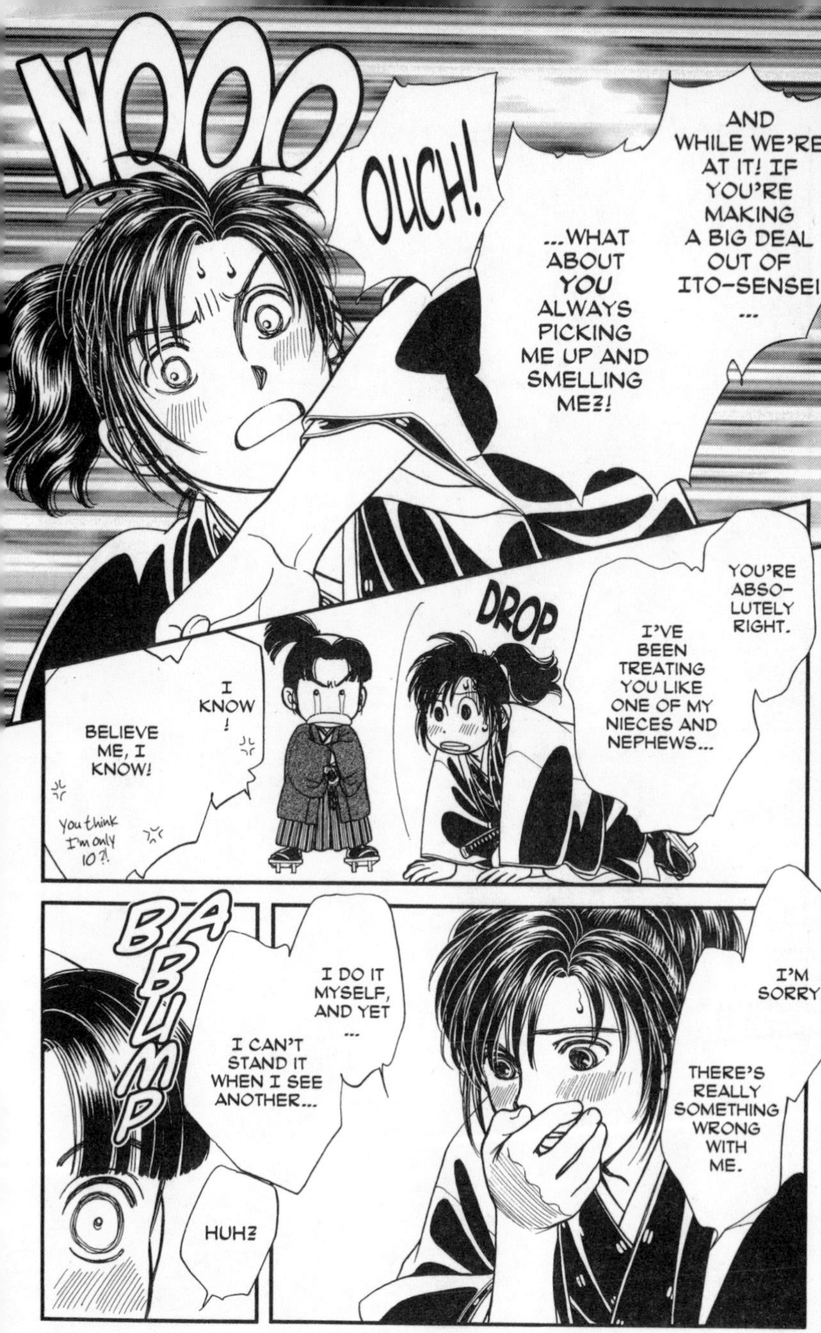
AND WHILE WE'RE AT IT! IF YOU'RE MAKING A BIG DEAL OUT OF ITO-SENSEI ...
...WHAT ABOUT YOU ALWAYS PICKING ME UP AND SMELLING ME?!
OUCH!
NOOO
YOU'RE ABSO-LUTELY RIGHT.
I'VE BEEN TREATING YOU LIKE ONE OF MY NIECES AND NEPHEWS...
DROP
I KNOW!
BELIEVE ME, I KNOW!
You think I'm only 10?!
I'M SORRY.
THERE'S REALLY SOMETHING WRONG WITH ME.
I DO IT MYSELF, AND YET ...
I CAN'T STAND IT WHEN I SEE ANOTHER...
BA-BUMP
HUH?

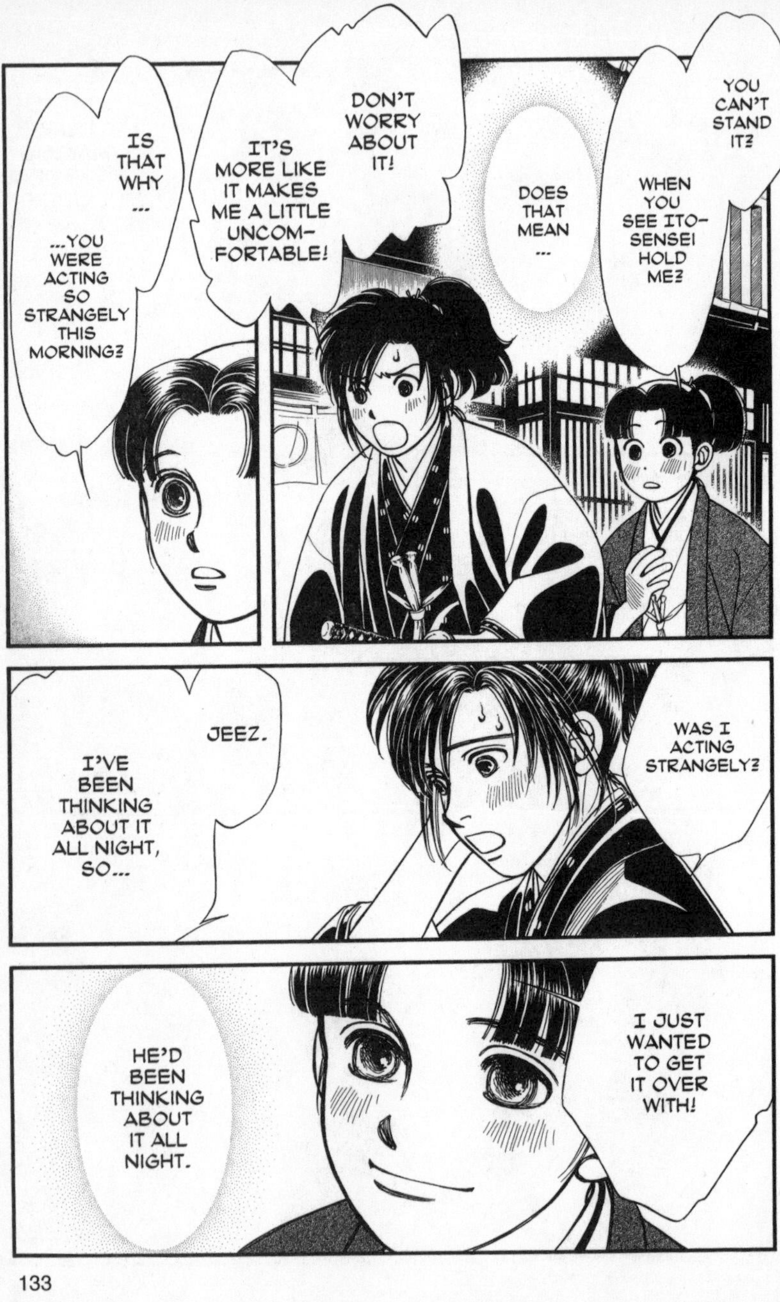
YOU CAN'T STAND IT?
WHEN YOU SEE ITO-SENSEI HOLD ME?
DOES THAT MEAN ...
DON'T WORRY ABOUT IT!
IT'S MORE LIKE IT MAKES ME A LITTLE UNCOM-FORTABLE!
IS THAT WHY ...
...YOU WERE ACTING SO STRANGELY THIS MORNING?
WAS I ACTING STRANGELY?
JEEZ.
I'VE BEEN THINKING ABOUT IT ALL NIGHT, SO...
I JUST WANTED TO GET IT OVER WITH!
HE'D BEEN THINKING ABOUT IT ALL NIGHT.

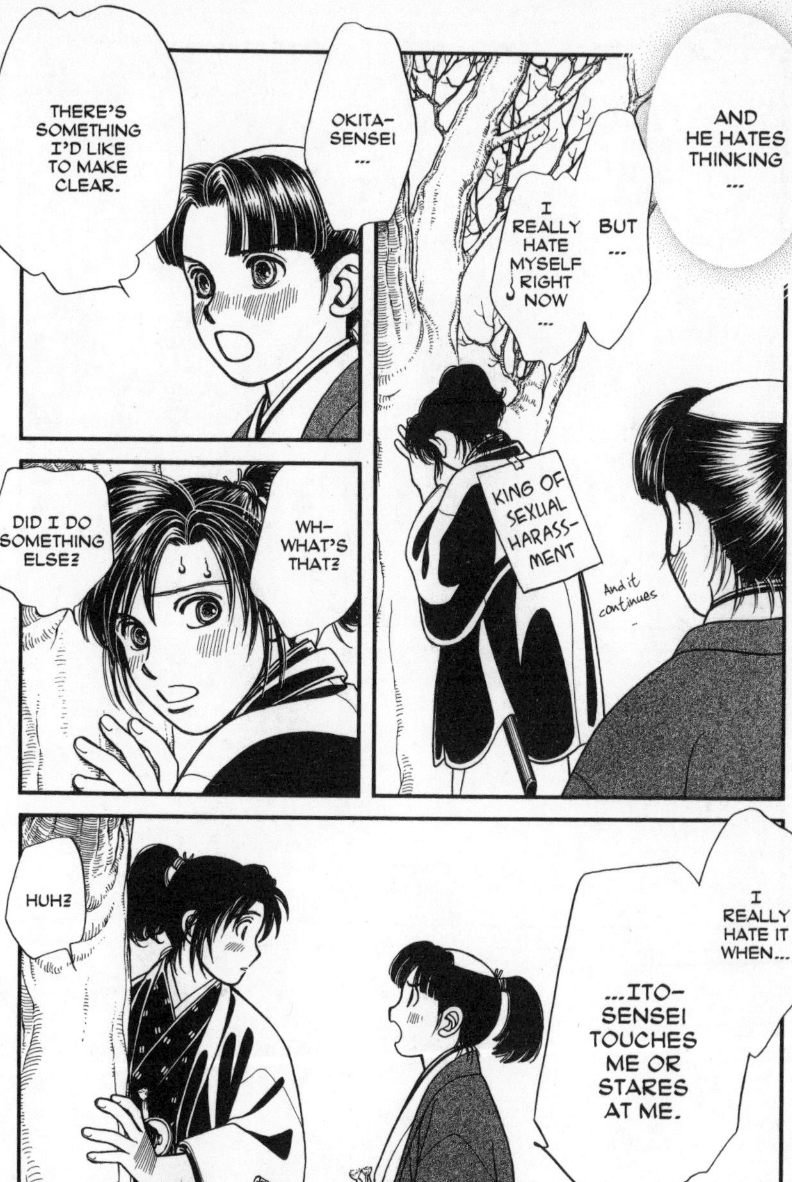
AND HE HATES THINKING ...
BUT ...
I REALLY HATE MYSELF RIGHT NOW ...
KING OF SEXUAL HARASS-MENT
And it continues
OKITA-SENSEI ...
THERE'S SOMETHING I'D LIKE TO MAKE CLEAR.
WH-WHAT'S THAT?
DID I DO SOMETHING ELSE?
I REALLY HATE IT WHEN...
...ITO-SENSEI TOUCHES ME OR STARES AT ME.
HUH?

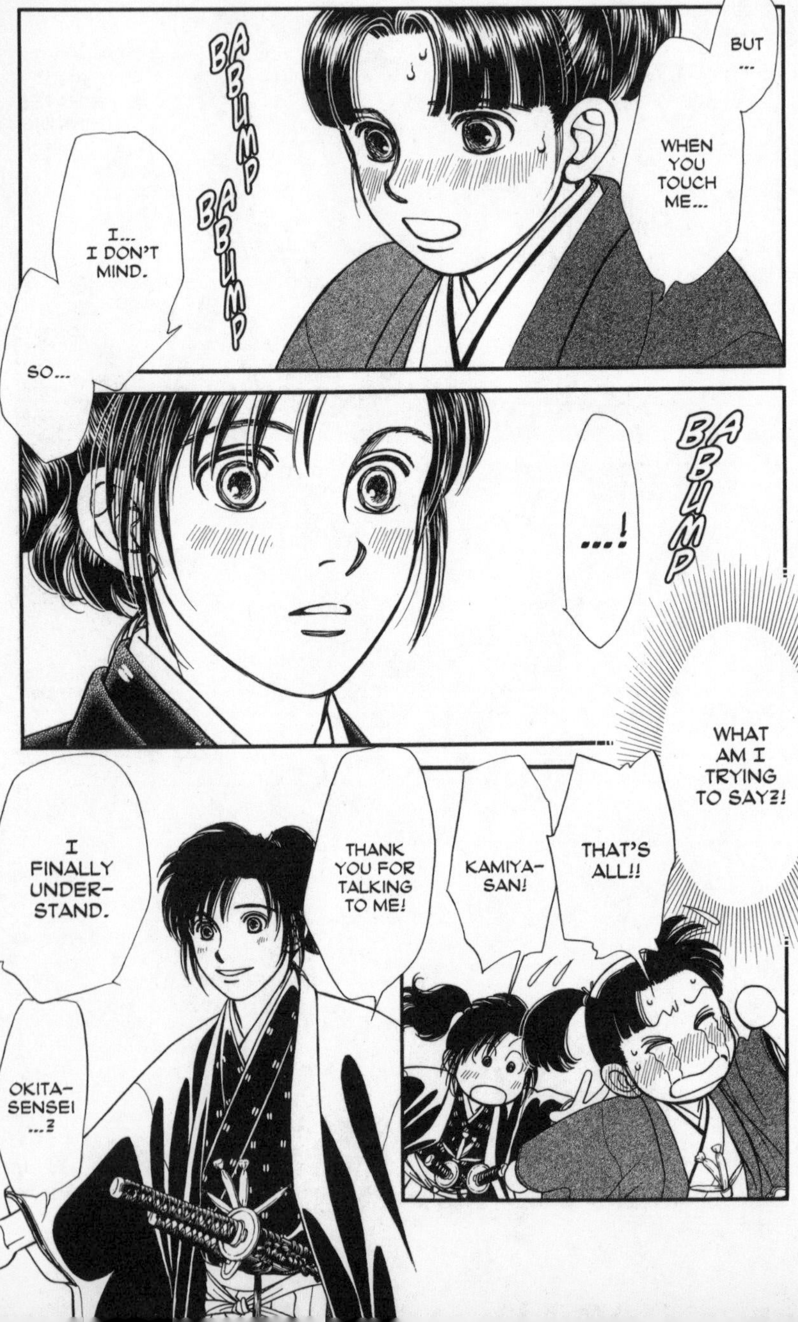
BUT...
WHEN YOU TOUCH ME...
BABUMP
BABUMP
I... I DON'T MIND.
SO...
BABUMP
...!
WHAT AM I TRYING TO SAY?!
THAT'S ALL!!
KAMIYA-SAN!
THANK YOU FOR TALKING TO ME!
I FINALLY UNDER-STAND.
OKITA-SENSEI...?

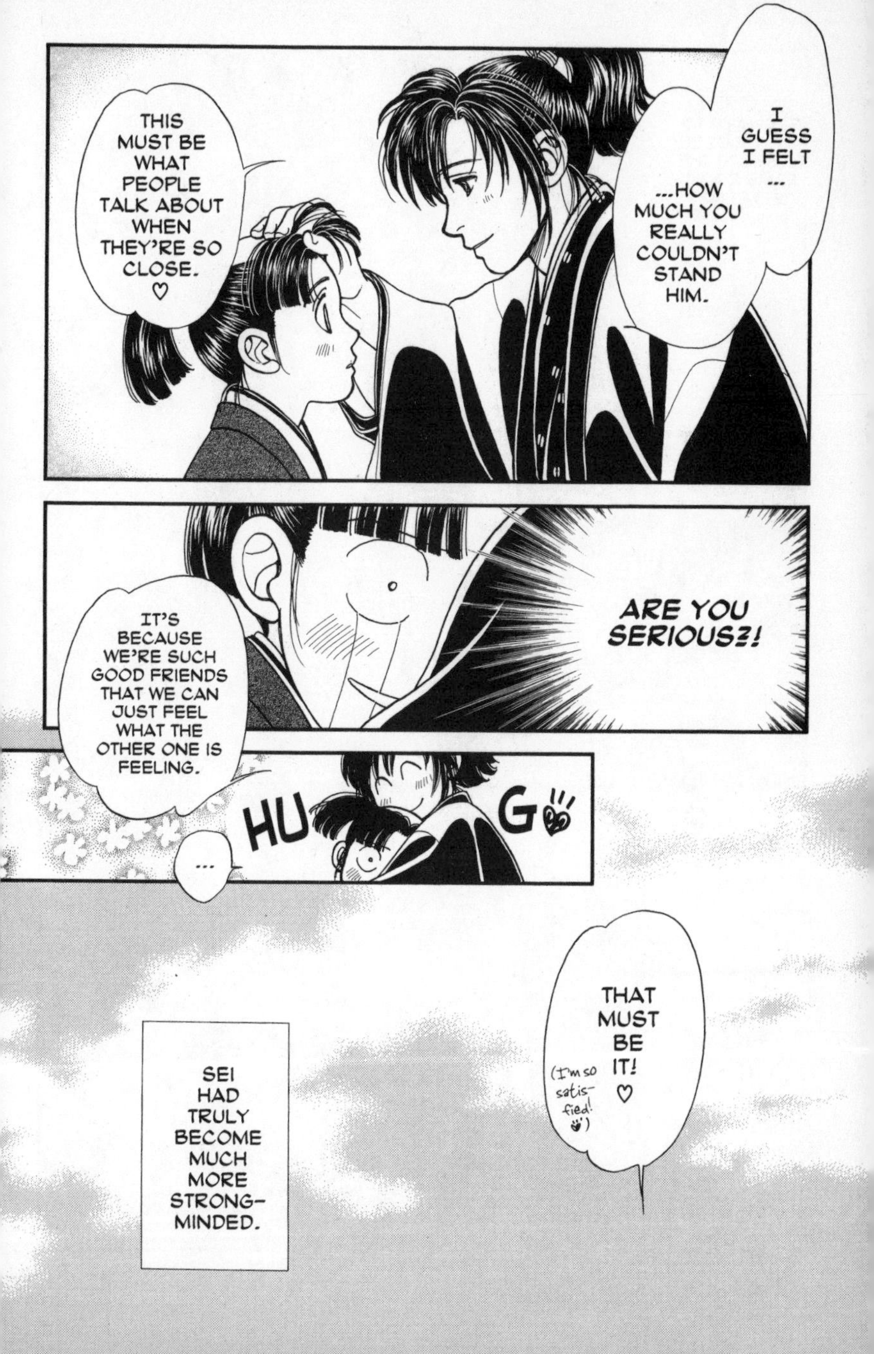
I GUESS I FELT ...
...HOW MUCH YOU REALLY COULDN'T STAND HIM.
THIS MUST BE WHAT PEOPLE TALK ABOUT WHEN THEY'RE SO CLOSE. ♡
ARE YOU SERIOUS?!
IT'S BECAUSE WE'RE SUCH GOOD FRIENDS THAT WE CAN JUST FEEL WHAT THE OTHER ONE IS FEELING.
HUG
...
THAT MUST BE IT! ♡
(I'm so satisfied!)
SEI HAD TRULY BECOME MUCH MORE STRONG-MINDED.

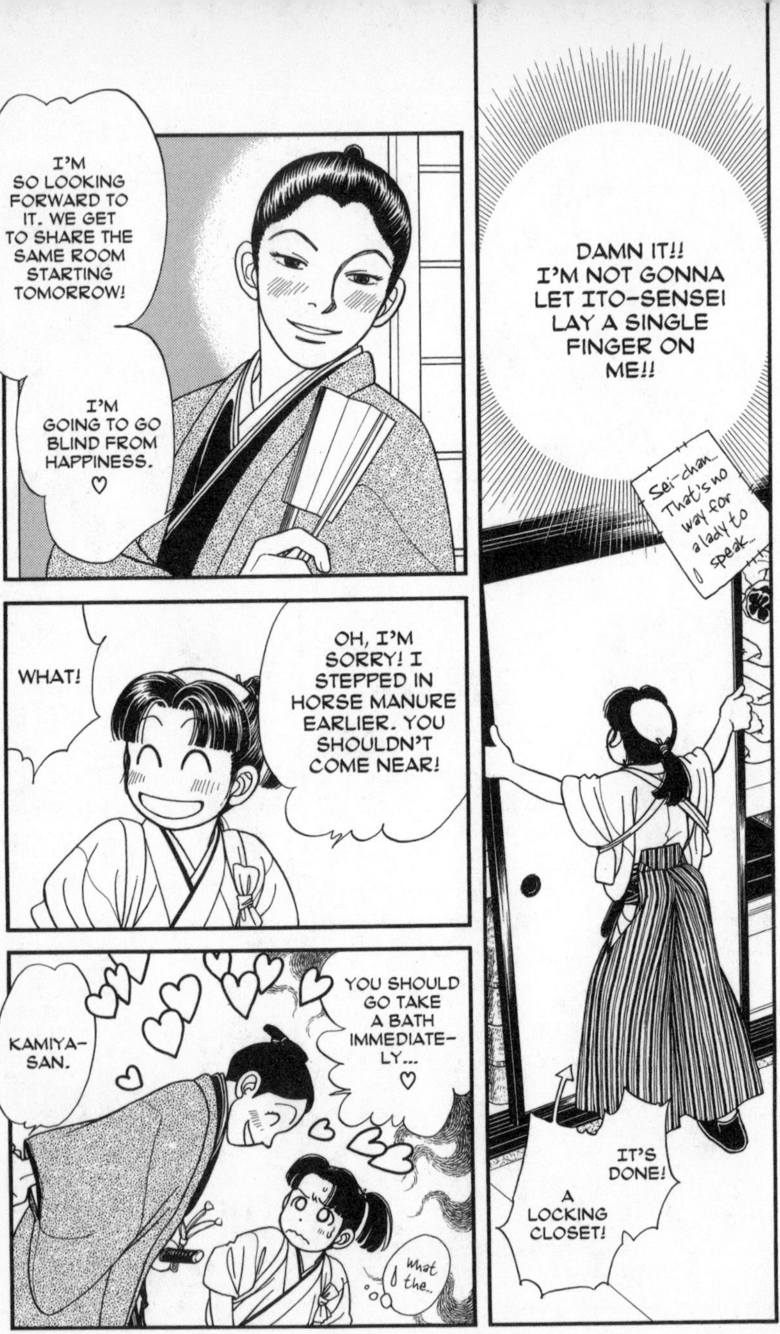
DAMN IT!! I'M NOT GONNA LET ITO-SENSEI LAY A SINGLE FINGER ON ME!!
Sei-chan... That's no way for a lady to speak...
IT'S DONE!
A LOCKING CLOSET!
I'M SO LOOKING FORWARD TO IT. WE GET TO SHARE THE SAME ROOM STARTING TOMORROW!
I'M GOING TO GO BLIND FROM HAPPINESS. ♡
OH, I'M SORRY! I STEPPED IN HORSE MANURE EARLIER. YOU SHOULDN'T COME NEAR!
WHAT!
YOU SHOULD GO TAKE A BATH IMMEDIATE-LY... ♡
KAMIYA-SAN.
What the..

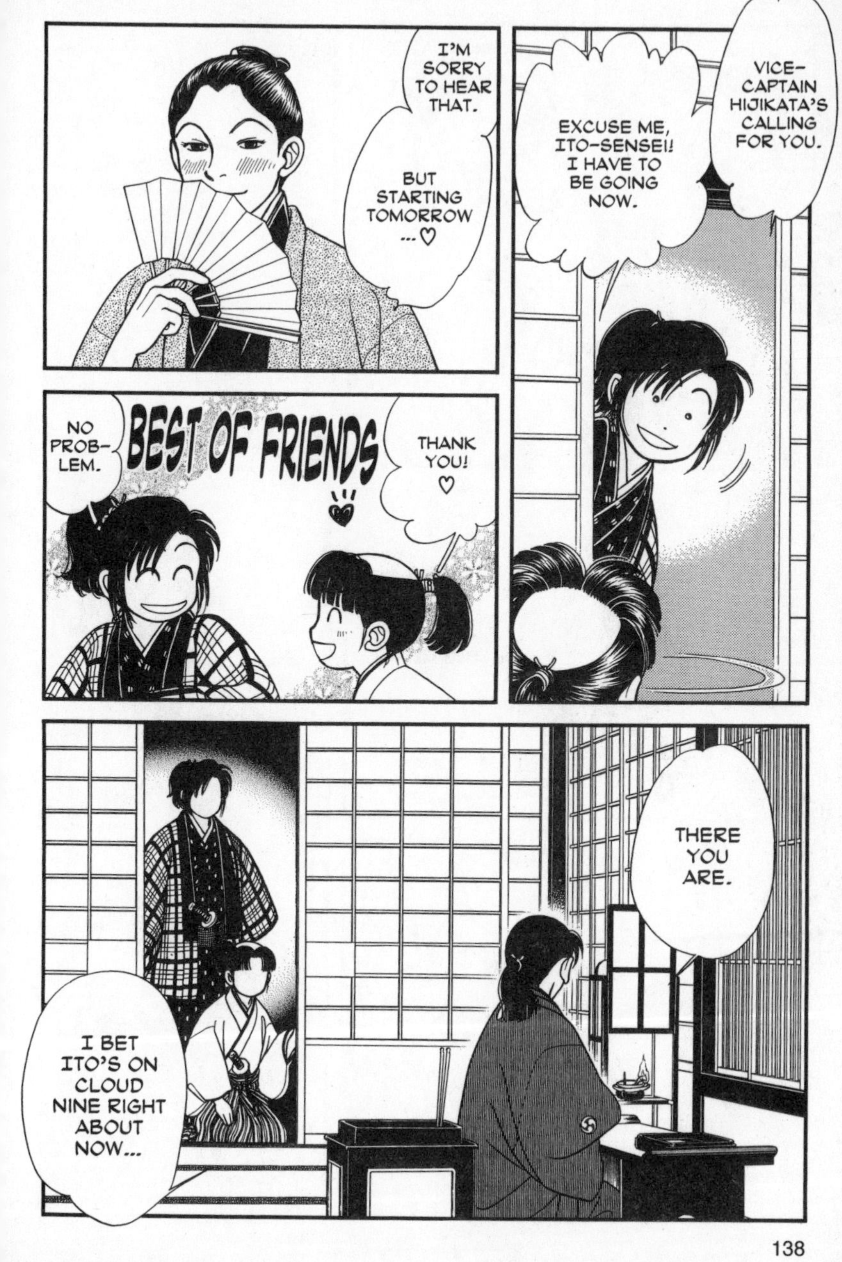
VICE-CAPTAIN HIJIKATA'S CALLING FOR YOU.
EXCUSE ME, ITO-SENSEI! I HAVE TO BE GOING NOW.
I'M SORRY TO HEAR THAT.
BUT STARTING TOMORROW ...♡
THANK YOU! ♡
BEST OF FRIENDS
NO PROBLEM.
THERE YOU ARE.
I BET ITO'S ON CLOUD NINE RIGHT ABOUT NOW...

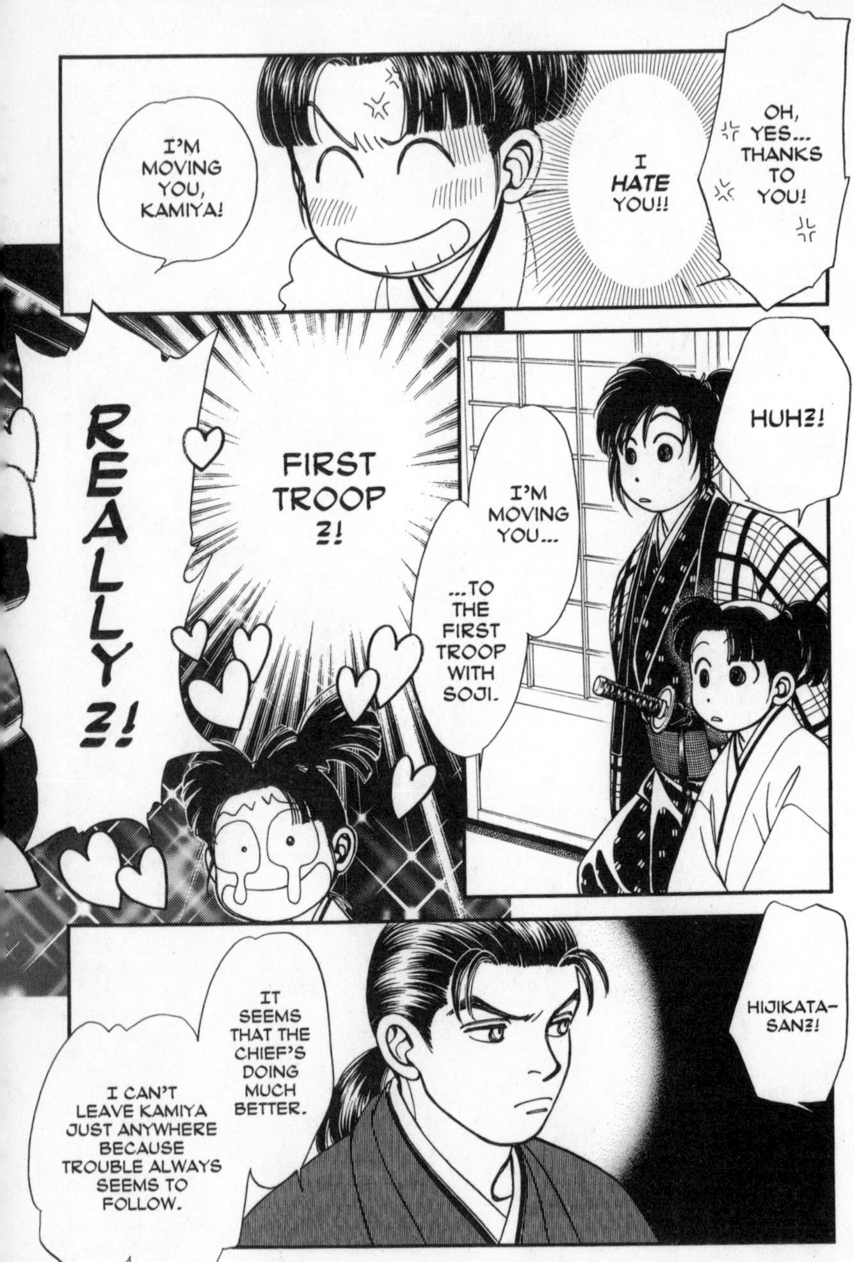
OH, YES... THANKS TO YOU!
I HATE YOU!!
I'M MOVING YOU, KAMIYA!
HUH?!
I'M MOVING YOU...
...TO THE FIRST TROOP WITH SOJI.
FIRST TROOP?!
REALLY?!
HIJIKATA-SAN?!
IT SEEMS THAT THE CHIEF'S DOING MUCH BETTER.
I CAN'T LEAVE KAMIYA JUST ANYWHERE BECAUSE TROUBLE ALWAYS SEEMS TO FOLLOW.

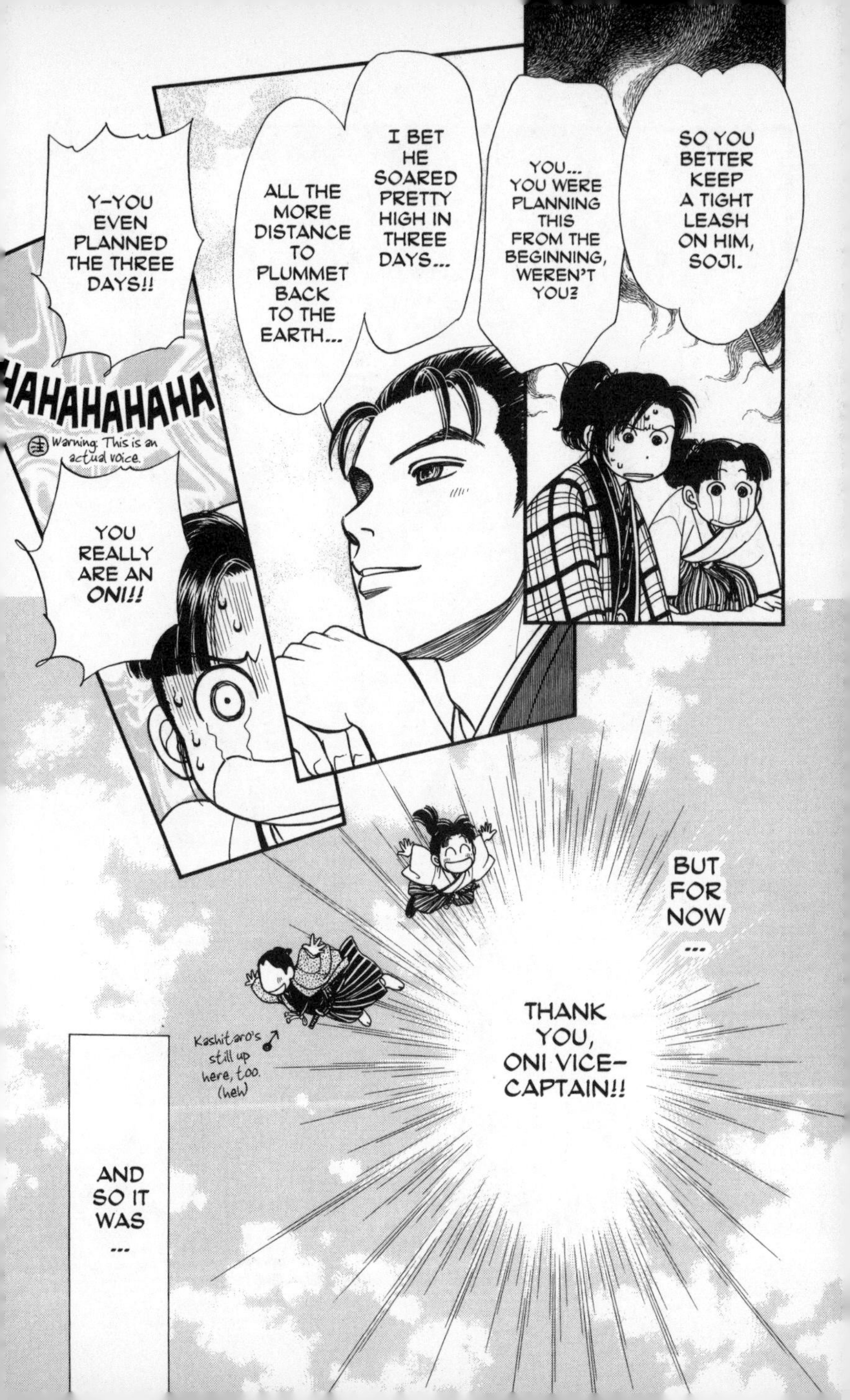
SO YOU BETTER KEEP A TIGHT LEASH ON HIM, SOJI.
YOU... YOU WERE PLANNING THIS FROM THE BEGINNING, WEREN'T YOU?
I BET HE SOARED PRETTY HIGH IN THREE DAYS...
ALL THE MORE DISTANCE TO PLUMMET BACK TO THE EARTH...
Y-YOU EVEN PLANNED THE THREE DAYS!!
HAHAHAHAHA
Warning: This is an actual voice.
YOU REALLY ARE AN ONI!!
BUT FOR NOW ...
THANK YOU, ONI VICE-CAPTAIN!!
Kashitaro's still up here, too. (heh)
AND SO IT WAS ...

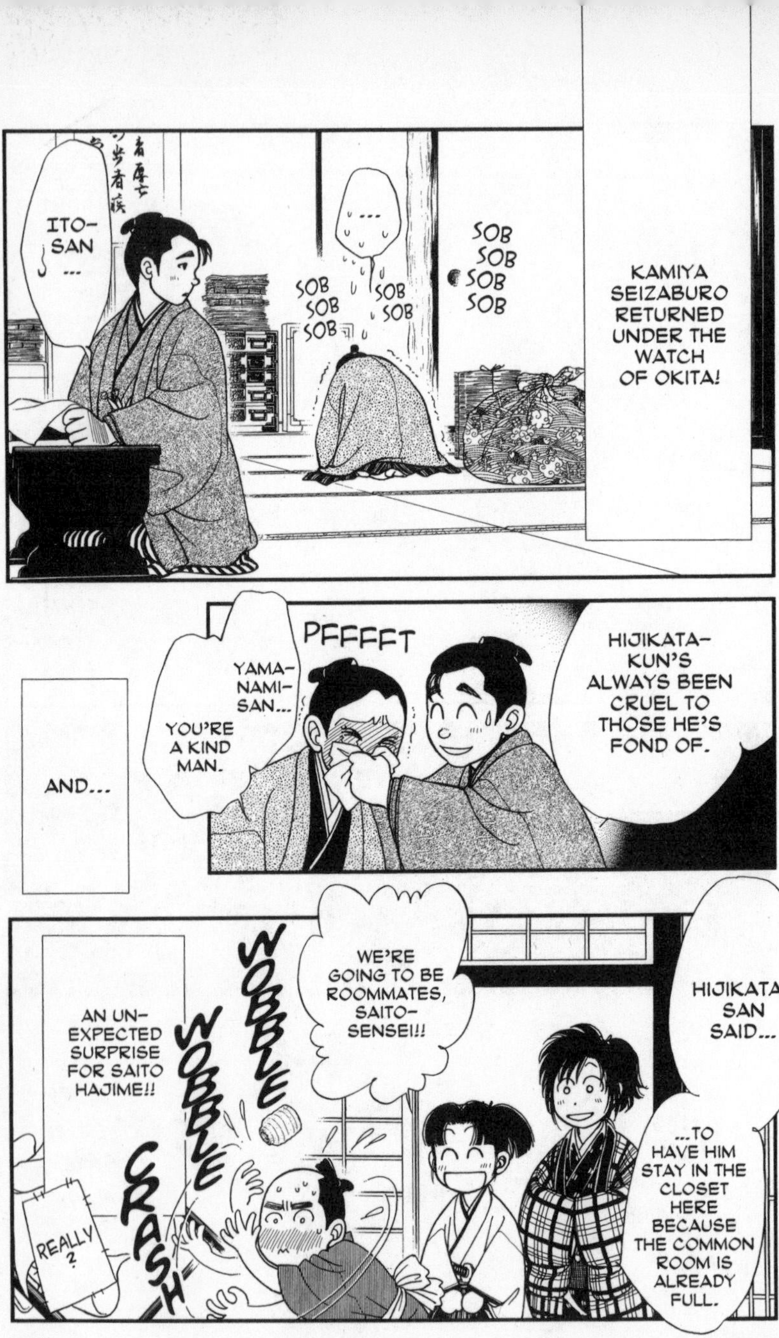

KAMIYA SEIZABURO RETURNED UNDER THE WATCH OF OKITA!
SOB SOB SOB SOB
...
SOB SOB
SOB SOB SOB
ITO-SAN...
HIJIKATA-KUN'S ALWAYS BEEN CRUEL TO THOSE HE'S FOND OF.
PFFFFT
YAMANAMI-SAN... YOU'RE A KIND MAN.
AND...
HIJIKATA-SAN SAID...
...TO HAVE HIM STAY IN THE CLOSET HERE BECAUSE THE COMMON ROOM IS ALREADY FULL.
WE'RE GOING TO BE ROOMMATES, SAITO-SENSEI!!
WOBBLE WOBBLE WOBBLE
CRASH
AN UNEXPECTED SURPRISE FOR SAITO HAJIME!!
REALLY?

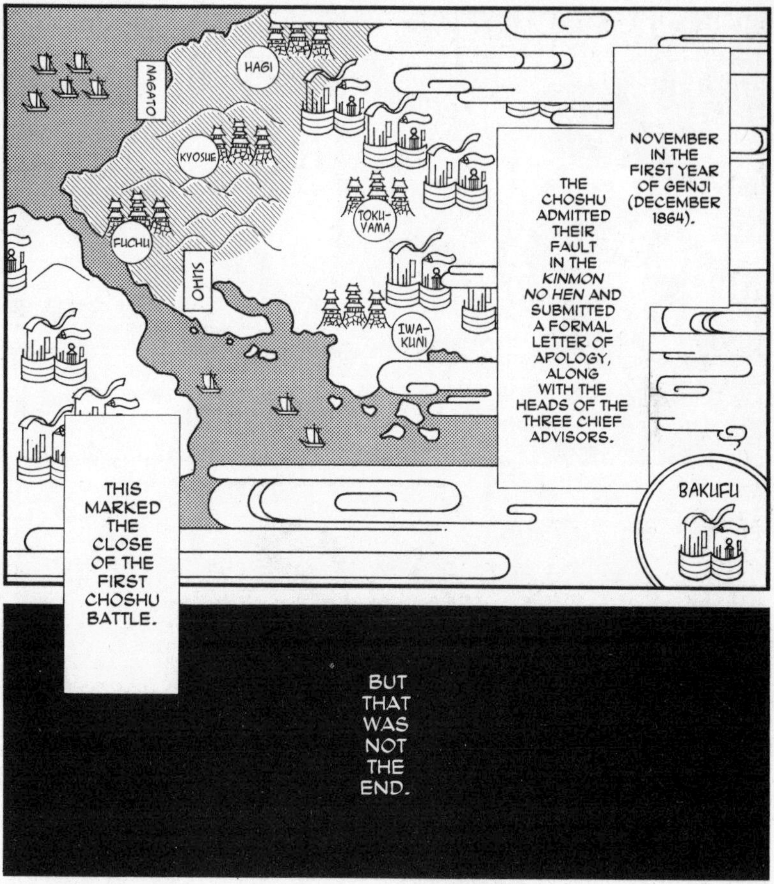
NOVEMBER IN THE FIRST YEAR OF GENJI (DECEMBER 1864).
THE CHOSHU ADMITTED THEIR FAULT IN THE *KINMON NO HEN* AND SUBMITTED A FORMAL LETTER OF APOLOGY, ALONG WITH THE HEADS OF THE THREE CHIEF ADVISORS.
HAGI
NAGATO
KYOSUE
TOKUYAMA
FUCHU
SUHO
IWAKUNI
BAKUFU
THIS MARKED THE CLOSE OF THE FIRST CHOSHU BATTLE.
BUT THAT WAS NOT THE END.

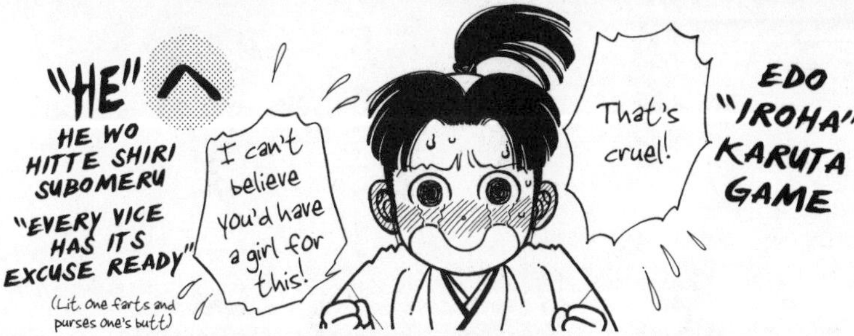
EDO "IROHA" KARUTA GAME
That's cruel!
I can't believe you'd have a girl for this!
"HE" へ
HE WO HITTE SHIRI SUBOMERU
"EVERY VICE HAS ITS EXCUSE READY"
(Lit. one farts and purses one's butt)

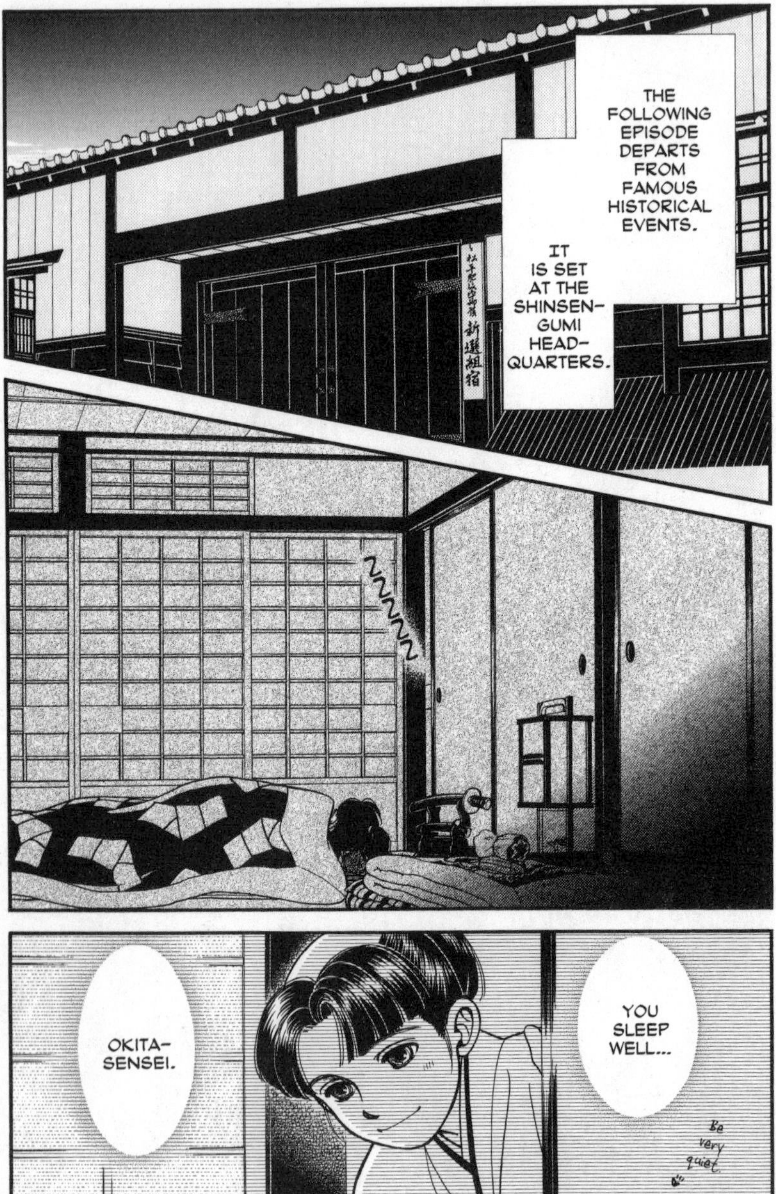
THE FOLLOWING EPISODE DEPARTS FROM FAMOUS HISTORICAL EVENTS.
IT IS SET AT THE SHINSEN-GUMI HEAD-QUARTERS.
新選組宿
ZZZZZ
YOU SLEEP WELL...
Be very quiet
OKITA-SENSEI.

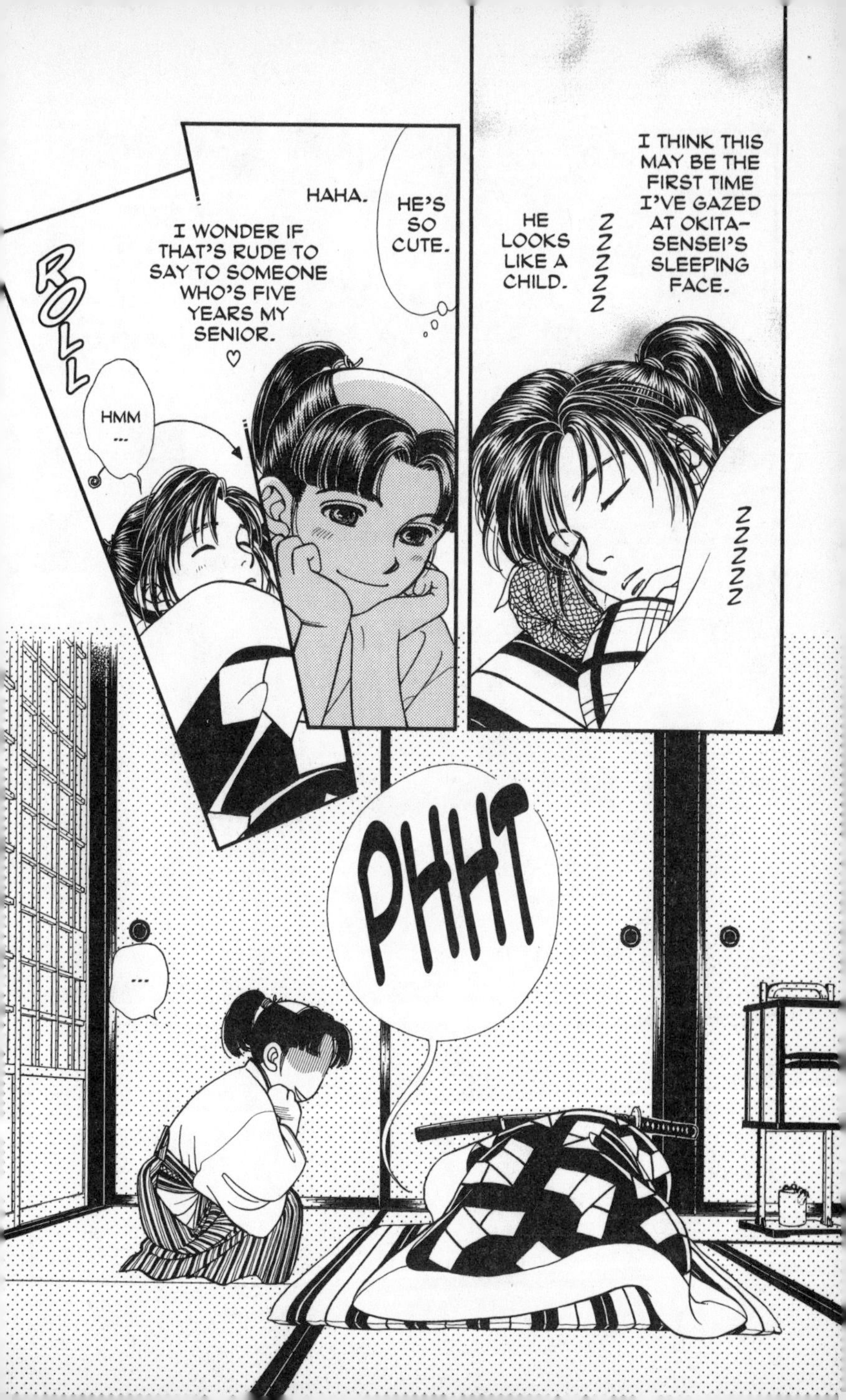
I THINK THIS MAY BE THE FIRST TIME I'VE GAZED AT OKITA-SENSEI'S SLEEPING FACE.
ZZZZZ
ZZZZZ
HE LOOKS LIKE A CHILD.
HE'S SO CUTE.
HAHA.
I WONDER IF THAT'S RUDE TO SAY TO SOMEONE WHO'S FIVE YEARS MY SENIOR. ♡
ROLL
HMM ...
PHHT
...

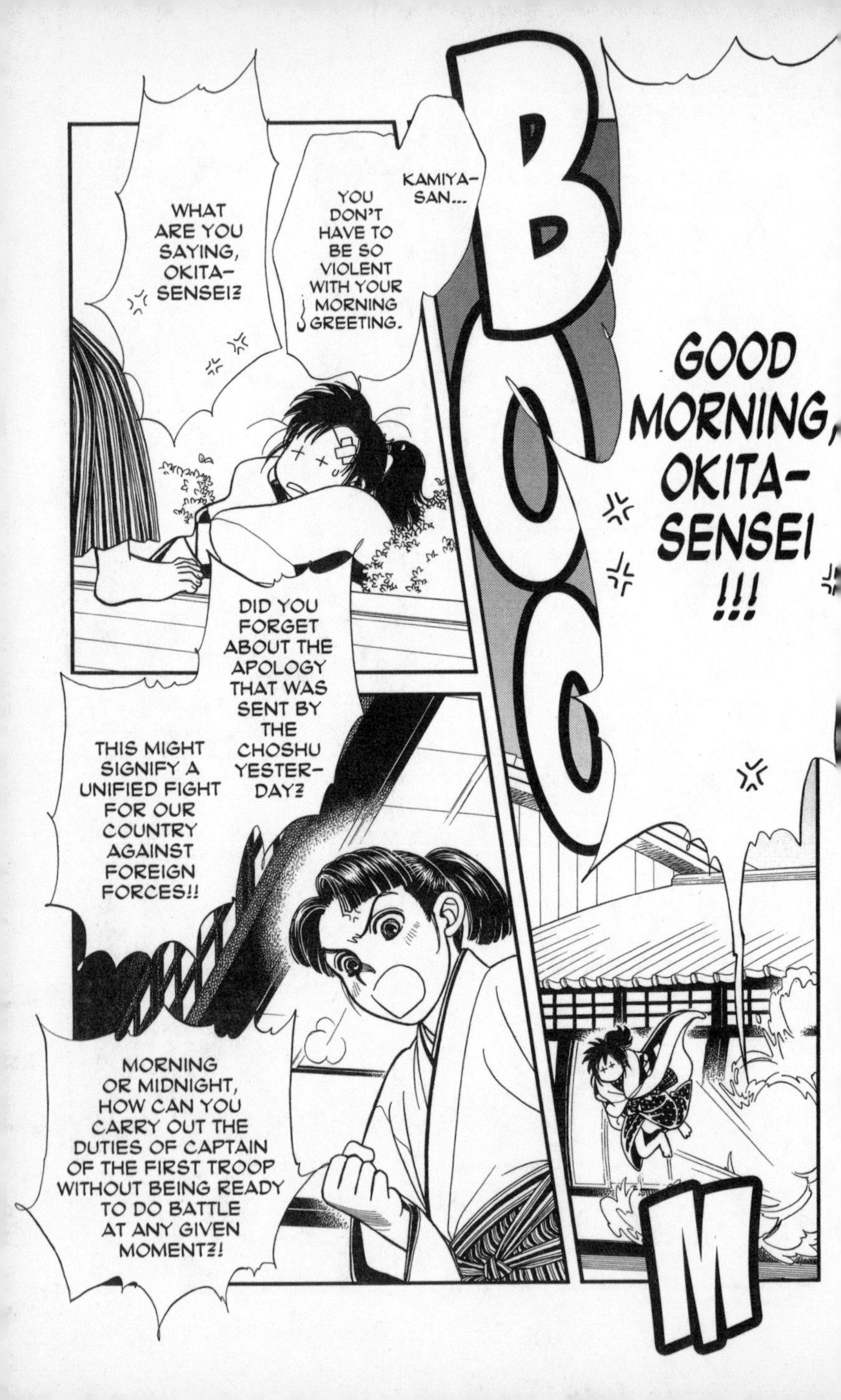
GOOD MORNING, OKITA-SENSEI!!!
BOOOM
KAMIYA-SAN... YOU DON'T HAVE TO BE SO VIOLENT WITH YOUR MORNING GREETING.
WHAT ARE YOU SAYING, OKITA-SENSEI!?
DID YOU FORGET ABOUT THE APOLOGY THAT WAS SENT BY THE CHOSHU YESTER-DAY!?
THIS MIGHT SIGNIFY A UNIFIED FIGHT FOR OUR COUNTRY AGAINST FOREIGN FORCES!!
MORNING OR MIDNIGHT, HOW CAN YOU CARRY OUT THE DUTIES OF CAPTAIN OF THE FIRST TROOP WITHOUT BEING READY TO DO BATTLE AT ANY GIVEN MOMENT!?!

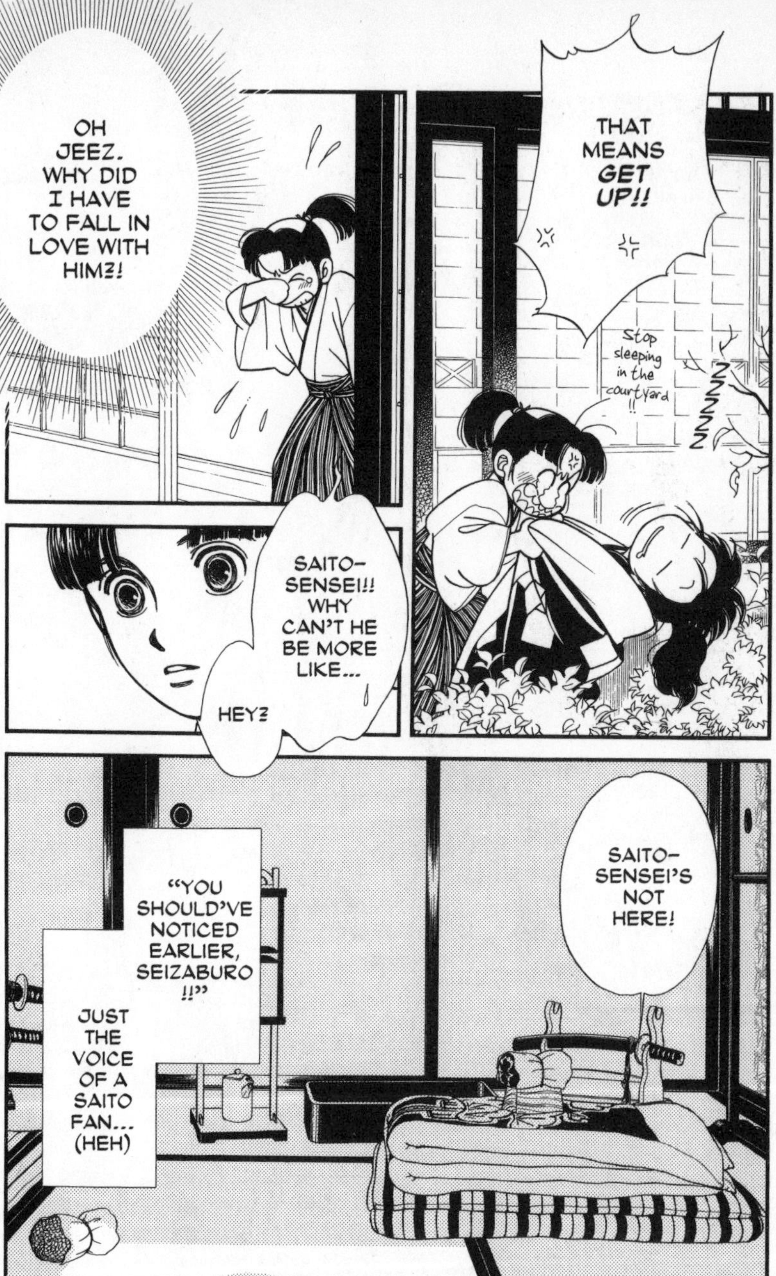
THAT MEANS GET UP!!
Stop sleeping in the courtyard!!
ZZZZZ
OH JEEZ. WHY DID I HAVE TO FALL IN LOVE WITH HIM?!
SAITO-SENSEI!!! WHY CAN'T HE BE MORE LIKE...
HEY?
SAITO-SENSEI'S NOT HERE!
"YOU SHOULD'VE NOTICED EARLIER, SEIZABURO!!"
JUST THE VOICE OF A SAITO FAN... (HEH)

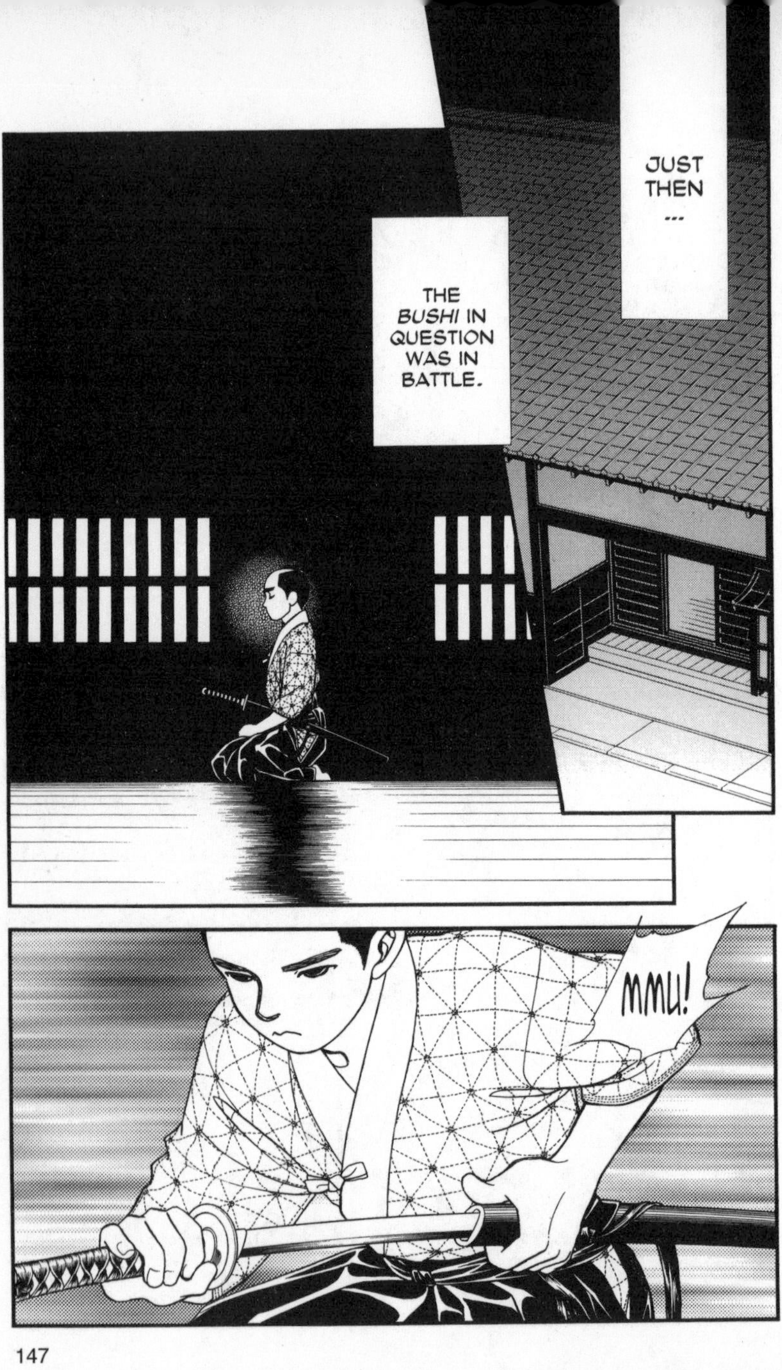
JUST THEN ...
THE *BUSHI* IN QUESTION WAS IN BATTLE.
MMU!

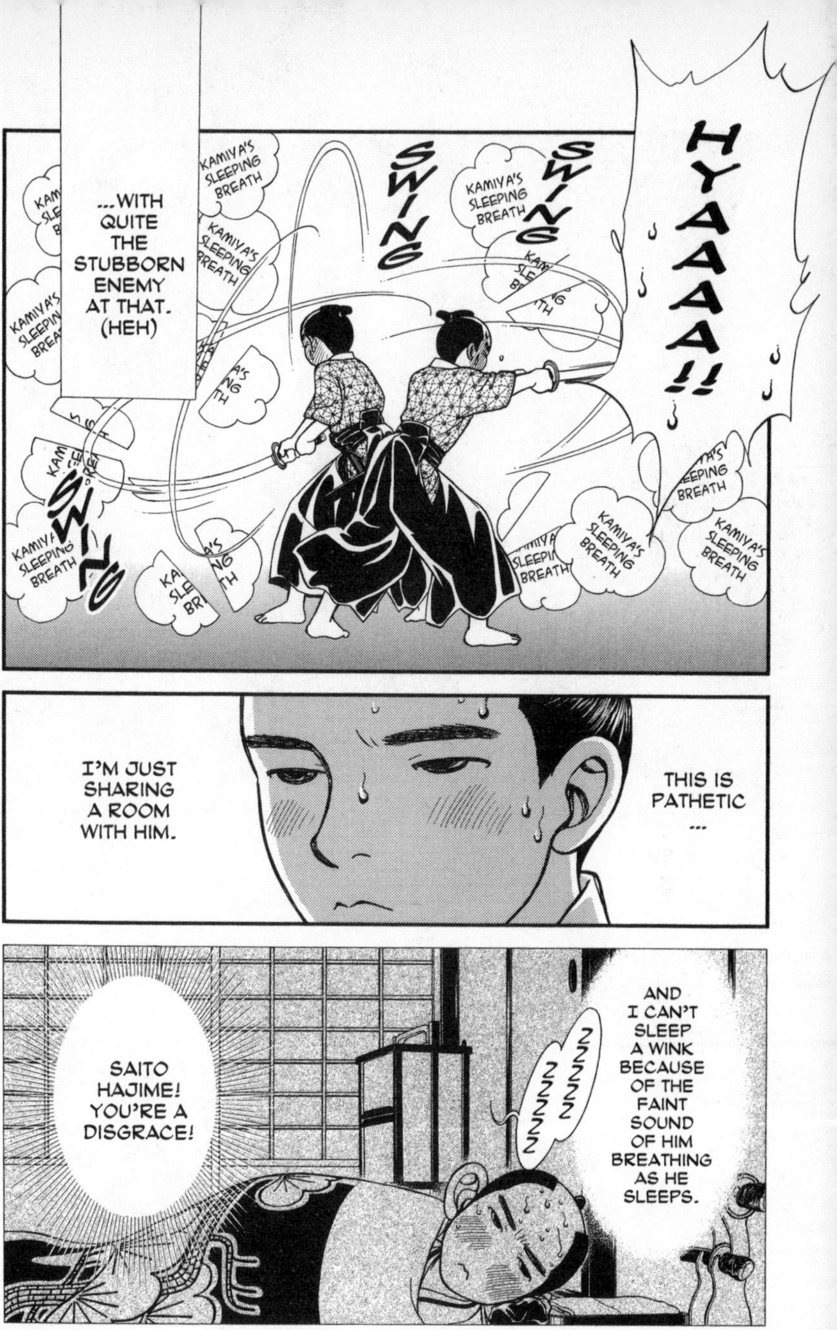
HYAAAA!!
SWING
KAMIYA'S SLEEPING BREATH
SWING
KAMIYA'S SLEEPING BREATH
...WITH QUITE THE STUBBORN ENEMY AT THAT. (HEH)
KAMIYA'S SLEEPING BREATH
KAMIYA'S SLEEPING BREATH
KAMIYA'S SLEEPING BREATH
SWING
KAMIYA'S SLEEPING BREATH
KAMIYA'S SLEEPING BREATH
THIS IS PATHETIC ...
I'M JUST SHARING A ROOM WITH HIM.
AND I CAN'T SLEEP A WINK BECAUSE OF THE FAINT SOUND OF HIM BREATHING AS HE SLEEPS.
ZZZZZ ZZZZZ
SAITO HAJIME! YOU'RE A DISGRACE!

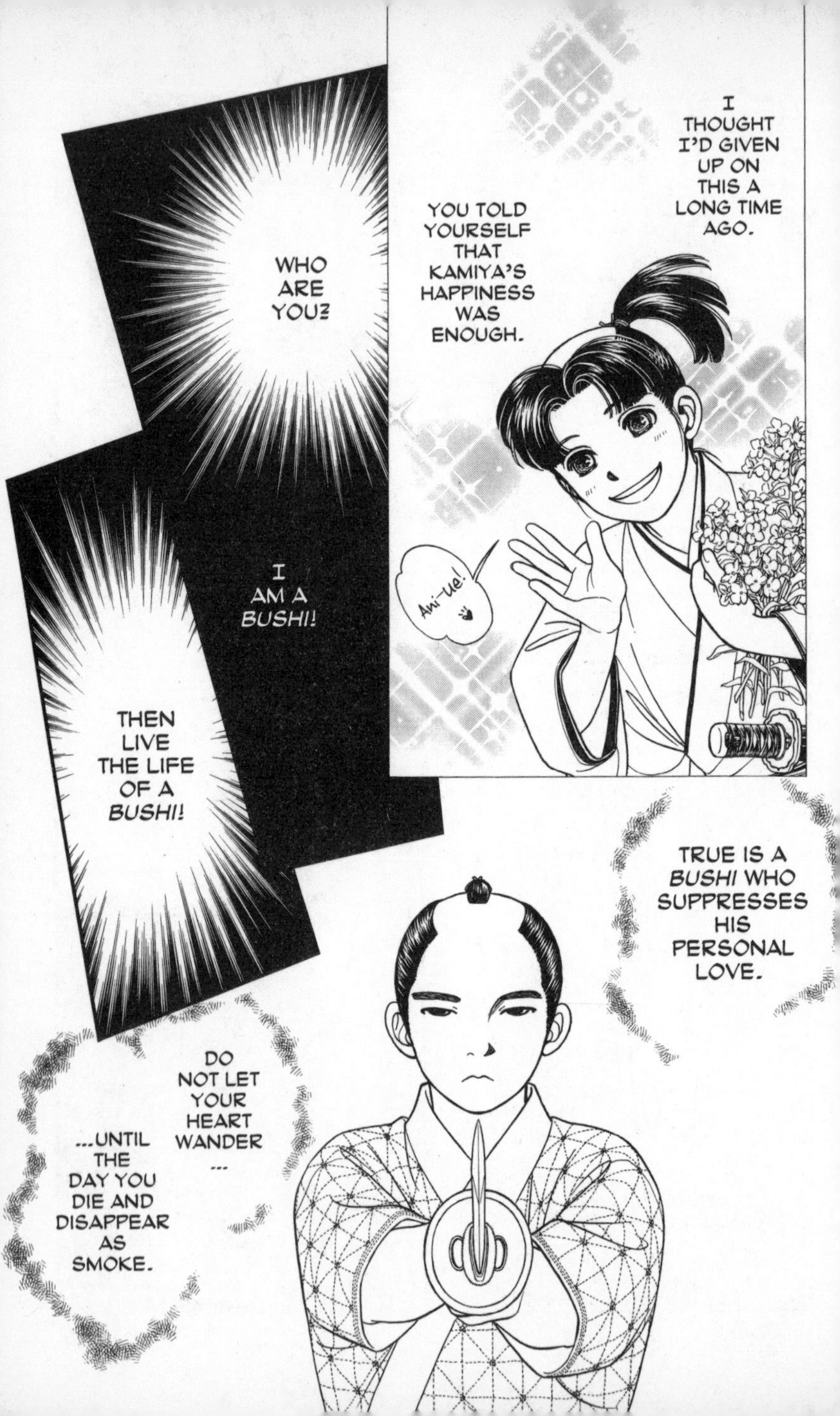
I THOUGHT I'D GIVEN UP ON THIS A LONG TIME AGO.
YOU TOLD YOURSELF THAT KAMIYA'S HAPPINESS WAS ENOUGH.
Ani-ue!
WHO ARE YOU?
I AM A *BUSHI*!
THEN LIVE THE LIFE OF A *BUSHI*!
TRUE IS A *BUSHI* WHO SUPPRESSES HIS PERSONAL LOVE.
DO NOT LET YOUR HEART WANDER...
...UNTIL THE DAY YOU DIE AND DISAPPEAR AS SMOKE.

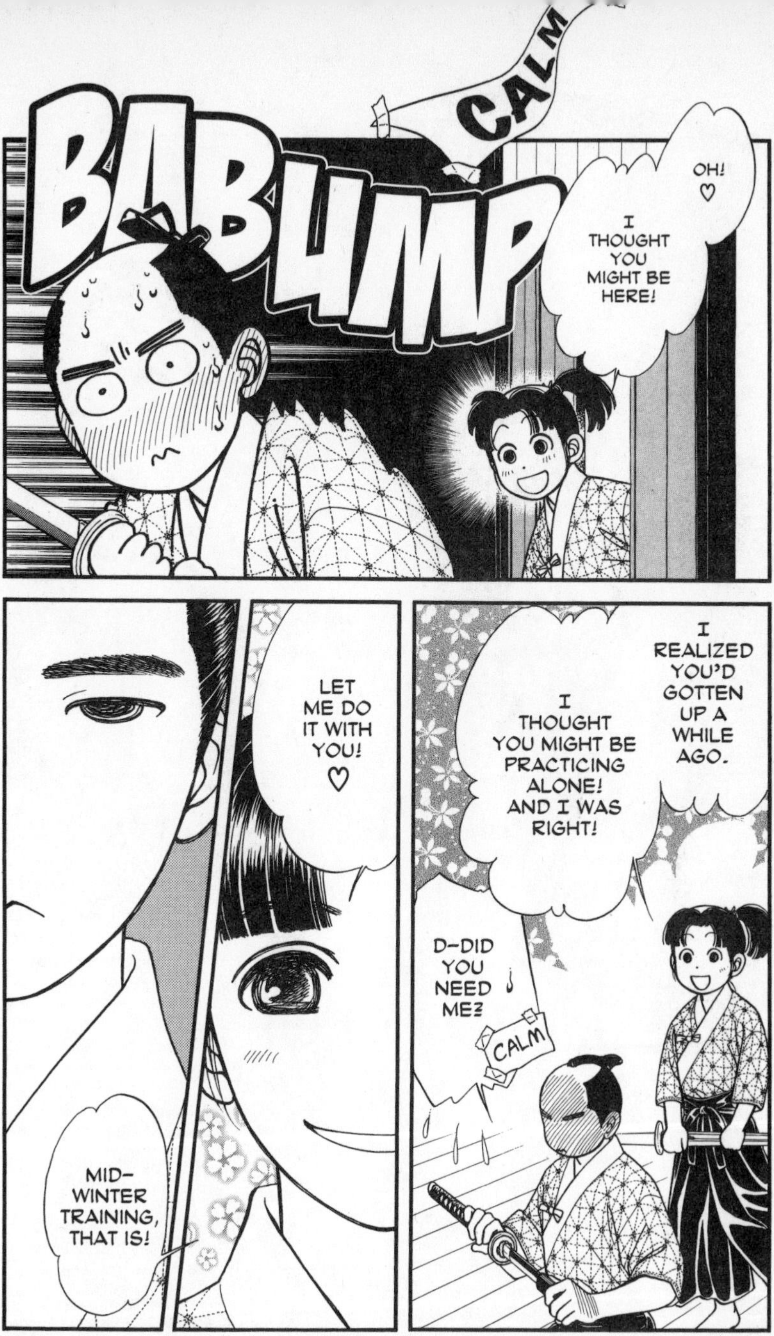
CALM
OH! ♡
I THOUGHT YOU MIGHT BE HERE!
BABUMP
I REALIZED YOU'D GOTTEN UP A WHILE AGO.
I THOUGHT YOU MIGHT BE PRACTICING ALONE! AND I WAS RIGHT!
D-DID YOU NEED ME?
CALM
LET ME DO IT WITH YOU! ♡
MID-WINTER TRAINING, THAT IS!

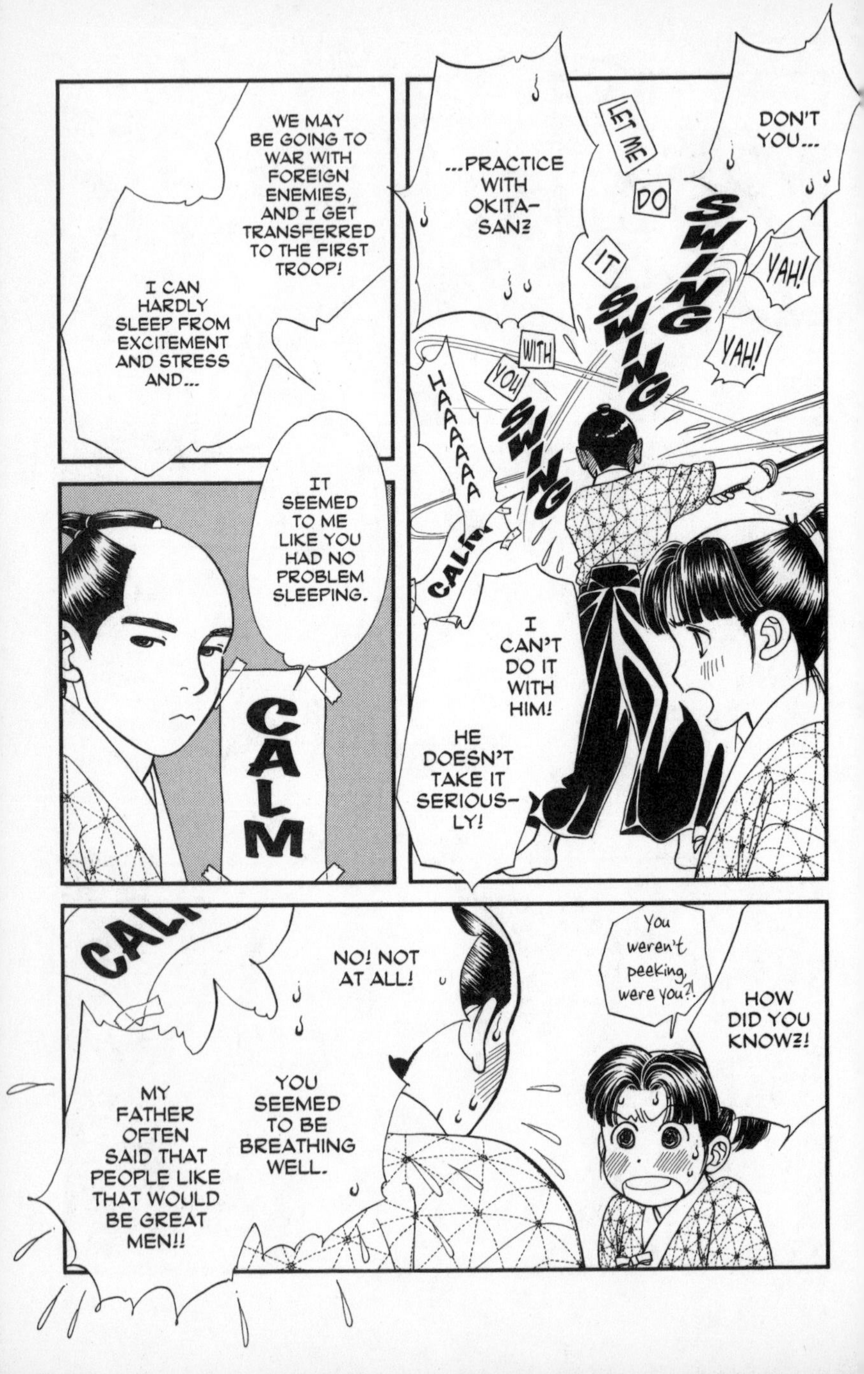

DON'T YOU...
LET ME DO IT WITH YOU
...PRACTICE WITH OKITA-SAN?
SWING
YAH!
YAH!
SWING
SWING
HAAAAAA
CALM
I CAN'T DO IT WITH HIM!
HE DOESN'T TAKE IT SERIOUS-LY!
WE MAY BE GOING TO WAR WITH FOREIGN ENEMIES, AND I GET TRANSFERRED TO THE FIRST TROOP!
I CAN HARDLY SLEEP FROM EXCITEMENT AND STRESS AND...
IT SEEMED TO ME LIKE YOU HAD NO PROBLEM SLEEPING.
CALM
You weren't peeking, were you?!
HOW DID YOU KNOW?!
NO! NOT AT ALL!
YOU SEEMED TO BE BREATHING WELL.
MY FATHER OFTEN SAID THAT PEOPLE LIKE THAT WOULD BE GREAT MEN!!

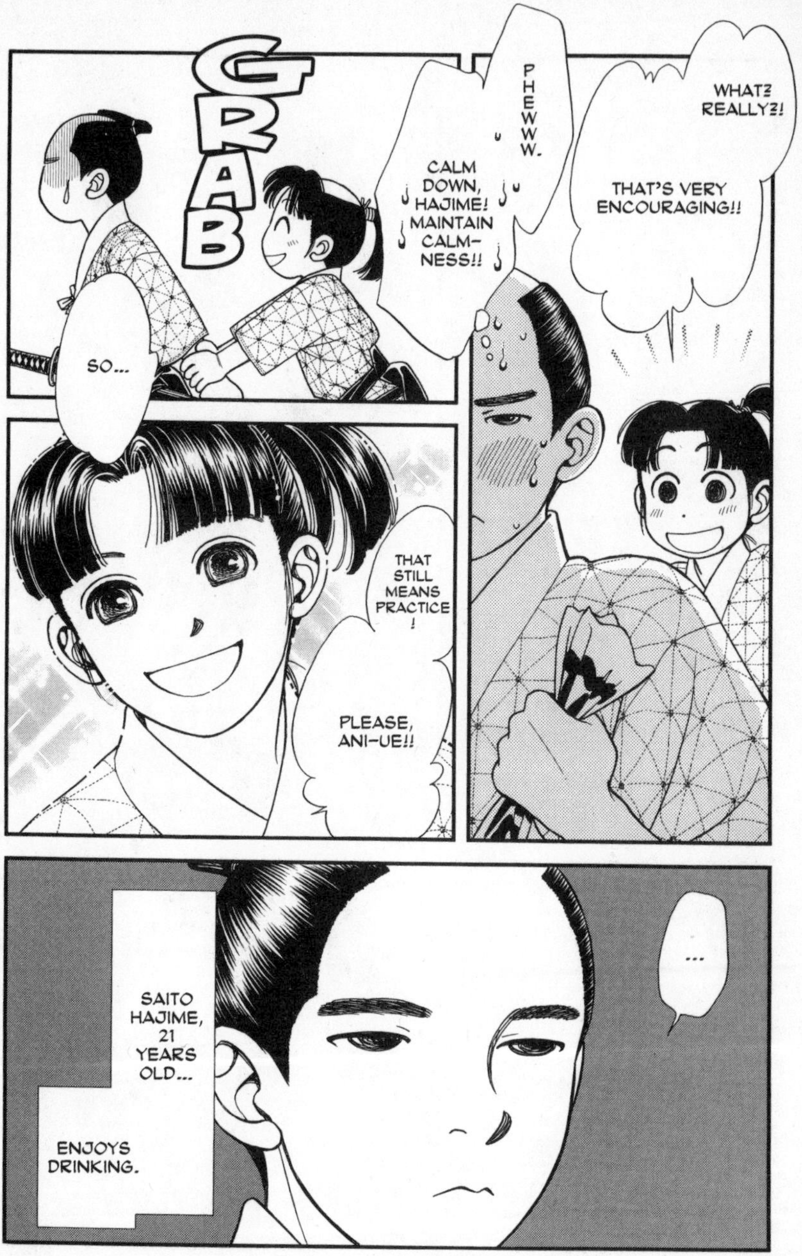
WHAT?! REALLY?!
THAT'S VERY ENCOURAGING!!
PHEWWW.
CALM DOWN, HAJIME! MAINTAIN CALMNESS!!
GRAB
SO...
THAT STILL MEANS PRACTICE!
PLEASE, ANI-UE!!
...
SAITO HAJIME, 21 YEARS OLD...
ENJOYS DRINKING.

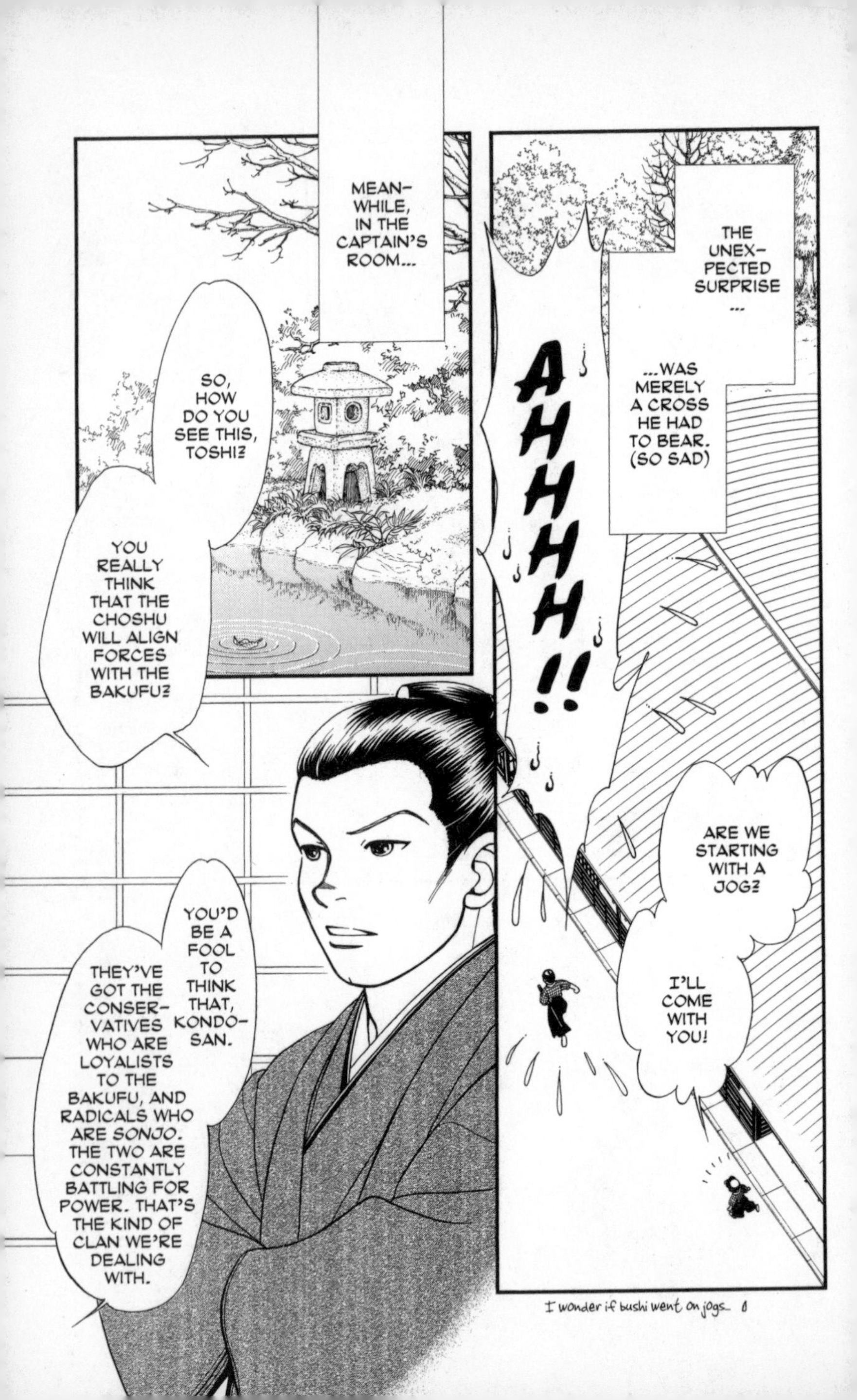
THE UNEXPECTED SURPRISE...
...WAS MERELY A CROSS HE HAD TO BEAR. (SO SAD)
AHHHH!!
ARE WE STARTING WITH A JOG?
I'LL COME WITH YOU!
MEANWHILE, IN THE CAPTAIN'S ROOM...
SO, HOW DO YOU SEE THIS, TOSHI?
YOU REALLY THINK THAT THE CHOSHU WILL ALIGN FORCES WITH THE BAKUFU?
YOU'D BE A FOOL TO THINK THAT, KONDO-SAN.
THEY'VE GOT THE CONSERVATIVES WHO ARE LOYALISTS TO THE BAKUFU, AND RADICALS WHO ARE *SONJO*. THE TWO ARE CONSTANTLY BATTLING FOR POWER. THAT'S THE KIND OF CLAN WE'RE DEALING WITH.
I wonder if bushi went on jogs ♪

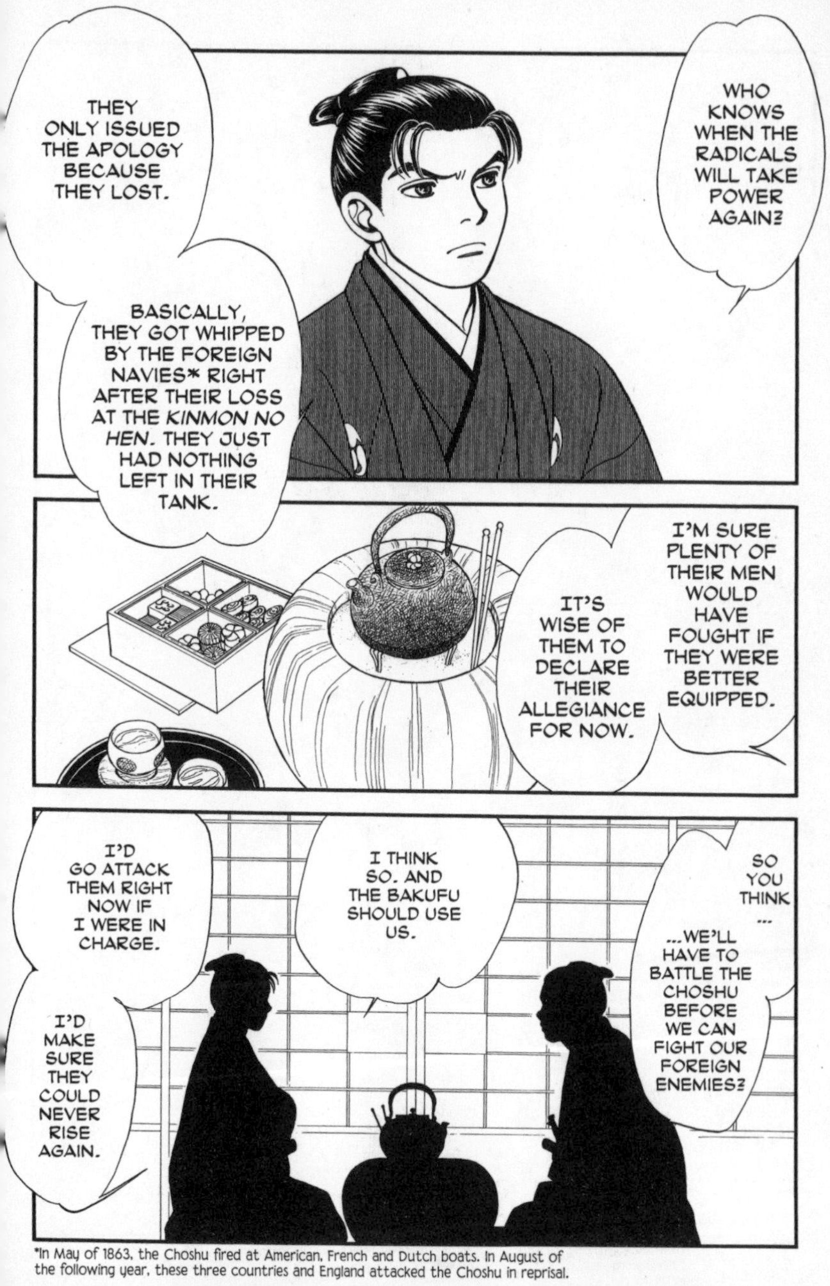
WHO KNOWS WHEN THE RADICALS WILL TAKE POWER AGAIN?
THEY ONLY ISSUED THE APOLOGY BECAUSE THEY LOST.
BASICALLY, THEY GOT WHIPPED BY THE FOREIGN NAVIES* RIGHT AFTER THEIR LOSS AT THE *KINMON NO HEN*. THEY JUST HAD NOTHING LEFT IN THEIR TANK.
I'M SURE PLENTY OF THEIR MEN WOULD HAVE FOUGHT IF THEY WERE BETTER EQUIPPED.
IT'S WISE OF THEM TO DECLARE THEIR ALLEGIANCE FOR NOW.
SO YOU THINK ...
...WE'LL HAVE TO BATTLE THE CHOSHU BEFORE WE CAN FIGHT OUR FOREIGN ENEMIES?
I THINK SO. AND THE BAKUFU SHOULD USE US.
I'D GO ATTACK THEM RIGHT NOW IF I WERE IN CHARGE.
I'D MAKE SURE THEY COULD NEVER RISE AGAIN.

*In May of 1863, the Choshu fired at American, French and Dutch boats. In August of the following year, these three countries and England attacked the Choshu in reprisal.

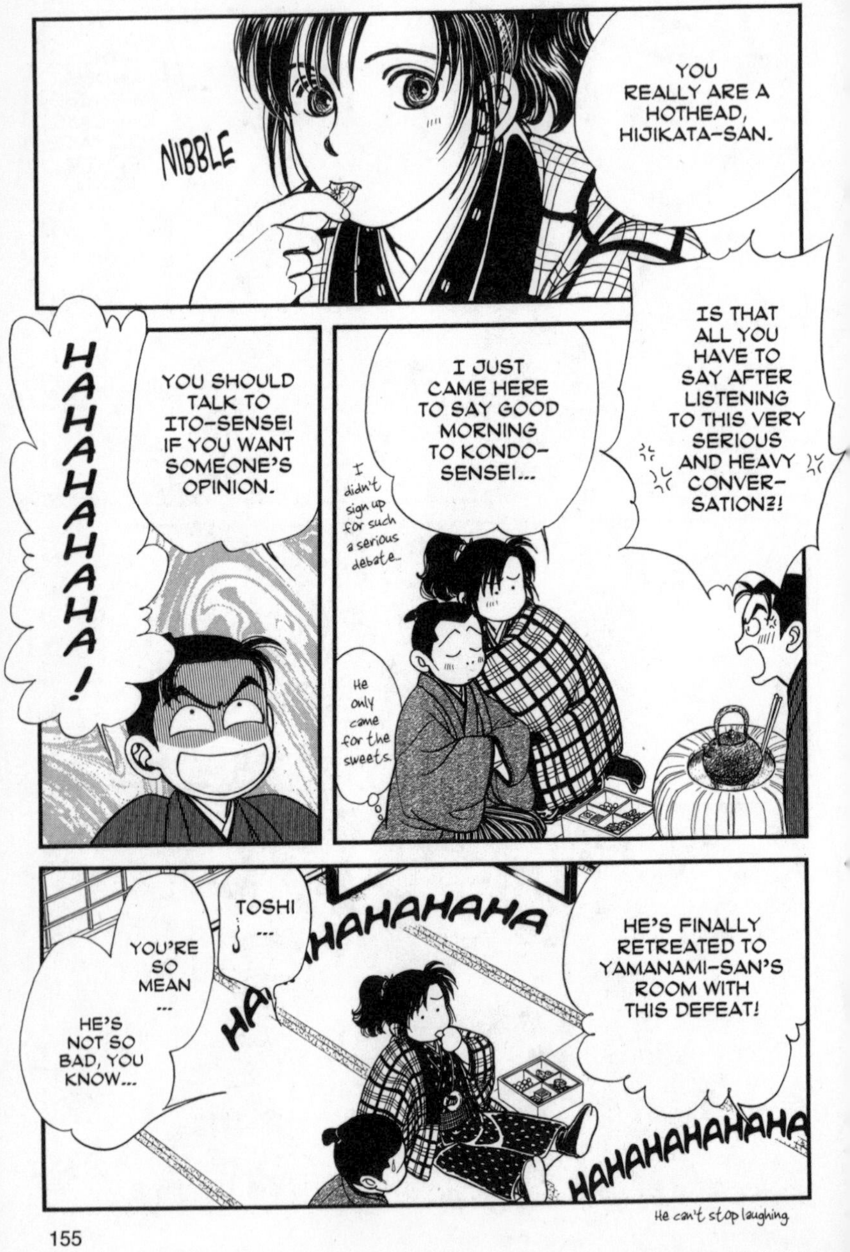
YOU REALLY ARE A HOTHEAD, HIJIKATA-SAN.
NIBBLE
IS THAT ALL YOU HAVE TO SAY AFTER LISTENING TO THIS VERY SERIOUS AND HEAVY CONVER-SATION?!
I JUST CAME HERE TO SAY GOOD MORNING TO KONDO-SENSEI...
I didn't sign up for such a serious debate...
He only came for the sweets.
YOU SHOULD TALK TO ITO-SENSEI IF YOU WANT SOMEONE'S OPINION.
HAHAHAHAHAHAHA!
HE'S FINALLY RETREATED TO YAMANAMI-SAN'S ROOM WITH THIS DEFEAT!
HAHAHAHAHAHA
HAHAHAHAHA
TOSHI...
YOU'RE SO MEAN...
HE'S NOT SO BAD, YOU KNOW...
He can't stop laughing

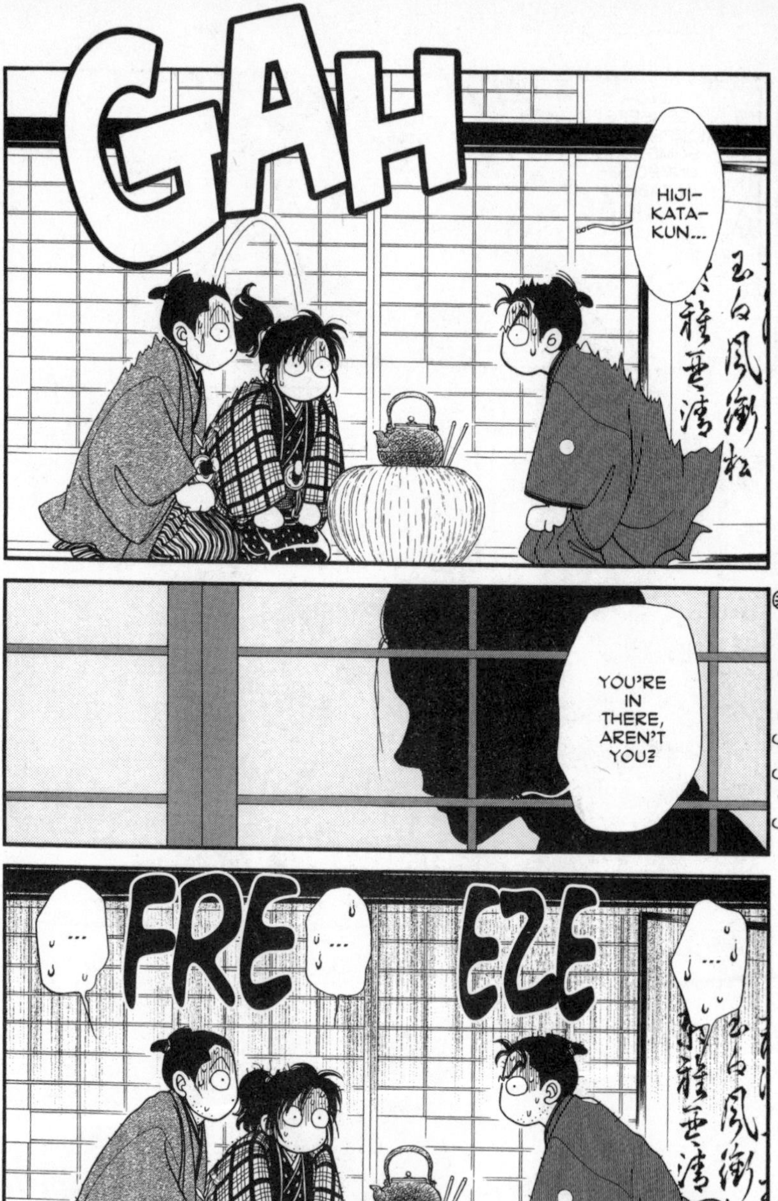
GAH
HIJI-KATA-KUN...
YOU'RE IN THERE, AREN'T YOU?
(注) Dramatic stage lighting.
FREEZE
...
...
...

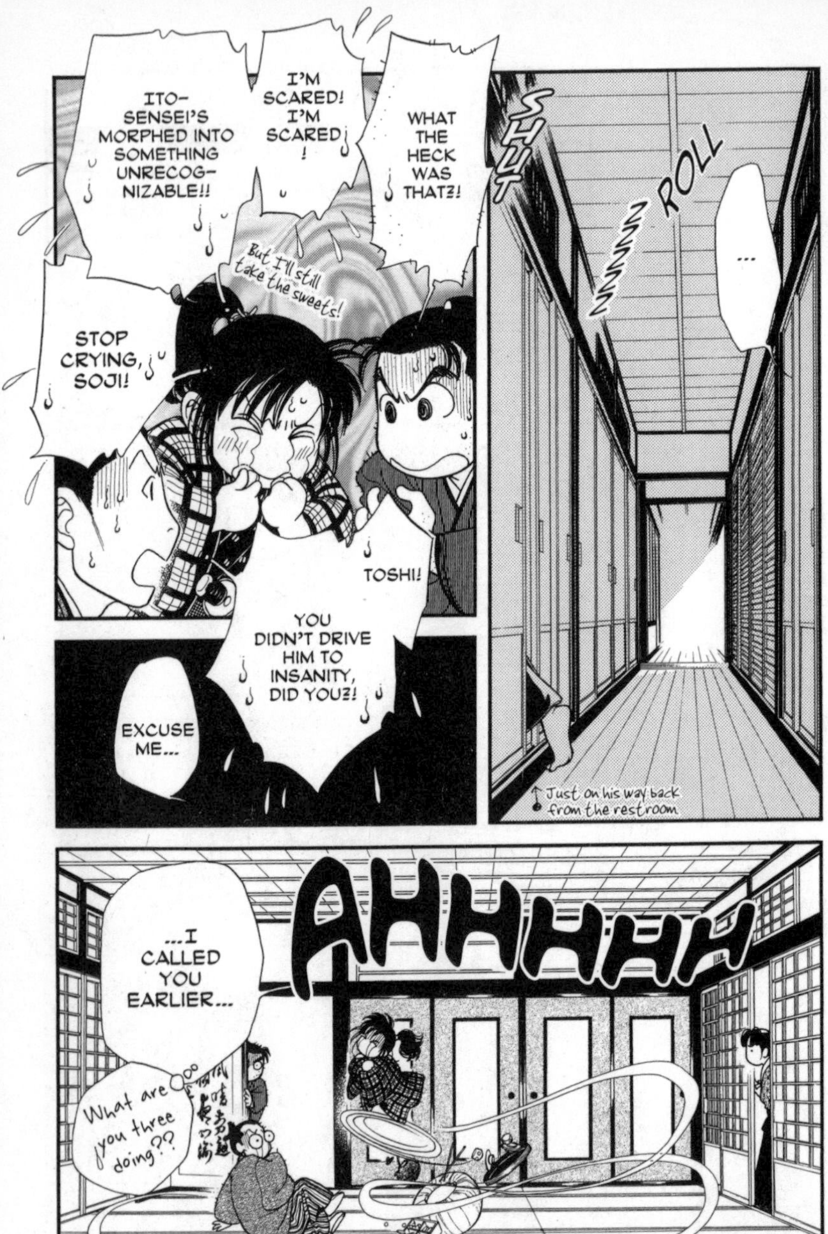
SHUT
ROLL
NNNNNN
...
Just on his way back from the restroom
WHAT THE HECK WAS THAT?!
I'M SCARED! I'M SCARED!
ITO-SENSEI'S MORPHED INTO SOMETHING UNRECOGNIZABLE!!
But I'll still take the sweets!
STOP CRYING, SOJI!
TOSHI!
YOU DIDN'T DRIVE HIM TO INSANITY, DID YOU?!
EXCUSE ME...
AHHHHHH
...I CALLED YOU EARLIER...
What are you three doing??

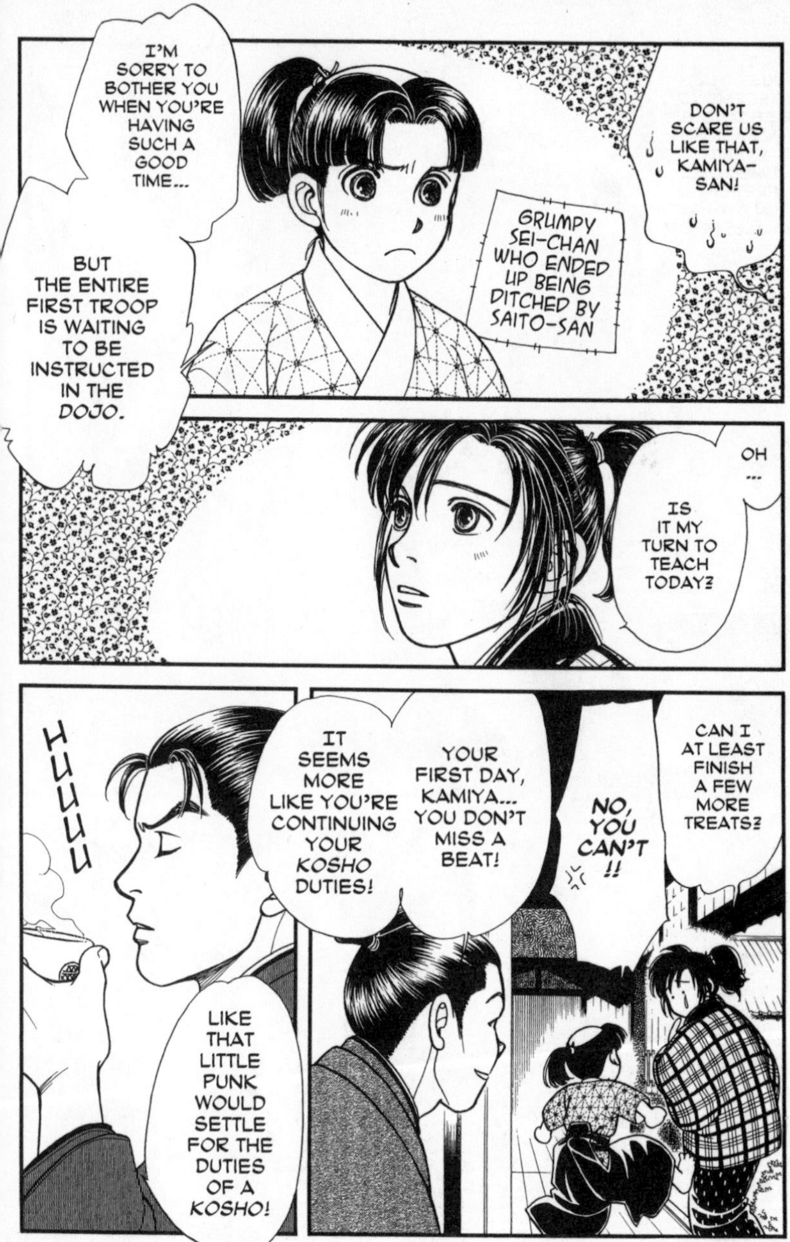
DON'T SCARE US LIKE THAT, KAMIYA-SAN!
GRUMPY SEI-CHAN WHO ENDED UP BEING DITCHED BY SAITO-SAN
I'M SORRY TO BOTHER YOU WHEN YOU'RE HAVING SUCH A GOOD TIME...
BUT THE ENTIRE FIRST TROOP IS WAITING TO BE INSTRUCTED IN THE *DOJO*.
OH...
IS IT MY TURN TO TEACH TODAY?
CAN I AT LEAST FINISH A FEW MORE TREATS?
NO, YOU CAN'T!!
YOUR FIRST DAY, KAMIYA... YOU DON'T MISS A BEAT!
IT SEEMS MORE LIKE YOU'RE CONTINUING YOUR *KOSHO* DUTIES!
HUUUU
LIKE THAT LITTLE PUNK WOULD SETTLE FOR THE DUTIES OF A *KOSHO*!

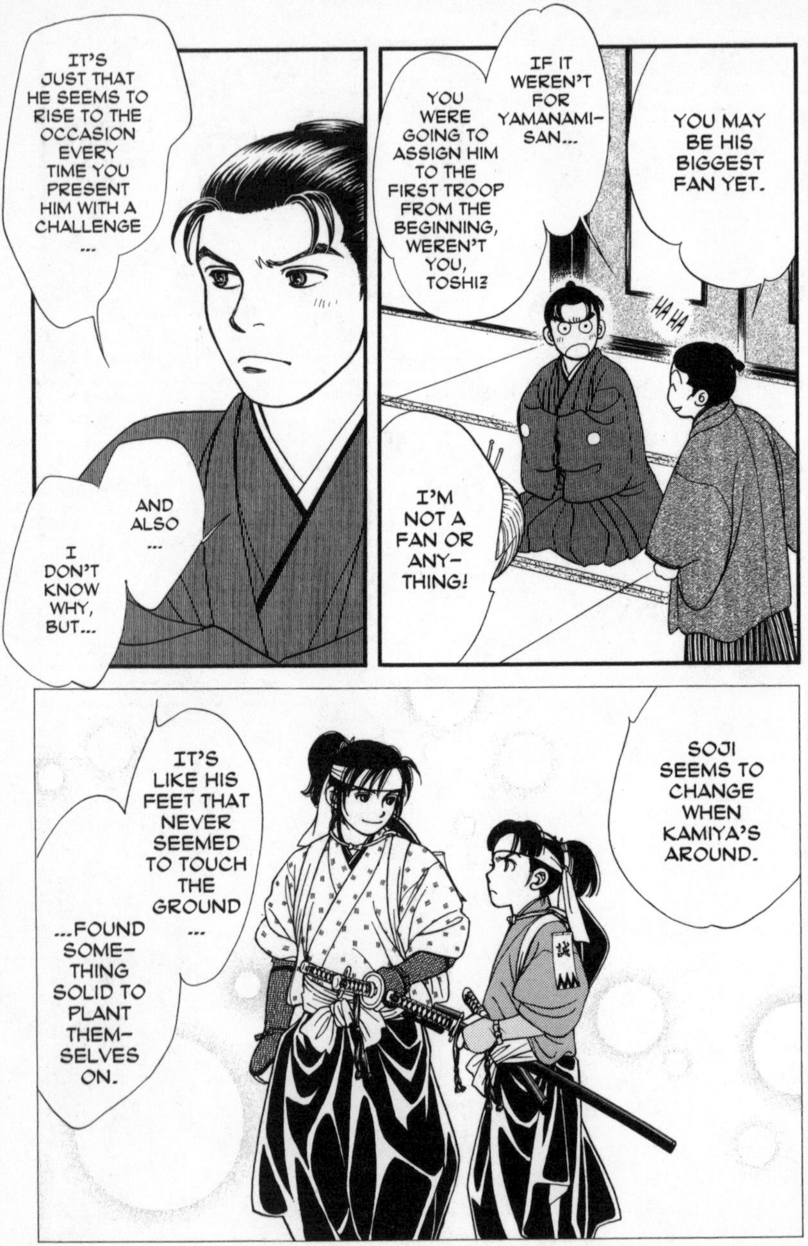
YOU MAY BE HIS BIGGEST FAN YET.
HA HA
IF IT WEREN'T FOR YAMANAMI-SAN...
YOU WERE GOING TO ASSIGN HIM TO THE FIRST TROOP FROM THE BEGINNING, WEREN'T YOU, TOSHI?
I'M NOT A FAN OR ANYTHING!
IT'S JUST THAT HE SEEMS TO RISE TO THE OCCASION EVERY TIME YOU PRESENT HIM WITH A CHALLENGE...
AND ALSO...
I DON'T KNOW WHY, BUT...
SOJI SEEMS TO CHANGE WHEN KAMIYA'S AROUND.
IT'S LIKE HIS FEET THAT NEVER SEEMED TO TOUCH THE GROUND...
...FOUND SOMETHING SOLID TO PLANT THEMSELVES ON.

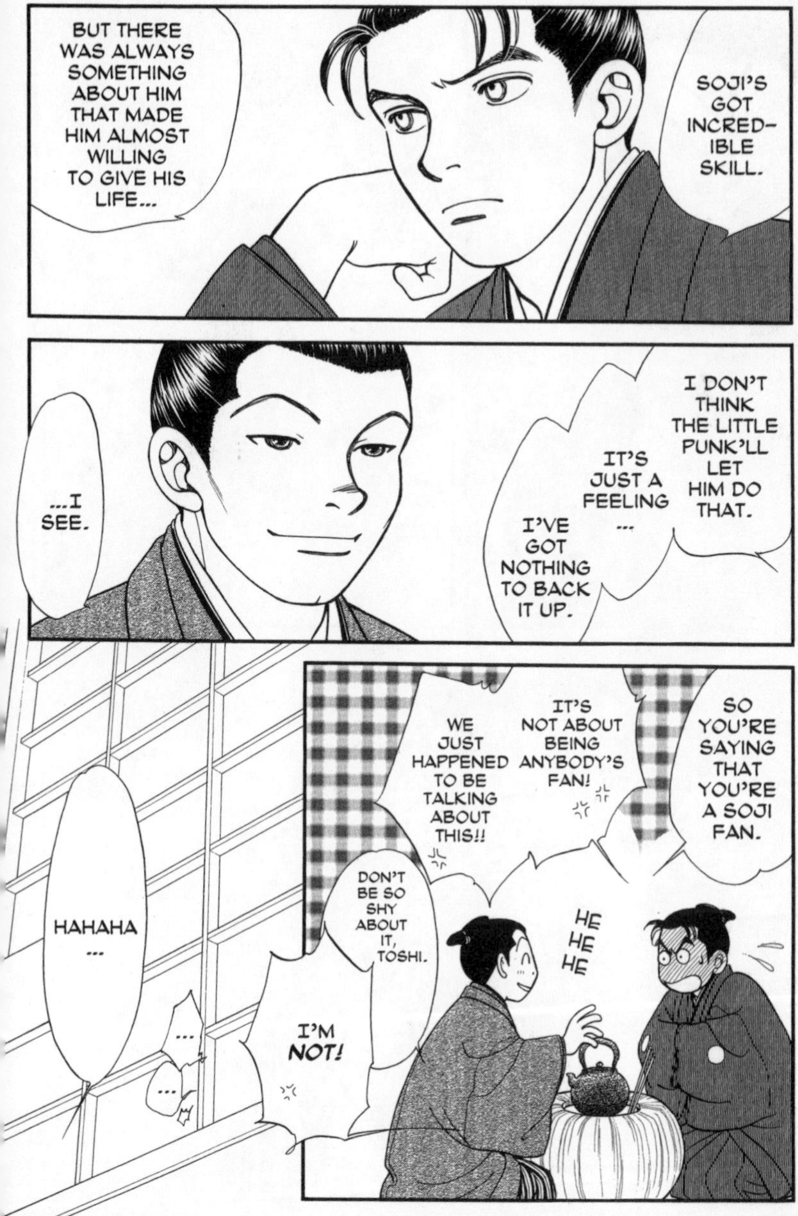
SOJI'S GOT INCRED-IBLE SKILL.
BUT THERE WAS ALWAYS SOMETHING ABOUT HIM THAT MADE HIM ALMOST WILLING TO GIVE HIS LIFE...
I DON'T THINK THE LITTLE PUNK'LL LET HIM DO THAT.
IT'S JUST A FEELING...
I'VE GOT NOTHING TO BACK IT UP.
...I SEE.
SO YOU'RE SAYING THAT YOU'RE A SOJI FAN.
IT'S NOT ABOUT BEING ANYBODY'S FAN!
WE JUST HAPPENED TO BE TALKING ABOUT THIS!!
HE HE HE
DON'T BE SO SHY ABOUT IT, TOSHI.
I'M **NOT!**
HAHAHA...
...
...

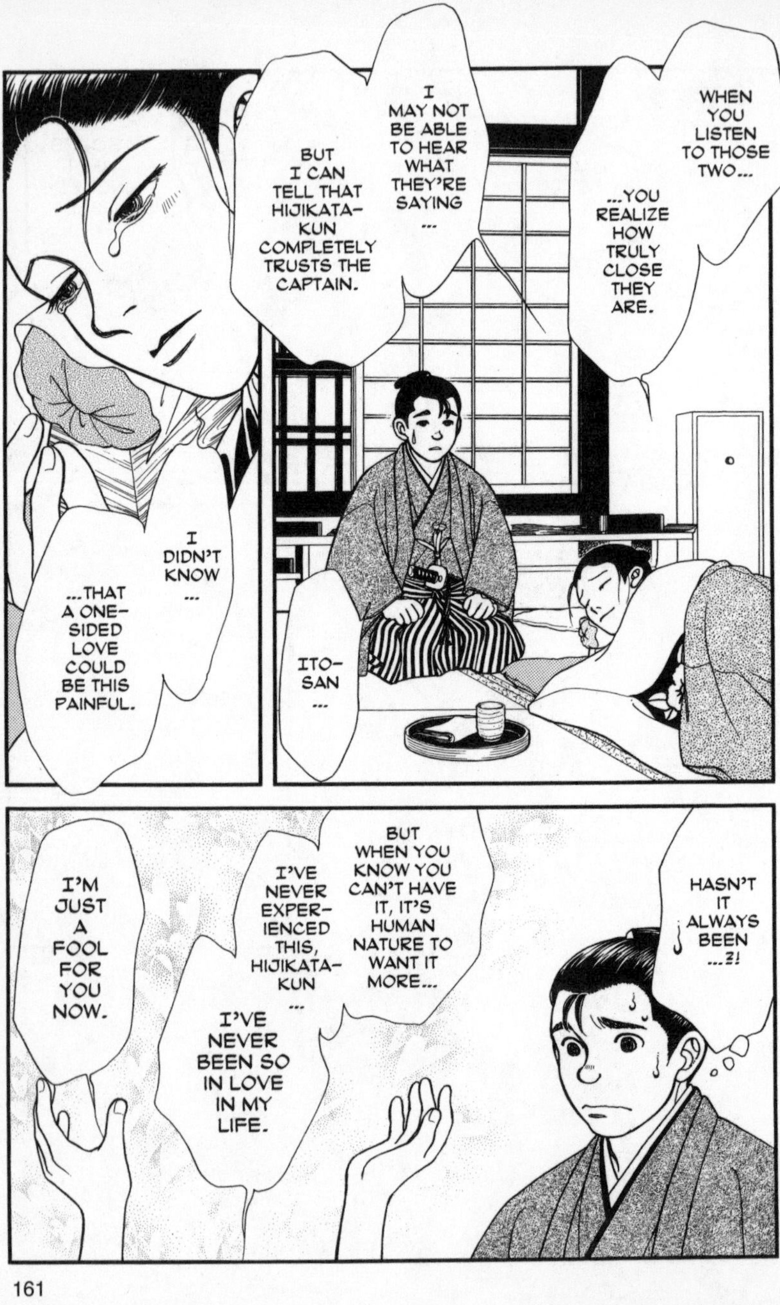
WHEN YOU LISTEN TO THOSE TWO...
...YOU REALIZE HOW TRULY CLOSE THEY ARE.
I MAY NOT BE ABLE TO HEAR WHAT THEY'RE SAYING...
BUT I CAN TELL THAT HIJIKATA-KUN COMPLETELY TRUSTS THE CAPTAIN.
ITO-SAN...
I DIDN'T KNOW...
...THAT A ONE-SIDED LOVE COULD BE THIS PAINFUL.
HASN'T IT ALWAYS BEEN...?!
BUT WHEN YOU KNOW YOU CAN'T HAVE IT, IT'S HUMAN NATURE TO WANT IT MORE...
I'VE NEVER EXPERIENCED THIS, HIJIKATA-KUN...
I'VE NEVER BEEN SO IN LOVE IN MY LIFE.
I'M JUST A FOOL FOR YOU NOW.

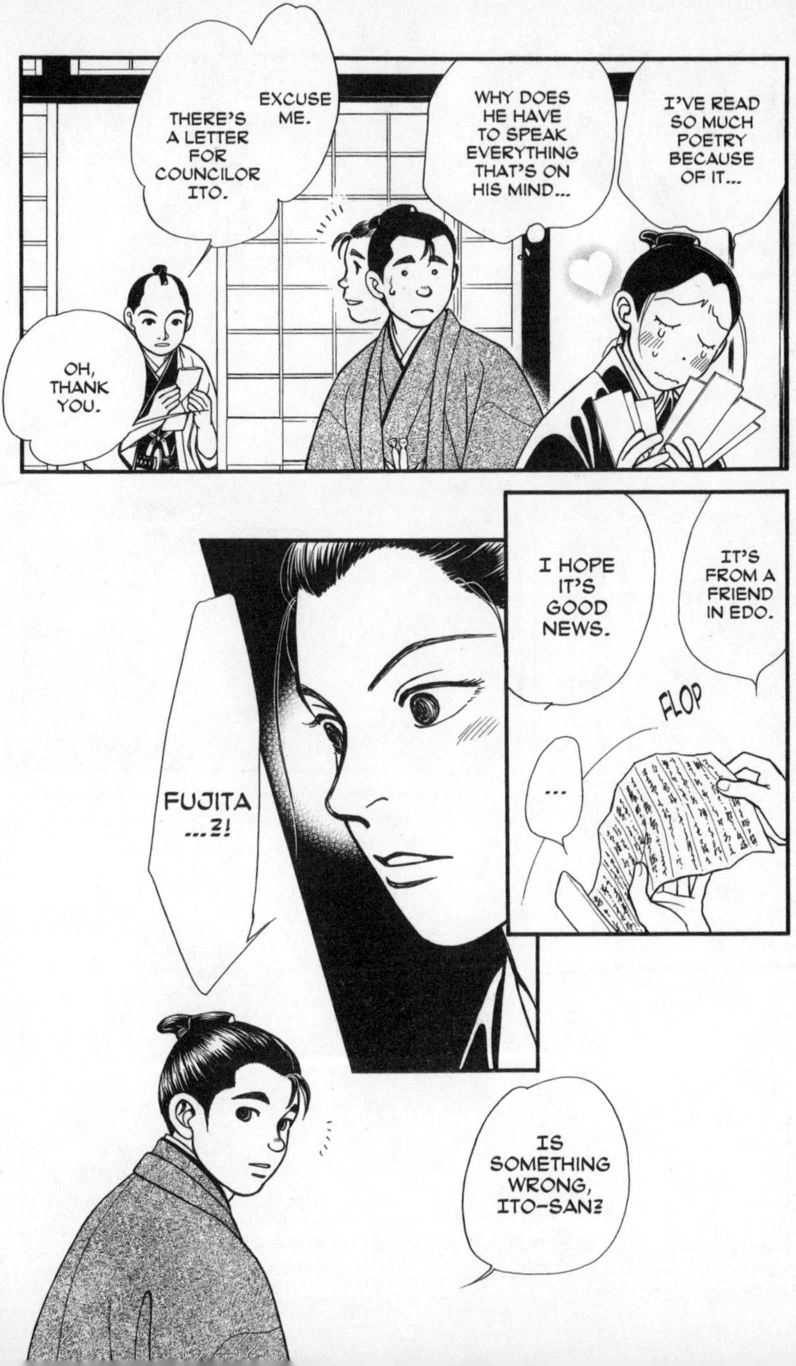
I'VE READ SO MUCH POETRY BECAUSE OF IT...
WHY DOES HE HAVE TO SPEAK EVERYTHING THAT'S ON HIS MIND...
EXCUSE ME.
THERE'S A LETTER FOR COUNCILOR ITO.
OH, THANK YOU.
IT'S FROM A FRIEND IN EDO.
I HOPE IT'S GOOD NEWS.
FLOP
...
FUJITA ...?!
IS SOMETHING WRONG, ITO-SAN?

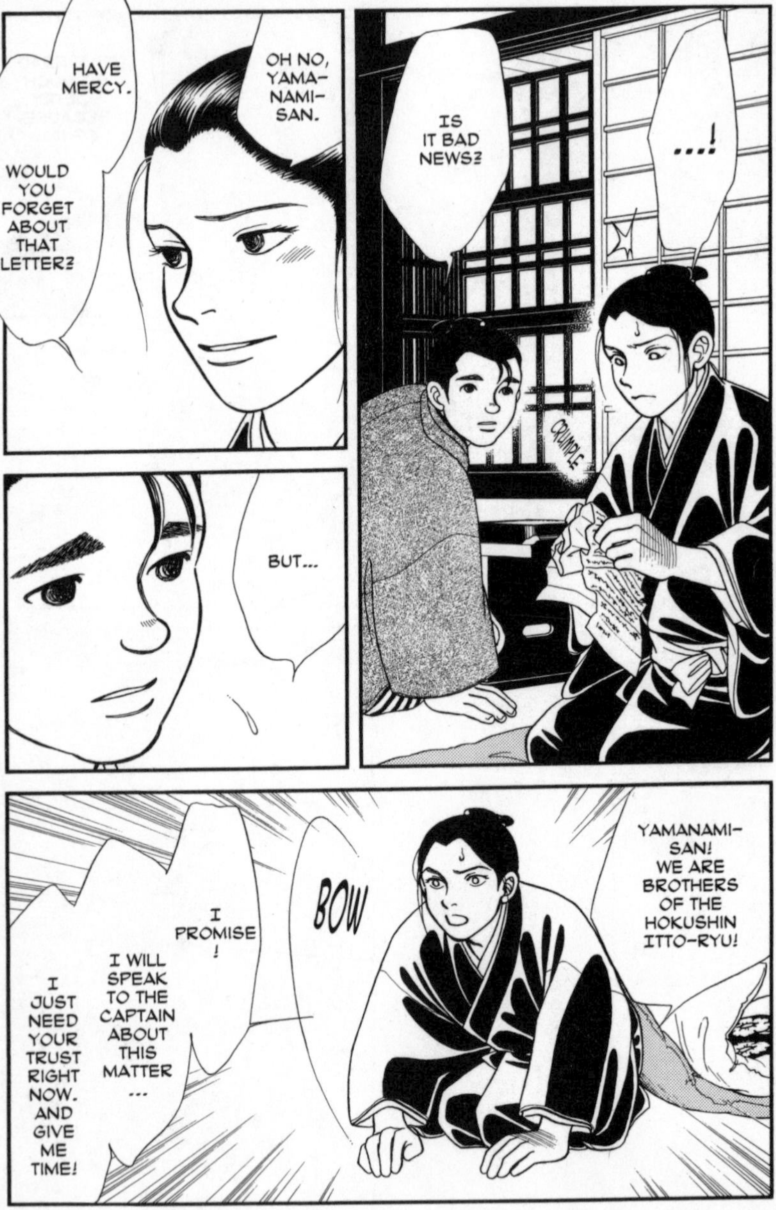

...!
IS IT BAD NEWS?
CRUMPLE
OH NO, YAMANAMI-SAN.
HAVE MERCY.
WOULD YOU FORGET ABOUT THAT LETTER?
BUT...
YAMANAMI-SAN! WE ARE BROTHERS OF THE HOKUSHIN ITTO-RYU!
BOW
I PROMISE!
I WILL SPEAK TO THE CAPTAIN ABOUT THIS MATTER...
I JUST NEED YOUR TRUST RIGHT NOW. AND GIVE ME TIME!

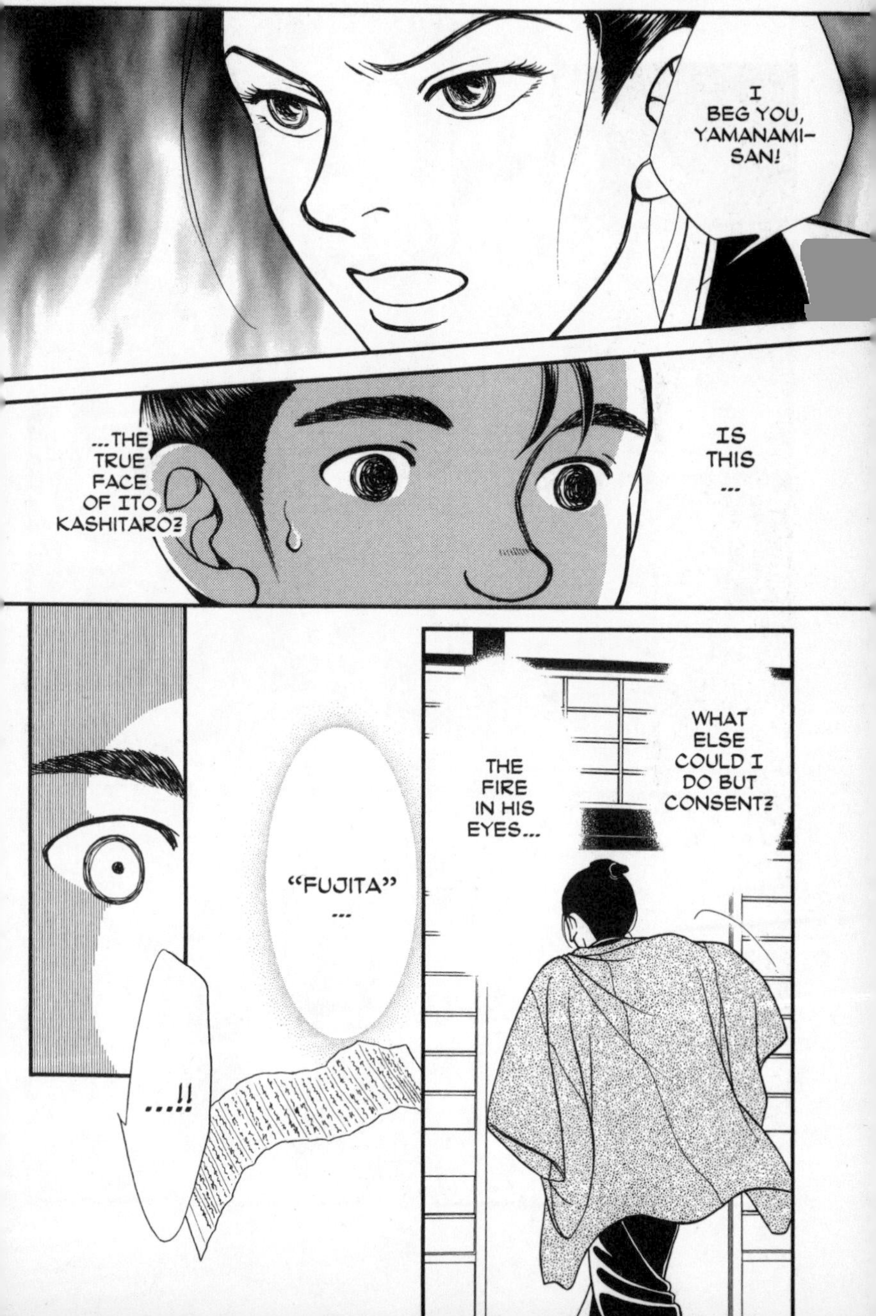
I BEG YOU, YAMANAMI-SAN!
IS THIS ...
...THE TRUE FACE OF ITO KASHITARO?
WHAT ELSE COULD I DO BUT CONSENT?
THE FIRE IN HIS EYES...
“FUJITA” ...
...!!

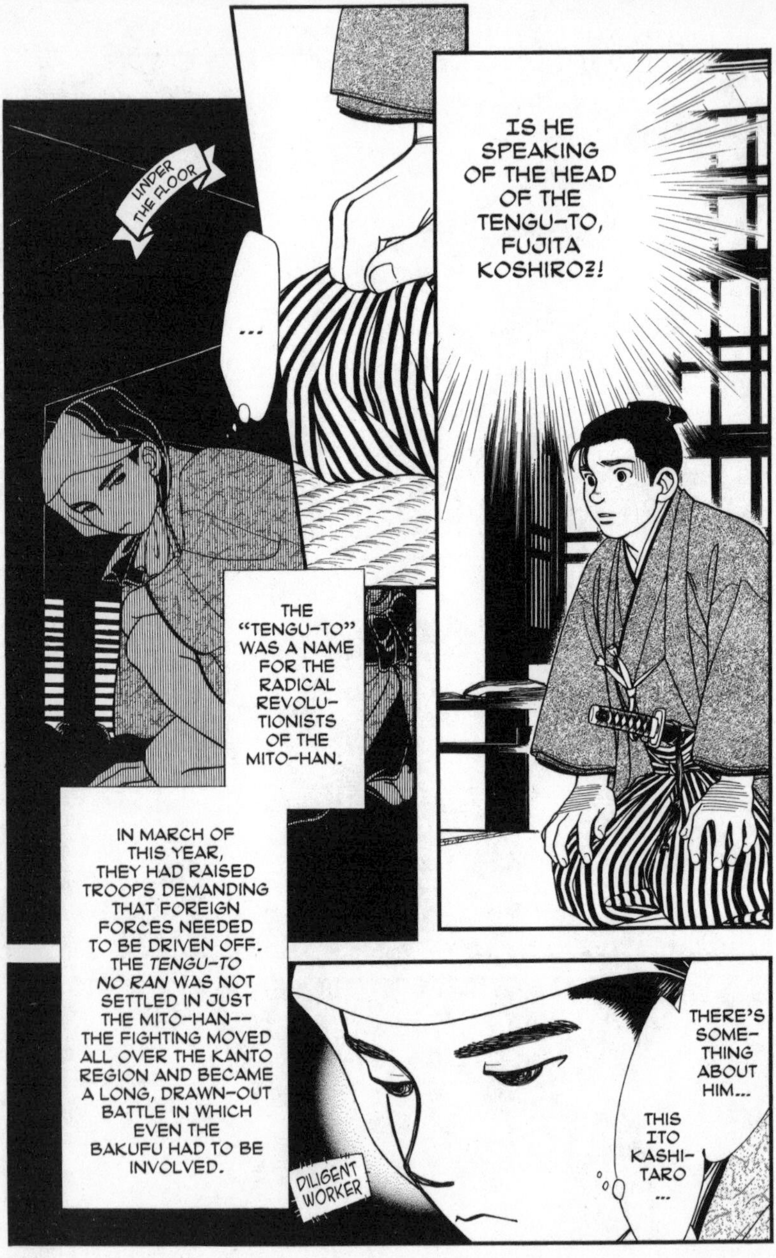
IS HE SPEAKING OF THE HEAD OF THE TENGU-TO, FUJITA KOSHIRO?!
...
UNDER THE FLOOR
THE "TENGU-TO" WAS A NAME FOR THE RADICAL REVOLUTIONISTS OF THE MITO-HAN.
IN MARCH OF THIS YEAR, THEY HAD RAISED TROOPS DEMANDING THAT FOREIGN FORCES NEEDED TO BE DRIVEN OFF. THE *TENGU-TO NO RAN* WAS NOT SETTLED IN JUST THE MITO-HAN-- THE FIGHTING MOVED ALL OVER THE KANTO REGION AND BECAME A LONG, DRAWN-OUT BATTLE IN WHICH EVEN THE BAKUFU HAD TO BE INVOLVED.
THERE'S SOMETHING ABOUT HIM...
THIS ITO KASHITARO...
DILIGENT WORKER

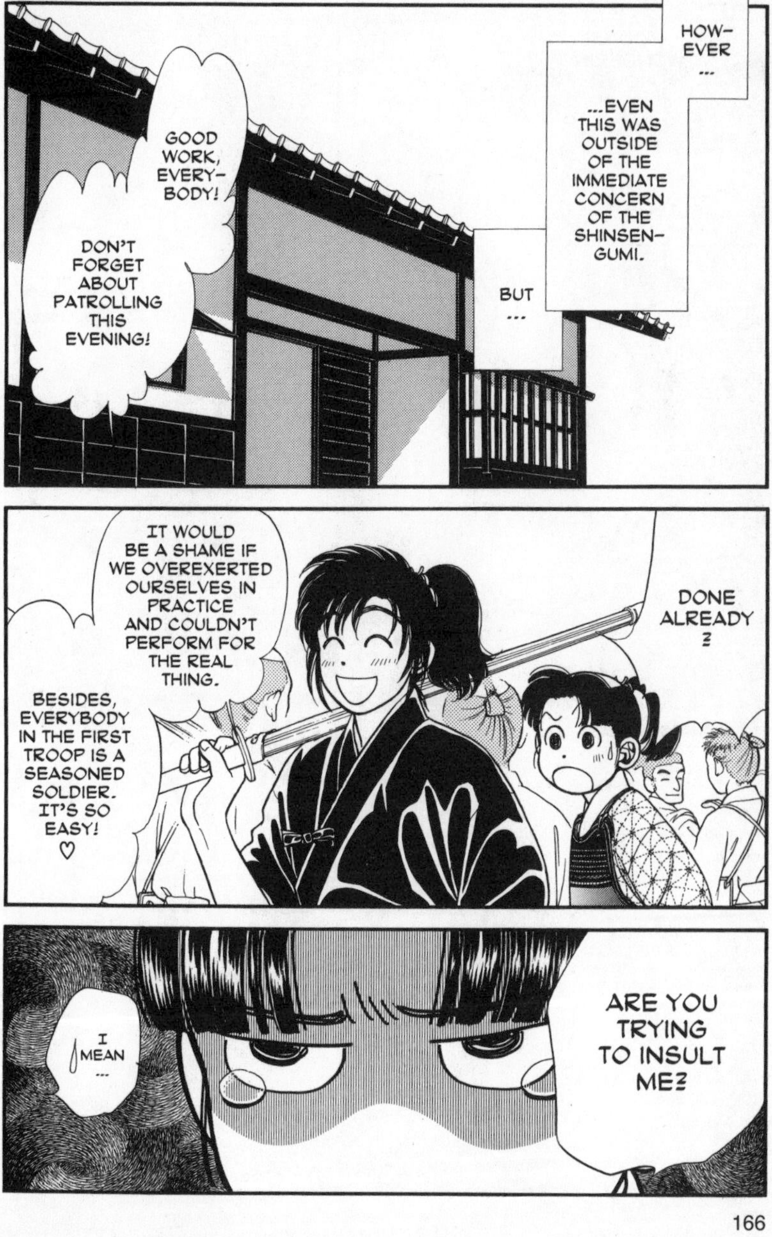
HOW-EVER...
...EVEN THIS WAS OUTSIDE OF THE IMMEDIATE CONCERN OF THE SHINSEN-GUMI.
BUT...
GOOD WORK, EVERY-BODY!
DON'T FORGET ABOUT PATROLLING THIS EVENING!
DONE ALREADY?
IT WOULD BE A SHAME IF WE OVEREXERTED OURSELVES IN PRACTICE AND COULDN'T PERFORM FOR THE REAL THING.
BESIDES, EVERYBODY IN THE FIRST TROOP IS A SEASONED SOLDIER. IT'S SO EASY! ♡
ARE YOU TRYING TO INSULT ME?
I MEAN...

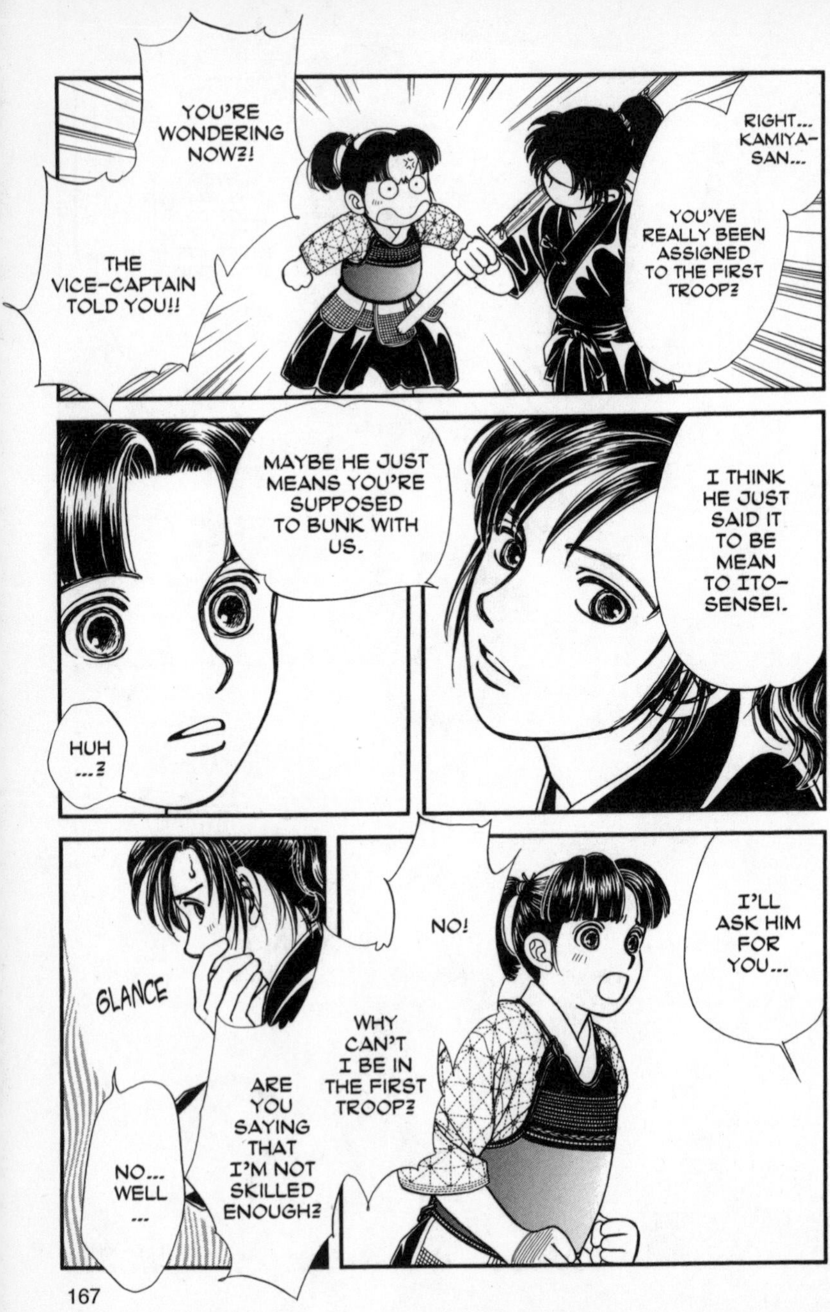
RIGHT... KAMIYA-SAN...
YOU'VE REALLY BEEN ASSIGNED TO THE FIRST TROOP?
YOU'RE WONDERING NOW?!
THE VICE-CAPTAIN TOLD YOU!!
I THINK HE JUST SAID IT TO BE MEAN TO ITO-SENSEI.
MAYBE HE JUST MEANS YOU'RE SUPPOSED TO BUNK WITH US.
HUH ...?
I'LL ASK HIM FOR YOU...
NO!
WHY CAN'T I BE IN THE FIRST TROOP?
ARE YOU SAYING THAT I'M NOT SKILLED ENOUGH?
GLANCE
NO... WELL ...

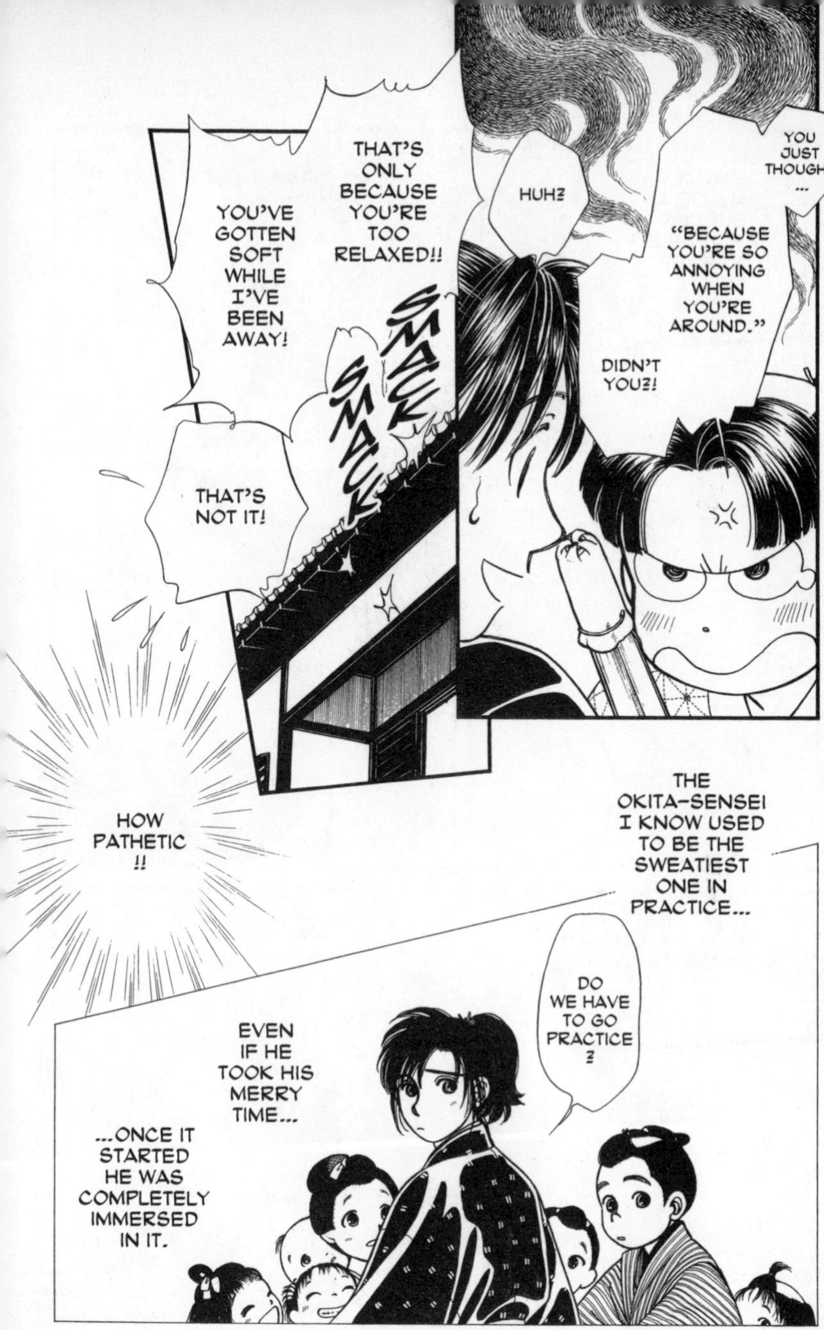
YOU JUST THOUGHT ...
"BECAUSE YOU'RE SO ANNOYING WHEN YOU'RE AROUND."
DIDN'T YOU?!
HUH?
THAT'S ONLY BECAUSE YOU'RE TOO RELAXED!!
YOU'VE GOTTEN SOFT WHILE I'VE BEEN AWAY!
SMACK
SMACK
THAT'S NOT IT!
THE OKITA-SENSEI I KNOW USED TO BE THE SWEATIEST ONE IN PRACTICE...
HOW PATHETIC !!
DO WE HAVE TO GO PRACTICE ?
EVEN IF HE TOOK HIS MERRY TIME...
...ONCE IT STARTED HE WAS COMPLETELY IMMERSED IN IT.

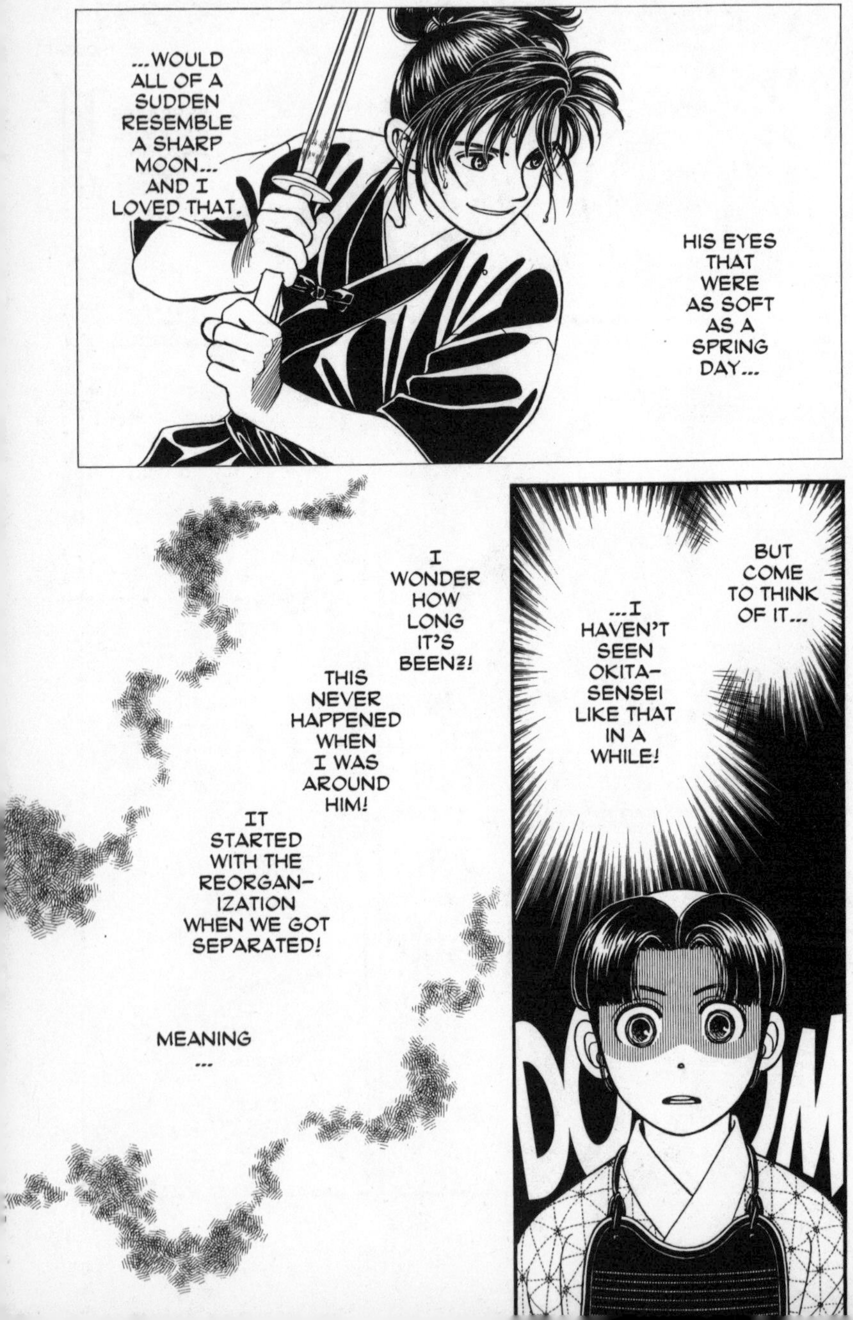
HIS EYES THAT WERE AS SOFT AS A SPRING DAY...
...WOULD ALL OF A SUDDEN RESEMBLE A SHARP MOON... AND I LOVED THAT.
BUT COME TO THINK OF IT...
...I HAVEN'T SEEN OKITA-SENSEI LIKE THAT IN A WHILE!
I WONDER HOW LONG IT'S BEEN?!
THIS NEVER HAPPENED WHEN I WAS AROUND HIM!
IT STARTED WITH THE REORGAN-IZATION WHEN WE GOT SEPARATED!
MEANING ...

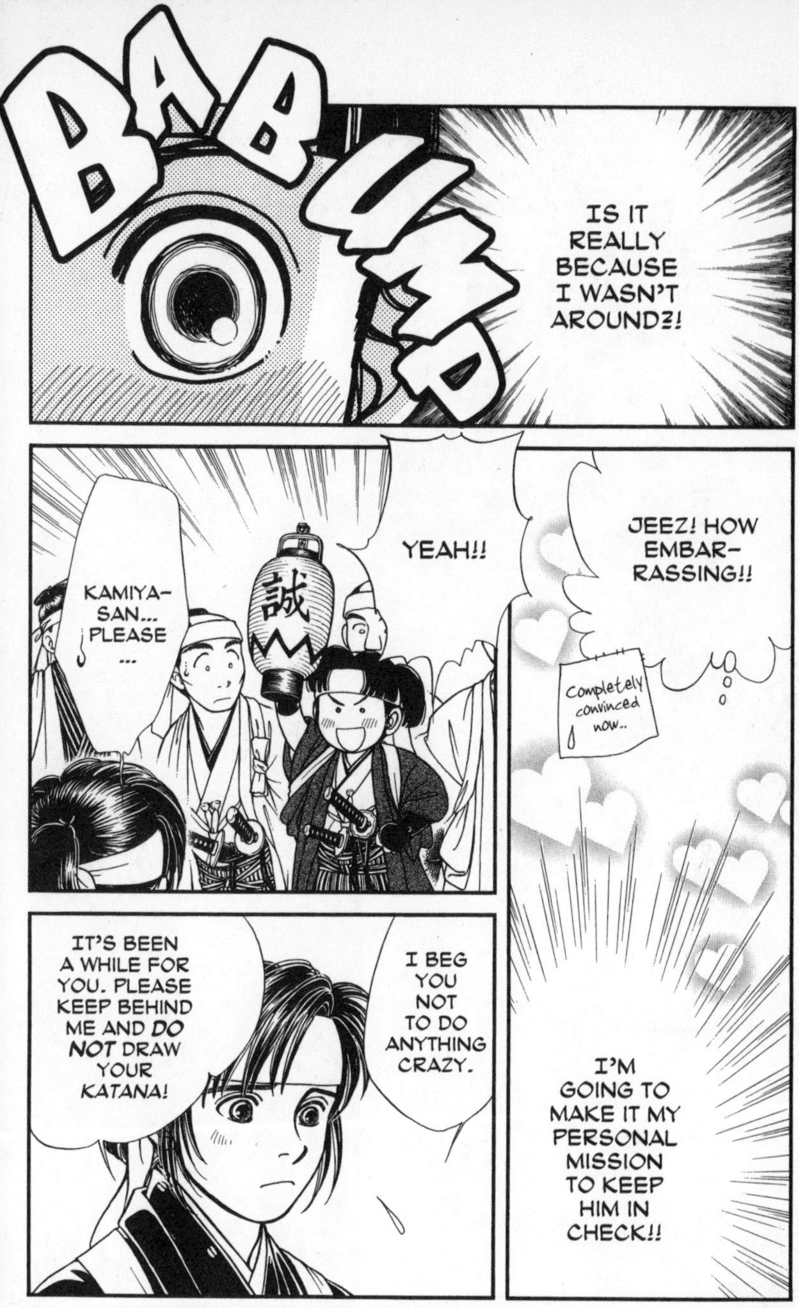
IS IT REALLY BECAUSE I WASN'T AROUND?!
BABUMP
JEEZ! HOW EMBAR-RASSING!!
Completely convinced now..
I'M GOING TO MAKE IT MY PERSONAL MISSION TO KEEP HIM IN CHECK!!
YEAH!!
KAMIYA-SAN... PLEASE ...
I BEG YOU NOT TO DO ANYTHING CRAZY.
IT'S BEEN A WHILE FOR YOU. PLEASE KEEP BEHIND ME AND *DO NOT* DRAW YOUR KATANA!

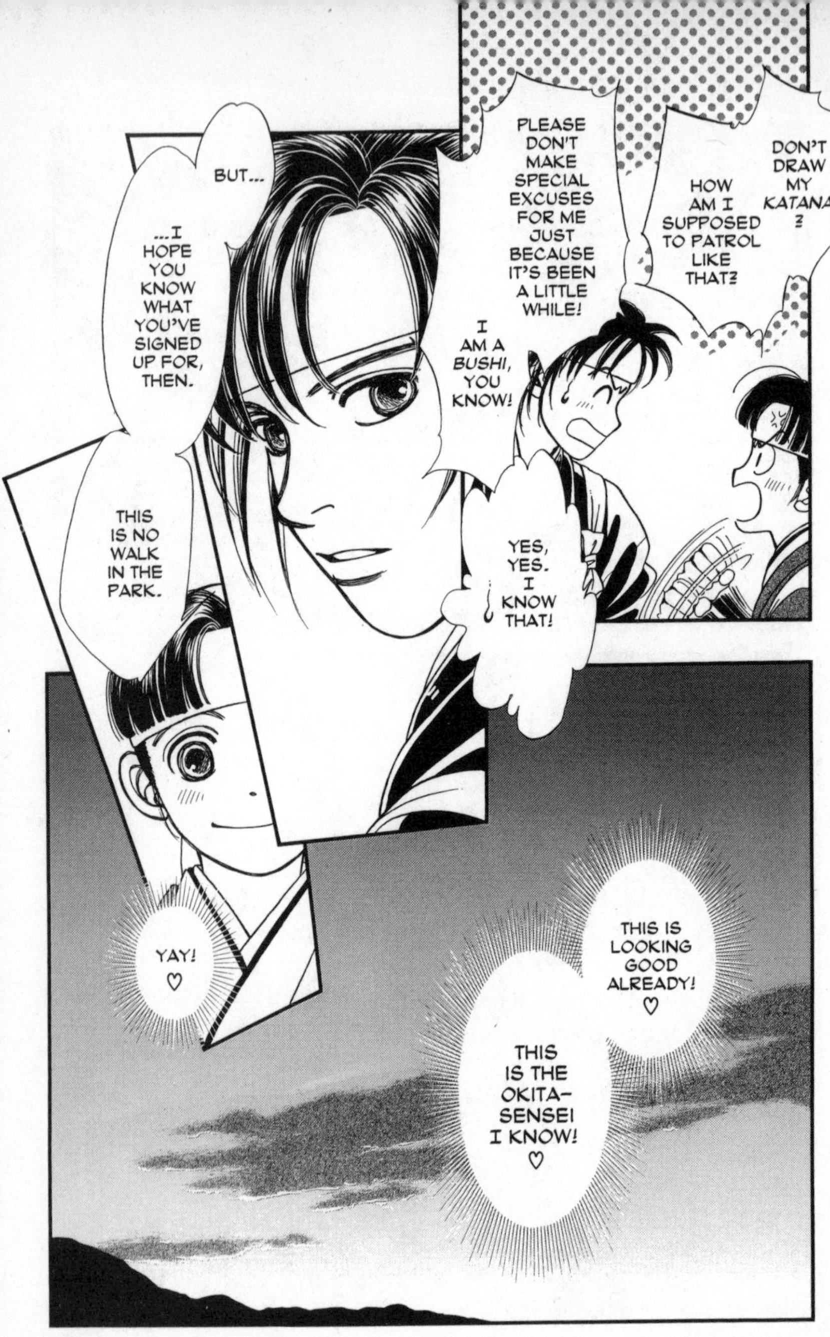
DON'T DRAW MY KATANA?
HOW AM I SUPPOSED TO PATROL LIKE THAT?
PLEASE DON'T MAKE SPECIAL EXCUSES FOR ME JUST BECAUSE IT'S BEEN A LITTLE WHILE!
I AM A *BUSHI*, YOU KNOW!
YES, YES. I KNOW THAT!
BUT...
...I HOPE YOU KNOW WHAT YOU'VE SIGNED UP FOR, THEN.
THIS IS NO WALK IN THE PARK.
YAY! ♡
THIS IS LOOKING GOOD ALREADY! ♡
THIS IS THE OKITA-SENSEI I KNOW! ♡

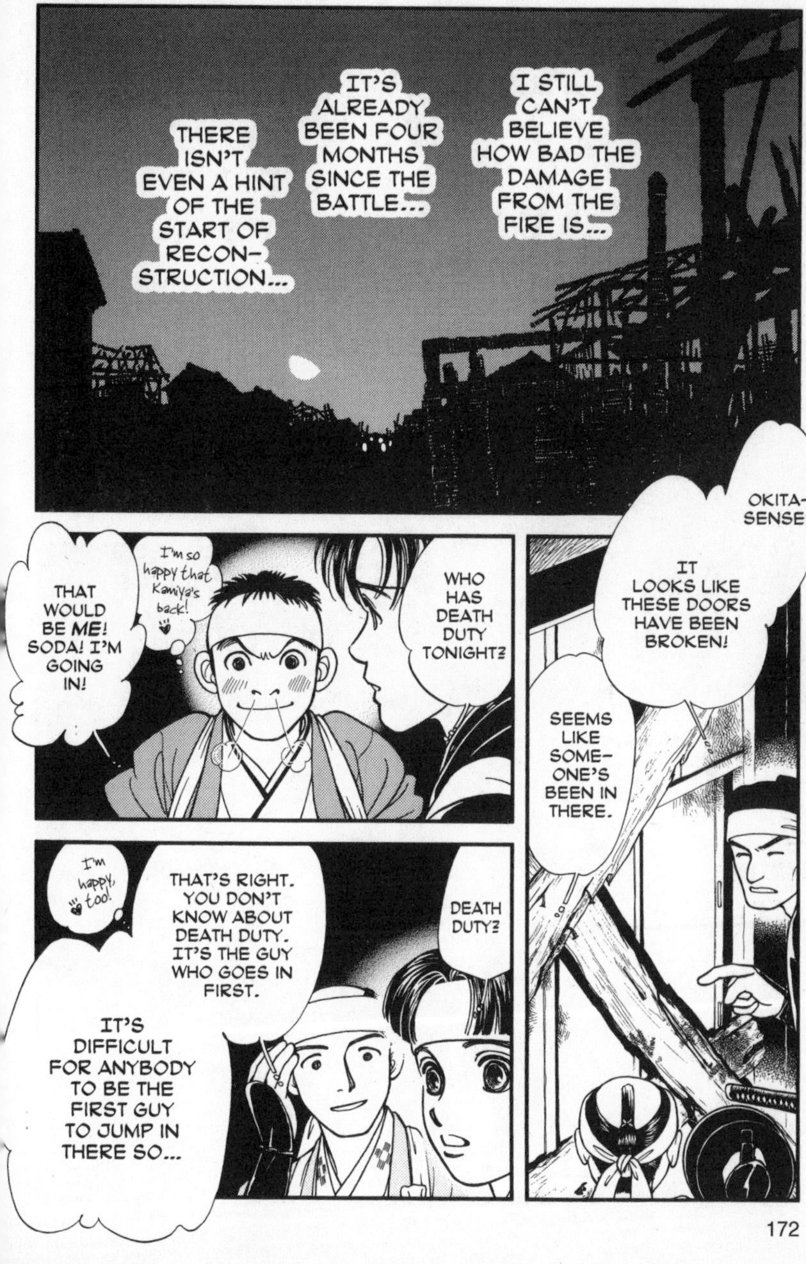
I STILL CAN'T BELIEVE HOW BAD THE DAMAGE FROM THE FIRE IS...
IT'S ALREADY BEEN FOUR MONTHS SINCE THE BATTLE...
THERE ISN'T EVEN A HINT OF THE START OF RECON-STRUCTION...
OKITA-SENSEI!
IT LOOKS LIKE THESE DOORS HAVE BEEN BROKEN!
SEEMS LIKE SOME-ONE'S BEEN IN THERE.
WHO HAS DEATH DUTY TONIGHT?!
I'm so happy that Kamiya's back!
THAT WOULD BE *ME*! SODA! I'M GOING IN!
DEATH DUTY?!
THAT'S RIGHT. YOU DON'T KNOW ABOUT DEATH DUTY. IT'S THE GUY WHO GOES IN FIRST.
I'm happy, too!
IT'S DIFFICULT FOR ANYBODY TO BE THE FIRST GUY TO JUMP IN THERE SO...

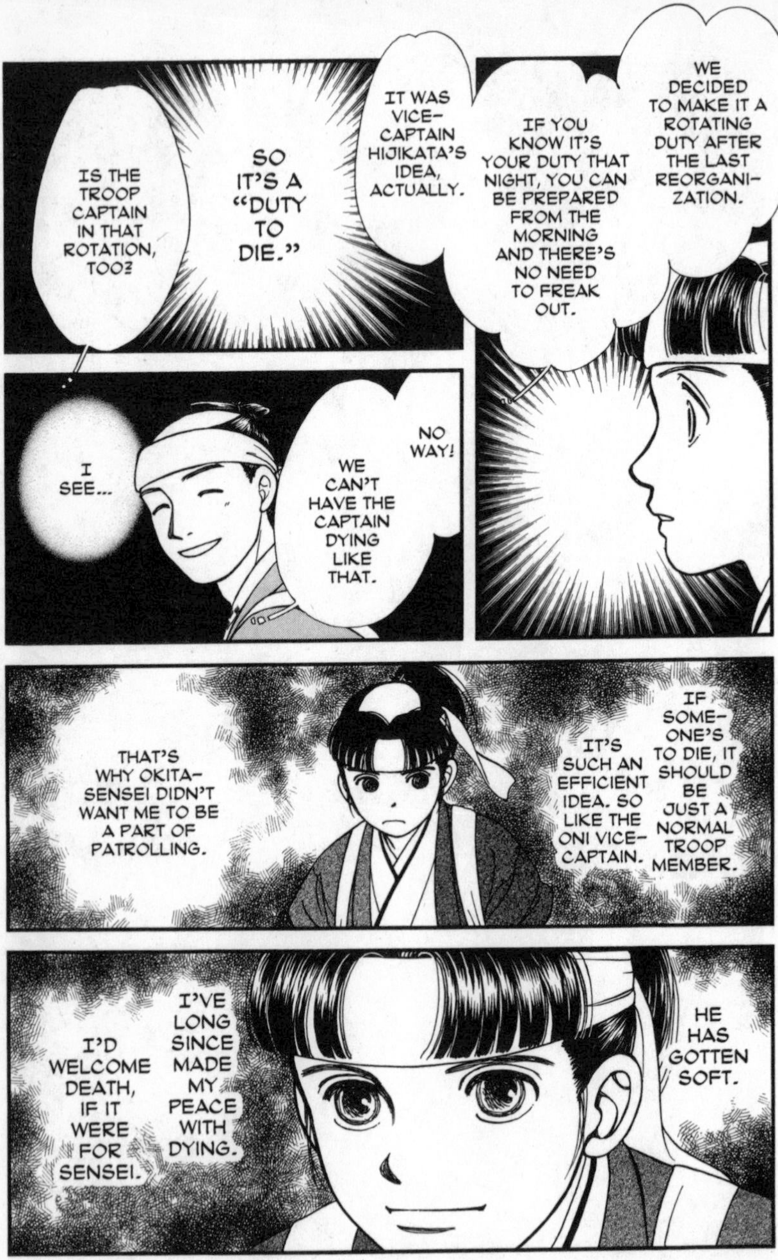
WE DECIDED TO MAKE IT A ROTATING DUTY AFTER THE LAST REORGANIZATION.
IF YOU KNOW IT'S YOUR DUTY THAT NIGHT, YOU CAN BE PREPARED FROM THE MORNING AND THERE'S NO NEED TO FREAK OUT.
IT WAS VICE-CAPTAIN HIJIKATA'S IDEA, ACTUALLY.
SO IT'S A "DUTY TO DIE."
IS THE TROOP CAPTAIN IN THAT ROTATION, TOO?
NO WAY!
WE CAN'T HAVE THE CAPTAIN DYING LIKE THAT.
I SEE...
IF SOMEONE'S TO DIE, IT SHOULD BE JUST A NORMAL TROOP MEMBER.
IT'S SUCH AN EFFICIENT IDEA. SO LIKE THE ONI VICE-CAPTAIN.
THAT'S WHY OKITA-SENSEI DIDN'T WANT ME TO BE A PART OF PATROLLING.
HE HAS GOTTEN SOFT.
I'VE LONG SINCE MADE MY PEACE WITH DYING.
I'D WELCOME DEATH, IF IT WERE FOR SENSEI.

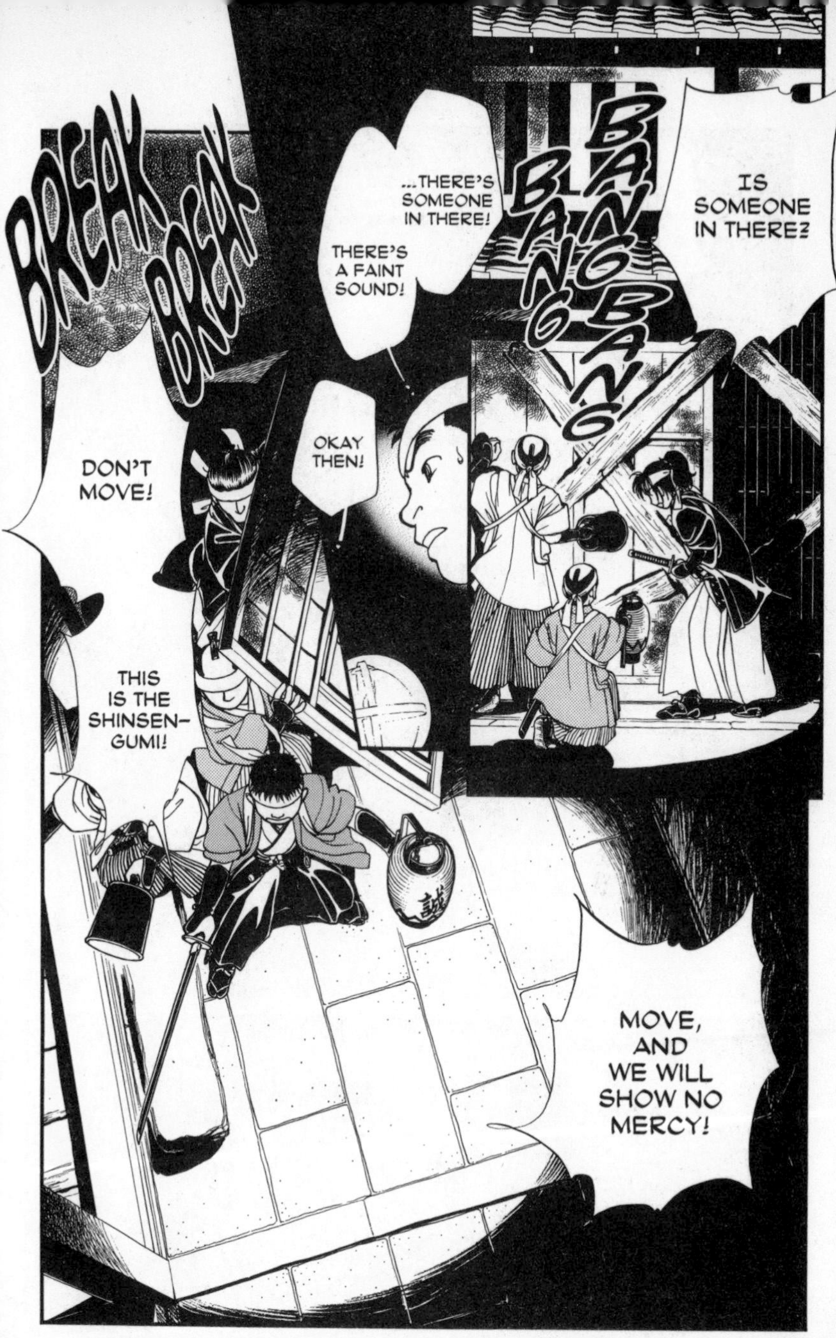
IS SOMEONE IN THERE?
BANG BANG
BANG BANG
...THERE'S SOMEONE IN THERE!
THERE'S A FAINT SOUND!
OKAY THEN!
BREAK
BREAK
DON'T MOVE!
THIS IS THE SHINSEN-GUMI!
MOVE, AND WE WILL SHOW NO MERCY!

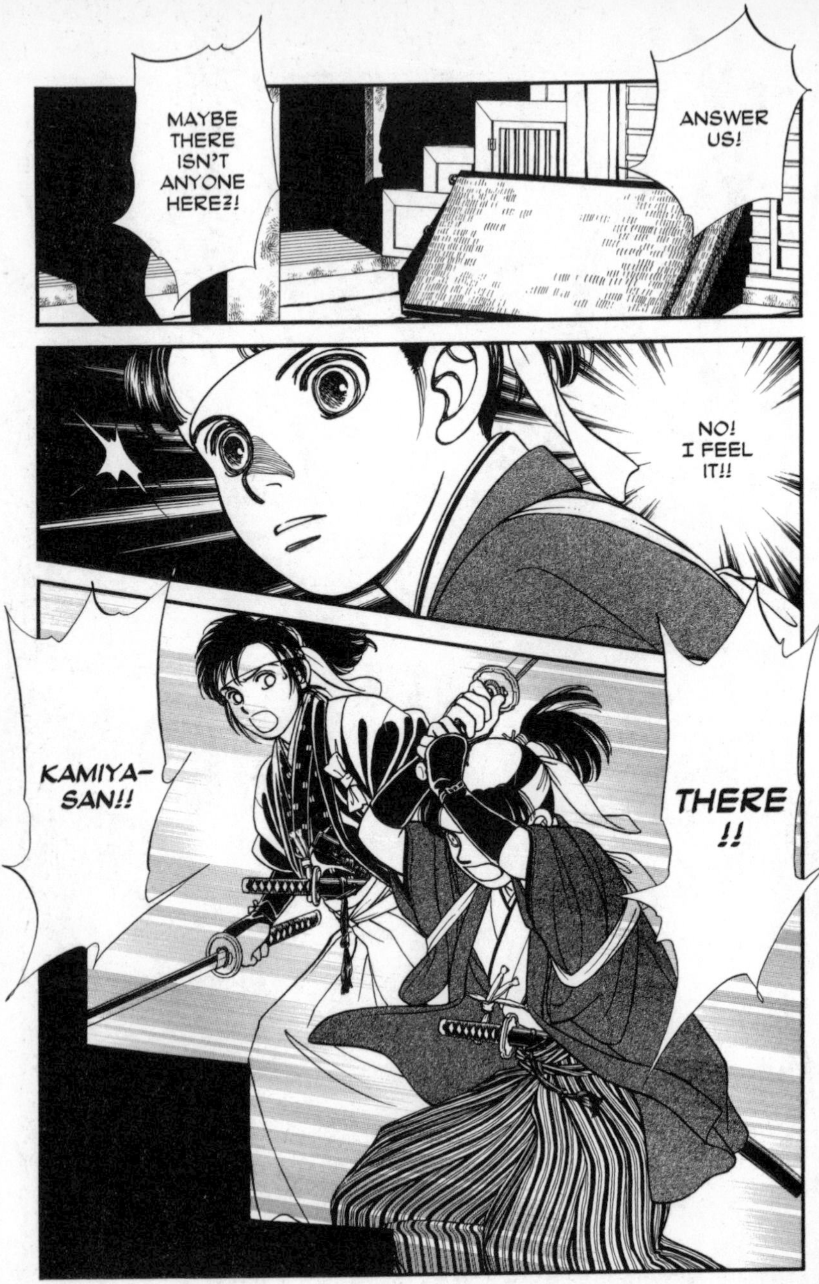
ANSWER US!
MAYBE THERE ISN'T ANYONE HERE?!
NO! I FEEL IT!!
THERE !!
KAMIYA-SAN!!

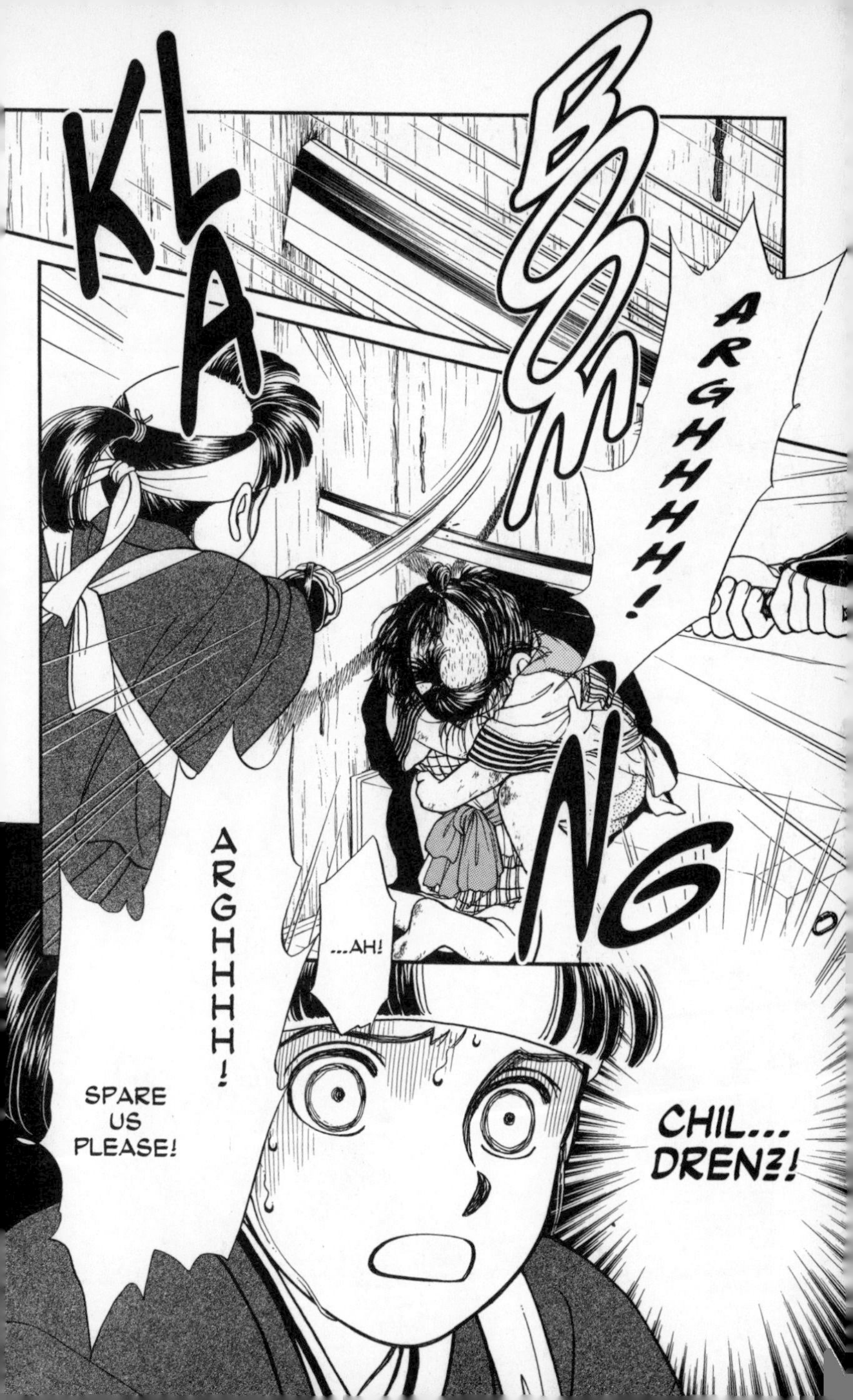
ARGHHHH!
BOOM
KLANG
CHIL... DREN?!
...AH!
ARGHHHH!
SPARE US PLEASE!

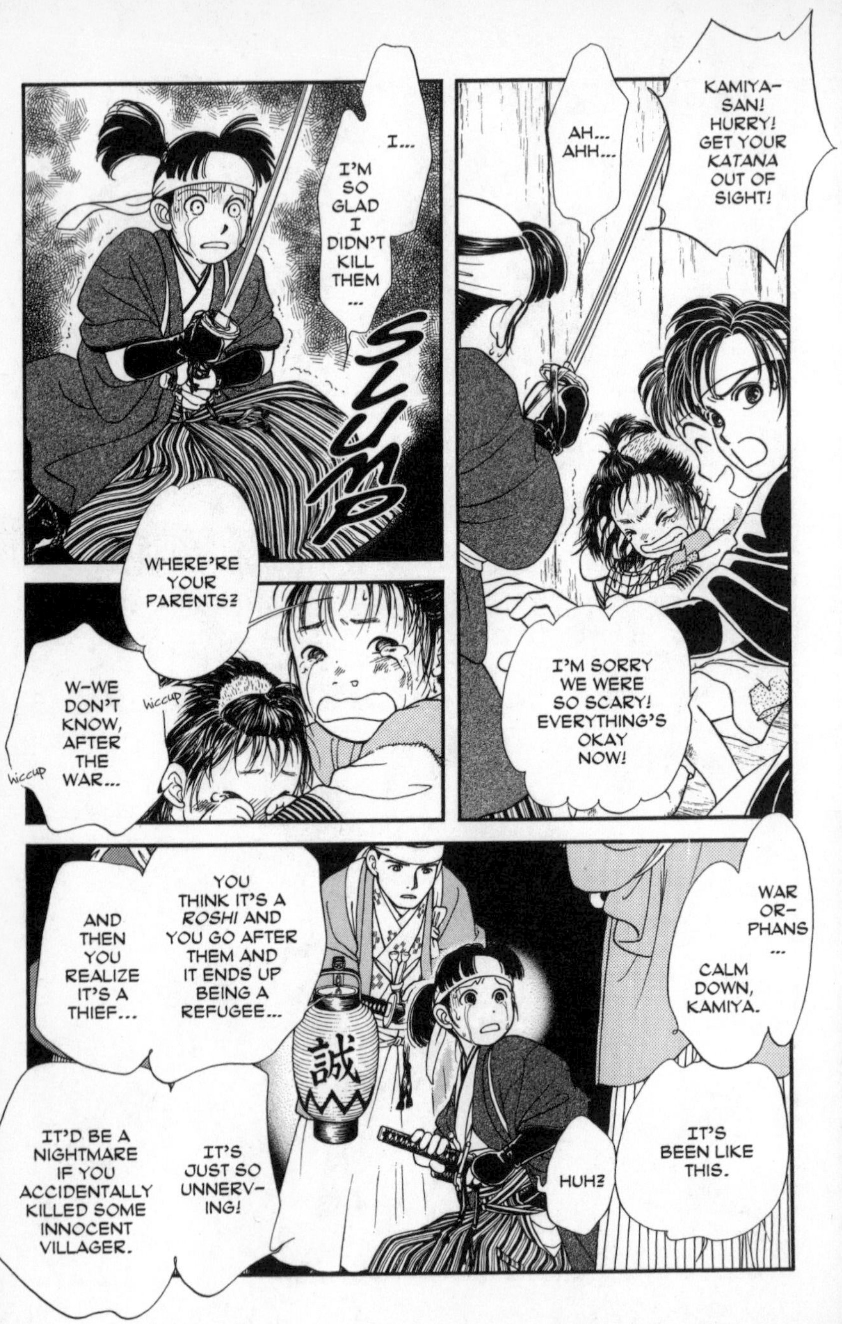
KAMIYA-SAN! HURRY! GET YOUR *KATANA* OUT OF SIGHT!
AH... AHH...
I'M SORRY WE WERE SO SCARY! EVERYTHING'S OKAY NOW!
I...
I'M SO GLAD I DIDN'T KILL THEM ...
SLUMP
WHERE'RE YOUR PARENTS?
hiccup
W-WE DON'T KNOW, AFTER THE WAR...
hiccup
WAR OR-PHANS ...
CALM DOWN, KAMIYA.
IT'S BEEN LIKE THIS.
HUH?
誠
YOU THINK IT'S A *ROSHI* AND YOU GO AFTER THEM AND IT ENDS UP BEING A REFUGEE...
AND THEN YOU REALIZE IT'S A THIEF...
IT'S JUST SO UNNERV-ING!
IT'D BE A NIGHTMARE IF YOU ACCIDENTALLY KILLED SOME INNOCENT VILLAGER.

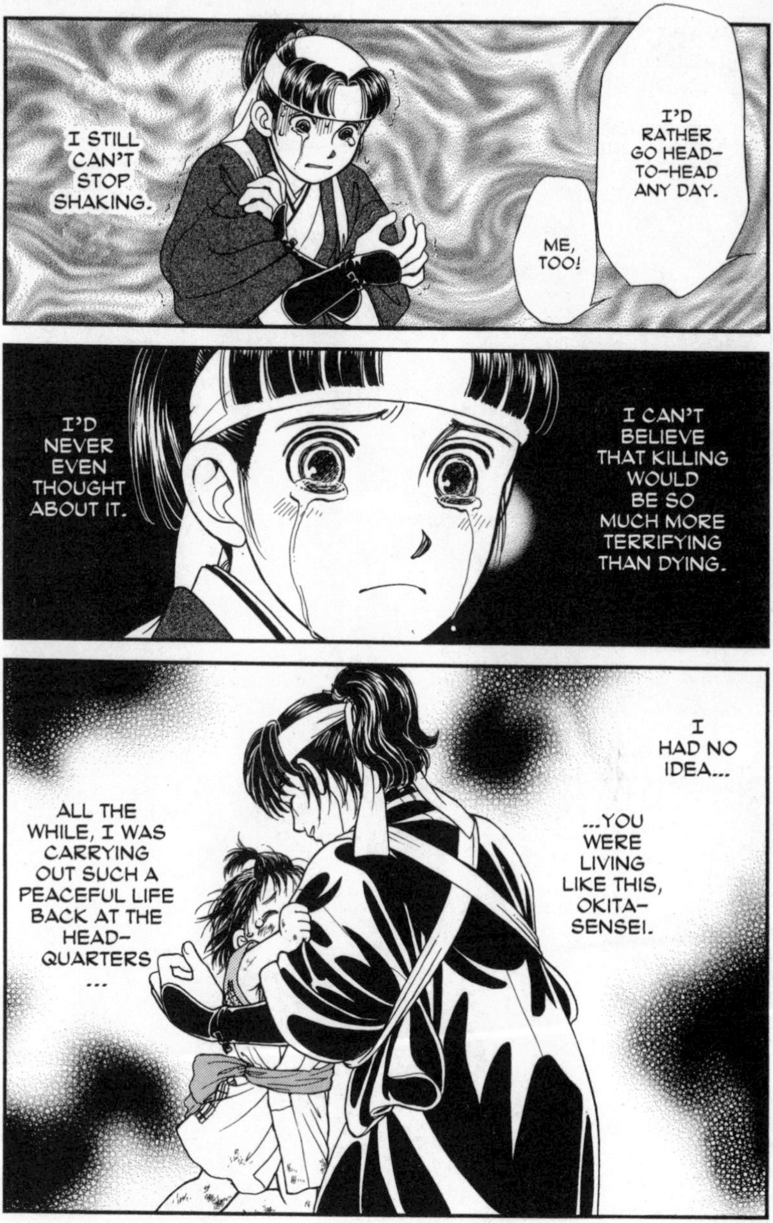
I'D RATHER GO HEAD-TO-HEAD ANY DAY.
ME, TOO!
I STILL CAN'T STOP SHAKING.
I CAN'T BELIEVE THAT KILLING WOULD BE SO MUCH MORE TERRIFYING THAN DYING.
I'D NEVER EVEN THOUGHT ABOUT IT.
I HAD NO IDEA...
...YOU WERE LIVING LIKE THIS, OKITA-SENSEI.
ALL THE WHILE, I WAS CARRYING OUT SUCH A PEACEFUL LIFE BACK AT THE HEAD-QUARTERS ...

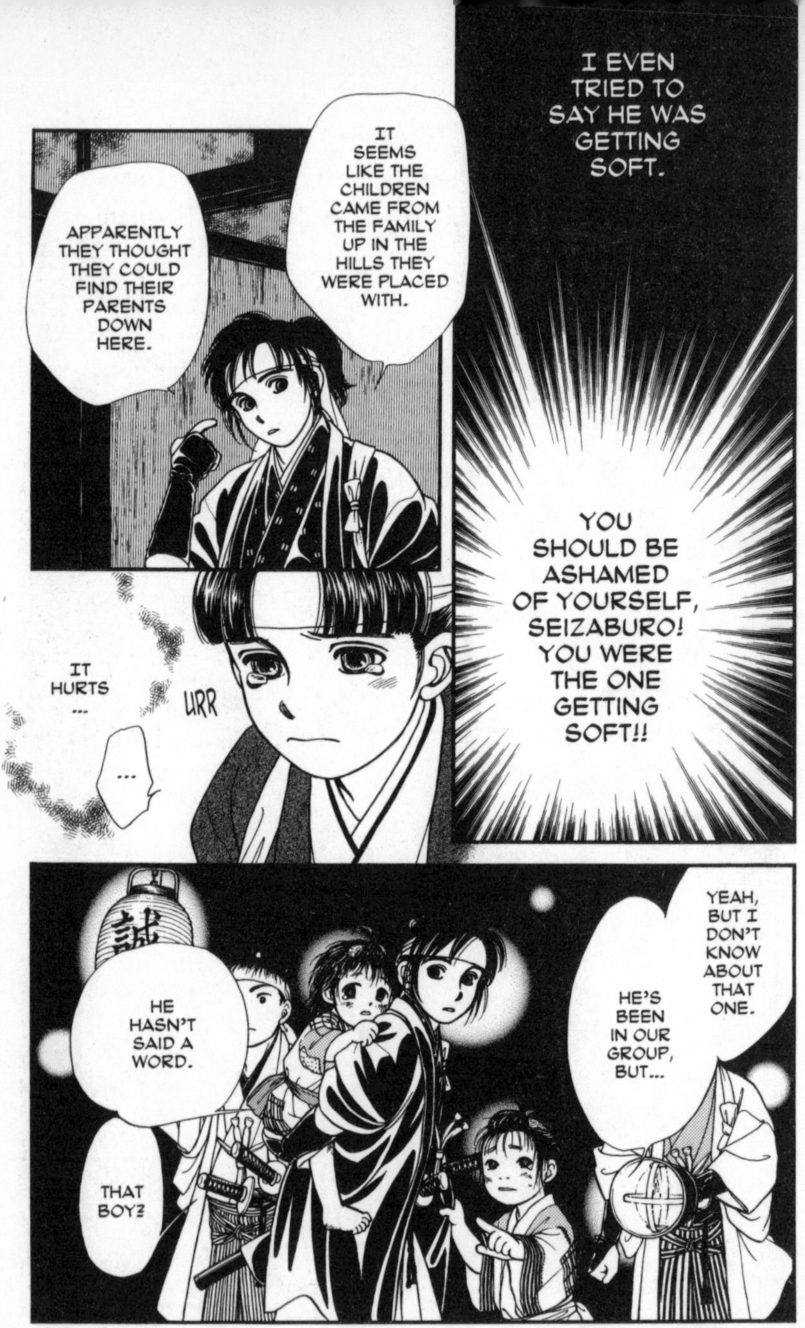
I EVEN TRIED TO SAY HE WAS GETTING SOFT.
YOU SHOULD BE ASHAMED OF YOURSELF, SEIZABURO! YOU WERE THE ONE GETTING SOFT!!
IT SEEMS LIKE THE CHILDREN CAME FROM THE FAMILY UP IN THE HILLS THEY WERE PLACED WITH.
APPARENTLY THEY THOUGHT THEY COULD FIND THEIR PARENTS DOWN HERE.
URR
IT HURTS ...
...
YEAH, BUT I DON'T KNOW ABOUT THAT ONE.
HE'S BEEN IN OUR GROUP, BUT...
HE HASN'T SAID A WORD.
THAT BOY?

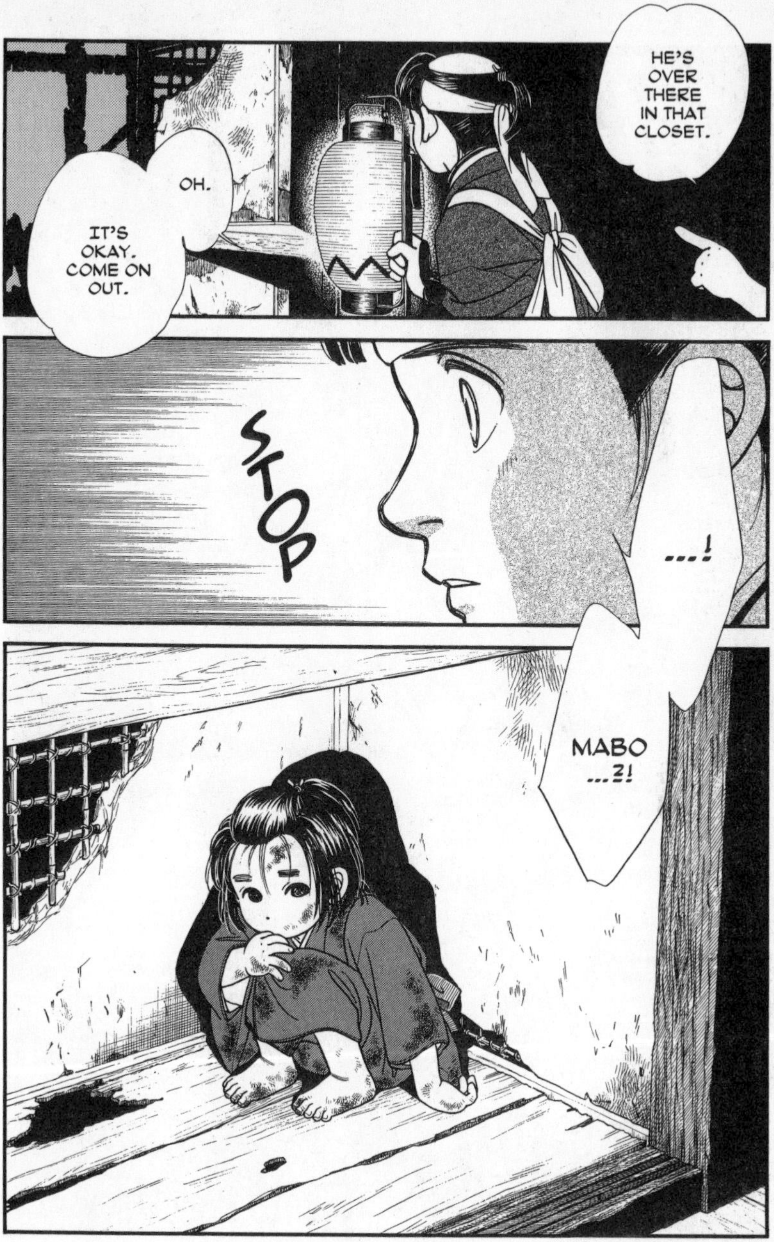
HE'S OVER THERE IN THAT CLOSET.
OH. IT'S OKAY. COME ON OUT.
...!
STOP
MABO ...?!

To Be Continued!

TAEKO WATANABE PRESENTS

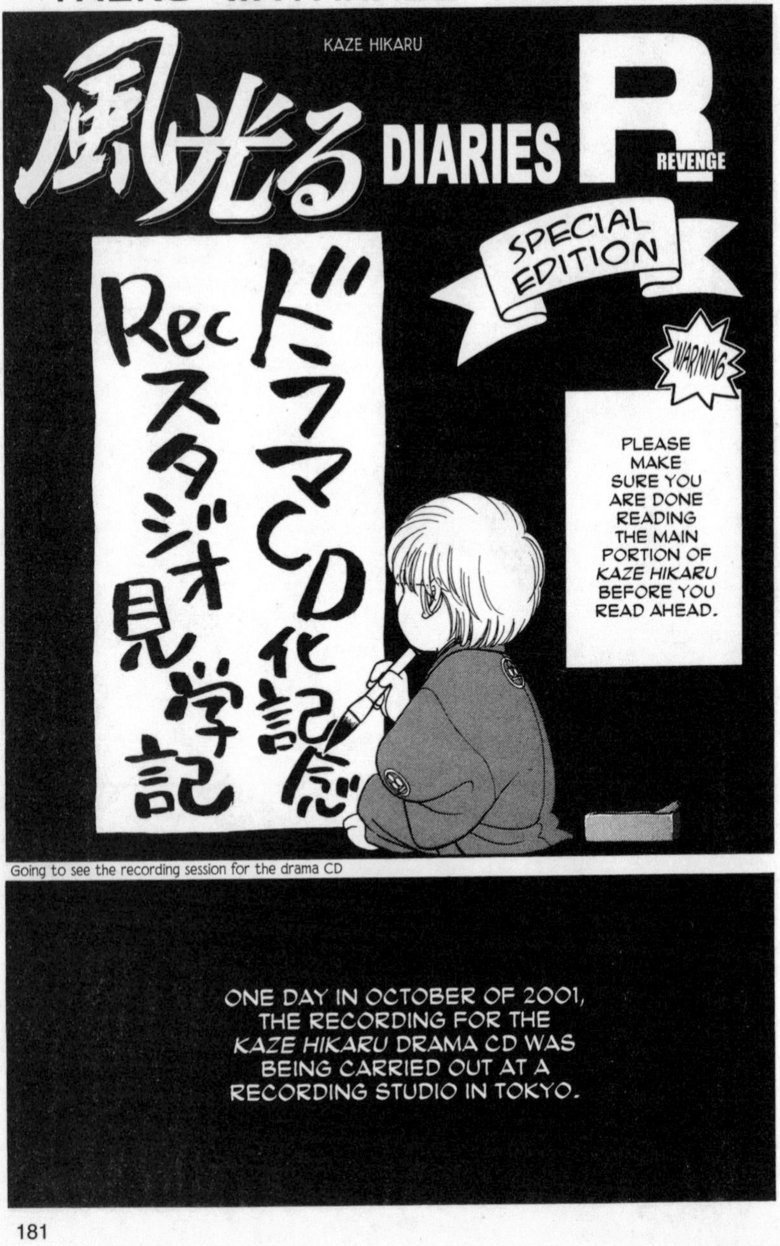
KAZE HIKARU
風光る DIARIES R
REVENGE
SPECIAL EDITION
ドラマCD化記念
Recスタジオ見学記
WARNING
PLEASE MAKE SURE YOU ARE DONE READING THE MAIN PORTION OF *KAZE HIKARU* BEFORE YOU READ AHEAD.

Going to see the recording session for the drama CD

ONE DAY IN OCTOBER OF 2001, THE RECORDING FOR THE *KAZE HIKARU* DRAMA CD WAS BEING CARRIED OUT AT A RECORDING STUDIO IN TOKYO.

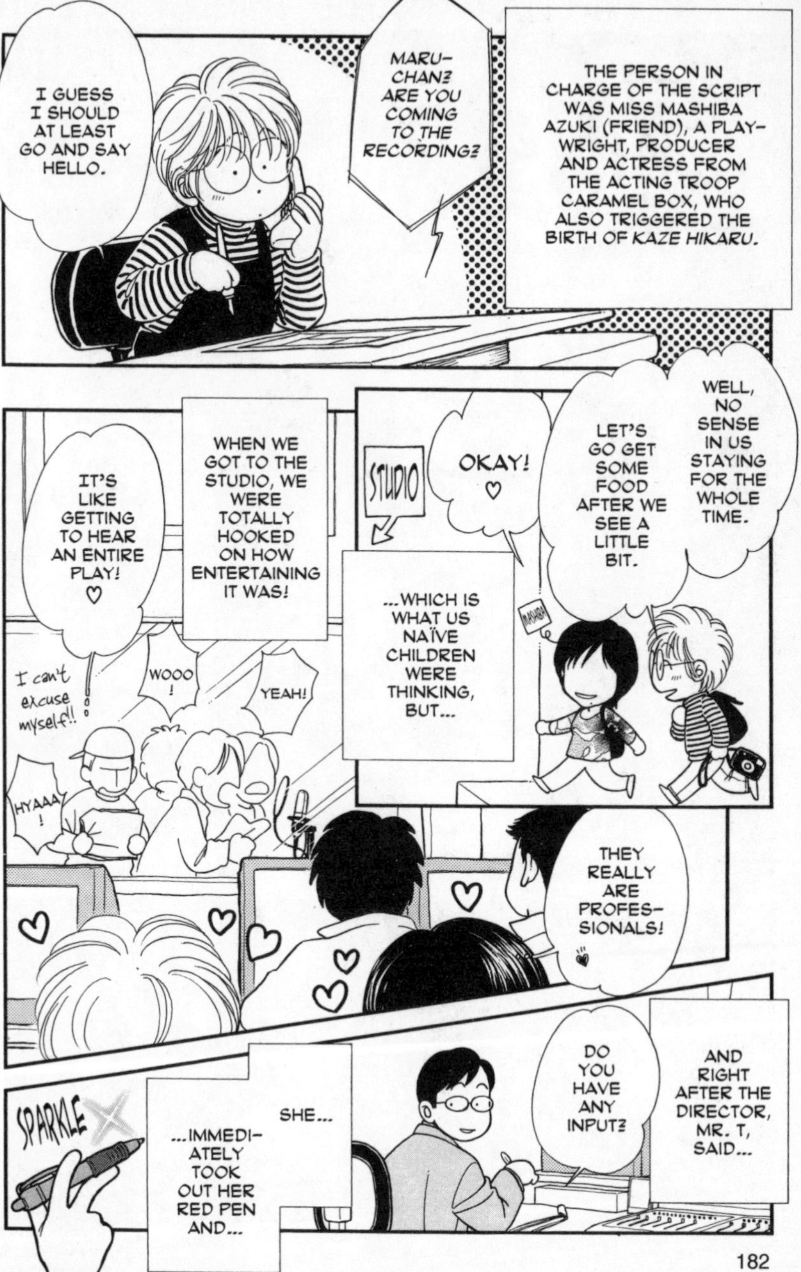
THE PERSON IN CHARGE OF THE SCRIPT WAS MISS MASHIBA AZUKI (FRIEND), A PLAY-WRIGHT, PRODUCER AND ACTRESS FROM THE ACTING TROOP CARAMEL BOX, WHO ALSO TRIGGERED THE BIRTH OF *KAZE HIKARU*.
MARU-CHAN? ARE YOU COMING TO THE RECORDING?
I GUESS I SHOULD AT LEAST GO AND SAY HELLO.
WELL, NO SENSE IN US STAYING FOR THE WHOLE TIME.
LET'S GO GET SOME FOOD AFTER WE SEE A LITTLE BIT.
OKAY! ♡
STUDIO
...WHICH IS WHAT US NAÏVE CHILDREN WERE THINKING, BUT...
WHEN WE GOT TO THE STUDIO, WE WERE TOTALLY HOOKED ON HOW ENTERTAINING IT WAS!
IT'S LIKE GETTING TO HEAR AN ENTIRE PLAY! ♡
YEAH!
WOOO!
I can't excuse myself!!
HYAAA!
THEY REALLY ARE PROFES-SIONALS!
AND RIGHT AFTER THE DIRECTOR, MR. T, SAID...
DO YOU HAVE ANY INPUT?
SHE...
...IMMEDI-ATELY TOOK OUT HER RED PEN AND...
SPARKLE

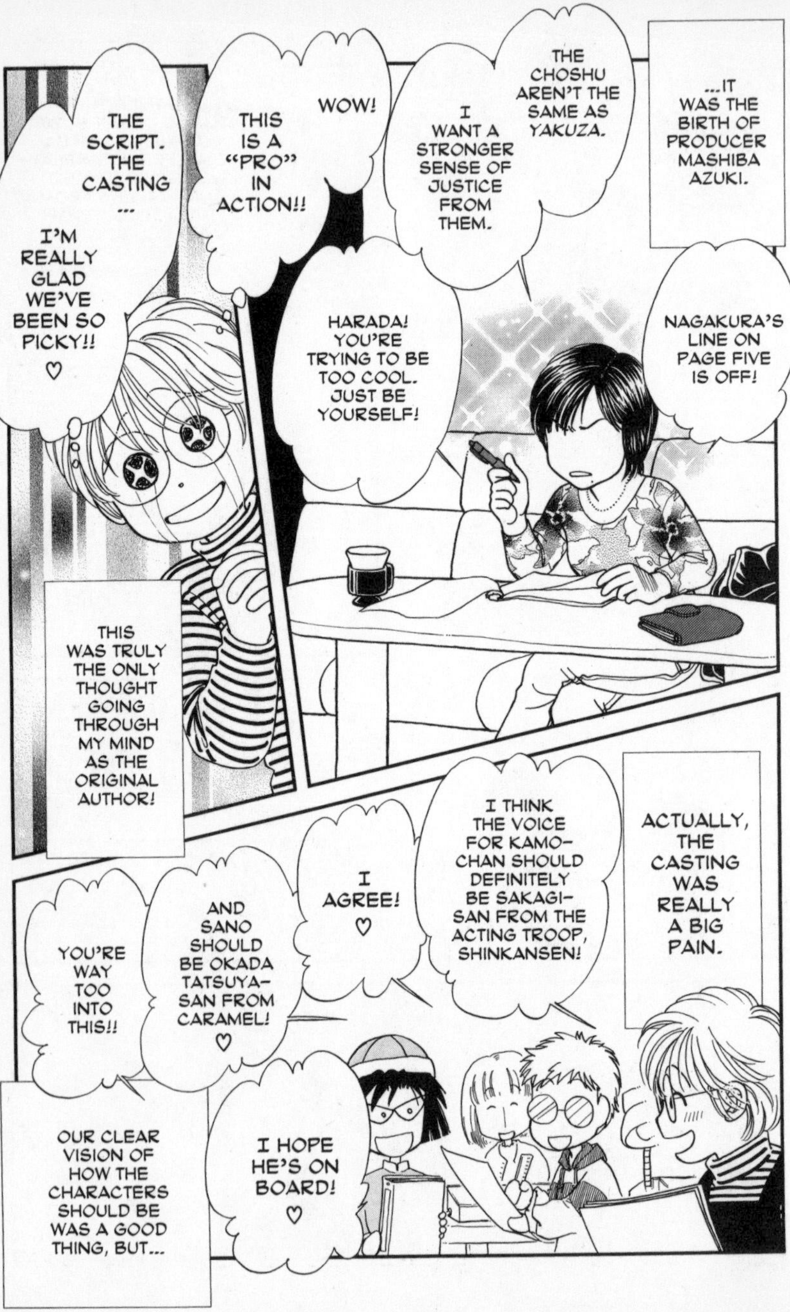
...IT WAS THE BIRTH OF PRODUCER MASHIBA AZUKI.
NAGAKURA'S LINE ON PAGE FIVE IS OFF!
THE CHOSHU AREN'T THE SAME AS YAKUZA.
I WANT A STRONGER SENSE OF JUSTICE FROM THEM.
HARADA! YOU'RE TRYING TO BE TOO COOL. JUST BE YOURSELF!
WOW!
THIS IS A "PRO" IN ACTION!!
THE SCRIPT. THE CASTING...
I'M REALLY GLAD WE'VE BEEN SO PICKY!! ♡
THIS WAS TRULY THE ONLY THOUGHT GOING THROUGH MY MIND AS THE ORIGINAL AUTHOR!
ACTUALLY, THE CASTING WAS REALLY A BIG PAIN.
I THINK THE VOICE FOR KAMO-CHAN SHOULD DEFINITELY BE SAKAGI-SAN FROM THE ACTING TROOP, SHINKANSEN!
I AGREE! ♡
AND SANO SHOULD BE OKADA TATSUYA-SAN FROM CARAMEL! ♡
YOU'RE WAY TOO INTO THIS!!
I HOPE HE'S ON BOARD! ♡
OUR CLEAR VISION OF HOW THE CHARACTERS SHOULD BE WAS A GOOD THING, BUT...

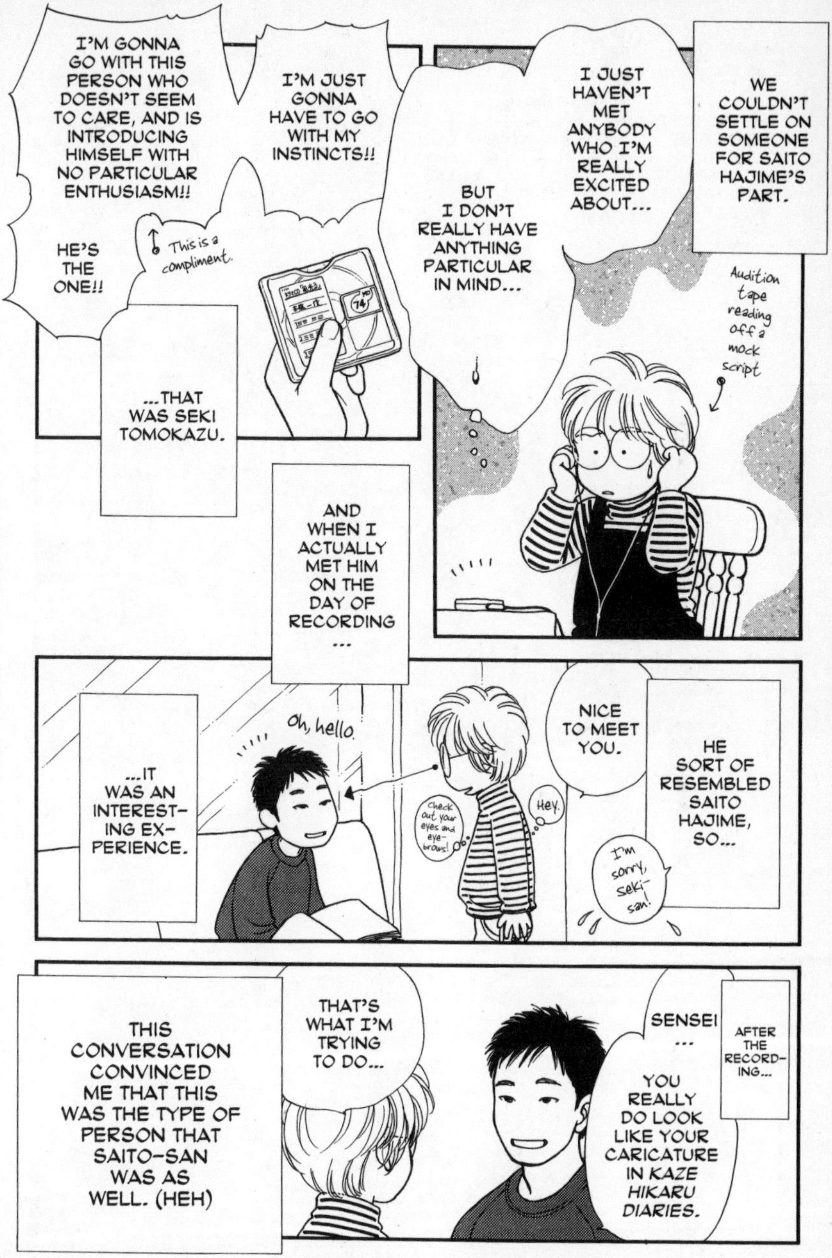

WE COULDN'T SETTLE ON SOMEONE FOR SAITO HAJIME'S PART.
I JUST HAVEN'T MET ANYBODY WHO I'M REALLY EXCITED ABOUT...
BUT I DON'T REALLY HAVE ANYTHING PARTICULAR IN MIND...
Audition tape reading off a mock script
I'M JUST GONNA HAVE TO GO WITH MY INSTINCTS!!
I'M GONNA GO WITH THIS PERSON WHO DOESN'T SEEM TO CARE, AND IS INTRODUCING HIMSELF WITH NO PARTICULAR ENTHUSIASM!!
HE'S THE ONE!!
This is a compliment.
...THAT WAS SEKI TOMOKAZU.
AND WHEN I ACTUALLY MET HIM ON THE DAY OF RECORDING ...
HE SORT OF RESEMBLED SAITO HAJIME, SO...
NICE TO MEET YOU.
I'm sorry, Seki-san!
Hey.
Check out your eyes and eye-brows!
Oh, hello.
...IT WAS AN INTERESTING EXPERIENCE.
AFTER THE RECORDING...
SENSEI...
YOU REALLY DO LOOK LIKE YOUR CARICATURE IN KAZE HIKARU DIARIES.
THAT'S WHAT I'M TRYING TO DO...
THIS CONVERSATION CONVINCED ME THAT THIS WAS THE TYPE OF PERSON THAT SAITO-SAN WAS AS WELL. (HEH)

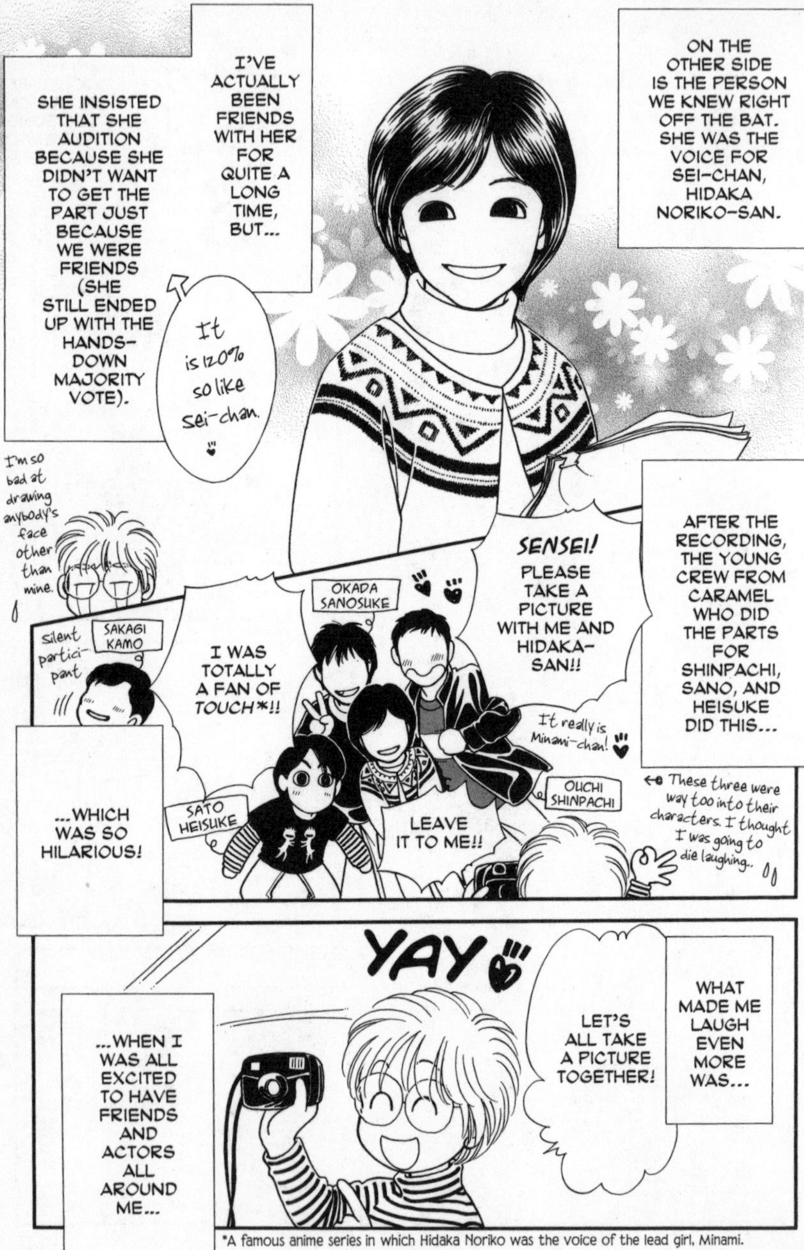
ON THE OTHER SIDE IS THE PERSON WE KNEW RIGHT OFF THE BAT. SHE WAS THE VOICE FOR SEI-CHAN, HIDAKA NORIKO-SAN.
I'VE ACTUALLY BEEN FRIENDS WITH HER FOR QUITE A LONG TIME, BUT...
SHE INSISTED THAT SHE AUDITION BECAUSE SHE DIDN'T WANT TO GET THE PART JUST BECAUSE WE WERE FRIENDS (SHE STILL ENDED UP WITH THE HANDS-DOWN MAJORITY VOTE).
It is 120% so like sei-chan.
I'm so bad at drawing anybody's face other than mine.
AFTER THE RECORDING, THE YOUNG CREW FROM CARAMEL WHO DID THE PARTS FOR SHINPACHI, SANO, AND HEISUKE DID THIS...
SENSEI! PLEASE TAKE A PICTURE WITH ME AND HIDAKA-SAN!!
OKADA SANOSUKE
I WAS TOTALLY A FAN OF TOUCH*!!
SAKAGI KAMO
Silent partici-pant
It really is Minami-chan!
OUCHI SHINPACHI
These three were way too into their characters. I thought I was going to die laughing..
LEAVE IT TO ME!!
SATO HEISUKE
...WHICH WAS SO HILARIOUS!
WHAT MADE ME LAUGH EVEN MORE WAS...
LET'S ALL TAKE A PICTURE TOGETHER!
YAY
...WHEN I WAS ALL EXCITED TO HAVE FRIENDS AND ACTORS ALL AROUND ME...

*A famous anime series in which Hidaka Noriko was the voice of the lead girl, Minami.

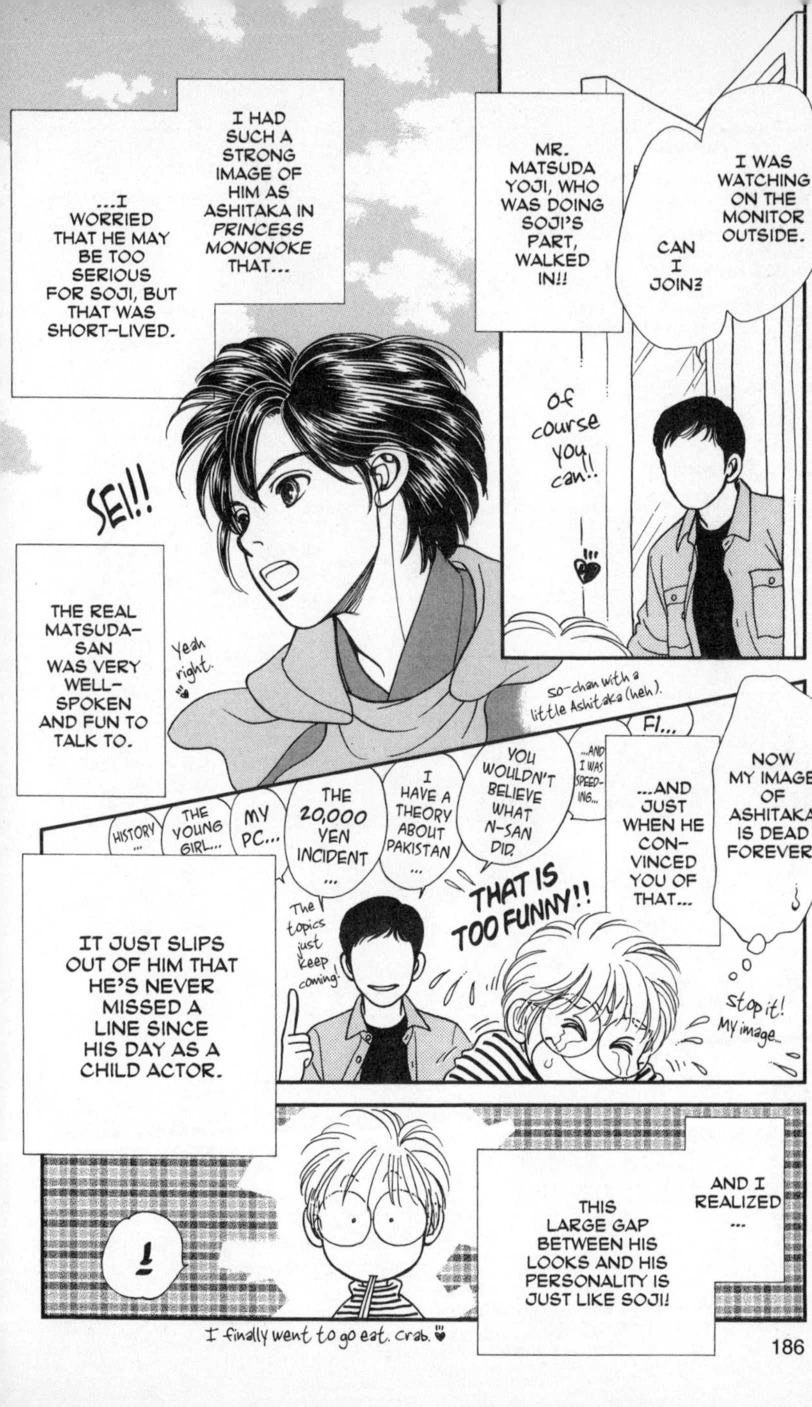
I WAS WATCHING ON THE MONITOR OUTSIDE.
CAN I JOIN?
MR. MATSUDA YOJI, WHO WAS DOING SOJI'S PART, WALKED IN!!
Of course you can!!
I HAD SUCH A STRONG IMAGE OF HIM AS ASHITAKA IN *PRINCESS MONONOKE* THAT...
...I WORRIED THAT HE MAY BE TOO SERIOUS FOR SOJI, BUT THAT WAS SHORT-LIVED.
SEI!!
THE REAL MATSUDA-SAN WAS VERY WELL-SPOKEN AND FUN TO TALK TO.
Yeah right.
NOW MY IMAGE OF ASHITAKA IS DEAD FOREVER!
...AND JUST WHEN HE CONVINCED YOU OF THAT...
FI...
So-chan with a little Ashitaka (heh).
...AND I WAS SPEEDING...
YOU WOULDN'T BELIEVE WHAT N-SAN DID.
I HAVE A THEORY ABOUT PAKISTAN...
THE 20,000 YEN INCIDENT...
MY PC...
THE YOUNG GIRL...
HISTORY...
Stop it! My image...
THAT IS TOO FUNNY!!
The topics just keep coming!
IT JUST SLIPS OUT OF HIM THAT HE'S NEVER MISSED A LINE SINCE HIS DAY AS A CHILD ACTOR.
AND I REALIZED...
THIS LARGE GAP BETWEEN HIS LOOKS AND HIS PERSONALITY IS JUST LIKE SOJI!
!
I finally went to go eat. Crab.

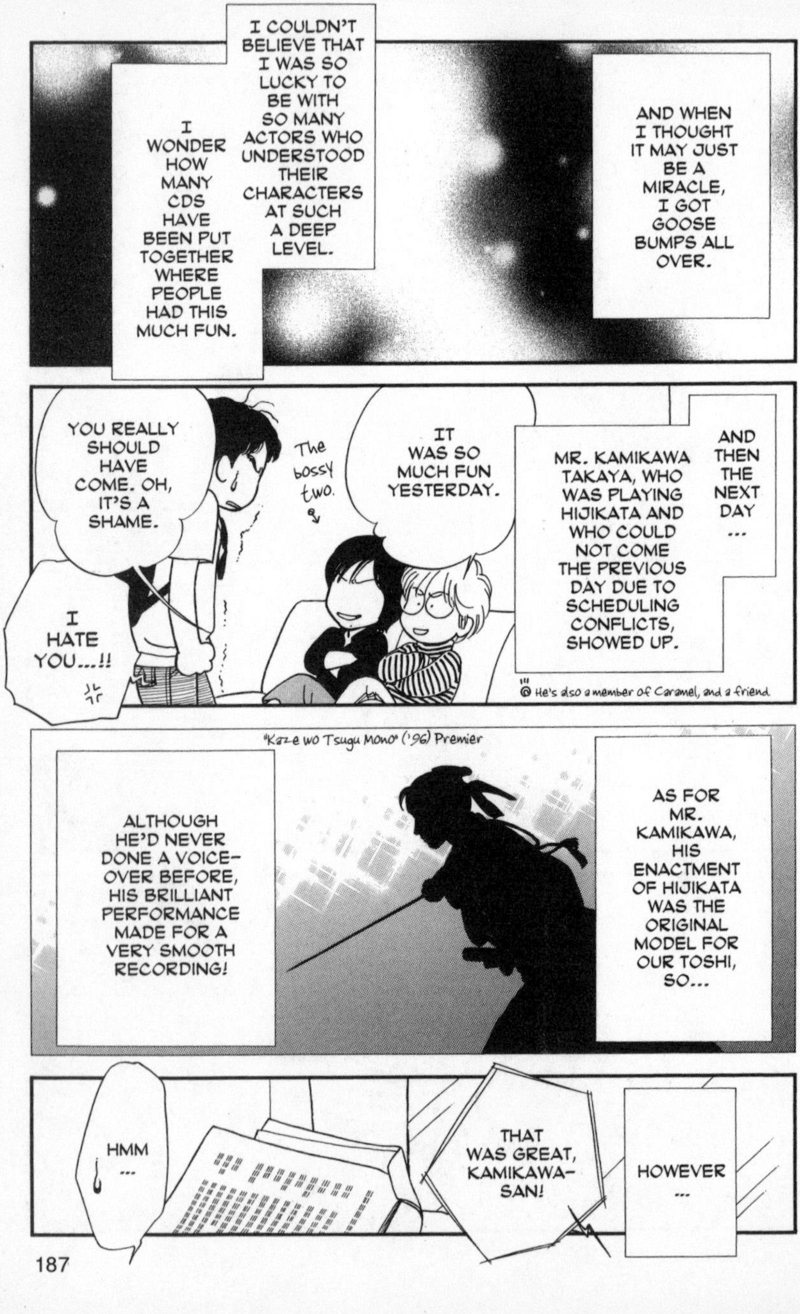
AND WHEN I THOUGHT IT MAY JUST BE A MIRACLE, I GOT GOOSE BUMPS ALL OVER.
I COULDN'T BELIEVE THAT I WAS SO LUCKY TO BE WITH SO MANY ACTORS WHO UNDERSTOOD THEIR CHARACTERS AT SUCH A DEEP LEVEL.
I WONDER HOW MANY CDS HAVE BEEN PUT TOGETHER WHERE PEOPLE HAD THIS MUCH FUN.
AND THEN THE NEXT DAY...
MR. KAMIKAWA TAKAYA, WHO WAS PLAYING HIJIKATA AND WHO COULD NOT COME THE PREVIOUS DAY DUE TO SCHEDULING CONFLICTS, SHOWED UP.
He's also a member of Caramel, and a friend.
IT WAS SO MUCH FUN YESTERDAY.
The bossy two.
YOU REALLY SHOULD HAVE COME. OH, IT'S A SHAME.
I HATE YOU...!!
"Kaze wo Tsugu Mono" ('96) Premier
AS FOR MR. KAMIKAWA, HIS ENACTMENT OF HIJIKATA WAS THE ORIGINAL MODEL FOR OUR TOSHI, SO...
ALTHOUGH HE'D NEVER DONE A VOICE-OVER BEFORE, HIS BRILLIANT PERFORMANCE MADE FOR A VERY SMOOTH RECORDING!
HOWEVER...
THAT WAS GREAT, KAMIKAWA-SAN!
HMM...

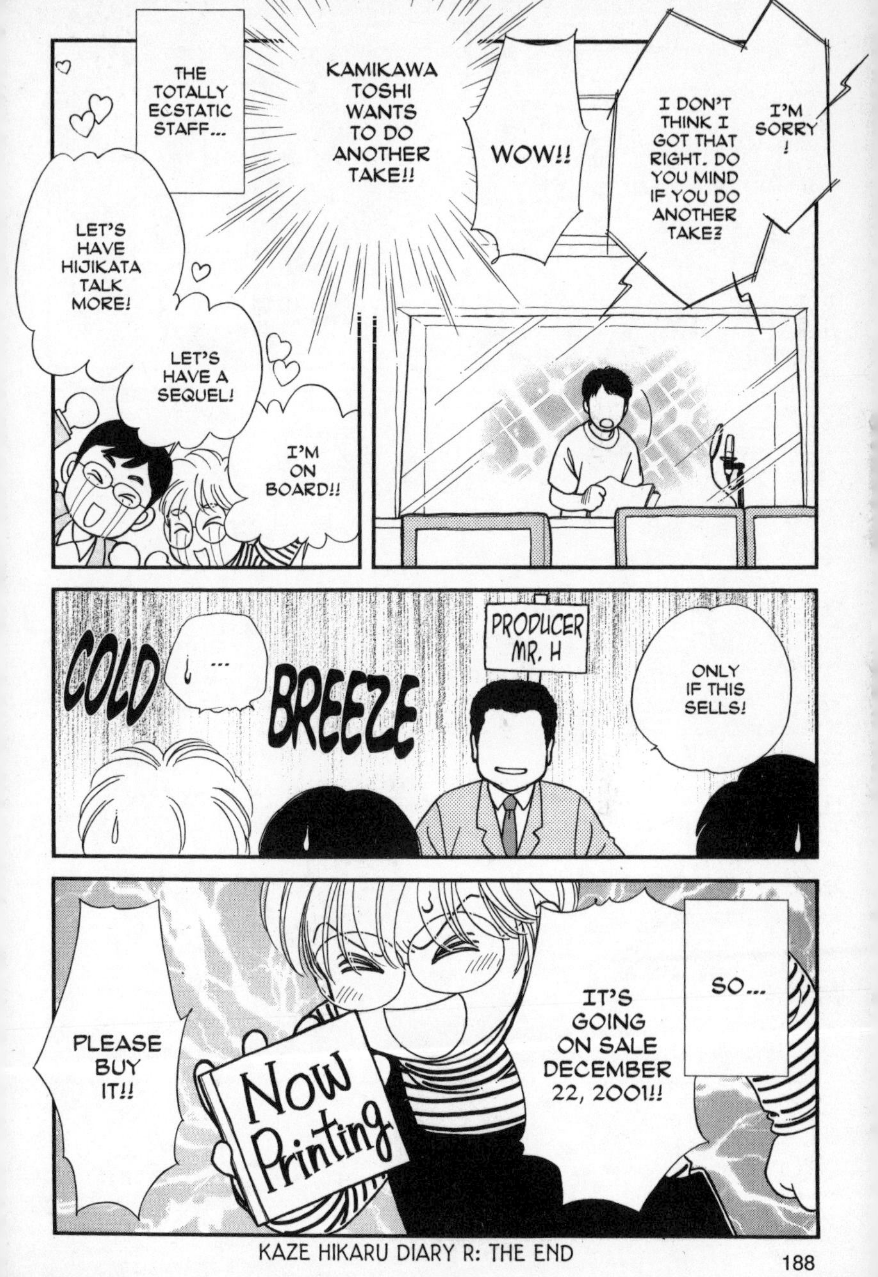
I'M SORRY!
I DON'T THINK I GOT THAT RIGHT. DO YOU MIND IF YOU DO ANOTHER TAKE?
WOW!!
KAMIKAWA TOSHI WANTS TO DO ANOTHER TAKE!!
THE TOTALLY ECSTATIC STAFF...
LET'S HAVE HIJIKATA TALK MORE!
LET'S HAVE A SEQUEL!
I'M ON BOARD!!
ONLY IF THIS SELLS!
PRODUCER MR. H
...
COLD BREEZE
SO...
IT'S GOING ON SALE DECEMBER 22, 2001!!
Now Printing
PLEASE BUY IT!!

KAZE HIKARU DIARY R: THE END

Decoding Kaze Hikaru

Kaze Hikaru is a historical drama based in 19th century Japan and thus contains some fairly mystifying terminology. In this glossary we'll break down archaic phrases, terms, and other linguistic curiosities for you, so that you can move through life with the smug assurance that you are indeed a know-it-all.

First and foremost, because *Kaze Hikaru* is a period story, we kept all character names in their traditional Japanese form—that is, family name followed by first name. For example, the character Okita Soji's family name is Okita and his personal name is Soji.

AKO-ROSHI:
The ronin (samurai) of Ako; featured in the immortal Kabuki play *Chushingura* (Loyalty), aka *47 Samurai*.

ANI-UE:
Literally, "brother above"; an honorific for an elder male sibling.

BAKUFU:
Literally, "tent government." Shogunate; the feudal, military government that dominated Japan for more than 200 years.

BUSHI:
A samurai or warrior (part of the compound word *bushido*, which means "way of the warrior").

CHICHI-UE:
An honorific suffix meaning "father above."

DO:
In kendo (a Japanese fencing sport that uses bamboo swords), a short way of describing the offensive single-hit strike *shikake waza ippon uchi*.

RONIN:
Masterless samurai.

RYO:
At the time, one *ryo* and two *bu* (four bu equaled roughly one ryo) were enough currency to support a family of five for an entire month.

-SAN:
An honorific suffix that carries the meaning of "Mr." or "Ms."

SENSEI:
A teacher, master, or instructor.

SEPPUKU:
A ritualistic suicide that was considered a privilege of the nobility and samurai elite.

SONJO-HA:
Those loyal to the emperor and dedicated to the expulsion of foreigners from the country.

TAMEBO:
A short version of the name Tamesaburo.

YUBO:
A short version of the name Yunosuke.

-HAN:

The same as the honorific –SAN, pronounced in the dialect of southern Japan.

-KUN:

An honorific suffix that indicates a difference in rank and title. The use of *kun* is also a way of indicating familiarity and friendliness between students or compatriots.

MEN:

In the context of *Kaze Hikaru*, *men* refers to one of the "points" in kendo. It is a strike to the forehead and is considered a basic move.

MIBU-ROSHI:

A group of warriors that supports the Bakufu.

NE'E-SAN:

Can mean "older sister," "ma'am," or "miss."

NI'I-CHAN:

Short for *oni'i-san* or *oni'i-chan*, meaning older brother.

OKU-SAMA:

This is a polite way to refer to someone's wife. *Oku* means "deep" or "further back," and comes from the fact that wives (in affluent families) stayed hidden away in the back rooms of the house.

ONI:

Literally "ogre," this is Sei's nickname for Vice-Captain Hijikata.

RANPO:

Medical science derived from the Dutch.

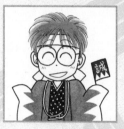

The cover for Volume 9 was a bigger adventure than the one for Volume 7. I had prepared myself for complaints that the characters were drawn too small and their faces couldn't be seen, but then I was surprised by all the letters I got claiming that this was the reader's favorite cover art. One person envisioned the cherry blossoms scattering when at the bookstore, another imagined the story before and after the depicted scene, and another gave the beautiful title of "Blessed" to the drawing... Every time I read a letter, I felt humbled by the readers' imagination, to which I had obviously not given enough credit. Kaze Hikaru has come to its tenth volume thanks to the support of its wonderful readers. I dedicate to you my renewed gratitude, love and respect.

Taeko Watanabe debuted as a manga artist in 1979 with her story *Waka-chan no Netsuai Jidai* (Love Struck Days of Waka). *Kaze Hikaru* is her longest-running series, but she has created a number of other popular series. Watanabe is a two-time winner of the prestigious Shogakukan Manga Award in the girls category—her manga *Hajime-chan ga Ichiban!* (Hajime-chan Is Number One!) claimed the award in 1991 and *Kaze Hikaru* took it in 2003.

Watanabe read hundreds of historical sources to create *Kaze Hikaru*. She is from Tokyo.

KAZE HIKARU VOL. 10
The Shojo Beat Manga Edition

STORY AND ART BY
TAEKO WATANABE

Translation & English Adaptation/Mai Ihara
Touch-up Art & Lettering/Rina Mapa
Design/Izumi Evers
Editor/Jonathan Tarbox

Editor in Chief, Books/Alvin Lu
Editor in Chief, Magazines/Marc Weidenbaum
VP of Publishing Licensing/Rika Inouye
VP of Sales/Gonzalo Ferreyra
Sr. VP of Marketing/Liza Coppola
Publisher/Hyoe Narita

Printed in Canada

Published by VIZ Media, LLC
P.O. Box 77010
San Francisco, CA 94107

Shojo Beat Manga Edition
10 9 8 7 6 5 4 3 2 1
First printing, August 2008

www.viz.com

PARENTAL ADVISORY
KAZE HIKARU is rated T+ for Older Teen and is
recommended for ages 16 and up. This volume
contains realistic violence, alcohol use, and sexual
themes.
ratings.viz.com

store.viz.com

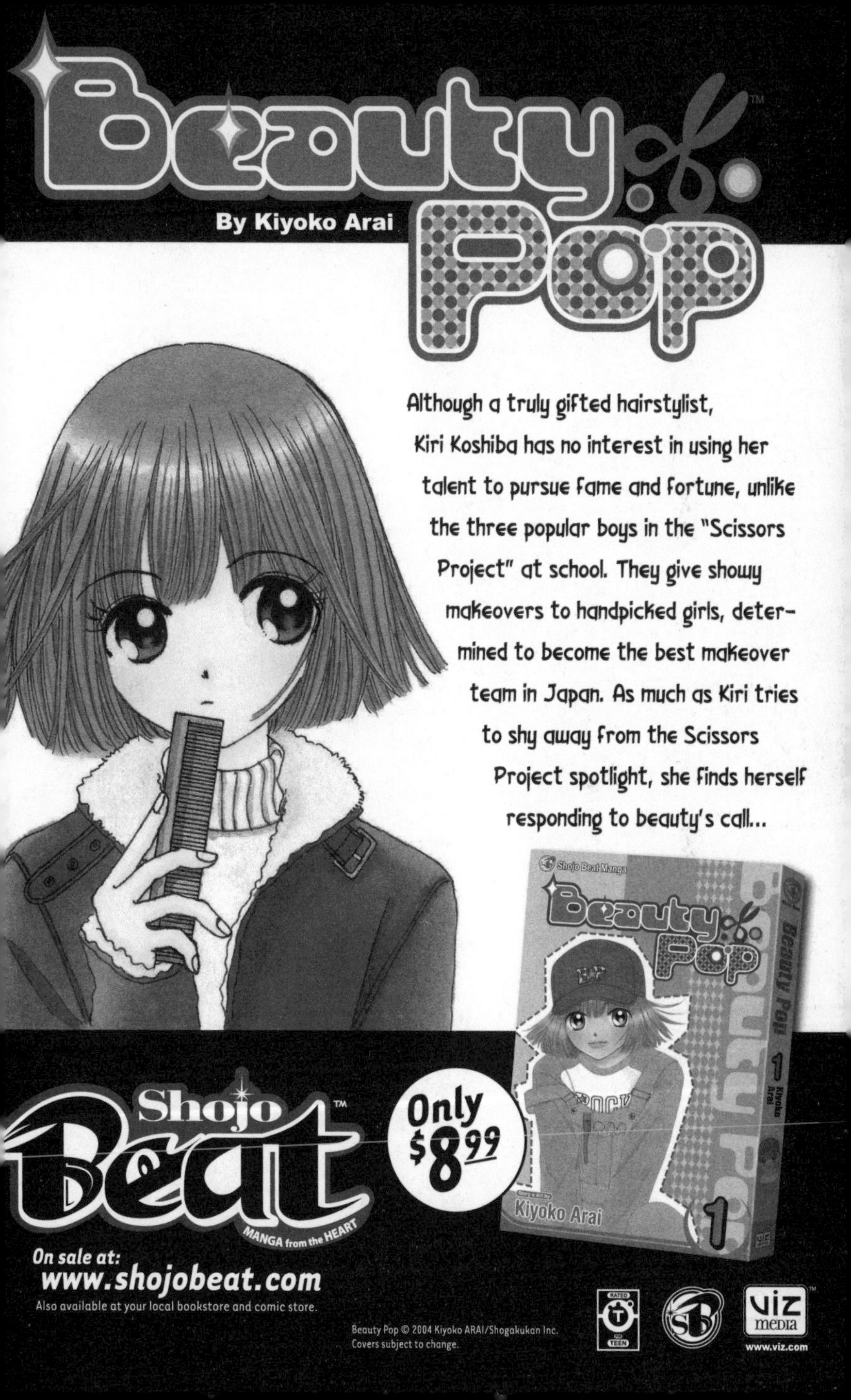
Beauty Pop™
By Kiyoko Arai
Although a truly gifted hairstylist, Kiri Koshiba has no interest in using her talent to pursue fame and fortune, unlike the three popular boys in the "Scissors Project" at school. They give showy makeovers to handpicked girls, determined to become the best makeover team in Japan. As much as Kiri tries to shy away from the Scissors Project spotlight, she finds herself responding to beauty's call...
Shojo Beat Manga
Beauty Pop
Kiyoko Arai
1
Only $8.99
Shojo Beat™
MANGA from the HEART
On sale at:
www.shojobeat.com
Also available at your local bookstore and comic store.
Beauty Pop © 2004 Kiyoko ARAI/Shogakukan Inc.
Covers subject to change.
RATED T TEEN
VIZ media
www.viz.com

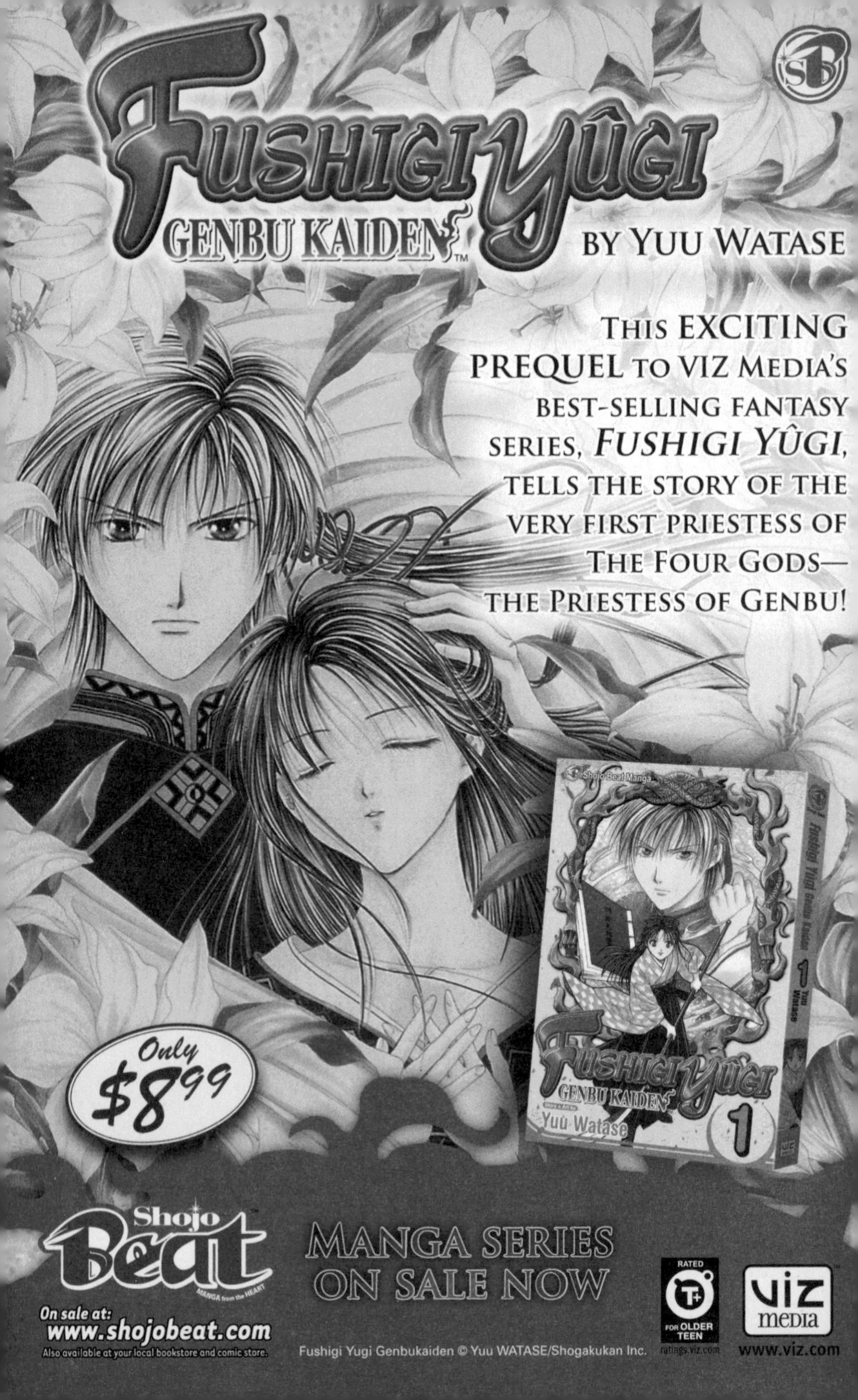

Fushigi Yûgi
Genbu Kaiden™
By Yuu Watase
This EXCITING PREQUEL to VIZ Media's best-selling fantasy series, Fushigi Yûgi, tells the story of the very first priestess of The Four Gods—the Priestess of Genbu!
Only $8.99
Shojo Beat Manga
Fushigi Yûgi Genbu Kaiden
Story & Art by Yuu Watase
1
Shojo Beat
Manga from the Heart
Manga Series On Sale Now
On sale at:
www.shojobeat.com
Also available at your local bookstore and comic store.
Fushigi Yugi Genbukaiden © Yuu WATASE/Shogakukan Inc.
Rated T+ for Older Teen
ratings.viz.com
viz media
www.viz.com

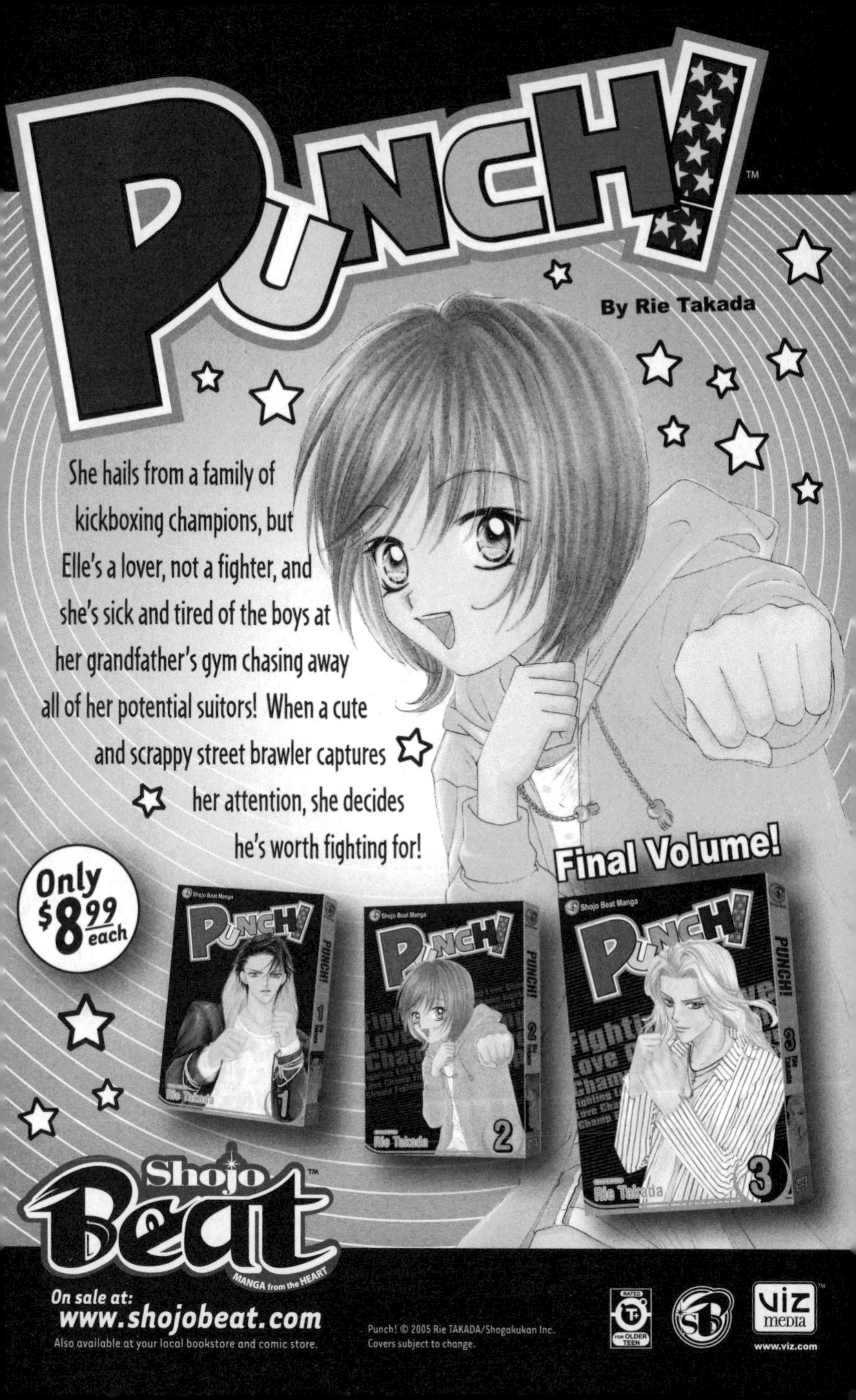

PUNCH!™
By Rie Takada
She hails from a family of kickboxing champions, but Elle's a lover, not a fighter, and she's sick and tired of the boys at her grandfather's gym chasing away all of her potential suitors! When a cute and scrappy street brawler captures her attention, she decides he's worth fighting for!
Only $8.99 each
Final Volume!
Shojo Beat Manga
PUNCH!
Rie Takada
1
2
3
Shojo Beat™
MANGA from the HEART
On sale at:
www.shojobeat.com
Also available at your local bookstore and comic store.
Punch! © 2005 Rie TAKADA/Shogakukan Inc.
Covers subject to change.
RATED T+ FOR OLDER TEEN
VIZ media
www.viz.com

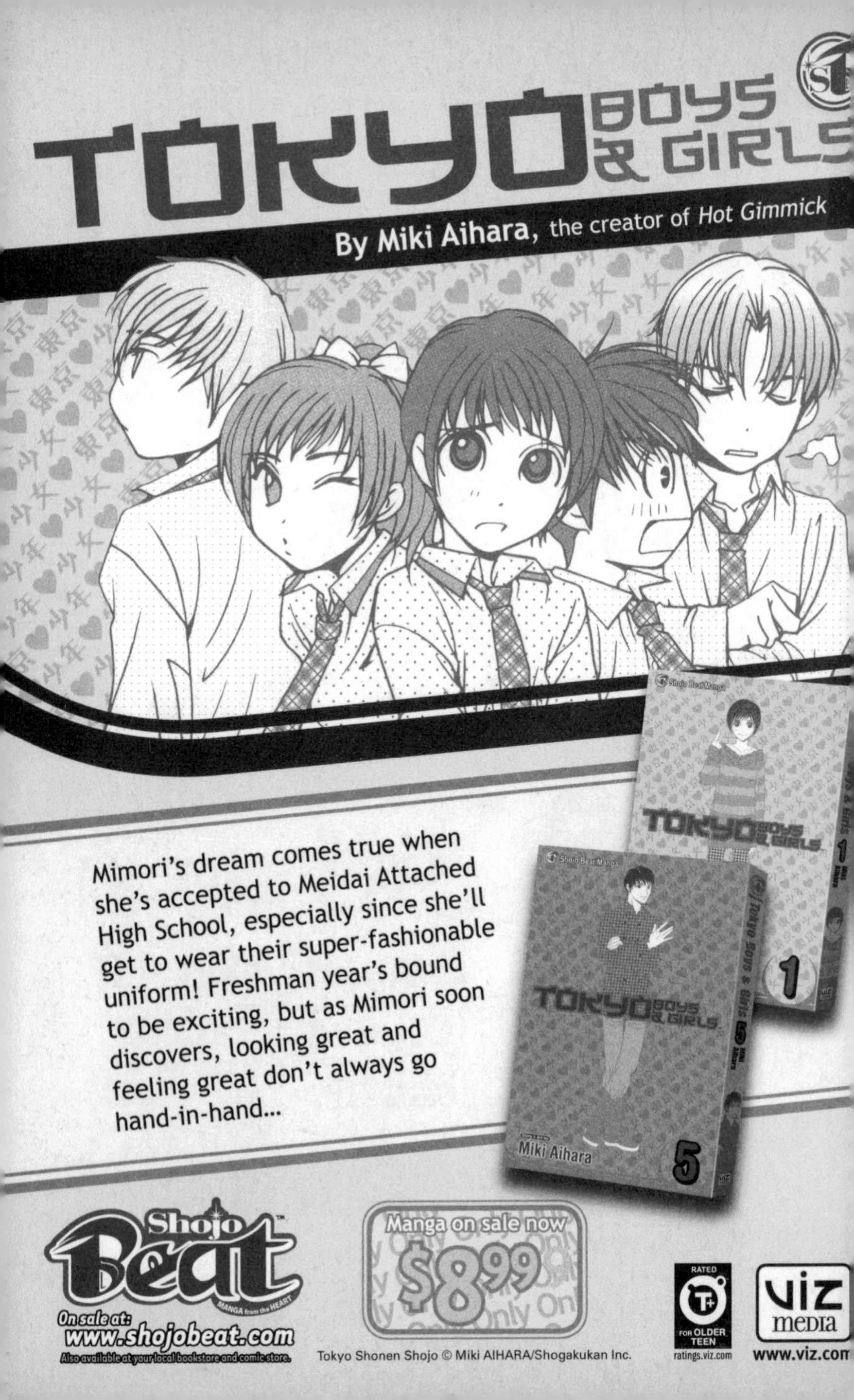
TOKYO BOYS & GIRLS
By Miki Aihara, the creator of Hot Gimmick
Mimori's dream comes true when she's accepted to Meidai Attached High School, especially since she'll get to wear their super-fashionable uniform! Freshman year's bound to be exciting, but as Mimori soon discovers, looking great and feeling great don't always go hand-in-hand...
Shojo Beat Manga
TOKYO BOYS & GIRLS
Miki Aihara
5
1
Shojo Beat
MANGA from the HEART
On sale at:
www.shojobeat.com
Also available at your local bookstore and comic store.
Manga on sale now
$8.99
Tokyo Shonen Shojo © Miki AIHARA/Shogakukan Inc.
RATED
T+
FOR OLDER TEEN
ratings.viz.com
VIZ media
www.viz.com

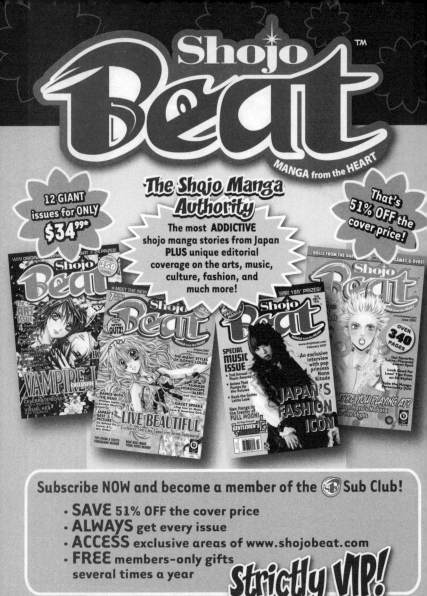

Save OVER **50%** o~~f~~

Shojo Beat
MANGA from the HEART

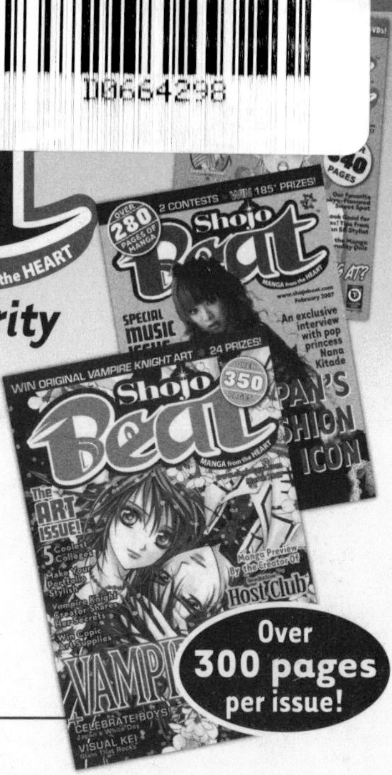

The Shojo Manga Authority

This monthly magazine is injected with the most **ADDICTIVE** shojo manga stories from Japan. PLUS, unique editorial coverage on the arts, music, culture, fashion, and much more!

☑ **YES!** Please enter my one-year subscription (12 GIANT issues) to *Shojo Beat* at the LOW SUBSCRIPTION RATE of **$34.99!**

Over **300 pages** per issue!

NAME

ADDRESS

CITY   STATE   ZIP

E-MAIL ADDRESS   P7GNC1

☐ **MY CHECK IS ENCLOSED** (PAYABLE TO *Shojo Beat*)   ☐ **BILL ME LATER**

CREDIT CARD: ☐ **VISA**   ☐ **MASTERCARD**

ACCOUNT #   ARAM PUBLIC LIBRARY   EXP. DATE
                            Delavan, Wisconsin 53115

SIGNATURE

CLIP AND MAIL TO ➤

SHOJO BEAT
Subscriptions Service Dept.
P.O. Box 438
Mount Morris, IL 61054-0438

Canada price for 12 issues: $46.99 USD, including GST, HST and QST. US/CAN orders only. Allow 6-8 weeks for delivery. Must be 16 or older to redeem offer. By redeeming this offer I represent that I am 16 or older.

Vampire Knight © Matsuri Hino 2004/HAKUSENSHA, Inc. Nana Kitade © Sony Music Entertainment (Japan), Inc.
CRIMSON HERO © 2002 by Mitsuba Takanashi/SHUEISHA Inc.

RATED
T+
FOR OLDER TEEN
ratings.viz.com